Politics at the Periphery

# Politics at the

# Periphery

*Third Parties in
Two-Party America*

*J. David Gillespie*

UNIVERSITY OF
SOUTH CAROLINA PRESS

Copyright © 1993 University of South Carolina
Published in Columbia, South Carolina, by the University of South Carolina Press
Manufactured in the United States of America

**Library of Congress Cataloging-in-Publication Data**

Gillespie, J. David, 1944–
    Politics at the periphery : third parties in two-party America /
J. David Gillespie.
      p.    cm.
    Includes bibliographical references and index.
    ISBN 0-87249-843-3
    1. Third parties (United States politics)—History.    I. Title.
JK2261.G55, 1993
324.273'8—dc20                             92-43973

# Contents

# Preface

You are entitled to know something about my approach to the topic of this book. I am not now, nor have I ever been, enrolled in any American third political party. Much that we associate with mainstream American politics I find to be bland and uninspiring. America's noblest political figures have been men and women possessing vision, though admittedly vision needs some tempering by pragmatism. I believe that the structural barriers placed on third-party participation in American politics have been more forbidding and debilitating than behooves the world's leading democratic nation.

I harbor considerable respect for the impulse to step outside two-party bounds, to craft third parties. That is because the impulse is driven so often by a vision of what should be. This does not mean that I find every third party's vision appealing. Some, I think, merit admiration, consideration, and possible devotion. Others are fun because they are so eccentric. Some third-party visions are mean-spirited, nasty, even downright dangerous.

I have devoted a lot of time over the last fifteen years to the thrill of the chase, in preparing for what you are about to read. I have pored over hundreds of government and private documents, election returns, financial records, biographies of third-party leaders, party platforms, newspapers, journals, and other materials. Southern Poverty Law Center's Klanwatch Project supplied information about the far right; the Hoover Institution at Stanford University provided data on the radical left. I spent half of a summer day in a cabin on Lake Superior talking Depression-era politics with a Farmer-Laborite ex-governor of Minnesota. The quest took me to the Arlington headquarters of a Nazi party, to the Manhattan home of the Communist party. I have attended third-party conventions and other meetings. I sat for an afternoon in a federal court listening to testimony in a Socialist Workers party suit against the FBI.

Leaders of many third parties—Citizens, Communist, Conservative, Expansionist, Industrial Union, Liberal, Libertarian, National States' Rights, Nazi, New Alliance, Progressive Coalition, Progressive Labor,

Prohibition, Revolutionary Communist, Socialist, Socialist Workers, and others—have talked politics with me and answered my questions. (Some of these, along with leaders of other third parties, also participated in a study I did of the beliefs and personalities of people in third-party leadership positions.) A few of the interviews were via telephone. Some took place in leaders' homes. Most were at parties' headquarters. A conversation with the cofounder of a revolutionary Maoist party had its setting in a coffee shop. It had nothing to do with avoiding FBI bugging devices. The party leader would have invited me home, he told me, but his wife had the flu.

Had I been doing the answering instead of the questioning, I might well have suspected the questioner's motives and fairness. It amazed me to find how open and forthcoming most of these people were. Some of the interviews were exciting and challenging. With one exception, maybe two, they all were informative, worthwhile encounters. None of those interviewed demanded, or even asked for, editorial control over what I would say about them or their associations. I appreciate the willingness of these people—many leading organizations that dwell far outside the mainstream—to trust that I would give an honest report.

I am grateful to Judi Gillespie, a proficient writer who happens to be my spouse and best friend too, for her limitless encouragement, her frank and helpful commentary on the various drafts, and so much else.

Within the guild of political science, I owe the most substantial debt of gratitude to Professor Laura R. Woliver, a first-rate scholar at the University of South Carolina, Columbia. This book is much stronger, certainly it is far more inclusive, because of Laura Woliver's recommendations. Warren Slesinger and Peggy Hill of the University of South Carolina Press have been unwaveringly generous in their encouragement, but also in their insistence that the manuscript be the best that it can be. Professor Leon Epstein of the University of Wisconsin has been very helpful in his observations and recommendations after reading a draft of this book. I appreciate the gracious support of Professors Frank Sorauf of the University of Minnesota and Earl Black of the University of South Carolina, Columbia. Professor Steven R. Brown of Kent State University taught me Q methodology and most of what I know about political psychology.

I am indebted to Professors Bill Moore of the College of Charleston, Jim Guth of Furman University, and Booker Ingram and Tom Weaver of Presbyterian College. I thank Presbyterian College for giving me sabbatical leave, summer research funds, and computer and other support services crucial to this project. Teresa Inman, Steve Owens, Doug Wallace, and Flo Dowdle know my debts to them in this project.

I have talked third-party politics, both in and outside classes, with large numbers of students over the years. The interest of many of them fueled my resolve to write this book, and their ideas have affected what I have written. I thank them one and all.

Politics at the Periphery

# Introduction

Not very long ago, American major parties occupied the central turf of this nation's electoral system. They also were potent agencies in the making of public policy. Recent decades have seen the rise of challengers to the power of major parties in the electoral and policy processes. Political Action Committees (PACs) may not be black holes of the American political process, but some observers believe that PACs gradually but inexorably are sucking away the life and vitality of the major parties. Candidates formerly dependent upon the funding and other services of their parties have come more and more to rely upon PACs. Interest groups sponsoring PACs expect at least friendly access for their lobbyists in return for services rendered to the successful candidates.

Mass media, especially television, also have come to intrude into the domain fomerly commanded by the Republican and Democratic parties. By virtually all accounts from political scientists, mass media today have replaced major parties as the principal intercessories or links between voters and candidates in presidential elections and in other elections too. It should come as little surprise that most American voters today are ticket-splitters, that they register unflattering opinions of the major parties, or that a surging wave of voters—young ones especially—has divorced itself from party identification and embraced the independent label. Some recent observers claim that the nation is entering into a politics without parties, and they lament what they say is passing away.[1]

Major parties have moved toward marginalization; but the Democratic and Republican parties remain for now far more than marginal actors. So much of the space reserved for parties still is appropriated by Democrats and Republicans that many readers may only vaguely be aware of the existence of the others—America's third parties.

You are about to become better acquainted with this nation's third parties, past and present, and with many of the men and women who have had the courage, tenacity, devotion, or pigheadedness to lead or support third parties. These individuals thereby entered into a peripheral realm normally far removed from the mainstream of American party politics; in short they marched to the beat of a different drummer. America's third-party tradition is almost as ancient as its pattern of two major parties. Third parties have been around in some form or another since the 1820s. If there has been a golden age for third parties, certainly that has not been the twentieth century. The nineteenth century brought, unlike the succeeding century, occasional tears or breaks in the national two-party fabric, thus furnishing opportunities for third parties to move in the direction of the mainstream.

Observing the partial atrophying of the Republican and Democratic parties today, third-party optimists like to prophesy new opportunities, maybe even a new golden age, as this nation moves toward the next century. The cards now are heavily stacked against third parties, as you will begin to see in chapter 1.

Even so, consider this: Two of the thirty-six state gubernatorial races held in 1990 brought victory to candidates not running under the banners of the major parties. Connecticut's Lowell Weicker and Walter Hickel of Alaska won election that year to four-year terms as chief executives of their states. Though billing himself an independent, Weicker ran on the "A Connecticut Party" (ACP) line. That "A" secured for Weicker first place on the ballot. By 1992, Weicker's new creation was beginning to behave like a real party. Lynn Taborak, ACP's 1992 nominee for Connecticut's fifth congressional district, took a quarter of the vote running against Republican and Democratic foes. Hickel in 1990 was the nominee of the Alaska Independence party, an organization claiming devotion to secession for the gigantic state.[2] One of the real problems faced by third-party and independent candidacies is the obscurity or lack of name recognition of most of their nominees. Weicker and Hickel, by contrast, held prominent records in politics, Weicker as a liberal Republican U.S. Senator, Hickel as Republican governor of Alaska and later as President Nixon's first secretary of the interior.

On the same day that Hickel and Weicker were taking their gubernatorial victories, Bernard Sanders won Vermont's seat in the U.S. House. Sanders is an avowed socialist, one of the very few to reach Capitol Hill since World War II. Sanders took the statewide election with 56.3 percent of the vote, beating Peter Smith, the Republican first-term incumbent; the Democratic challenger; and the nominee of a Vermont third party named Liberty Union. Two years later Sanders faced Republican and Democratic opponents and also the anti-incumbent wrath of the voters. Yet he won his return to the House with a 60 percent share of the vote. Although running as an independent, Sanders is well known to Vermont voters as leader of Burlington's Progressive Coalition (PC). The PC is a

## Important Third-Party and Independent Candidacies
## in Gubernatorial Races, 1990

**Alaska**

| | | |
|---|---|---|
| Walter J. Hickel, Alaska Independence party | 75,721 | (38.9%) |
| Tony J. Knowles, Democratic party | 60,201 | (30.9%) |
| Arlis Sturgulewski, Republican party | 50,991 | (26.2%) |
| Jim Sykes, Green party | 6,563 | ( 3.4%) |
| Michael O'Callaghan, Political party | 942 | ( .5%) |

**Connecticut**

| | | |
|---|---|---|
| Lowell P. Weicker, A Connecticut party | 460,576 | (40.4%) |
| John G. Rowland, Republican party | 427,840 | (37.5%) |
| Bruce A. Morrison, Democratic party | 236,641 | (20.7%) |
| Joseph A. Zdonczyk, Concerned Citizens party | 16,044 | ( 1.4%) |

**Other Third-Party and Independent Candidacies Receiving at**
**Least Eight Percent of Gubernatorial Vote**

| | |
|---|---|
| Conservative party (New York) | (20.4%) |
| Independent (Kansas) | ( 8.8%) |
| Independent (Maine) | ( 9.3%)* |
| Independent (Oklahoma) | ( 9.9%) |
| Independent (Oregon) | (12.9%) |

**Source:** "For the Record: Election '90 Results," *Congressional Quarterly Weekly Report*, 49 (February 23, 1991), 493–500.

*After the election, the Maine independent "awarded" his votes to the Maine Libertarian party, making that party eligible for automatic ballot access.

local third party that has come closer than the Democrats or Republicans in the years since 1981 to majority control of the Board of Aldermen of Vermont's largest city. Sanders held Burlington's mayoralty from 1981 until 1989.

Third parties find congenial ground in widely scattered locations. After election day 1992, an Alaska Independent, three New Hampshire Libertarians, three Vermont Progressives, and a half dozen independents held state legislature seats. The Libertarian party claimed over 100 elected government officials in 1992. At the same time, members of local Greens parties held twenty city council and five county commission seats in various places and the mayoralty of small Cordova, Arkansas.[3]

Independent candidate Ross Perot was a major player in the presidential campaign of 1992. Except for two former presidents who went on to run as third-party challengers, Perot's 19 percent was the best in history for a presidential candidate not running under the banner of a major party. Perot's wealth and the $60 million or more that the candidate willingly spent on his "world class" campaign partly account for this phenomenal result. But Perot also showed how frayed and vulnerable the two major parties have become. After Bill Clinton's election, Perot himself observed that the time may be nearing for the launch of a national third party capable of doing real battle.

America is fundamentally a pragmatic nation—some commentators have said that pragmatism is the only authentic American contribution to philosophical thinking—and this nation's third parties have not been immune from pragmatism's sway. Ironically, pragmatism really is anti-philosophical; it judges right or worthiness in terms no loftier or more visionary than the efficiency of the method in solving a defined problem or achieving a specific objective. Many third parties, as you will see, either have gone through successive purist and pragmatic phases or have divided themselves into pragmatic v. purist camps. Third-party purists prefer being right than successful if the choice must be made. The prag-matists are more willing to shift weight toward the other foot.

This nation's major parties are owned body and soul by pragmatism. They pursue what the political philosopher Glenn Tinder calls "the pol-itics of convenience."[4] This character has a big impact on third parties. The major parties are essentially nonideological. Alabama's George Wallace, in a moment of venture into third-party waters, spoke consid-erable truth when he said of the Democrats and Republicans that "there's not a dime's worth of difference." Like a porous sponge, the major parties soak up through cooptation  (theft is a blunter but just as accurate a term) others' popular ideas, including those popularized by third parties. This is a big burden to the longevity and sustained vitality of those smaller parties, even if a benefit to mainstreaming their demands.[5]

Major parties are open associations normally welcoming back their renegades who ventured episodically onto third-party paths. Consider, for example, the Republican security blankets now cast off by Alaska's Hickel and Connecticut's Weicker, and think where these men are likely to go if they should find their third parties too constraining. Ponder Strom Thurmond's 1948 detour into Dixiecratic politics and his safe return first to the Democrats and now the Republicans. Think of George Wallace's swerve into the third-party periphery and his painless return to the Democratic fold—painless until the senseless act of a would-be assassin felled and paralyzed Wallace at a presidential campaign stop in Maryland on May 15, 1972. All this, of course, burdens third parties as sustained forces in American politics.

Few third parties ever fully escape the powerful attraction of the magnet which is pragmatism. Some of them either never produce a grand vision or, deserting it, become conscious and occasionally successful instruments for influencing the major parties. Despite all this, the third-party temperament comes much closer than that of the major parties to what Tinder calls "the politics of redemption." Redemptionists believe that the goal of politics must be a better world. It rarely has been fashionable in third-party circles to say that "politics is the art of the possible." For their purists but even their relative pragmatists, being right carries its own rewards. In this sense, people who participate in third-party politics truly are heeding the sounds of a different drummer.

Time may bear out the hopeful prophecies, the wishful thinking, of the third-party optimists, or it may crash them in obscurity. Whatever the future holds, I predict that you will remember the major parties' blandness, their nonideological devotion to the center, their pragmatic focus upon winning and winning alone and find fascination in the some-times very different characters of the other parties about which you will be reading in the pages that follow. In those faint and distant drumbeats, you may even find one toward which you yourself will resonate.

## Notes

1. For example, David S. Broder, *The Party's Over* (New York: Harper and Row, 1972).

2. The new Alaska governor's rhetoric, style, and policy initiatives somehow managed to alienate Alaskans of almost every stripe. According to a May 1991 national report about Hickel, "the feminists are furious. The natives are restless. The Democrats are dyspeptic. The Republicans are riled. And even some of the more independent elements of the [Alaska] Independence party are circulating a petition demanding the recall of their man in the Governor's Mansion—a move the party chairman dismisses as a CIA plot." Philip Gold, "Profile: Walter J. Hickel: Alaska Warms Up to Wally World," *Insight on the News*, 7 (May 13, 1991), 43.

3. Jay Walljasper, "Why the Democrats Matter," *Utne Reader* (November/ December 1992), 150–151.

4. Glenn Tinder, *Political Thinking: The Perennial Questions*, 4th. ed. (Glenview, Ill.: Scott, Foresman and Co., 1986), 172–173.

5. See Leon Epstein, *Political Parties in the American Mold* (Madison: University of Wisconsin Press, 1986); and his *Political Parties in Western Democracies* (New York: Frederick A. Praeger Publishers, 1967).

# On the Outside Looking In:

## Third Parties and the Political Mainstream

> If a man does not keep pace with his companions,
> perhaps it is because he hears a different
> drummer. Let him step to the music which
> he hears, however measured or far away.
> —from *Walden* by Henry David Thoreau

The place is Birmingham, Alabama. It is late June 1979. Delegates from around the nation have come together for the national convention of the *Prohibition party*. Their party was born in 1869. It is the third most ancient American party living today, only fifteen years junior to the GOP (the Republicans) and four decades younger than the world's oldest active party, the Democrats.

What these delegates will do—nominate candidates for president and vice-president, adopt a platform, and rally to capture what free media attention may come their way—is pretty standard stuff for most American national parties. Even so, the setting and scene are likely to surprise the uninitiated. This convention is not being held in one of the mega-arenas the Democrats and Republicans select. The location, Motel Birmingham, has been carefully and deliberately chosen to reward this city's only dry (no-alcohol-allowed) lodging facility.

These delegates number under 100, not the 4,000 who attended Prohibition's 1892 Cincinnati convention or the thousands who show up for Republican and Democratic affairs today. Some of the delegates at Motel Birmingham are Woman's Christian Temperance Union (WCTU) members who still remember the glory days of the Prohibition era. Almost all of these folks are old. Before departing, they will eulogize Prohibition saints who have died in the four years since their party last met.

Their platform will bear planks embracing a host of conservative issues resembling those on which Republican Ronald Reagan also will run next year. But the centerpiece of this Prohibition document will be, as always, alcohol: "We . . . favor the prohibition of the manufacture, distribution, and sale of all alcoholic beverages." To prepare the way, the Reverend Charles Ewing will deliver a stirring keynote, "Liberty and the Liquor Traffic." His speech will feature the allegory of a mule and a leech:

> One hot summer day a mule was sensing the heat and thought he'd go down into the river and take a swim and cool off. After he'd splashed around a while and refreshed himself, he climbed out on the bank and looked down and saw a leech that had fastened itself to his leg. The mule said, "Now look here, Mr. Leech. I don't like your company. You just detach yourself from me right now." The leech looked up and said, "Now let's not get hasty about this. I have a proposition to make, which if you accept will result in our mutual benefit. . . . You license me to suck your blood. And for every six and a half drops I suck, I'll give you back one drop in revenue. And that way you can pay off your debts and balance your budget." The mule said, "Why, I never saw it that way before. I'll just take you up on that."
>
> Up in the top of a tree a wise old owl was listening to the whole conversation. He shook his head and said, "Only a jackass could fall for a line like that." I'm not sure whether the mule was a Democrat or Republican.

Local media watchers never will hear of this speech or its allegory. The media, in fact, will be quite inattentive to the goings-on at Motel Birmingham: a few humorous clips on local television news, a newspaper article or two. One on the front page of the afternoon paper will tell of the eccentricities of these Prohibition windmill-tilters.

These delegates harbor no illusions about their chances in the upcoming election. The person presenting presidential nominee Benjamin Bubar to his party will call their candidate "the man who *should be* the next president of the United States." Before leaving for home, these Prohibitionists will sing their party's old hymn, "I'd Rather Be Right Than President":

> I'd rather be right than President, I want my conscience clear;
> I'll firmly stand for the truth and right, I have a God to fear.

I'll work and vote the way I pray—No matter what the scoffers
   say—
I'd rather be right than President, I want my conscience clear."

Ben Bubar, who would manage to make it to the ballots of just eight
states in 1980, bagged 7,100 votes. Party fortunes have been just as
meager since. That may bother the rank and file less than you think.
Many of them bask in the glories of their party's past.

Although the Prohibition party itself never left the periphery to
enter the national mainstream, this party's past has been impressive. Its
crowning achievement, one for which Prohibition must share credit with
an array of other early twentieth-century temperance, women's, and
progressive movements and interests, was the **Eighteenth Amendment**.*
That 1919 federal constitutional addendum banned the manufacture, sale,
transportation, importation, or exportation of "intoxicating liquors." In
1932 the Twenty-first Amendment repealed the Eighteenth, the only
amendment so far to suffer such a fate. To this day, Prohibitionists say
that the major parties sandbagged prohibition's enforcement, thus en-
suring its failure.

According to this party's own official account of its history, Prohibition has trekked through three distinct phases: the Prophetic period (1869–
1896), the Pragmatic period (1896–1932), and the Fundamentalist period
(since 1932).[1] During the Prophetic phase, the Prohibitionists confidently
forecast that their party would bring about an "evangelistic transformation" to a higher social order in America. Pragmatic leaders of the second
phase held no such grandiose designs or illusions. Accepting the reality
that their party was not going to supplant either the Republicans or the
Democrats in the ranks of the major parties, they led their own third party
into coalitions with other temperance, woman suffrage, and progressive
associations. In its current Fundamentalist period, the party, deserting its
traditional attachments to progressive causes, has been born again as a
small, very peripheral band of conservative Protestant Christians.

Although the party scored its most impressive presidential vote result
in the Prophetic period—in 1892, some 270,770 voters, one of every
forty-four in the nation, voted Prohibition for president—evidence suggests that the party really enjoyed its heyday during its Pragmatic phase.
That was when the Eighteenth Amendment became the law of the land.

---

*Throughout this book key terms appear in bold type. These terms are defined in the
Glossary.

CHAPTER ONE

It was the time when, in 1916, Prohibition's Sidney J. Catts won 47.71 percent of the vote and the governorship of Florida,[2] when Los Angeles area voters sent Prohibitionist Charles H. Randall to three consecutive terms (1915–1921) in the U.S. House of Representatives.

You still may be unimpressed by Prohibition's longevity, its stand on alcohol, its occasional electoral victories in the past, or by the quixotic fidelity and commitment of its partisans today. If so, consider one final fact that may validate the claim that Prohibition has been a party worth knowing. Through the course of its Prophetic and Pragmatic phases, Prohibition held strong commitments to the woman suffrage movement — the organized effort to secure, by and for women, the right to vote. Prohibition's contribution to the ultimate success of that movement was far from minor.

In 1869, more than half a century before the ratification of the woman suffrage **Nineteenth Amendment**, Prohibition granted full participating delegate rights to the women attending the party's very first national convention. The women who took their seats at that Chicago meeting were the first ever accorded that prerogative by any American party. The Woman's Christian Temperance Union first organized itself in 1874 as the women's arm of the Prohibition party. During the two decades in which Prohibitionist Frances Willard (the first woman ever honored by a likeness in the Capitol's Statuary Hall) led it, WCTU far outstripped in importance its partisan parent. It became the largest women's organization of the nineteenth century. The WCTU was the very heart of the organized demand for prohibition and women's rights as well as for prison and labor reform, public support for neglected children, for peace, in short, for a transformed society dedicated to social justice.

Long before the 1880s birth of the Equal Rights party as the first national women's rights party, Prohibition had placed within its 1872 platform a plank demanding the vote for women. Other third parties would take up that charge, but Republican and Democratic platforms demurred from that position until 1916. Many women forged for themselves places of leadership and influence in the Prohibition party. In 1920, with national woman suffrage barely in place, Prohibition nominated Ella A. Boole of New York and Leah Cobb Marion of Pennsylvania for the U.S. Senate. Boole took 159,477 votes, Marion 132,610.

## Third-Party Types

The late V. O. Key observed two kinds of regionally or nationally organized third parties.[3] Key called one of these types the **continuing**

**doctrinal party.** You will be reading about continuing doctrinal parties in chapter 5 of this book.

Prohibition is one of the continuing doctrinal parties; so too are left-wing party associations like Socialist Labor, Socialist, Socialist Workers, and the Communist party. George Lincoln Rockwell's right-wing American Nazi party lived long enough to qualify for this category also. The Libertarian party (LP) born in 1971 bills itself with some justification as "the third largest party in America today." Libertarians hope that someday they either will supplant one of the two now-existing major parties or increase the number of majors to three; but the best bet for now is that LP will hold its present place as a continuing doctrinal third party.

Parties of this type sustain themselves for at least several decades. Most continuing doctrinal third parties regularly or occasionally nominate candidates, and on rare occasions their nominees have won local, state, even congressional office. But these parties' stability and continuity, their long lifespans, result more from their activists' faithful commitment to party doctrine or creed than from any genuine hope of electoral victory. Even their pragmatists, when pragmatists exist in their ranks, find their gratification in being right.

A student once observed that continuing doctrinal third parties reminded her of asteroids, those bits of rock and dust that orbit the sun in the general vicinity of two much larger planets. Though far from perfect, her metaphor is intriguing. Sometimes a party of this kind does influence the mainstream. Prohibition had something to do with enactment of the Eighteenth Amendment. Socialist party platforms influenced the development of Social Security and other New Deal programs, and that party governed Milwaukee as recently as 1960. The Communist party enjoyed some influence in the labor, minority, and academic communities of the 1930s and 1940s. But parties of this type never seriously threaten the dominance of the major parties. They are, as Key observed them, "in a sense outside the system."[4]

Beyond the constraints that keep all third parties out on the national periphery, continuing doctrinal parties often are alienated from the political and electoral mainstream by the radicalism of their creeds and by their activists' fidelity to creed. No presidential candidate running solely as nominee of a continuing doctrinal party ever has won more than 6 percent of the popular vote. Some of these parties regard the whole American election process to be a sham or fraud and do not normally offer candidates for office.

Because of this chasm separating continuing doctrinal parties from the mainstream, some scholars prefer to call them minor parties.[5] The third-party designation, they say, should be reserved for parties belonging to V. O. Key's second type, the "recurring, shortlived . . . party eruptions." Short-lived parties are the subject of chapters 2 and 3 of this book.

A **short-lived party** usually originates either as a movement of economic protest or as a splinter from one of the major parties. Antimasons and Free Soilers, Populists, Progressives, Dixiecrats, and others have proven unable to sustain themselves as significant actors in American politics. Even so, these short-lived parties sometimes score impressive results in elections: the Know Nothings (1856), Populists (1892), Bull Moose Progressives (1912), La Follette Progressives (1924), and American Independents (1968) as well as John Anderson's National Unity Campaign (1980). Through "appropriation" of their ideas by major parties, some of these transient parties strongly influence the development of public policy. Their early deaths thus do not necessarily indicate that they have failed, at least in the policy area. The irony here is supreme; success at forcing its policy demands on the mainstream may write the death warrant for a third party.

Some third-party leaders strongly aver that to Key's two third-party types an additional category must be added: the third party that came in from the cold. The national pattern of only two major parties has existed with but a few breaks since the 1790s: Federalists v. Democratic-Republicans, Democrats v. National Republicans, then Whigs, and finally Republicans. The brief deviations have been interludes of one-partyism rather than multi-partyism. Even so, some people claim that the Republicans originated as a third party in 1854 and then quickly supplanted the Whigs within the national two-party system. Libertarians and others find hope in that. Some historians concur with this analysis, though others contend that the Whigs already were being consigned to the ashcan of history by the time the GOP was born. Even if the hopeful contention is true, any third party today must count it improbable that the scenario will replay to its benefit.

Whatever the validity of this claim from Republican history, there surely is one other genuine third-party type. You will be reading about the parties of this kind, the **non-national significant other,** in chapter 6. Virginia Readjusters of the last century; the Wisconsin Progressive party during the Depression and World War II; the Progressive Coalition of today's Burlington, Vermont; and the Liberals, Conservatives, and Right-to-Lifers in contemporary New York all are or have been parties of this type. Non-national significant others find an influential place for themselves in the politics of their state or community, some even becoming major party actors there. Some have sent nominees to Congress. But in their electoral base they remain confined, either by external circumstance or their own choice, to their own originating boundaries.

Take, for example, the Minnesota Farmer-Labor party. Born around the close of World War I, Farmer-Labor quickly upended the Democrats as the main party opposition to Minnesota's dominant Republicans. Later, in the depths of the Depression, it overtook the GOP as the principal governing party in that state. In 1944 it merged with the Democrats. To this day Minnesota voters find on their ballot the Democratic-Farmer-Labor party, which is now the state's affiliate of the national Democratic party. The old Farmer-Labor party achieved major party status in Minnesota.[6] But like the other non-national significant others, it remained a third party from the national perspective because it never extended beyond the boundaries into which it was born.

## Major Parties, Third Parties, and the Two-Party System

The political scientists Dan Nimmo and Thomas D. Ungs have defined a political party as "a coalition of fairly stable, enduring, and frequently conflicting interests, organized to mobilize support in competitive elections in order to control policy making."[7] They obviously had an American **major party** in mind, because their definition hits these parties right in the eye. The Democrats and Republicans do attract some people for reasons of principle, even ideology; but these major parties mainly seek to win elections and, through winning, to control the political system and its policy processes. In pursuit of these goals, each big party becomes like an umbrella accessible to various interests and their constituencies. The late Lee Atwater, a master campaign strategist, liked to think of the major parties, especially his own GOP, as big tents.

Although the Nimmo and Ungs definition is partly valid when applied to major parties in other nations with two-party systems, it is less suitable to those parties than in characterizing American Republicans and Democrats. Great Britain and many of the English-speaking nations possess two-party systems; but a lot of these countries have third parties, like Britain's Liberal Democrats, that have managed to sustain themselves and win parliamentary seats over a very long time. In the transient nature of its most significant third parties, the United States is extraordinary in the Anglo world.

The reader dissatisfied with the large umbrella (or big tent) metaphor when thinking of American major parties would do well to ponder a porous sponge.[8] In their singleminded devotion to winning, the Democrats and Republicans above all else include. America's major parties are not, of course, totally devoid of ideological differentiation; the soul of the GOP does rest a few degrees to the right of the Democrats'. But for America's big parties, the game is to hover close to the center in order to seek as much support as they can. It is an overstatement that they say all things to all people. They just say as much as they can to all they can reach.

There are many, some political scientists among them, who lament the bland, centrist, relatively nonideological and undifferentiated characters of American major parties. In a famed but noninfluential 1950 report, the Committee on Political Parties of the American Political Science Association strongly recommended the revamping of each American major party as a **responsible party** on the order of Britain's major Conservative and Labour parties. The Democratic and Republican parties, this report said, should become more centralized, more internally cohesive and disciplined, more externally differentiated than they have been in the past.[9]

This relative irresponsibility of the Democratic and Republican parties accounts in part for the low opinion that Americans hold for their major parties. Third parties often present themselves as principled alternatives to the nonprogrammatic majors, and some third-party leaders genuinely have hoped that their movements might cash in on the fact. Ironically, just the opposite holds true. It seems almost to be natural law: the more formidable a third party's challenge to the central place of the major parties, the more likely it is that the third party's life will be transient and short.

> These transient American examples support the paradoxical conclusion that a third party is a functioning element in two-party competition. In a sense, a third party represents dysfunction. If two-party competition functioned perfectly, the two major parties would contain all important political forces. . . . But the two-party competition is never perfect. *It comes closest to being so in the United States, where the [major] parties can be loosely organized and hospitable to divergent interests.*[10] (Emphasis added.)

In their inclusive strategy and style, America's open and undisciplined major parties impose few if any penalties upon their renegades, their Strom Thurmonds and George Wallaces and legions of others, who set out for, then return from, third-party destinations. This saps away the sustained vitality of the third party by draining off its strong leadership. Another reason for the transient lives of America's most threatening and significant third parties is the major parties' ability and willingness to take ideas and programs that third parties show to be popular. It is not always by design or preference of the organization folks in a major party. Party primaries empower dissenters and dissenting opinions to penetrate major party ranks; a more closed system of nominating major party candidates might otherwise drive dissent toward a sustained third-party course.[11]

## "Third Party": A Definition

An association that calls itself a party should be considered a party. This truth seems self-evident despite elitist penchants of many scholars for imposing definitions from above. Neither Nimmo and Ungs nor other conventional approaches illuminate the search for a meaningful working definition for third party.

In function some American third parties resemble interest groups as much as they do the major parties. Like interest groups, third parties tend to be much better at articulating interests than at interest aggregation. For some third parties, the issue focus or the array of primary interests is in fact as narrow as that of the single issue interest groups; consider, for example, the anti-abortion reason for existence of New York's Right-to-Life party. Many short-lived parties do try to create large aggregative umbrellas. Most fail at this, and none sustain what they have built. Continuing doctrinal parties are unwilling to revise credal commitments just to become more popular or win elections. Prohibitionists, as you know by now, would rather be "right than president." So too would those, at least those who are purists, in the ranks of the other continuing doctrinal parties.

Interest groups, social scientists say, may be vitally concerned with (and decisive in) election outcomes, but they do not formally nominate candidates for office. The vast majority of third parties do, like major parties, nominate candidates, on some occasions at least. However, many third parties find insurmountable problems of ballot access, and few enter into campaigns with real hope of electoral victory. Third parties sometimes run token campaigns hoping that by capturing free media coverage they can begin to educate the public. Many third parties (the National Woman's party is an example) have found their clout in methods—lobbying, picketing, demonstrations—that many people hold to be more characteristic of interest groups than of parties.

Through most of its history this nation has experienced a rather stable pattern of two major parties.[12] Third parties include all those parties proving unable either to transform the national party system into a multi-party arrangement or to replace one of the existing major parties within the national two-party framework. Because Republicans and Democrats have held center stage nationally since the Civil War, the third-party appellation belongs to all post-1865 self-designated parties other than the Democratic and Republican parties.

A **third party** is an organized aggregate of leaders, members, and supporters that 1. designates itself a party, 2. articulates perceived interests of its devotees, 3. presses these interests upon or in contradistinction to the American political and party systems using electoral and/ or other political methods, and 4. either never attains or is unable to sustain the primary or the secondary share of loyalties of people making up the national body politic.

## Three-Dimensional Parties

One of the insights gleaned by political scientists who have studied American major parties is that they are three-dimensional in nature: (1) **party organization** (outside the formal government), (2) **party in the electorate,** and (3) the **party-in-government.**[13] This is important to third parties, for when the characteristics in one of the major party dimensions change these changes can affect the viability and fate of third parties. Moreover, third parties sometimes become three-dimensional themselves.

### Party Organization

American major party organizations are much less centralized than the parties of the European democracies; and in contrast to the European **mass membership party** type, in which many partisans in the electorate also hold formal ("card carrying, dues paying") membership in their party's organization, the Democrats and Republicans have **cadre party** organizations: here only a small percentage of party identifiers in the electorate become active in their major party's organization. Due mainly to direct primaries, television, interest group electioneering activities, and the decline of patronage, the major party organization and its cadre have forfeited a lot of their previous control over party matters like nominating and the supervision and management of campaigns. As a result, elected partisans in government become more independent of their party's non-governmental organization and maybe more dependent upon partisans in the electorate.

Third parties organize themselves in various ways. Some that emphasize electoral objectives copy the major parties and build cadre structures. One reason is that state legislators, Democrats and Republicans, pass the statutes regulating both election and the character of party electoral organizations. One intrinsic weakness of short-lived third parties is their inability to organize effectively, especially at the grassroots. There is a real Catch 22 here. Effective organization, important for any successful party, is vital to third parties' mastery of the statutory hurdles to their securing a place on the ballot. But the short-lived party's popular appeal often peaks in the party's infancy, when its organization is inexperienced, underdeveloped, and poorly financed.

Many American third parties are, unlike the Republican or Democratic parties, formal membership organizations. But third parties rarely are able to develop into European-type mass membership bodies. There have been a few; the Socialist party, which took nearly a million presidential votes in 1912, had 118,045 dues-paying members that year. Many doctrinal parties are both centrally organized and closed, internally controlling recruitment. Some Marxist-Leninist parties see themselves as an elite vanguard leading the workers' struggle. Nazi associations sometimes organize along quasi-military lines, and they claim to confine their membership to racial Aryans.

### Party in the Electorate

The breadth and depth of popular devotion to the major parties has been diminishing since the 1950s. Independents and weak partisans grow in proportion to the numbers of strong major party identifiers. Some scholars have seen such **dealignment** as the first step toward **realignment,** with the Republican Party. They suggest that Reagan and Bush-era Republicans became expert umbrella-builders, that the GOP went far toward replacing the Democrats' New Deal coalition as the majority party in America.[14] Third parties hope on the other hand that dealignment, coupled with low voter turnout, signals real popular disenchantment with both major parties and an opening door for a third party. But with the exception of blue collar whites (especially in the South), many of whom shifted gradually to the Republicans in the 1970s and 1980s, the main trend so far seems to be detachment from any party.[15]

Public opinion surveys are the most effective measures of partisanship in the electorate. But survey research is a young science providing little useful information from before World War II. It is unknown, for instance, how many voters considered themselves to be personally affiliated with a third party in 1912, when third-party presidential candidates took 35 percent of the popular votes. Survey responses reveal that in 1984 only 2 percent of the national electorate called themselves something other than Democrats, Republicans, or independents.[16] It is unlikely that more than 3 percent at any time since then have considered themselves to be affiliated with a third party. Election victory or even a decent showing thus requires third parties to present issues so compelling and candidates attractive enough to mute ingrained affinities for the majors. Compounding their problem is the perception heartily encouraged by the major parties that a third-party vote is futile; worse, that through diversion it may help elect the major party and candidate less congenial to the voter's views.

### Party-in-Government

In the United States each major party-in-government finds nearly impossible its dream of becoming the exclusive governing party. This wildly contrasts with the two major parties in parliamentary Britain, where one party governs and the other serves—pending the next national elections—as Her Majesty's Loyal Opposition. In America Republicans and Democrats share both in governance and opposition. One reason is separation of powers and federalism, architectural division of governmental functions among three branches and two (or three) levels of government, that militates against one-party control of the whole game.[17] The constitutional framers designed this architecture to provide such barriers because they feared the tyrannical potential of **faction**—an interest-holding segment of society, be it party, interest group, or whatever. Through divion they hoped to conquer and neutralize that potential.[18]

Another barrier to single-party monopoly is that the two major parties in Congress and state legislatures have lacked most of the discipline, cohesion, and differentiation one finds in Britain and other countries. There is some evidence that during the Reagan years congressional Republicans and Democrats moved very modestly in the responsible party direction. But on divided legislative votes in Congress, it still is normal to find a coalition of Democrats and Republicans opposing a coalition of Democrats and Republicans.

Third parties are not major direct players within the institutions of national government. Antimasons did hold many U.S. House seats in 1833–1835 and Know Nothings were a very substantial minority in the House during 1855–1857. Both of these were times of major party flux and transition. Lincoln's Republicans still may have been in transition to major party status as of 1860; Lincoln won with 40 percent of the popular vote but 59 percent of the electors in a four-way race. It is, however, almost axiomatic that third parties do not win the American presidency.

Presidents appoint personal supporters and their own party's devotees to the administration. Even when congressional statutes limit single-party appointment to the regulatory commissions, the main beneficiary of these limits is the nonpresidential major party. One should be very skeptical of those who characterize the federal judiciary as nonpartisan (even non-political). Studies show that presidents appoint people of their own (major) party more than 90 percent of the time to positions on the federal bench.[19]

Third parties have had some position in Congress. Except in certain Congresses of the 1830s, 1850s, and 1890s, their numbers have been marginal. Those numbers have declined precipitously since the passing of the 1930s Great Depression. Third parties nearly have been shut out of the chambers of Congress since 1945. Just two candidates have won U.S. House elections on third-party ballot lines since World War II, the last in 1948. Since 1951, except for a handful of independents, the House has been entirely in Democratic and Republican hands.

Vermonters in 1990 elected independent socialist Bernard Sanders to fill their only seat in the House. Fearing recrimination from Republicans, the House Democrats rejected an entreaty from this Vermont "radical" for admission to the Democratic caucus; but they made an arrangement for his appointment to House committees. On divided votes Sanders usually found himself on the same side as most of the Democrats. He voted against the resolution authorizing President Bush to initiate the Desert Storm operation.[20]

One third partisan and two independents have won U.S. senatorial election since World War II. The two most recent senators elected or reelected without benefit of major party ballot position were Harry Byrd, Jr., and James L. Buckley. Son of a prominent Virginia Democratic family, Byrd first won his senate seat as a Democrat. An independent during his second and third senate terms (1971–1983), he connected with the Senate Democrats, especially the southern conservative "boll weevil" group. Buckley was elected to a six-year term in 1971 on the New York Conservative party ticket. He had the blessing of President Richard M. Nixon and tacit support from part of the state GOP establishment. In the Senate he associated with the Republican Conference.

Third-party people in Congress may serve their constituents ably.

They may be effective legislators as well, either in coalition with Democrats or Republicans or on essentially nonpartisan matters; but their numbers are far too small to enact third-party platform commitments without support from many in one or both major parties. Thus, assuming that third-party numbers remain relatively small, numbers are not the most crucial thing determining whether a third party will influence the policy-making process. That influence is more likely when a major party takes for itself an issue position that the third party has advanced previously.

## The Usefulness of Third Parties: A Utilitarian Analysis

In dealing with political phenomena, scholars often use a technique called role analysis. They write of roles presidents play: chief executive, head of state, commander in chief. Party specialists also use role analysis. Just about any book on the subject will tell you that the main role of political parties—usually the writer is thinking about the major parties—is to link people with their political system. In doing so, parties discharge related roles or functions: (1) helping organize the political selection process, especially elections; (2) mobilizing citizen participation; (3) contributing to popular understanding of politics; (4) channeling and reducing conflict, thus helping build the consensus that democracy needs; (5) organizing and running the government and/or opposition.

Third parties also play roles. Though a third party may differ from the major parties or from another third party in the manner and impact of its role performance, Rosenstone and his colleagues rightly observe that third parties do play many of the roles also played by the Democrats and Republicans.[21]

Third parties carry out two additional roles that the major parties do not. First, they are a way for the dissident, the disaffected, to "blow off steam." Thus they serve, often quite unintentionally, to undergird and stabilize the political system, including the pattern of just two major parties. Second, a third party may assist, by the example of its own popular appeal, in correcting the policy stands, even the ideological course, of a major. A third party therefore is, as Leon Epstein sees it, "a functioning element in two-party competition."[22]

There is, however, a severe and inherent limit on the usefulness of such role analysis when applied to third parties. Just think about it. When speaking of role playing one cannot escape thoughts of an assigned part within the already-written script of a play. In this case the play is

**Table 1.1: Third-Party Presence (Excluding Independents) in U.S. Congress, By Period**

*Average Third-Party Percentage of All Seats in Congresses of the Period*

| Period | House | Senate* |
|---|---|---|
| 1829–1871 | | |
| 21st-41st Congress | 4.96 | 1.70 |
| 1871–1911 | | |
| 42d-61st Congress | 1.69 | 2.74 |
| 1911–1951 | | |
| 62d-81st Congress | .95 | .94 |
| 1951–1991 | | |
| 82d-101st Congress | .00 | .15 |

*Prior to 1913 ratification of the 17th Amendment, which mandated popular election of U.S. Senators, members of the Senate were selected by the legislatures of their respective states.

the American political process (system) and the main script is the constitutional framework for that process. Although its users may deny it or even not know it, role analysis carries a built-in conservative or system-maintaining bias. Role players are expected to follow the script and to contribute to the overall success of the play.

Third parties and their devotees really dislike that kind of interpretation of what they do. Revolutionist third parties feel profoundly alienated from the very essence of the present system. In democratic theory's distinction between loyal and disloyal opposition, their leaders and followers may see themselves in the latter ranks even if reticent to say so publicly. Some of the spirit of insurgency exists in all third parties. The very existence of a third party bears a conviction that there is at least a defect in electoral and policy processes emasculating all viewpoints that the majors do not steal. Nonrevolutionist parties may work to reform these processes to end such closure. But the concept of system-maintaining role playing really is alien to third-party impulse and spirit.

Consider now a different approach—utilitarian analysis—to assessing third parties' usefulness. Classical **Utilitarianism** was a nineteenth-century school of thought founded by Jeremy Bentham, whose followers and descendants included such major luminaries as James Mill and John Stuart Mill. These Utilitarians rejected traditional metaphysical notions of the Good and replaced them with good defined and implemented by individuals in terms of a pleasure-pain principle. For these Utilitarian thinkers good is what brings pleasure to a particular person, and evil (or bad) is what inflicts on that person pain. Each individual is free to define these things for oneself. The rub comes in implementation, for one person's pleasure pursuit can impede or checkmate that of another. The good society must yield the greatest good (or happiness) for the greatest number. For classical Utilitarians this meant a society in which each individual has maximum discretion to pursue that person's own good, subject only to the constraints (think of them as fences) that society must impose to protect every other individual's prerogative to do the same thing. Most societies are not good, because they build their fences too high; the individual feels the tyranny of the collective. The earlier Utilitarians feared structural fences, those institutional constraints enacted and enforced by government. One of the important later ones, John Stuart Mill (*On Liberty,* 1859), showed more concern about social fences: high walls constructed in the court of public opinion.

In this chapter's last section the reader will be looking at both kinds of fences, social (cultural constraints) and institutional (structural constraints), and their design for the purpose and effect of consigning third parties to the periphery. Before that you will be observing the usefulness of third parties: their individual and social utility.

### Individual Utility

Some people find a lot of emotional gratification in associating with third parties. One reason is what can be called the Don Quixote syndrome. Studies show that most people have bandwagon psyches; they are attracted to a winner. People who have the Don Quixote syndrome are just the opposite. They feel attraction to lost causes and reality and significance in a vision that stands no chance of fulfillment. It is easy to find lost causes and attractive visions in the myriad of third parties.

A man in his seventies revealed to me in an interview that he has voted in every presidential election since he turned twenty-one. Only once has he voted for a major-party candidate. His 1972 ballot went to George McGovern—a decision that he came to regret. Every other time he voted for someone on the third-party left, usually the Socialist nominee. He always repudiated the observation of others that "politics is the art of the possible," along with their objection that his third-party votes may have helped elect conservative presidents. He had a very different view of politics, a vision of human beings living in true community. The ancient Greeks would have understood what he meant.

Many will concede that there is something admirable in dreaming impossible dreams, in preferring to be right than president. Few will deny that Don Quixote can be a powerful magnet attracting people to third parties.

A second magnet may be less noble, but it too has strong pulling power. This is the big fish in a little pond syndrome. Think how much easier it would be to attain a position of third-party leadership—with a grandiose title like regent, executive director, national chairman, member of the central committee, national director, or national leader, or even to found a third party—than to find a place as member of the Republican National Committee, delegate to the Democratic National Convention, or as a major party nominee for an important office. Many people enter politics with egos in need of stroking. It often is easier to do that in the context of third-party activity.

Harold Lasswell, in a classic psychoanalytical work, revealed that among political figures there are two dissimilar personality types, the **political agitators** and **political administrators**.[23] Political administrators are pragmatic, goal-centered people who are most effective and personally gratified in positions of governmental leadership and influence. Agitators are more rigid people who invest their psychic energies in a mission or cause. They pitch their political appeals in emotional and exhortative language and they vituperate their adversaries as enemies of all that is good and right. Their gratification comes in the heat of political contest (the crusade or struggle) far more than in daily routines of governing. In 1968 Alabama Governor George Wallace ran a most impressive third-party presidential campaign. Wallace biographers characterize their man as the epitome of Lasswell's political agitator type. Given their consignment to the political periphery and the devotion of many of them to mission or cause, it would seem quite likely that third parties attract more than their share of political agitators. A 1980s study of leaders of twelve contemporary third parties bears testimony that this is true, especially for third parties with values most distant from the mainstream.[24]

This study also indicates that some third parties attract authoritarian personalities. Personalities of this type appear in heavy concentrations in parties of the ultraright. This evidence supports what might be inferred logically. T. W. Adorno, in his renowned 1950 psychological explanation of fascism's appeal, wrote that authoritarian personalities draw rigid boundaries between "us" and "them." They see human relationships (politics included) in terms of conflict and manipulation.[25]

Some principled people who come to a third party because of its program or vision would find gratification in their party's success. These people follow a cause because they believe it is right, not because it is lost. They may be convinced of a wrong that cannot or will not be remedied by the major parties, at least not without third-party pressure. Third parties, like other groups, also attract people seeking friendship, community, or more intimate relationship with people who share common bonds. Moreover, in those rare circumstances of a significant third-party presence in government, third-party devotees may seek and find patronage or other tangible material payoffs.

### Social Utility

There are some weird and eccentric third parties. Members of the Minnesota Twin Cities-based Archonist party insist that Zionism completely controls American government. They assume that any American war will be fought for Zionism's benefit. Archonists are not alone in that particular view. What is unique is their proposed remedy, what Archonists call their "Klinger Plan." In the event of war or the draft's resurrection, they intend to counsel young men to follow the lead of M*A*S*H's Corporal Klinger: dress in drag to render themselves undraftable.

The National Hamiltonian party rests on a saner side of the Daffy Kingdom. National Hamiltonians are an elitist group wanting to sack democracy and replace it with aristocracy. There is as well the Manhattan-based Expansionist party (XP), claiming 450 members. "Formed by homosexuals for all people," XP seeks American statehood for Puerto Rico, the Virgin Islands, English-speaking Canada, Australia, and New Zealand and an eventual political union of the United States, Britain, Ireland, and Western Europe under a revamped Constitution. A noble if narrow cause inspired the American Vegetarian party in the 1950s. The Theocratic party contested for the presidency in the 1960s.

Even parties like these, notable for nothing if not their eccentricity, may benefit society. Americans consider themselves, as others hold them, to make up the leading free pluralist society on earth. The existence and tolerance of organized eccentricity testifies to Americans and the world that the United States indeed is (or comes close to) what it claims to be.

Third parties, especially those which many Americans deem dangerous to the nation's security, sometimes become barometers of popular commitment to freedom. In doing so, they may assist the nation in eventually springing to freedom's defense. Think for a moment about the dark years of McCarthyism, about congressional investigations, and the blacklisting that came with the onset of the Cold War. Soviet influence in America and the Communist Party-USA with its links to Moscow were presumably this witch-hunt's main targets. Its many victims included almost the entire non-Communist left, prominent liberals and progressives portrayed either as Communist fellow travelers or as soft on communism. Another casualty of this hunt was the very freedom to associate without being presumed guilty by association. In 1951 the Supreme Court sustained the Smith Act,[26] notorious legislation declaring it a crime to teach, advocate, or to conspire to teach or advocate the overthrow of the government; to join or conspire to join any group so teaching, advocating, or conspiring; or even to correspond with such a group. Retrospectively scholars have described the nearly prevailing attitude of that time as "in order to save democracy we may have to destroy it." A spokesman for the Libertarian party may have been thinking of this McCarthy period when he said in an interview that Republicans and Democrats have done far more to undermine American democracy than American Communists (or Nazis) ever have.[27]

Today most Americans believe it good that the nation has pulled away from the paranoia of the McCarthy era; but in the late 1960s, fully a decade after the witch-hunt's passing, J. Edgar Hoover, then director of the FBI, privately set forth through the bureau a new Counterintelligence Program (**COINTELPRO**). Aimed nominally at radicals of both left and right for the protection of safety and national security, COINTELPRO mainly targeted leftist organizations, especially the Black Panther, Communist, and Socialist Workers parties. Hoover's successors kept COINTELPRO afloat for years after his 1972 death. The bureau sent agents and paid informants to infiltrate associations. It used dirty tricks to sow intergroup hatred and violence. The bureau manufactured prosecution evidence and suppressed documents supporting the defense in some trials of targeted group activists. It sometimes arranged for and carried out the deaths of association leaders. When revelation came COINTELPRO's defenders raised national security and public safety to justify what had been done. Freedom and security do conflict sometimes, and both are important goals. If there is anything positive in the McCarthy and COINTELPRO legacies, it is that the experience may have taught Americans that freedom demands some substantial risk taking, that liberty for all requires defense of the rights even of those who, if in power, might deny them to others.

Their greatest social utility lies in what third parties contribute to our relatively free marketplace of ideas. Many of America's noblest and most far-reaching advances in freedom were third-party proposals years before major parties touched them with even the longest pole. The Liberty party was struggling against slavery twenty years before the Civil War.

In the late nineteenth century, Prohibition and other third parties demanded woman suffrage. The 1892 Populists demanded equal rights for men and women. Fulfillment of that vision via an Equal Rights Amendment lies still undone a century later.

Of course, most of the issues that third parties raise die at a distance far removed from the mainstream. An American Nazi dream to consolidate Canada and the western, midwestern, and northeastern regions of the U.S. into an Aryan Republic of North America and to consign all American blacks to a separate black nation in the Southeast rightly died in obscurity. But many issues for which third parties early test the waters do, unlike the parties themselves, sail into the mainstream.

Observing that a third party raised an issue later taken up by mainstream parties and politicians does not prove that the issue's success can be attributed to the third-party effort. Interest groups indeed usually have been more potent pushers than third parties. The Eighteenth (Prohibition) Amendment fulfilled the generating dream of the Prohibition party; but historians say that groups like the Anti-Saloon League were more powerful locomotives for the Eighteenth Amendment than the party was.

The same is true of civil rights. Groups such as the Southern Christian Leadership Conference, the National Association for the Advancement of Colored People, and the Student Nonviolent Coordinating Committee were the organizational core of the modern civil rights movement. No third party either fostered or led that movement, despite some charges to the contrary by movement opponents. Yet decades before the 1955 Montgomery bus boycott, Communists and other American radicals were speaking out strongly on behalf of the rights of African-Americans. No doubt political motivations in part underlay these voices, as cynics have charged. But politics also motivated the silence of most early twentieth-century major party politicians on the issue of minority rights.

Historians believe that the Populists were America's most successful third party in transferring ideas into the mainstream. This is partly because in 1896 the Democrats swallowed most of the People's party program, virtually cannibalizing the third party in the bargain.

## Third-Party Constraints

Third parties can be useful. So what? Harold Lasswell, one of this century's most renowned political scientists, said politics is who gets what, when, and how. Nobody believes that life is always fair. If Lasswell's

**Table 1.2: Appropriation and Enactment of Third-Party Issues**

| Third-Party Platform(s) and Issues | Indications of Appropriation: Major Party Platform(s) | Subsequent Enactment: Constitutional Amendment or Congressional Statute |
|---|---|---|
| **Prohibition Party (late 19th century)** | | |
| Prohibition | — — | 18th Amendment (1919); 21st Amendment (repealed 18th) (1933) |
| Female Suffrage | Democrat (1916); Republican (1916) | 19th Amendment (1920) |
| Direct Election: U.S. Senate | Democrat (1908) | 17th Amendment (1913) |
| Initiative and Referendum | — — | None. But enacted in many states. |
| **Populist (People's) Party (1892)** | | |
| Direct Election: U.S. Senate | Democrat (1908) | 17th Amendment (1913) |
| Initiative and Refendum | — — | None. But enacted in many states. |
| Free Coinage of Silver | Democrat (1896) | Defeat of issue with passage of Gold Standard Act |
| Government Ownership of Railroads | — — | — — |
| Immigration Restrictions | Democrat (1896) | Many statutes, particularly in early 1920s |
| (Graduated) Income Tax | Democrat (1908) | 16th Amendment (1913) and subsequent legislation |
| Shorter Working Hours | Democrat (1908)— limited application | Wages and Hours Act (1938); earlier laws in many states |

**Table 1.2—continued**

| Third-Party Platform(s) and Issues | Indications of Appropriation: Major Party Platform(s) | Subsequent Enactment: Constitutional Amendment or Congressional Statute |
|---|---|---|
| **Socialist Party (1904–1912)** | | |
| Female Suffrage | Democrat (1916); Republican (1916) | 19th Amendment (1920) |
| Initiative and Referendum | —— | None. But enacted in many states. |
| Government Ownership of Railroads | —— | —— |
| (Graduated) Income Tax | Democrat (1908) | 16th Amendment (1913) and subsequent legislation |
| Shorter Working Hours | Democrat (1908)— limited application | Wages and Hours Act (1938); earlier laws in many states |
| Abolition of U.S. Senate | —— | —— |
| Abolition of Child Labor | —— | Keating-Owen Act (1916) and state statutes |
| **Socialist Party (1928)** | | |
| Public Works for the Unemployed | Democrat (1932, 1936) | Statutes passed in 1933 |
| Unemployment Insurance | Democrat (1932, 1936) | Social Security Act (1935) |
| **American Independent Party (1968)** | | |
| Toughness on Crime | Republican (1968) | Omnibus Crime Control and Safe Streets Act (1968) and subsequent legislation |

**Sources:** Arthur M. Schlesinger, Jr., ed., *History of U.S. Political Parties*, Vols. II–IV (New York: Chelsea House, 1973); and *National Party Conventions, 1831–1980* (Washington, D.C.: Congressional Quarterly, 1983).

idea is true, in politics there always will be big dogs who get a lot and the little ones receiving little or nothing. Remember that as you assess the peripheral status of third parties.

Social Darwinists believed that in the natural order of things the fittest survive. A line from an old song corrupts their meaning just slightly: "them what has is them what gets." The language and some of the implications of Social Darwinism rightly were discarded long ago. Even so, some of the factors that help usher third parties to the margins do not seem especially unjust. These include:

1. The open and inclusive nature of the major parties, including access by dissidents to the major parties through primaries;
2. Democratic and Republican appropriation of third-party issue positions and of former third-party leaders and supporters;
3. voter rejection of particular third-party candidates because they are politically inexperienced (most are), rigid and doctrinaire (many are), or mediocre unattractive persons;
4. third party vulnerability in organization, finance, and access to mass media, insofar as these problems are not results of legal/ institutional provisions that discriminate, or condone discrimination, against nonmajors.

Your concern should be instead with two other kinds of restraining forces. First, there are cultural constraints, those values in American political culture and elements in the public perception that delimit or constrain the fortunes and influence of third parties. Living in the restrictive social environment of Victorian Britain, John Stuart Mill feared the impact of cultural constraints upon the free will of minority individuals and groups. Today one may wish for more inclusive cultural values and a more tolerant public opinion while recognizing that Americans' values are more inclusive, their opinions more tolerant than the opinions and values either of the Victorian English or McCarthy-era Americans. Far more controversial are structural constraints: all those features of the American constitutional system and provisions of law that by effect and often apparently by design relegate third parties to the periphery.

### Cultural Constraints

Somehow this nation avoided any sustained experience with feudalism, monarchy, or a state church. Thus the sharp ideological divisions and class consciousness found elsewhere never really sprouted here. What developed instead, and in consequence, is a cultural consensus about core values, particularly liberty, individualism, and equal rights. These central values define and delineate the political mainstream. Major parties routinely defer to this cultural consensus. Any other group or (third) party unable to verify its faithful devotion to the values underlying this consensus is consigned—consigns itself—to the periphery.[28]

Sharing as they do in this consensus about core values, mainstream Americans also manifest a cultural duality probably inherited from the British. There is an old saying that in France the number of opinions, and of political parties to express them, precisely equals the number of French citizens. In America issues more frequently divide opinion into two main camps: Federalist versus Anti-Federalist, North versus South, urban versus rural, labor versus mangement, pro-life versus pro-choice. This duality naturally undergirds and supports a system of just two major parties.[29]

Third parties are beset by a **political socialization** process that (1) signals to each new generation that multiparty deviations from national two-party patterns are "unAmerican" and (2) normally engenders either loyalty for the GOP or Democrats or a nonpartisan disposition ("vote for the person, not the party"). Few children learn to devote themselves to the Communists or Libertarians, because there are so few Libertarians or Communists to teach them.

### Structural Constraints

It is with regard to the structural constraints that some dispassionate scholars join third-party defenders in charging that the system divests third parties, diminishes voters' freedom to choose, and thus violates democratic principles to which the nation claims devotion.

America's constitutional framers opposed the spirit and preponderance of any faction; but the political system they initiated normally mandates an electoral arrangement sustaining two dominant parties. This electoral device is called the **single-member district plurality system.** Think, for example, of elections to the national House of Representatives. If your state is entitled by virtue of its population size to more than one House seat, your state government must carve up the state into districts, each equal in population and each represented by a single House member. Every two years, when each district's voters elect a representative to the House, the candidate and party winning the largest share of votes take the seat. It is very possible that a party could win 10, 20, even 30 percent of the votes in the state but not come in first in any one district. Under this system that party wins no seats for its effort. The two principal beneficiaries of this arrangement have a vested interest in appealing to third-party supporters to avoid the temptation to cast a futile vote. This system of election is one reason why third parties are virtually shut out of Congress and most other elected bodies in America.

Some other democracies have adopted an alternate arrangement called **proportional representation (PR)**. This at-large system might assign U.S. House seats to the parties competing in your state in proportion to each party's share of the statewide vote. A party winning 20 percent of the vote in a state entitled to ten seats could expect two seats. Members of the Knesset or parliament of the small nation of Israel win based on their parties' shares of the vote in a nationwide PR system. It is not surprising that Israel and other nations adopting PR have developed multiparty systems.

PR is not unknown in this country, and it has been used in some local elections. New York City voters adopted a version of it in 1936. During its PR days, the Big Apple sent Communist party members Peter Cacchione and Benjamin Davis and allied leftists from the American Labor party to its city council. In 1947, the city abandoned PR as an early casualty of the Cold War.[30]

Presidential and vice-presidential elections are unique on the American scene in that for them the Constitution mandates the **electoral college.** Scholars quarrel over whether this system substantially burdens the third-party cause. The election of a third party presidential nominee seems as inconceivable in a direct popular election system as it now is through the electoral college. Someday the electoral college may even tangibly benefit a third-party campaign. If, for example, the November results entitle a third-party nominee to enough electors to deprive either major candidate of the prize, the third-party nominee, or nominee's electors, might try to negotiate with one of the major candidates. The third-party campaign might offer its electoral votes in return for a presence in or a policy promise from the new administration. If no such **quid pro quo** were worked out, the decision would be thrown to Congress; the House would choose the president, the Senate the vice-president, and a significant third party possibly could influence the decisions in those chambers. Both of these scenarios fueled the unfulfilled hopes of 1968 third-party nominee George Wallace. Neither scenario has come even close to fruition in any presidential election up to now. The electoral college system has failed on only three occasions to elect a president—1800, 1824, and 1876. None of these three exceptional cases involved a third party in any way.[31]

Offsetting this potential third-party benefit is a feature of the electoral college that usually (1) yields to the winner a larger proportion of the electoral votes than his share of the November popular vote and (2) locks (or virtually locks) out third parties from any electoral votes. This is the state-by-state winner-takes-all arrangement in which the candidate taking a state's popular plurality gets all its electoral votes. This prevails by law or custom in the District of Columbia and in forty-eight of the states. Even very popular third parties rarely win the largest vote (entitling them to electoral votes) in a state. In 1980 John Anderson took no electoral votes despite his national popular tally of nearly 7 percent. The same is true of Ross Perot, who earned a 19 percent share of the people's votes in 1992.

Only when the appeal of a third party heavily concentrates upon a particular region can the party expect its electoral vote share to approximate its percent of the popular vote. Since the Civil War just one third party campaign has garnered a larger proportion of the electoral than of the popular vote: in 1948 States' Rights Democrat (Dixiecrat) Strom Thurmond won 7.3 percent of the electors for his November popular share of 2.4 percent. Twenty years later George Wallace's American Independent party attracted nationwide support, but was particularly potent in the South. Even Wallace won but 8.5 percent of the electors for his 13.5 percent of the national popular vote.

Contemporary national policy places discriminatory burdens upon third-party efforts to obtain vital presidential campaign funds. Democratic and Republican campaigns reap the benefits. When Congress passed the 1974 **Federal Election Campaign Act,** the senators and representatives intended to clean up national elections following Watergate and to reduce wealthy donors' ("fatcats'") power over Washington politicians. But FECA also serves as "a major party protection act."[32]

The FECA process allocates very substantial sums for the Republican and Democratic presidential nominees to use in their general election campaigns. It is normally impossible for a third-party nominee to take federal money during the fall campaign, when the funds are most needed. This makes it more likely that private lenders will turn down third-party loan petitions as too risky. If the party received 5 percent of the presidential popular vote four years earlier, its present nominee may receive federal money to wage the campaign. The receipt by such a third-party campaign would be prorated on the basis of that party's share of the popular presidential votes four years ago; its allocation always would be far less than the funds given in equal shares to the Republican and Democratic campaigns. Otherwise, the campaigns of third-party presidential nominees may qualify for funds (on a prorated basis) only after the November election and only if they have received at least a 5 percent slice of the votes.

Candidates seeking their party's presidential nomination may qualify for federal matching funds, and on some occasions third-party candidates have qualified. Lenora Fulani of the New Alliance party took federal matching money in 1988. Money accrued to the new Natural Law party by this procedure in 1992. But to qualify a candidate must show viability by raising $100,000 in small private donations: $5,000 from small givers in each of twenty states. Libertarian party candidates, who qualified several times for matching funds, long refused on principle to accept funds which they contend are "stolen" from the American taxpayers.[33]

The senators and representatives who enacted FECA were Democrats and Republicans. At the least they must have intended some major party turf-guarding. Some also may have been thinking of their personal aspirations for the White House. The nation did need some campaign Lysol after 1972, and it may well be that FECA's critics dwell too exclusively upon its negatives. But it is a significant burden for third parties, probably the most substantial ever coming from the U.S. Congress.

One other FECA provision damages the third-party cause, in effect if not intent. The Federal Election Campaign Act of 1971 required public disclosure (name, address, occupation, employer) of donors giving as much as $200 to a presidential or congressional campaign. Later amendments, including the important ones incorporated into the 1974 FECA, left these disclosure requirements in place. Mandated disclosure deters donations to third-party campaigns. Givers know that the disclosure may damage their community standing. Sometimes they justifiably suspect more serious repercussions.

The Supreme Court has built some slack into the disclosure for the benefit of some aggrieved small parties. The high court in 1976 overturned forced disclosures by minor parties able to demonstrate "reasonable probability" that disclosure subjects the identified givers to "threats, harassment, or reprisals."[34] Based on that ruling, the Federal Election Commission in 1979 granted a five-year exemption from disclosure to the Socialist Workers party, a Trotskyist Marxist-Leninist group. SWP since has won two renewals of that exemption.[35] Communist Party-USA secured immunity from FECA-compelled disclosures in 1982.[36] That same year the Supreme Court found for such parties a First Amendment protection from state disclosure mandates as well. This case overruled an Ohio law and found in favor of the Socialist Workers party, an association that, the court said, "historically has been the object of harassment by government officials and private parties."[37] Even now the burden of proof remains in principle with the third party claiming exemption from disclosure requirements.

Financially disadvantaged as they are by federal law, most third

CHAPTER ONE

parties lack the resources to purchase much access to the public via expensive newspaper, radio, and television advertising. Mass media could provide free access, and to some degree they do. But the exposure the mainstream media normally give third parties is tiny. Researchers studying three leading national newspapers and the three weekly news magazines discovered that in 1980 these media gave Carter and Reagan ten times the coverage received by the other eleven candidates combined.[38] Given the significance of the Anderson bid that year, it is certain that the gap in most years is much larger still.

Print media have almost free rein under the First Amendment to decide what to publish. Like most of their functional kin in electronic broadcasting, the print folks keep profit in mind. They are convinced that their readers care mainly about campaigns that may win. The media view the campaign as a horse race. They generally train their binoculars upon the Republican and Democratic front-runners.

Television, of course, is now the most potent mass communicator. Television and radio broadcasters lament that their First Amendment privileges do not equal those belonging to print media. Congress and the Federal Communications Commission (FCC) have regulated radio and television for years. Underlying this regulation is a "scarcity rationale" (now arguably lamer in an era of multiple radio and television options, including cable) that assigns a public interest obligation to the custodians of the all-too-few broadcast frequencies.

Initially the broadcasters' obligation to serve the public interest gave third parties access to radio and television audiences. The 1934 Communications Act required broadcasters opening up to any candidate to provide equal opportunities for all other legally qualified candidates for the office. The FCC in 1949 advanced the **Fairness Doctrine** compelling broadcasters to cover issues of public importance and to reflect the range of differing views on these issues.

Recent decades have deeply eroded third-party access prerogatives. Congressional acts beginning in 1959 place broadcasters on firm legal ground when they ignore third parties in newscasts, candidate interviews, and documentaries or give gavel-to-gavel coverage of major party national conventions.[39]

Autumn television debates are ascendant rituals of presidential politics. A Republican or Democratic nominee refusing the challenge gives his major party opponent a ready-made issue. Ross Perot did participate in the three fall 1992 presidential debates, and Perot's running mate took part in the one meeting of vice-presidential nominees. But normally third-party or independent candidates cannot beg their way onto the debate stage.[40]

Whatever remaining value the Fairness Doctrine bore for third-party access died in 1988 when the FCC repealed that doctrine. The repeal fit the deregulatory ethos of the Reagan administration, and that president gave it his blessing.[41]

Protecting its own, national policy thus both denies third parties equal access to funds and refrains from recognizing for them a right to free contact with the public via the mass media. But in the states there is yet another constraint that for the nonmajors may be the severest of all.

One feature that distinguishes America from most other nations is the federal system. Under its particular division of governmental authority, states remain the principal overseers of elections. This may be supported, as Americans justify federalism in general, on the grounds of grassroots discretion and checks against overcentralization. But state control of elections brings what is probably the heaviest structural burden most third parties face: ballot access requirements that severely sap nonmajors' very limited organizational and financial resources and ultimately prove insurmountable for many of these parties. Write-in possibilities do exist in most states for candidates failing to master ballot-access requirements. But write-in campaigns are difficult, and the returns sometimes go uncounted. In one of its most controversial decisions of 1992 (*Burdick* v. *Takushi*), the Supreme Court sustained a Hawaii law prohibiting write-in votes.

Until the 1890s, when states began to adopt the secret ballot, political parties rather than states printed ballots (tickets) and distributed them to voters. This older system may have deterred third-party voting in two ways. Votes were cast in public, and a voter deserting the two main parties necessarily uncloseted himself before God and community. Moreover, because it was hard or impossible to cast a split ticket, voters hesitated to take a third-party ballot. This may have been especially true when the third party failed to nominate candidates for all the elected offices. But in principle at least this system allowed all parties equal access to voters on election day.[42]

The "Australian" secret ballot used since the 1890s challenges electoral fraud and reduces voter intimidation; but substantial burdens for third parties accompany these more general benefits. Parties yielded to state authorities the prerogative to print election ballots. The states then initiated requirements for positions on the ballot.[43]

States intended through these laws and regulations to support both the two-party system and the dominance of the two existing majors within it. They developed loftier and more persuasive rationalizations for these acts: keeping the ballot more comprehensible to voters, deterring dangerous radicalism, facilitating consensus building and mandate giving. Many states assumed the major parties' right both to appear on the ballot and to keep their ballot positions from election to election. Some states did impose on major parties the same ballot access stipulations that third parties faced. But even those states were initiating burdens that were hard or impossible for third parties but relatively easy for the resource-rich major parties.

For third parties the barriers rest on two planes. First, individual state requirements often have been formidable. One particularly notorious case was in Ohio, where a statute locked out all third parties from a position on the presidential ballot for four consecutive elections (1952–1964). In 1968 the George Wallace campaign discovered that under this law it faced an impossibility. It would have had to produce a petition signed by nearly a half-million voters and to have filed it by February before the November election. In a Wallace challenge to the Supreme Court, Ohio admitted its motivation to preserve the hegemony of two major parties. The Court struck down this law but left many less draconian ones.[44]

A second difficulty lies in the almost unfathomable state-to-state variation in access requirements. Ballot access is so complex that serious third-party presidential campaigns virtually require legal experts specialized in election law.

In the fifteen elections from 1920 through 1976 no third-party or independent campaign mastered all requirements to place its presidential candidate on the ballots of every constituency. Progressive nominee Robert La Follette in 1924 made all but one of forty-eight state ballots, but his name appeared in the forty-seven under four different party labels. By grace of the Supreme Court, a body he often condemned for "judicial tyranny," George Wallace cracked all fifty state ballots (not that of Washington, D.C.), though under six different labels.

State and federal litigation initiated between 1968 and 1980 eased third parties' ballot access burdens. Third parties today owe a lot of thanks to Wallace but also to Eugene McCarthy and John Anderson, who as third-party or independent candidates took their ballot access cases to court. In 1980 Anderson and his National Unity Campaign made all fifty-one ballots. So did Libertarian nominee Ed Clark. Both mastered odds that remain substantial. Each was required to file state access petitions bearing well over one million names. Anderson spent more than half of the $7.3 million his campaign collected between March and September on petition drives and legal fees. Meanwhile the Democratic and Republican campaigns allocated their much larger resources (including FECA funds) to campaign tactics for reaching voters before election day.[45]

No third-party or independent presidential candidacy made all fifty-one ballots in 1984. Four years later just New Alliance's Lenora Fulani joined the Republican and Democratic presidential nominees on every ballot in the country. Fulani's party estimates that 70 percent of the $2 million it collected went to finance the drive for the 1.5 million petition signatures necessary to make all the ballots.[46] In 1992 independent Ross Perot and Libertarian Andre Marrou appeared with Clinton and Bush on all fifty-one. Nineteen other presidential candidates had their names on from one to forty ballots.

Today the most universal requirement for ballot access for a new party or one not receiving a fixed percentage of the vote in a recent election is the voter petition. Petition requirements vary widely state-to-state with respect to several questions: How many people must sign? When must the petitions be filed? Must the signers include a fixed minimum from each county or congressional district in the state? Do signers by their act disqualify themselves from participating in major party primaries?[47]

Despite serious questions as to the constitutionality of their prohibition, some states retained rules forbidding ballot access to the Communist party, to a campaign in whose name the word Communist appeared, or to a party advocating the revolutionary overthrow of American government. Communist party nominee Gus Hall appeared on twenty-three ballots in 1984 but under the Communist label in only twelve. In states where his name accompanied the People Before Profits tag, voter appeal may have been the campaign's principal consideration. Sometimes Hall ran as an independent because some states make ballot access easier for independents than for third parties. But on five ballots, Hall's name followed the designation Communists. It appears to have been a deliberate and artful dodge; that letter "s" may have been crucial to circumventing rules banning the word Communist from the ballot.[48]

## Conclusion

Third-party spokespeople believe or proclaim at least that once upon a time the Republicans resided, as third parties now do, on the periphery. Third-party folks must like a line from Simon and Garfunkel's "Sound of Silence": "words of the prophets are written on the subway walls." Many third-party leaders see themselves as prophets relegated for now, like the prophets in that song, to obscurity. In their unknown publications or rare appearances in mainstream media they sometimes prophesy that history will repeat, that somehow, like the GOP fourteen decades ago, their party may propel itself into the American mainstream. Next, they say, it may catapult the nation into a golden age.

Some of these hopes have decent foundations on which to rest. After all, Connecticut's Lowell Weicker and Alaska's Walter Hickel won gubernatorial elections on third-party tickets in 1990, the year that independent Bernard Sanders was capturing Vermont's U.S. House seat. Americans in droves followed Ross Perot as he moved beyond two-party bounds in 1992. Survey data reveal that Americans have no great love affair with either of their major parties.[49] Republican and even Democratic shifts to the right since 1980 leave some people disaffected and with the uncanny feeling that their presence in major party ranks is less than enthusiastically welcomed. Reagan-era redistributive policies from poor to rich fostered millions of newly have-not Americans,[50] some of whom, with a proper push, might seek a new third-party home.

But it would be premature and risky now to proclaim that a golden third-party era is impending or likely. In national politics America's third parties historically have been either transient or obscure. Americans' conviction late in the twentieth century about the basic legitimacy or "Americanism" of the two-party system has seemed more firmly entrenched than it was in the nineteenth century. Right or wrong, many people equate the vitality and future of that system specifically with the continuing dominance of the Republican and Democratic parties.

More imposing still are the structural edifices, fences barring the third-party path from periphery to mainstream. Those fences are now a lot higher than in the mid-nineteenth century. If you climb to the top you find them lined with barbed wire and broken glass.

You have read that third parties, though operating at the margins, are useful both to their devotees and to society at large. You may or may not be convinced of that. At the least, they are fascinating creatures marching as they do to different drummers. Some past and present third parties you may come to admire. Others you may well despise. Whether because of the impact of some third parties upon the central stages of American politics, their potential (however small) to enter the mainstream themselves, or because of third parties' utility, or just because they are interesting, third parties warrant your further exploration.

## Notes

1. Roger C. Storms, *Partisan Prophets: A History of the Prohibition Party* (Denver: Colo.: Prohibition National Foundation, 1972).

2. The definitive biography of Sidney Catts also is a fascinating one: Wayne Flynt, *Cracker Messiah: Governor Sidney J. Catts of Florida* (Baton Rouge: Louisiana State University Press, 1977).

3. V. O. Key, Jr., *Politics, Parties, and Pressure Groups*, 5th ed. (New York: Thomas Y. Crowell, 1964), 255.

4. *Ibid.*

5. For example, Leon Epstein, *Political Parties in Western Democracies* (New York: Frederick A. Praeger Publishers, 1967).

6. Millard L. Gieske, *Minnesota Farmer-Laborism* (Minneapolis: University of Minnesota Press, 1979), and John E. Haynes, *Dubious Alliance* (Minneapolis: University of Minnesota Press, 1984).

7. Dan Nimmo and Thomas D. Ungs, *American Political Patterns*, 3d. ed. (Boston: Little, Brown and Co., 1973), 275.

8. See Leon Epstein, *Political Parties in the American Mold* (Madison: University of Wisconsin Press, 1986).

9. Committee on Political Parties, APSA, "Toward a More Responsible Two-Party System," *American Political Science Review,* 44, Supplement (September 1950).

10. Epstein, *Political Parties in Western Democracies,* 68.

11. Daniel A. Mazmanian, *Third Parties in Presidential Elections* (Washington D.C.: Brookings Institution, 1974), 3.

12. Some scholars contend that American history has known five successive national two-party systems and that a sixth may have been emerging in the 1980s. See, for example, Alan R. Gitelson, *et al., American Political Parties* (Boston: Houghton Mifflin, 1984), 24–35.

13. See, for example, Paul A. Beck and Frank J. Sorauf, *Party Politics in America,* 7th ed. (New York: Harper Collins, 1992).

14. For example, Gerald Pomper, *et al., The Election of 1984* (Chatham, N.J.: Chatham House, 1985), 84–86. In a 1991 *New York Times*/CBS study, 34% of the 14,695 respondents identified themselves as Democrats and 31% as Republicans.

15. In 1989, following the Democrats' third consecutive presidential defeat, Gary C. Jacobson proclaimed a phenomenon he called "split-level realignment." The American electorate, as Jacobson saw it, had attached itself for the long term to congressional Democrats and presidential Republicans. Jacobson, "Congress: A Singular Continuity," in *The Elections of 1988,* ed. Michael Nelson (Washington, D.C.: CQ Press, 1989), 127–152. Clinton's election in 1992 calls into question the validity of Jacobson's claim.

16. Center for Political Studies (University of Michigan) 1984 National Election Study.

17. Many American scholars criticize this feature of the American constitutional setup for its retarding effect upon party government. See the classical critique by James MacGregor Burns, *The Deadlock of Democracy* (Englewood Cliffs, N.J.: Prentice-Hall, 1963).

18. The clearest and most compelling statement of this fear and of divide-and-conquer as intended remedy is *The Federalist* No. 10 by James Madison.

19. Gitelson, *et al., American Political Parties*, 296–297.

20. Andrew Kopkind, "Bernie Sanders Does D.C.," *The Nation*, 252 (June 3, 1991), 728–732.

21. Steven J. Rosenstone, *et al., Third Parties in America* (Princeton, N.J.: Princeton University Press, 1984), 9.

22. Epstein, *Political Parties in Western Democracies*, 68.

23. Harold D. Lasswell, *Psychopathology and Politics* (Chicago: University of Chicago Press, 1930).

24. J. David Gillespie, "Third Party Leaders and the American Ideological Mainstream," paper presented in 1984 meeting of Northeastern Political Science Association.

25. T. W. Adorno, *et al., The Authoritarian Personality* (New York: Harper and Row, 1950).

26. *Dennis v. the United States*, 341 U.S. 494 (1951).

27. July 7, 1981 interview with Eric O'Keefe, Libertarian party national director, Washington, D.C.

28. Louis Hartz put forth these ideas in his classic treatise on American thought and practice, *The Liberal Tradition in America* (New York: Harcourt, Brace, and World, 1955), esp. 5–14.

29. Mazmanian, *Third Parties*, 1–2.

30. Simon W. Gerson, *Pete* (New York: International Publishers, 1976).

31. The 1800 House election resulted from a defect in the electoral college procedure later rectified by the Twelfth Amendment. The first two-party system disintegrated by 1820, and in 1824 four factions of the dominant Democratic-Republican party waged the presidential contest. None of the four factional standardbearers won an electoral majority and the House elected the president. A bipartisan commission was charged with the task of determining the outcome of the disputed presidential election of 1876.

32. Rosenstone, *et al., Third Parties*, 26.

33. In 1991 two Libertarians seeking their party's 1992 presidential nomination debated the issue of accepting federal matching funds. The purist Dick Boddie said he would never accept such funds. The more pragmatic Andre Marrou, who won LP's nomination, claimed that stolen funds should be taken back and used in a campaign serving the taxpayers. See *Libertarian Party News*, February 1991.

34. *Buckley v. Valeo*, 424 U.S. 1 (1976).

35. Greg McCartan, "Socialists Fight Disclosure of Campaign Contributors," *The Militant*, June 8, 1990.

36. Before clarification of the disclosure issue to the benefit of his organization, Communist party head Gus Hall proclaimed that his party would "never—and I mean *never*—under any circumstances do anything to permit the names of its members and contributors who wish to remain anonymous to fall into the hands

of the FBI." Gus Hall, *Labor Up Front* (New York: International Publishers, 1979), 88.

37. *Brown et al.* v. *Socialist Workers '74 Campaign Committee (Ohio) et al.*, 459 U.S. 87 (1982).

38. Rosenstone, *et al.*, *Third Parties*, 33.

39. Mazmanian, *Third Parties*, 104–105.

40. The only exception prior to 1992 was John Anderson, who debated Reagan in September 1980. Carter refused to join in a three-way debate, but he did debate Reagan a week before election day.

41. Paul Starobin, "'Fairness Doctrine' Has Had a Tangled Past," *Congressional Quarterly Weekly Report*, 46 (February 27, 1988), 482.

42. Rosenstone, *et al.*, *Third Parties*, 18, 24–25.

43. *Ibid.*, 19.

44. *Williams* v. *Rhodes*, 393 U.S. 23 (1968).

45. Rosenstone, *et al.*, *Third Parties*, 23–24.

46. November 1, 1988, telephone interview with Annie Roboff, New Alliance party press secretary.

47. Rosenstone, *et al.*, *Third Parties*, 20–22. South Carolina has required petition signers to provide their precinct name and voter registration number, information usually not readily accessible when a third-party campaign approaches a potential signer "on the street."

48. The Communist party constitution promises expulsion to any member "who is . . . engaged in espionage, . . . or who advocates force and violence or terrorism, or who participates in the activities of any group which seeks to undermine or overthrow any democratic institution through which the majority of the American people can express their right to determine their destiny."

49. See Gitelson, *et al.*, *American Political Parties*, 131–132.

50. See Kevin Phillips, *The Politics of Rich and Poor* (New York: Random House, 1990).

# CHAPTER TWO

# Brightly Blazing Candles:

## Transient National Third Parties in the Nineteenth Century

*My candle burns at both ends;*
*It will not last the night;*
*But ah, my foes, and oh my friends—*
*It gives a lovely light!*
—"First Fig" by Edna St. Vincent Millay

Have you ever heard this line from an old country music song? "I want to live hard, love fast, and die young, and leave a beautiful memory." Third parties were far from the mind of the person who wrote that song, but the line seems to say something about them anyhow. America's most significant third parties have indeed "died young," leaving behind substantial and potent legacies. Their brief lives are hard ones endured at the periphery of American politics. Full respectability never seems to come their way. Many of these parties would not even welcome a grant of legitimacy that the mainstream might confer upon them. Righteous indignation, a passion for justice, even vengeance or hate, are far more likely than love to be the emotions conveyed by or about these parties; those kinds of feelings can be as powerful as love in mobilizing people to political action.

In this chapter, you will be reading about the important transient national third parties of the nineteenth century. If there has been a golden age for third parties in American national politics, that golden age was in the nineteenth century. Chapter 3, "Candles in the Wind," is devoted to the short-lived parties that have come and gone in the national politics of your own twentieth century.

# Nineteenth- and Twentieth-Century Short-lived Parties: Some Generalizations

Significant transient parties usually arise, in a spirit of protest, as self-appointed agencies of reform or change. Their demands may be in support of the underdog, for reconstruction of the party system and other revisions in the political process, for reordering the priorities and substance of public policies, or for many or all of these things. There have been exceptions, to be sure; for example the Constitutional Union party, a pre-Civil War association strongest in the southern and border region. Constitutional Unionists were what the British would call Yesterday's Men. They sought quiet and stability at a time when the old order was unraveling. For most short-lived parties and their supporters, however, the spirit has been much more akin to that famous line from the movie *Network*: "I'm mad as hell, and I'm not going to take it anymore." The revisionism and agitation of these parties may capture the mood and support of large, disaffected segments of the electorate. They breed suspicion or hostility in people who, happy with the status quo, demand "legitimacy and civility" in party rhetoric and programs.

The genesis of parties of this particular kind has taken two different forms. Some of these parties begin as factions that secede from one or the other of the major parties. Their leaders try to take with them many voters who gave their support in the past to the major party. A **secessionist party** may seek by its withdrawal to punish the major party and to force it to reformulate its being and essence. The secessionists may intend, if not that, to leave for good and to work to alter the party system itself. Most of the significant short-lived parties begin independently, not as factions seceding from one of the major parties. They may, like the Antimasons, come to life during breaks or tears in the national two-party fabric. Sometimes they spring up when the two-party system seems healthy and viable. Their founders and leaders may even include prominent former Republicans or Democrats. But their outreach to supporters of both major parties, to independents, and on occasion to people devoted to other third parties shows that they have undertaken a strategy somewhat unlike the one that secessionist parties tend to use.

The defining characteristic of these transient parties is their short life spans. They are, as V. O. Key said of them, "shortlived . . . eruptions." Twentieth-century short-lived parties have tended to have even briefer lives than did their predecessors of the last century. The primary appeal of a party of this type lasts for a decade at most; often it centers upon a single election round. A shell of the old partisan structure may continue

**Table 2.1: Significant National Short-lived Parties**

**Parties Seceding From Democratic Party**
  Southern Democrats, 1860
  States Rights' Democrats (Dixiecrats), 1948

**Parties Seceding From Republican Party**
  Liberal Republican party, 1870s
  Progressive party (Bull Moose), especially 1912

**Other Important Transient Parties**
  Antimasonic party, 1827–1836
  Liberty party, 1840–1848
  Free Soil party, 1847–1854
  American party (Know Nothing), late 1840s, 1850s
  Constitutional Union party, especially 1860
  Greenback party, 1876–1888
  People's party (Populist), 1890s
  Progressive party, 1924
  Union party, 1936
  Progressive party, 1948 (and 1952)
  American Independent party, 1968 (and 1972)
  National Unity Campaign, 1980

on a while longer. The Populists were at their electoral peak in the first six years of the 1890s. Populist diehards held together the ghost of the old People's party until 1908. A few years after George Wallace's remarkable presidential showing in 1968, his American Independent party split into two small sects. Badly withered, both still showed pulses (barely) as the 1990s dawned. But the American Independent party as most Americans knew it really died when, in 1972, Wallace left it to return to the Democratic party.

Transient parties die quickly because their appeal proves transitory. It is difficult to organize effectively for the long haul. American major parties, pragmatic beings that they are, always keep the upcoming election in their sights. A major party, like a sponge, sops up—appropriates or steals—things that have value or that pose a threat to the position and the electoral objectives of that major party. The more popular an idea or issue put forth by a third party, the more likely it is that one of the major parties (one at least) will take it for itself. The purpose is, of course, to win over to the major party's electoral coalition all but the third party's most irredeemable loyalists. Major parties rarely if ever punish those who defect to organizing roles or leadership positions in new third-party ventures; the Democratic and Republican parties are far more inclined to embrace their prodigal sons and daughters and reward them for their return. Thus, short-lived parties, often quite at odds with their own deliberate and stated goals, become corrective agencies assisting in the care and maintenance of the two-party system.

Also constraining the transient parties are things they share with third parties of other kinds, with the continuing doctrinal parties and the non-national significant others. Third parties generally suffer problems of ballot and media access and a host of other troubles about which you have read in the last chapter.

The most significant of the short-lived parties have profoundly affected mainstream politics. Not all transient parties enjoy even short-term success. Most, in fact, do not, and the emphasis of this chapter and the next on the most successful short-lived parties should not lead you to false conclusions. Even so, the historical ledger confirms that more than a few short-lived parties nearly left the periphery for a place in the political mainstream. Some of these parties have influenced the content of major party platforms and the development and reform of public policies. Voter support of transient parties in some presidential elections determined which major party candidate won.

Nineteenth- and twentieth-century third-party campaigns before 1992 won more than 10 percent of the presidential popular votes seven times; two of these campaigns took over 20 percent. In all seven cases the third party (or more important party in a fusion campaign) was a short-lived party. In addition, in two elections transient parties entered into presidential fusion campaigns with the Democratic party: the Liberal Republicans in 1872 and the Populists in 1896.

Third parties have won some forty state gubernatorial popular elections. Twenty-four of these successful campaigns for governor featured national or regional parties of the transient kind or fusion campaigns in which the principal party was short-lived. Fifteen other gubernatorial wins went to parties not organizing electorally beyond the particular state. Only once in history has a governorship gone by election to a national continuing doctrinal party.

Short-lived parties sometimes have been highly personalistic undertakings to serve the political objectives of their prominent founders. The American Independent party of 1968 was in essence George Wallace. Wallace's fame as the segregationist, law and order, states' rights Alabama governor, his charisma, and his agitational skills in reaching

## Table 2.2: Indicators of Electoral "Success" for Third Parties, 1826–1990

| Indicator | Short-lived (Transient) | Continuing Doctrinal | Non-national Significant Other |
|---|---|---|---|
| Successful gubernatorial elections[a] | 24 | 1 | 15 |
| Total presidential electoral vote since 1832[b] | 334 | 1[c] | — |
| Number of times received 1–4.99% of presidential popular vote | 9 | 14 | — |
| Number of times received 5–9.99% of presidential popular vote[d] | 3 | 1[d] | — |
| Number of times received 10–19.99% of presidential popular vote | 5 | — | — |
| Number of times received over 20% of presidential popular vote[b] | 2 | — | — |

**Sources:** Joseph E. Kallenbach and Jessamine S. Kallenbach, *American State Governors, 1776–1976*, Vol. I (Dobbs Ferry, N.Y.: Oceana Publications, 1977) and *Presidential Elections Since 1789* (Washington, D.C.: Congressional Quarterly, Inc., 1975).

[a]Beyond these numbers, there have been many other elections involving third-party fusions with one or the other nationally recognized major party.

[b]Excludes 1872 Democratic-Liberal Republican and 1896 Democratic-People's parties fusion campaigns.

[c]In 1972 a Virginia GOP elector cast one vote for John Hospers, nominee of the Libertarian party (a continuing doctrinal party).

[d]History's best showing for a presidential candidate running solely as the nominee of a continuing doctrinal party was for Eugene V. Debs, candidate of the Socialist party, in 1912. Debs won 5.99% of the vote.

conservatives who wanted to "send a message" to the nation's political establishment determined what success his party was to enjoy.

Theodore Roosevelt, the main architect of the 1912 Progressive, or Bull Moose party, was also that party's primary reason for coming to life. As the Progressive party presidential nominee in 1912, Teddy Roosevelt, the popular ex-president who had proclaimed the presidency to be a "bully pulpit," won 27.39 percent of the popular vote. That left just 23.18 percent for the incumbent president, Republican William Howard Taft, and 41.84 percent for Woodrow Wilson, the Democratic challenger. That election signaled history's only unambiguous occasion in which a third-party nominee finished second in a presidential election.[1]

Many, though not all, historians who have commented find in the record much to suggest that the Bull Moose party nominee played the spoiler role that year. As these scholars see it, Roosevelt split the GOP (the Republican party), thus throwing the election in effect to the Democrat, Woodrow Wilson. The Republican party was at the time clearly the nation's majority party, and it would hold on to that position until the Great Depression. Wilson first won the presidency in a **deviating or idiosyncratic election** in which candidate factors, among them loyalties to Teddy Roosevelt, more than counteracted the natural advantage of the majority party. Wilson's reelection in 1916 resulted in part from advantages that an incumbent normally has.

## The Nineteenth Century as Third-Party Golden Age

The Antimasonic party, America's very first nationally organized third party, set itself up in 1827–1828. It lasted for just under a decade. The 1850s brought history's most spectacular national third-party electoral eruption. During its 1854–1857 peak, the American party sent at least forty-three of its own to the U.S. House for the Thirty-fourth Congress (the American party's Nathaniel Banks was Speaker), elected governors in six states, and enjoyed major party status in more than half of the thirty-one states in the Union. By the time of the People's party demise, mainly through absorption into the Democratic party at the close of the nineteenth century, Populists had achieved what many scholars believe to be a more broad-ranging and permanent legacy of influence upon process and policy than any other third party in our history. It is no wonder that third-party critics of the major parties so often speak of the nineteenth century as if it were for third parties the shining era of Camelot.

That century brought occasional ruptures and discontinuities in the national two-party system. Sometimes third parties stood to become short-term beneficiaries of these dislocations. Antimasonic organization and success were in part a result of Federalist party demise after 1816 and the factionalization of the remaining Democratic-Republican party in the 1820s. National dominance by Republicans and Democrats has proven far less pregnable in the twentieth century, and this century's third parties have found the windows of opportunity to be less substantial in national politics. (Sometimes during the twentieth century they have discovered some shining light in states and communities.)

Nineteenth-century third-party voter appeal was a cause, not just an effect, of those occasional tears in the two-party fabric. American party power, more than the later rise of the GOP, conditioned the decline and fall of the Whig party, although sectionalism and the slavery issue also delivered death blows to the Whigs. Populist fortunes in the last decade of the nineteenth century helped bring about, in 1896, what political scientists see as the rarest of all election types—a **converting election**, in which the partisan allegiances of many voters shift, some going over to one major party but others to the other major party. To the chagrin of Populist leaders and activists, most of whom (especially in the nonsouthern quarters of the People's party) were more favorably disposed to the Democrats, the net effect of all these conversions was to strengthen the GOP as the prevailing major party of the time.[2]

### The Antimasonic Party

The Masons, those men who belong to the Free and Accepted Masons, take part in the world's largest secret fraternal society. Although it originated in the stonemasons' and builders' guilds of the Middle Ages, Freemasonry has in modern times attracted many men from higher professions and social stations. Masons must affirm their belief in a supreme being and in the eternal nature of the human soul. The very secrecy with which Masons discharge their ritual and carry out their fraternal life has for centuries fed charges by the order's enemies that Freemasonry is a worldwide conspiracy against Christianity, or democracy, or the rights and privileges of ordinary men and women. Freemasonry long ago received the bitter condemnation of the Roman Catholic Church, and it has been banned by law in the twentieth century in many Communist and Third World nations.

A maxim, more deserving of consideration than it usually gets, says this about seekers of ogres or villains: "We have met the enemy and he is us!" By an act they took on September 12, 1826, some western New York Masons incalculably damaged their own Masonic order. Their act triggered the party that dedicated itself to unshrouding Masonic secrets and to toppling what Antimasons thought to be an elite, conspiratorial monopoly in American politics. The Antimasonic Party was to be America's first national third party. Third-party history thus began in western New York on a late summer day in 1826.

If you have heard the recent antiestablishment, fundamentalist Christian assault on secular humanism, that may give you some inkling about early nineteenth-century critics' indictment of Freemasonry. The Masons had been a part of the secular spirit of the Enlightenment. Freemasonry had included George Washington, Benjamin Franklin, the Marquis de Lafayette, Patrick Henry, and a lot of other people who had helped launch this new nation. Many of these men had held the views of secular deism which were very unlike the articles of faith of orthodox Christians. Opponents smelled a false god of humanism. They alleged that Masonry used the cross and other sacred symbols in perverse and sacrilegious rites. Presbyterians and Methodists passed resolutions sharply condemning the order.[3]

Equally devastating was the claim that the order's secrecy masked a conspiracy to deprive ordinary men of their liberty and their share of power in the republic. It could not escape anyone's notice that prominent people, Henry Clay and Andrew Jackson among them, continued to feel its attraction or to be recruited by it. Jackson was to become the leading target of Freemasonry's antagonists. The fraternal order's English connections and its secret titles of nobility were constant grist for the propaganda mill. William Morgan, an ex-Mason, wrote a book exposing the secrets and oaths of the order. It was news of the impending publication of Morgan's exposé, *Illustrations of Masonry*, that apparently pushed those New York Masons over the edge.

Morgan was far from the wealth and power attributed by Antimasonry to men of the Masonic order. A spiritual heir to Freemasonry's medieval European beginnings, he was a traveling stonecutter who lived in small Batavia in western New York. Marxists might interpret his break with what Masonry had become as a victory for class consciousness. As Morgan's book neared release and those standing to profit began their publicity hype, Masonic agents of law and order arrested Morgan for theft, let him go, then retook him for a $2.69 debt. A donor, probably Masonic, made good the debt. As Morgan left jail, some revenge-minded Masons kidnapped him. Morgan ended up in the Niagara River with weights tied to his body.[4]

Morgan's murder could not stop the presses. Incensed both by the book's revelations and the failure of Masonic judges and juries to indict

Morgan's kidnappers (and likely murderers), Antimasons spread their message like wildfire. It could be said that it spread like a weed: the *Enquirer,* founded and edited by Thurlow Weed, became Antimasonry's most effective propaganda agent.

Already by 1828 Antimasons were a major party in New York; with seventeen state assembly and four senate seats they were the party in opposition to the state's Jacksonian establishment. The Antimasonic party's 1830 gubernatorial candidate there took 48 percent of the vote in a losing effort.

In Pennsylvania and Vermont as well, the party came to hold major party status; it came very close to it in Massachusetts too. Antimasons won the 1835 Pennsylvania gubernatorial race, and they took and held the Vermont governorship through four successive campaigns (1831–1834). At their national peak (1833–1835) they held at least twenty-five seats (10.4 percent of the total) in the U.S. House.[5]

The Antimasonic message—opposition to secrecy, elitism, and secularism—was a populist one. The party drew its devoted followers disproportionately from the poor and from revival-minded Protestants. There was a lot of overlap in the ranks of these two demographic groups. Yet the party also drew to it men of fame and ambition: William Henry Seward, Frederick Whittlesey, Francis Granger, and Thaddeus Stevens.

Surprisingly, considering its available talent pool, Antimasons nominated William Wirt for their one and only presidential try. In his 1832 quest for the presidency, Wirt proved to be an ineffective campaigner who carried a damaging and most ironic load: the nominee was a Mason who had not repudiated his connection with the enemy order! Still, he took 7.78 percent of the nation's popular vote and the seven electors of Vermont. Less than 1 percent of his votes came from states south or west of Pennsylvania.

The life of this first national transient third party was a scant nine years. By 1836 Antimasonry was a memory but also a legacy. The Whig party firmly established itself as a new national major party by the middle of the 1830s. Partisan Antimasonry was largely absorbed into that new Whig party. Through this cooptation, the dying party passed into the rising one a spirit of egalitarianism and evangelism, and at least a residue of agitation for political reform.[6]

Antimasonry had been the very first party to use a national convention to nominate a presidential candidate and write a platform. America's premier national convention, the Antimasonic, met in Baltimore late in September 1831. Their innovation was a sizable democratic step away from the oligarchial closed caucus nominating procedure used by previous political parties. The Democrats, following suit, have convened every four years since 1832. The Whigs did likewise until their own demise in the 1850s. The GOP, buying into the same tradition, has conducted its affairs through quadrennial national conventions ever since 1856.

Antimasonic suspicion of secrecy may have left permanent marks on the national landscape. Freemasonry suffered very substantial injury from the Antimasonic assault. Other secret orders, notably Phi Beta Kappa, unveiled themselves in response to Antimasonic agitation. Universities' campaigns today against secrecy and elitism in their fraternity and sorority Greek systems bear at least coincidental resemblance to Antimasonic populism. Federal and state freedom of information acts have given Americans some access to government dossiers about themselves. Late twentieth-century sunshine laws open governmental deliberations to the scrutiny of press and public. Do you think it farfetched to relate such sunshine to a legacy of openness left by history's first national third party? Maybe so.

### Liberty and Free Soil

By the time of the firing on Ft. Sumter—the second "American shot heard 'round the world"—an antislavery party, the Republican party, already was a well-established actor in national politics. The GOP began its life with a spectacular claim to major party status: in 1854, the year of its birth, it won a plurality (over 46 percent) of the seats in the U.S. House. Liberty and Free Soil were earlier antislavery parties that never came in from the third-party cold. They paved the way for the GOP.

Differing points of view divided the antislavery cause in the decades before 1860. Antiextensionists wanted to close new territories and states to slavery, and sometimes they fought battles opposing the interstate slave trade and slavery in the District of Columbia. Antiextensionists were, however, pragmatic folks unwilling to push the cause to the lengths the abolitionists would take it. Sometimes, when the more radical view seemed futile, people who were abolitionist at heart became, in practice, antiextensionists.

**LIBERTY**  The Liberty Party (1840–1848) was in soul and philosophy abolitionist, although its leaders and program conceded that the federal government lacked authority to abolish slavery by fiat. The Liberty party's principled stand for abolitionism and its refusal to adopt secondary issues with vote-drawing power curtailed the party's appeal. Also limiting what the party could achieve was the disdain that many abolitionists felt toward partisan politics. Quite a few of the most prominent abolitionists rejected, in fact, political action of any kind. The cause, as they saw it, was moral, not political.

The Liberty party scored miserably in its 1840 bid for the presidency. Nominee James G. Birney took only one of every 400 votes in the nation. Two-thirds of his votes were from New York and Massachusetts. Birney won 2.3 percent four years later. His New York state tally in 1844 was 15,812. Democrat James K. Polk beat Whig Henry Clay in New York by just 5,106. Since Clay would have won the presidency had he received New York's electors, Libertymen laid justifiable claim to having determined the outcome.

FREE SOIL    The Free Soil party, born in 1847–1848 as Liberty's direct partisan descendant in the antislavery struggle, was a more pragmatic association given to coalition building. To purists' charges of expediency, some Free Soilers replied that to be right and fail is no victory for the right. In its ascendant days Free Soil brought three groups together: Libertymen from the older party, New York-based Barnburner Democrats (reformers so named because, it was said, "they would burn the barn to destroy its rats"), and Massachusetts-centered Conscience Whigs.[7] Many of the Barnburners and Conscience Whigs came much closer to antiextension than to abolition.

The Wilmot Proviso, an 1846 proposal to prohibit slavery in new lands purchased from Mexico, was the common bond that allied these three groups. The Wilmont Proviso was, in substance, no more important than other pre-Civil War antiextentionist proposals. That measure, in fact, failed to pass in Congress; but as a symbol around which the Free Soil party's three principal groups could unify, it was crucial to the party's development.

Free Soil pragmatism appeared in the party's eclectic concern for issues other than slavery; and in their 1848 selection of Martin van Buren, who had won the presidency in 1836 as a Democrat (he was renominated but defeated in 1840), Free Soilers showed some expedient devotion to election returns. Van Buren was an antiextensionist but no abolitionist, and his public record bore some embarrasing early remarks which seemed to defend slavery. Van Buren took 10.12 percent of the popular vote in 1848, a significant tally but one disappointing to most Free Soilers. Van Buren failed to take a state popular vote plurality; he and his third party therefore took not a single electoral vote. The party did not even circulate its ballots in any state south of Maryland.

As the Free Soil party entered the 1850s, it faced a dilemma it never mastered. Devotion to antislavery was leading Free Soilers to build ties with the Democrats, particularly in New York, Ohio, Wisconsin, and

Indiana. This new Free Soil-Democratic quid pro quo sent Free Soilers Charles Sumner and Salmon Chase (who was later to become Supreme Court Chief Justice) to the U.S. Senate, and it was responsible for the election of several Free Soilers to the House. Although these working relationships tangibly strengthened the antislavery voice in Washington, they also sapped the party's vitality as an independent force. Free Soil's fiercest loyalists, as it turned out, were its **purists,** not the **pragmatists.**[8]

Control of Free Soil party organization affairs fell by default to doctrinaire abolitionists, and the party became both purer and less widely appealing. John P. Hale from Free Soil's Libertymen branch was the party's 1852 presidential nominee. Hale won just under five percent of the vote.

When the Republican Party was born in 1854, that brand new party easily absorbed Free Soil's surviving remnants. It would be the Republicans' achievement to organize the antislavery movement into a partisan force with the power, by 1860, to take the presidency.

### The American (Know Nothing) Party

Slavery and its companion issues, sectionalism and union, were gravely important matters. They were by far, as later events would show, the most significant public business that the nation faced. But they were not, however, the only issues of the time. When the Compromise of 1850 passed, many optimists erroneously felt that slavery and sectional division were resolved forever. The Compromise of 1850 admitted California as a free state; organized other Mexican acquisitions as New Mexico and Utah territories; vested the citizens of these new territories with the right to settle the issue of slavery within their boundaries by popular sovereignty; and gave Texas $10 million in return for its renunciation of claims to New Mexico Territory. The 1850 Compromise forbade the slave trade—but not slavery itself—in Washington, D.C. The Fugitive Slave Law, the most controversial single element of the Compromise, promised decisive federal action to stop the practice of assisting runaway slaves.

For a while after passage of the Compromise of 1850, another issue threatened to crowd out slavery and sectionalism for the number one place on the national agenda. Promulgator and chief beneficiary of this challenging issue in the 1850s was the American party, a new association that came to be known as Know Nothing. The issue those Know Nothings raised still evokes a lot of controversy and strife today.

So self-evident, it sounds almost trite to say that America is a heterogeneous land of immigrants and their descendants. *E Pluribus*

*Unum*, the nation's motto, brings about thoughts of the melting pot, but also pride in the ethnic, racial, and religious diversity of the United States. The inscription on the Statue of Liberty is eloquent in its welcome to new immigrants. Americans saw the global power of that statue's symbolism when Chinese students demanding freedom built their own statue in Tiananmen Square.

From the first new waves of immigration in the early nineteenth century, American nativists have joined together to demand immigration restrictions as well as to make life difficult for new arrivers. Nativist influence produced laws that in the past severely restricted immigration, especially of people from the world's nonwhite areas. The shabby treatment of Japanese-Americans during World War II and today's organized pressure to mandate English as the official language (eighteen states had done so by 1991) demonstrate that the United States is far from unanimous consensus about its own ethnic character. Some of the ugliest recent episodes of the kind featured Ku Klux Klan violence against newly arrived Vietnamese refugees fishing in the Gulf of Mexico. The political lexicon today bears a term for reactionary bigots. They go by the name "know nothings."[9]

New Yorker Horace Greeley, a figure well-known in nineteenth-century journalism and liberal political circles, thought up that term and applied it pejoratively to the American party of the 1840s and 1850s. New York state gave birth to the American party as it had to Antimasonry. The appeal of these two parties hit a responsive chord in common men suspicious of the motives of public policies produced by unresponsive elites. There were basic differences between the two third parties as well. Antimasons hated secrecy and the conspiracies that they believed secrecy produces. The Know Nothings, who knew that the appeal of their message far exceeded the popularity of the party that preached it, were secretive. Often they went to considerable lengths to conceal from voters the party nominees' links to the party. Since they claimed to know nothing, Greeley named them Know Nothings. People came to call it the Know Nothing party.[10]

This was to be one of the very earliest forms of American nativist revolt. The American party began as an anti-immigrant and anti-Catholic association, the appeal of which to native-born Protestants was fed by the huge new wave of largely Catholic immigration in the 1840s. Know Nothing was the most spectacular nativist eruption ever to take the form of an organized political party. Like dozens of other third parties, this one would fail in its quest to become a nationwide major party; but of all these failed ventures, the Know Nothings' came closest to that ultimate success. The Republican party would finally fill the void that was left by collapsing Whiggery; but for a number of years it seemed a fair bet that the American Party would be the beneficiary to step into that vacuum.

Know Nothing concern for secrecy explains why estimates range so widely, from forty-three to seventy, about the number of American party U.S. House seats at the party's prime, the Thirty-fourth Congress (1855–1857). The Know Nothings' share of that chamber's seats, between 18.4 and 29.9 percent, was larger than that of any other party in history except for those that achieved national major party status. The American party's Nathaniel Banks was the only third-party House member ever elected by that chamber to the position of House speaker. Despite its congressional presence and the House's presiding gavel, the party was a bust in the Washington legislative process. Congress failed to enact nativist proposals for a twenty-one-year naturalization period and for immigration bans on "foreign paupers, criminals, idiots, lunatics, insane, and blind persons."[11]

Know Nothing victories in state and local elections were nothing short of phenomenal. By 1854 the party controlled the legislatures of Rhode Island, New Hampshire, Connecticut, Maryland, and Kentucky, and it was the principal opposition in nearly a dozen others. Between 1854 and 1857, the American party took governorships in Massachusetts, California, Connecticut, Kentucky, New Hampshire, and Maryland.

Outside the South the party appealed both to nativist and to anti-Catholic feeling. Its propaganda about Catholicism was, if anything, more virulent than its Americanist message. But in the South the party's appeal and essence were of a different sort. Relatively few immigrants went south in the first half of the nineteenth century. Moreover, not many places south of the Mason-Dixon line held heavy concentrations of Catholics. Even in places like Catholic south Louisiana, Catholic populations tended to be native born and southern. American party organizations in the southern states divested themselves of most of the nativist and anti-Catholic message pushed by their northern counterparts; they assumed in its place a more traditional party role as loyal opposition to the usually dominant Democrats.[12] Louisiana Know Nothings in 1855 nominated a Catholic and very nearly elected him governor.

By 1856 slavery and sectionalism again were supplanting nativism as the nation's most potent and explosive issue. The 1854 Kansas-Nebraska Act seemed to be undoing the most hopeful efforts of northerners and southerners to hold the Union together. That federal act formally rescinded the Missouri Compromise of 1820. The Missouri

Compromise had admitted Missouri as a slave state, but had closed the remaining Louisiana Purchase tract lying north of the 36° 30' parallel to slavery. The Kansas-Nebraska Act horrified anti-extensionists because in the form in which it finally passed, it reopened the specter of slavery in yet-to-be-organized lands above 36° 30'. Antislavery people would never forgive Illinois Democratic Senator Stephen A. Douglas, the bill's chief sponsor, for capitulating to southern demands in order to secure passage of the bill. The Kansas-Nebraska Act organized the remaining lands north of 36° 30' into the Kansas and Nebraska territories and empowered citizens of these new territories to settle by vote the issue of slavery within their boundaries. Just as Douglas had anticipated, proslavery sentiment proved too weak in Nebraska, the more northern territory, for slavery to become much of an issue there. But troubling reports of the ugly campaign, amounting to civil war, in Bleeding Kansas inflamed public opinion in the North. From this point on, no remedy would be enough to stop the avalanche toward war between sections.

The center of gravity in the American party shifted dramatically toward the South in 1856. Northern antislavery delegates to the 1856 Know Nothing national convention demanded that their party nominate someone opposed to slavery north of 36° 30'. When the convention gave the nod instead to Millard Fillmore, many of these northerners bolted and went home to take part in history's first Republican presidential campaign.

The 1850 death of Whig Zachary Taylor had brought Fillmore to a two-and-one-half year interim as president.[13] As president and later even as nominee of the Americans, Fillmore was no nativist. Just prior to his 1856 nomination, word came to him that the pope had granted him an audience.[14] His campaign muted and largely ignored the nativist theme, avoided slavery, and concentrated on "preserving the Union." A remnant of the Whig party went through the motions of nominating American nominee Fillmore for the presidency in 1856. Fillmore's campaign should not, however, be regarded as a fusion campaign. Whiggery, hopelessly divided over slavery, was by now dormant, and Whig organizational support was inconsequential to Fillmore's election results.[15]

Fillmore took 21.53 percent of the nation's votes, 41.79 percent of those cast in the South, and a quite remarkable 48.48 percent of the votes from the border states. Fillmore's Maryland majority gave him that state's eight electoral votes. The party's showing was much more anemic in the North. Less than 6 percent of New Englanders' popular votes went to the American party.

Northern Know Nothing support rapidly dissipated, the party's former followers deserting to the GOP. In the South, where support for the anti-slavery Republicans was all but nonexistent, the Know Nothings continued until the end of the 1850s as the Democrats' main opposition. Know Nothing candidate Sam Houston won the Texas state governorship as late as 1859; but the Know Nothing party as a national movement was by that time almost to the point of extinction. The disease killing the party was sectionalism and slavery.

### Constitutional Union and Southern Democrat.

No other issue in history has rivaled slavery and sectionalism in their impact upon the American political parties. Opposition to slavery was the raison d'être for Liberty and Free Soil and the rallying cry for ascendant Republicanism. Whig inability to speak with clarity to the issue delivered the death blow to that party. Sectionalism and slavery destroyed the Know Nothings and very nearly the Democrats. In 1860, they were the impetus for a unique four-party contest for the presidency as the nation rolled inexorably toward civil war.

Abraham Lincoln, the second Republican presidential nominee (John C. Fremont had run four years earlier), won the presidency in 1860. All surveys of historians and political scientists rank Lincoln among America's five greatest presidents. Many place him at number one. But his 39.82 percent of the popular vote gave him one of the most tepid mandates of any elected president in history. He did much better in the electoral college, garnering 180 of 303 electors. Lincoln took every state in the Midwest and Far West and all but three electors in the Northeast. He won 23.7 percent of Delaware's popular votes but did poorly in the other border states. His Republicans did not bother to distribute ballots in any southern state below Virginia. It would have been futile, perhaps even hazardous, to do so there.

Slavery, irreconcilably dividing Americans, built the 1860 stage for two regionally based presidential contests. Lincoln's only significant opponent in the Midwest and in every northeastern state except Pennsylvania was the Democratic nominee, Stephen A. Douglas. The Democrat finished second in the national voting with 29.46 percent. Douglas was the election's only candidate to take popular votes in every state where voters participated that year. He won popular pluralities and electoral votes only in New Jersey and border-state Missouri. Three of New Jersey's seven electors went for Douglas, the others for Lincoln.

Douglas had managed somehow to alienate important interests throughout the land. He antagonized Democratic President James Buchanan and his administration. Antislavery voters still nursed their grudge over Bleeding Kansas. Southerners were mad at Douglas for leading the opposition to Kansas's admission to statehood under its proslavery Lecompton Constitution. Slavery interests had stacked the cards, winning approval in Kansas for a constitution that did not really have the blessing of most of the territory's citizens. Even so, southerners saw Lecompton's defeat in Congress as a violation of a gentlemen's agreement in the Kansas-Nebraska Act.[16] Douglas's share of the southern vote was an unimpressive 8.4 percent.

The real contest in the South and in Maryland and Kentucky pitted the nominees of two transient third parties against each other. Tennessean John Bell, a former U.S. Senator, took his home state plus Kentucky and Virginia as the choice of the *Constitutional Union party*. The rest of the South plus Maryland and Delaware went to Kentucky's John C. Breckinridge. Vice-president in the Buchanan administration (1857–1861), Breckinridge ran as the presidential nominee of the *Southern Democratic party*.

Long before 1860, Constitutional Unionism had been a wisp in the eye of some folks living below the Mason-Dixon line. As far back as 1851, Howell Cobb had won the Georgia governorship on ballots labeled Constitutional Union. The same year ten elected Unionists left their homes in Mississippi, Alabama, and Georgia to take seats in the U.S. House. But the party did not organize to do presidential battle until 1860. It came crashing down after Lincoln's victory, the utter futility of its one desire—to preserve the Union—underscored by the seceding South and the rise of the Confederacy.

Third-party people sometimes console themselves with the thought that their day will come, that what they envision will be popular enough someday to come into the mainstream. Constitutional Unionists had no such future vision; they were reactionaries linked to a world already lost. As a party, they hoped only to wish away all the divisiveness over slavery and to save a Union that really could be restored only by force of arms. Their platform, all two hundred words of it, skirted or ignored every other issue. The party drew its leadership from the ranks of ex-Whigs and ex-Know Nothings. Bell himself had left the Senate in 1859 still wearing the label of the extinct Whig party. Party activists were Yesterday's Men; delegates attending its convention in May "were or appeared to be venerable gentlemen representing a generation of almost forgotten politicians, [most of whom] had retired from public life involuntarily."[17] A journalist observing the scene wrote that the convention was inundated by "virtuous twaddle."[18]

Of the two third parties, Constitutional Union had the more

aristocratic ambiance. Southern Democrats, especially the rank and file, had a grittier, more populist, and more redneckish character. Southern Democrats ran best in rural counties where there were few slaves. Constitutional Unionists found their support among large landowners and in the commercial interests of the cities.[19]

The Southern Democratic party was the only nationally significant American party ever to speak unequivocally in defense of slavery. Historians sometimes refer to this party as Secessionist Democrat. That appropriate label carries a double meaning. The party was the first ever to begin life in formal secession from a major party. Its leaders, moreover, were willing, even eager, to think the unthinkable: the withdrawal of slave states from the United States of America. Breckinridge was to go on himself to become a Confederate major general. As the Civil War drew to a close, Breckinridge was serving as Confederate secretary of war.

The Southern Democratic party came to life at two 1860 conventions of the national Democratic party: the first in April at Charleston, the other in Baltimore two months later. In Charleston, southern delegates demanded that the national Democratic platform include some measures for the defense of slave interests. When the convention refused and resolved instead to call upon the Supreme Court to settle the issue of slavery, delegations from the Deep South and some of the delegates from Arkansas and Delaware withdrew in protest.[20]

Failing to nominate a presidential candidate, the national Democrats reconvened in Baltimore in June. Forces supporting Douglas, who won the nomination there, manipulated the process to secure Douglas's selection. Most crucially, they denied reinstatement to, and replaced instead, many of the delegates who had walked out at Charleston. When this happened, delegations from the rest of the South but also from distant California and Oregon headed for the doors of the Balitmore convention hall. Delegates who had walked out of the Baltimore meeting reconvened in rump session and nominated Breckinridge. Another group of southerners, many of them veterans of the Charleston convention, met in Richmond and endorsed Breckinridge as well. Their Southern Democratic party was born. Its last gasp, like that of Constitutional Union, would come with Lincoln's 1860 presidential victory.[21]

Another third party eighty-eight years later would give weight to propositions that sometimes history really does repeat itself. This new party took States' Rights Democratic party for a name. Far better known as Dixiecrat, that 1948 segregationist party took race and sectionalism nearly as far as an electoral party could take it, given what the Civil

**Table 2.3: Regional Division in Support for Four Principal Presidential Candidates/Parties, 1860**

| | Parties/Candidates: Percent of Total Popular Vote and Number of Electoral Votes by Region[a] | | | |
| --- | --- | --- | --- | --- |
| | Republican/ Lincoln | Democrat/ Douglas | Southern Democrat/ Breckinridge | Constitutional Union/ Bell |
| **National Totals:** | | | | |
| 4,685,561 popular | 39.82% | 29.46% | 18.09% | 12.61% |
| and 303 electoral | 180 | 12 | 72 | 39 |
| votes | electoral votes | electoral votes | electoral votes | electoral votes |
| **Regions:** | | | | |
| Northeast | 56.36% | 29.39% | 11.90% | 2.35% |
| (9 states, 110 | | | | |
| electoral votes) | 107 | 3 | 0 | 0 |
| Midwest | 53.11% | 43.33% | 1.93% | 1.63% |
| (7 states, 66 | | | | |
| electoral votes) | 66 | 0 | 0 | 0 |
| Far West | 32.74% | 31.31% | 29.01% | 6.93% |
| (2 states, 7 | | | | |
| electoral votes) | 7 | 0 | 0 | 0 |
| Border States | 5.83% | 21.76% | 31.95% | 40.46% |
| (4 states,[c] 32 | | | | |
| electoral votes) | 0 | 9 | 11 | 12 |
| South[d] | 0.22% | 8.40% | 51.03% | 40.36% |
| (11 states, 88 | | | | |
| electoral votes) | 0 | 0 | 61 | 27 |

Data computed from *Presidential Elections Since 1789* (Washington: Congressional Quarterly, Inc. 1975).

[a]The Democrats (Douglas) received votes in all 33 states. Southern Democrats and Constitutional Unionists ran in every state except New Jersey, New York, and Rhode Island. Republicans did not distribute ballots in any southern state south of Virginia.

[b]California and Oregon.

[c]Delaware, Kentucky, Maryland, and Missouri.

[d]Southern electoral vote total includes eleven states seceding from the Union in 1860–1861. Popular vote percentages for South exclude South Carolina. That state did not institute popular participation in selection/instruction of electors until after the Civil War.

War had settled. Dixiecrats seceded, like their 1860 Southern Democratic forebears, from the national Democratic party. Both of these third parties were southern-based and proud of it. But the 1860 Southern Democratic party was far more national in its outreach than either its Constitutional Union contemporary or its Dixiecrat ideological descendant. Southern Democracy drew support from slavery defenders outside the South. In Pennsylvania, where much of the Democratic establishment supported the southerners, the contest really was between Lincoln and Breckinridge. Breckinridge won 37.5 percent of all popular votes that Pennsylvanians cast; Lincoln took 56.3 percent of those votes. Douglas's pitiful 3.5 percent share in Pennsylvania barely edged out the Constitutional Union candidate for a distant third place. Breckinridge did well indeed in the two far western states. Oregon's 14,758 voters put the Southern Democrat just 254 votes short of victory there. Breckinridge finished a close third in California, where he took 28.4 percent of all popular votes cast. Lincoln won California with his 32.3 percent popular vote share. Douglas took 31.7 percent in the Golden State.

## Important Short-lived Parties After the Civil War

The Civil War temporarily stymied third-party development. America had focused so much of its attention upon sectionalism and slavery. As military arms settled the issue of slavery (though not sectionalism), it also severed the rationale for creating new parties to defend or to challenge the peculiar institution. Election campaigns in the Union during the war pitted the GOP (the Republican party) against a Democratic party weakened by the temporary loss of its southern base. There was no room at all for third parties. In the Confederacy, elections were nonpartisan affairs. Some say this was because the beleaguered South could not afford the luxury of partisan division. Certainly the Confederacy never had the time to develop or evolve a party system of its own.

### Liberal Republican Party

In the more congenial environment of post-Civil War America, new parties were destined to grow up and pose powerful if transient challenges to the major Republican and Democratic parties. The Liberal Republican party (LRP) first threw down the gauntlet in the 1870s. These Liberals actually accomplished little of any lasting importance. As a party they committed suicide in a fit both of expediency and eccentricity.

LRP was the first secessionist party that began its life by breaking away from the GOP. Liberal Republicans never intended their third party to be a distinct and independent challenger over the long term. Many of them envisioned it instead as the agency for correcting the course that the Republican party was taking; they were very unhappy that commercial and industrial interests were coming to master and command the GOP, and to remold it into a bastion of high-tariff protectionism. Liberal Republicans also wanted civil service reform, and they recoiled at the corruption in the Republican administration of Ulysses S. Grant.

The LRP did have its principles; but one of the things for which it stood bore the seeds of expediency. The Liberals opposed the radical Reconstruction of the South, especially continuation of military occupation and control for years after pacification of the region. Liberals and Democrats found themselves with that overlapping interest, and each saw in the other an enticing potential partner in election battles with Republican regulars.

The Liberal Republican movement began in Missouri in 1870, the brainchild of Republican U.S. Senator Carl Schurz. Liberal Republican-Democratic fusion tickets threw out the Republican establishment and won the Missouri governor's office for Democrat B. Gratz Brown on election day 1870. Two years later, Missouri voters again delivered the governor's office to a candidate of the two parties in fusion.

Prairie winds blew this fusionist Missouri Model in southeasterly directions during the years 1872–1876. Despite Reconstruction measures that temporarily disenfranchised many Confederate war veterans, successful Democratic-Liberal Republican campaigns seized the governorships of Georgia, Tennessee, and Louisiana. Fusion nominees came very close to taking the reins of power in Alabama, Arkansas, and Florida.

In 1872 the Democrats, desperate to unseat President Grant, committed themselves to the Missouri Model in a fusion presidential campaign. The 1872 Democratic convention gave that major party's nominations to the candidates that earlier the Liberal Republicans had selected to run for president and vice-president. *New York Tribune* editor Horace Greeley ran for the presidency that year as the Liberal Republican and Democratic candidate. His running mate was a well-known Missouri fusionist, B. Gratz Brown. The Democrats also adopted verbatim LRP's vaguely worded platform.

Greeley's selection was, for both parties, a colossal mistake. Historians with tender hearts sometimes call Greeley a Don Quixote type. Greeley certainly was tactless, alienating, and eccentric. He had an uncanny knack for fighting hopeless causes.

Soon after Ft. Sumter he had urged Lincoln to make peace with the Confederacy on their own terms. Then he became an enthusiastic champion of military conquest. [Even while he was seeking] Democratic support for his candidacy, he said he would not endorse any Democratic nominee for office. Most Democrats [and Liberal Republicans] opposed high tariffs ... But Greeley was a protectionist. . . .

The campaign was a disaster. Greeley made a series of blunders. He denounced a Union soldier's convention as "rekindling the bitterness and hatred . . . of civil war." He called Negroes "ignorant, deceived, and misguided" for voting against him. He even said he would accept secession if the southerners voted for it in a fair and open election.[22]

Some of this did play well in the South, where Greeley took Georgia, Tennessee, and Texas. His other victories were in border states: Missouri, Maryland, and Kentucky. Grant won 56 percent of the national popular vote, and every other state in the country.

Greeley died soon after the November election, before the members of the electoral college could cast their votes. The sixty-six electors pledged to Greeley then scattered their votes. B. Gratz Brown, Greeley's running mate, received just eighteen presidential electoral votes. Three of the eleven Georgia electors insisted on voting for Greeley; Congress refused to certify electoral votes for a dead candidate.

Southern advocates of the Missouri Model continued their coalitions for four more years; but the Liberal Republican movement as a presidential factor ended, as it had begun, in 1872. Greeley's death had nothing to do with it. Greeley's disastrous campaign did.

Some of the policies for which LRP stood did find their way to enactment. Very little evidence exists that any of these measures were legacies of LRP itself. Reconstruction was ended and southern home rule restored, but not because LRP had desired it and worked toward that goal. After the presidential election of 1876, one of the most disputed in history, a bipartisan commission voted, on a strict 8–7 party-line split, to hand the presidency to Republican Rutherford B. Hayes. Democrat Samuel J. Tilden, who had won a majority of popular votes, prevailed on his supporters in Congress to accept the commission's decision. Tilden's act of statesmanship very well may have been the first part of a Machiavellian quid pro quo prearrangement with Hayes and other key Republicans. Very soon thereafter, Hayes announced that he was ending military occupation of the South.[23]

In 1883, Congress adopted the Pendleton Act, a major early step toward replacing the old spoils system with merit-based civil service.

Had it been still alive, LRP might have welcomed that act, but the long-dead party had nothing to do with Pendleton's passage.

Many of the third-party developments in the nineteenth century's closing decades were important for reasons other than election payoffs or challenges presented to the major parties. You will be reading more later on about some of these. The oldest American third parties living today first came to be after the Civil War. The Socialist Labor party, the most ancient surviving American Marxist party, was born more than a century ago. Older than that, the Prohibition party is today the oldest continuing doctrinal party in the United States. In 1872, the three-year-old Prohibition party became the nation's first party to put forth a plank demanding the vote for women. Twelve years later, the Equal Rights party, a tiny flash in the pan, was the first American party ever to offer for president a woman, Belva Lockwood, who met the constitutional requirements for that office. The situation was ironic: nothing in the U.S. Constitution barred women from the presidency, but women were disenfranchised almost everywhere.[24] Lockwood's 1884 tally, 4,149 votes, came entirely from men.

Most late nineteenth-century national third parties stood to the left of the major parties. Many were organized farmer and worker reactions to frustrations rendered by industrial capitalism, by what Marxists believed to be capitalism's inherent contradictions: owning haves versus producing have-nots and cycles of boom and bust. These parties sought relief from the miseries of capitalism. Their various prescriptions were for reform, roll-back, even overthrow. Most such parties were not avowedly or self-consciously Marxist; but their rhetoric raised the specter of class struggle for the first time in American party history.

The United Labor party embraced the remarkable "single tax" proposal of economist Henry George, who nearly won New York City's mayoralty in 1886. George theorized that landowners were drawing unjustifiable but ever more lucrative profits from their increasingly scarce commodity. His single tax plan, which would continue to rally support well into the twentieth century, called on government to confiscate all income from bare land (though not from improvements to the land), and to abolish all other taxes. He calculated that his single tax would multiply government revenues, the bulk of which were to go for social services for the needy. The plan, he said, was to redistribute on two sides. It would give out the burdens to the wealthy and the benefits to the poor.

Related to United Labor and almost identical in name, the Union Labor party was a socialist coalition of some elements in the Knights of Labor workers' organization and some radical farm groups. In 1888 Union Labor presidential nominee A. J. Streeter of Illinois took 1.29 percent of the national vote. Despite its name, the Union Labor took few of its votes from workers in the urban industrial Northeast. It ran best in the rural South and Midwest. Streeter took 11.4 percent of the Kansas vote, 8.2 percent of the votes cast in Texas, and 6.8 percent of the votes in Arkansas.

### Greenbackers and Populists

GREENBACK  *The National party,* better known as Greenback, was the most influential by far of the leftist parties springing forth in the nation's politics of the 1870s and 1880s. Nationally organized in 1876, Greenback peaked in the last three years of the 1870s. Events of the 1880s steadily diminished party influence and strength, and in 1888 the remnant of Greenbackers formally consigned their dear old party to the history books. Many ex-Greenbackers went on to work in the Populist movement during the last decade of the nineteenth century.

During Greenback's glory days it enjoyed broad appeal, its swelling ranks of farmers and workers responding to two stimuli. First, exorbitant rates charged by monopolistic and heavily subsidized railroads for shipping farm products to market brought down the wrath of midwestern and southern farmers and their demand for federal and state regulation of the railroad industry. Farmers organized for independent political action through their semisecret associations called granges. These grangers produced the quasi-partisan Antimonopoly Movement which went on to win key 1873 state elections in California and several midwestern states.

The grangers' struggle against railroad injustices could not, by itself, have produced a party with the national appeal and clout of Greenback.[25] In the 1870s a sharp downturn in the industrial cycle brought suffering to millions of industrial workers and led many to doubt more than ever the capitalist system. The Panic of 1873, followed by miserable years of industrial depression, temporarily paralyzed the stock market, brought bank failures and thousands of plant and business shutdowns, and sent many workers to the breadlines. Conditions of American industrial boom and bust, and therefore America's 1870s economic woes, were deeply affected by European credit and investment activity; but destitute have-nots were inclined to search for their ogres in profit-gouging American captialists. Reckless speculation by railroads did play a part in the Panic of 1873 and the subsequent downward economic spiral. The granger campaign and industrial depression unleashed powerful voices for a new party to represent have-not farmers and workers.

The 1870s depression led many to seek easy money solutions to the problem of hard to obtain capital. Their first national platform alluded to "the necessities of the people whose industries are prostrated, whose labor is deprived of its just reward by a ruinous policy which the Republican and Democratic parties refuse to change." They would go on to name their new association the National party.

Everyone knew them as Greenbackers. During the Civil War, the Union had raised a lot of revenue by issuing greenbacks—paper treasury notes that, unbacked by specie (gold, silver, or other metal), were fully used as legal tender. The new Greenbackers were protesting new deflationary, "hard money" post-Civil War policies, especially the return to what was, in effect, a gold standard. They demanded the unlimited circulation of greenbacks.

Always stronger among farmers than workers, Greenback was nonetheless America's first third party to achieve truly national significance by coalescing agrarian and labor interests. Twentieth-century parties like Minnesota Farmer-Labor owe something to this Greenback coalition-building experiment.

The late nineteenth century was to be the heyday of interparty fusion campaigns. Greenbackers showed quite a willingness to work alongside other parties when it was politically advantageous to do so. Greenbackers found common ground with national and independent state labor parties. They also discovered overlapping issue concerns with the Readjusters, a Virginia third party briefly enjoying major party status in that state in the early 1880s. Greenback **fusion strategy** in the South usually linked the party electorally with the Republicans. Southern Greenbackers were the first indigenous southern party—most white southerners still regarded, and would for years to come, the GOP as the party of foreign conquest—to appeal openly for the votes of African-Americans. Eventually a political liability when regional Democrats brought home the message that Greenbackers were committing race treason, Greenbacks' interracial appeal at first benefitted the cause. Non-southern Greenbackers were more likely to join with the Democrats than with the GOP.

Never quite penetrating the invisible barrier separating political periphery from mainstream, Greenback did come to the threshold of major party status in a half-dozen widely scattered states. Greenback-Democrat fusion tickets won gubernatorial elections in Michigan, Maine, and Massachusetts. Congressional elections in 1878, Greenback's peak year, brought at least thirteen Greenbackers to the House. These Greenbackers filled seats from four midwestern, three northeastern, and three southern states.

Greenback returns in its three presidential contests were quite another matter. The party never won a single electoral vote. Its first nominee in 1876 took less than 1 percent of all popular votes, its last (in 1884) just 1.74 percent. Greenback's best presidential showing, and even it was disappointing, was for the 1880 candidacy of Iowa Greenback Congressman James B. Weaver.

A hardworking candidate, Weaver was the first nominee of any party to take his campaign to every corner of the nation. His party distributed Weaver ballots in all but four of the thirty-eight states. (The future would call him to campaign again, as the 1892 nominee of the People's party.) But the depression had ended by 1880, and with it the vitality of Greenback's farmer-worker coalition. Accurately or not, the Republicans convinced many voters that the economic recovery was because of the GOP's own hard money policy. Both major parties warned against wasted, dysfunctional third-party votes. Given the fact that Weaver's tally far exceeded Republican James A. Garfield's tiny victory margin (less than .1 percent) over Democrat Winfield S. Hancock, Greenback votes well may have determined the major party winner. Weaver took 3.32 percent of the national vote in that 1880 election.

He did better than that in three southern and three border states. Texas voters gave him his largest single state share, 11.7 percent. The party's best regional showing was in the agricultural Midwest, where six states gave him percentages higher than his national average. The 1880 Greenback presidential campaign washed out in the industrial Northeast.

The Greenback party fielded a range of issues secondary to the one giving the party its popular name. Many issues in Greenback platforms were important to the party activists themselves, not just to the party's outreach to voters. Greenbackers demanded federal regulation of interstate commerce, and that Washington retake vast amounts of the land the national government had given the rail corporations. The reforms called for in its 1880 platform showed the maturation of a party seeking to move from a "mad as hell" protest position to one demonstrating the responsible capacity to govern:

> all money to be issued and its volume controlled by the national government, an eight hour work day, enforcement of a sanitary code in industrial establishments, curtailment of child labor, the establishment of a Bureau of Labor Statistics, . . . a graduated income tax, the ballot for women, and equal voting rights for blacks.[26]

Although they were considered radical at the time Greenbackers proposed them, most of these things have long since become fixtures of the American polity. Firm assessments of cause and effect are difficult, of course. Greenback's strength, like that of almost every other third party of any national signficance, was sapped by major party appropriation of some of its most popular issues. Greenbackers had demanded interstate commerce regulation; their party was still clinging to life when an 1887 congressional act produced the Interstate Commerce Commission and authorized it to regulate railroading and other kinds of interstate commerce.

But Greenback passed most of its eventually enacted proposals on to its third-party heir, the far more influential People's party. As in a relay race, Populism's calls in turn helped set the agenda for the Progressive Era, the twentieth century's first fifteen or twenty years. The Greenback party had been dead for thirty-two years when, in 1920, one of its demands, woman suffrage, entered the U.S. Constitution.

Greenback still lived as a party when Edward Bellamy wrote his famed utopian novel, *Looking Backward.* That manifesto for humanizing the industrial system was to become one of the most influential American literary works ever. Nationalism was the word Bellamy used for the good society he wanted to see. That term he took from the National party, Greenback's more formal name. Borrowing in turn from Bellamy, Theodore Roosevelt, looking to retake the presidency in 1912 (he would run on the Bull Moose Progressive ticket), gave his program a theme: "The New Nationalism." Later presidents likewise would tag their visions for America: New Freedom, New Deal, Fair Deal, New Frontier, Great Society. Greenbackers had some hand in all that.

**POPULIST** The direct Greenback impact and legacy never came close to that of the Populist, the common name for followers of the People's party. Historians say that the People's party was to influence more directly this nation's course than any other third party ever. Populism itself, as a political term, is attributable to a large extent to the *People's party* story.

The People's party was founded as a national organization in 1892; some of what would become its state affiliates came to life just before the close of the 1880s. The Greenback party was partisan Populism's immediate third-party ancestor, and anyone studying them both feels struck by a sense of déjà vu. The national government extended gold backing to greenbacks in 1879: people holding those treasury notes were empowered to redeem them for gold. Easy money veterans of the old Greenbacker movement then moved on to support bimetalism: they demanded silver coinage along with the coinage of gold. The free coinage of silver became the rallying cry of the new People's party. It won support for the party in the silver-mining western states as well as from folks nationwide who wanted currency expansion. Populism's center of gravity always was in the midwestern and southern agricultural heartland and in the silver states of the West; but like its Greenback forebear, the People's party coalesced farm and labor interests.

The populism of this People's party was radical in the animus that it inherited from the Greenback movement, especially toward capitalism and its ownership class. This was the Gilded Age, the time of capitalist robber barons. Although many of the People's party reform issues were to make their way into the mainstream, Americans viewed them as radical when the party first raised them. When their party, itself still at the periphery, died, quite a few of the Populist leaders went on to nourish both the progressive and the socialist movements early in the twentieth century. There was something reactionary too about these Populists' vision. The Populists looked back nostalgically at a yeoman agrarian participatory democracy that seemed in the process of being devoured by urban big business industry and commerce.[27]

Domestic overcultivation and competition from foreign agricultural imports combined to bring about a serious decline in agricultural commodity prices late in the nineteenth century. That commodity price decline aggrieved American farmers and fed the development of organized Populism.[28] Farmers' rancor toward the railroads continued as well. Their grievances led them to organize sectional interest groups, the Northern Alliance and the Southern Alliance. African-American farmers, residing mainly in the South, joined together in the National Colored Farmers Alliance.

Most nonsouthern Populists wanted to leave behind the two national major parties in order to construct a strong partisan third force.[29] The third-party course also had its southern advocates. The South would produce Populist leaders of national stature: Georgia's Thomas E. Watson and Marion Butler of North Carolina. Tom Watson was one of those southern Populists who spoke out courageously in support of African-Americans. Radical agrarians, white and black, began to construct a truly biracial Populist farmers' movement in the South.

But there were many white southern populists who, hesitant about or hostile to the Populist movement's inclusion of blacks, decided at first to stick with the regionally dominant Democrats, the party of their ancestors, the party promising to serve as the frontline of defense for white supremacy. Some, like South Carolina's "Pitchfork Ben" Tillman (nicknamed for his vow to "tickle the ribs" of the establishment's Grover Cleveland), never broke with the Democratic party. In 1895 U.S. Senator

# Radical Agrarianism and "Southern Values":
## Has the South Always Been America's Most Conservative Region?

The American South has been the nation's dissenting region. The decades following World War II brought white southern resistance to civil rights. In the 1980s the South, despite party loyalties of the region's African-American population, was the section most inimical to Democratic party hopes of retaking the presidency. Not since 1964 has a Democratic presidential nominee taken a majority of southern white votes. Recent ones have not even come close; white southerners in 1980 gave Ronald Reagan 60 percent of their votes, southern "favorite son" Jimmy Carter, 35 percent. Just four of the eleven southern states voted for the all-southern Clinton-Gore ticket in 1992.

The late nineteenth century brought southern dissent of a very different sort. Southern radical agrarians—the region's Populists especially—were to be the soul and energy of resistance to capitalists' post-Reconstruction vision of an urban industrial New South. These southern radicals may have longed, along with their agrarian allies in other regions, for a world that was lost; but their political instincts and objectives were anything but conservative. Radical agrarians sought to empower ordinary men and women and to secure their protection from the miseries and dislocations of an emerging industrial system.

Radical agrarianism left its counter-conservative legacy upon both the values and the political practice of the southern region. Southern members of Congress nourished the progressivism of the Woodrow Wilson administration, and they gave substantial backing to liberal measures of Franklin Roosevelt's New Deal program. Ladd and Hadley, political scientists who examined public opinion survey data compiled in the 1930s, concluded that "during the New Deal the South was the most liberal section of the country—providing the highest measure of [popular] support for national Democratic programs."

The agrarian legacy is one reason why genuine southern populists have arisen on occasion, years after the People's party was relegated to the history books. There was, for example, "Big Jim" Folsom (he was also called "Kissin' Jim," a discreet allusion to his well-known womanizing). Folsom was governor of Alabama from 1947 to 1951 and from 1955 until 1959. Folsom's first election signaled a real populist revolt against the Big Mules, Alabama's corporate and planter elite. As governor, Folsom sought, mostly without success, to redistribute power to the common folk of the state. He was extraordinary among southern political notables in winning the enthusiastic support of organized labor. He was most exceptional in reaching out to black Alabamians, most of whom, disenfranchised and segregated in the Jim Crow circumstances of the time, were unable, if eager, to reward him for his inclusiveness. Folsom worked fruitlessly for repeal of the poll tax that disenfranchised most black, and thousands of poor white, Alabamians. He petitioned all the way to the U.S. Supreme Court in his failed bid to bind Alabama's 1948 Democratic electors to vote for Harry Truman, not segregationist Dixiecrat Strom Thurmond. In his Christmas 1949 message to the state, he declared that "as long as the Negroes are held down by deprivation and lack of opportunity, all the other people will be held down alongside them. Let's start talking fellowship and brotherly love, and doing unto others. And let's do more than talk about it; let's start living it."

Political scientist Daniel Elazar observed, at the close of the 1960s, that most of the South then possessed a traditionalist political culture. Elazar's point was valid, despite the South's radical agrarian heritage. On three fundamental issues, at least, the South has been the most tradition-minded and the most conservative of regions. One of these, of course, has been race. A second is the region's hostility toward labor unions. The third has been southerners' gender attitudes. During the first two decades of the twentieth century, the South proved to be infertile ground for building support for national woman suffrage. Some southerners' unenthusiastic response to feminism and the women's movement today may be attributed to growing up in the region's conservative Protestant milieu.

In the 1970s and 1980s, America grew more conservative while its southern section (perhaps) was becoming less traditional. Values no longer mutually alienate the nation and the South as they did in the past. Southerners' values, even on race, are today far less distinguishable from those of people living outside the South. From

Tillman (a former governor) pushed through a state constitutional amendment that effectively disenfranchised most South Carolina blacks. Tom Watson, the Populist leader in neighboring Georgia, roundly condemned the amendment.[30]

Due largely to such quarrels about strategy and race, the birth of the national People's party was delayed until 1892. Populist parties already were electorally active in some nonsouthern states by 1890. Eight of their nominees won seats in the U.S. House, and many others took state and local offices. Two Populists, choices of the Kansas and South Dakota legislatures, sat in the U.S. Senate before the national People's party was even born. In 1890, Alliance-backed populist Democrats were winning local, state, even congressional seats in some southern states.

At a February 1892 conference attended by 800 delegates representing the black and two white regional farmer Alliances, the Knights of Labor, and nineteen other farm and labor associations, Minnesota's Ignatius Donnelly, one of Populism's most eloquent orators, brought them to their feet with a rousing call to action:

> We meet in the midst of a nation brought to the verge of moral, poli'ical, and material ruin. Corruption dominates the ballot box, the legislatures, the Congress, and touches the ermine of the bench. The people are demoralized. . . . The fruits of the toil of millions are boldly stolen to build up colossal fortunes, unprecedented in the history of the world, while their possessors despise the Republic and endanger liberty. From the same prolific womb of governmental injustice we breed the two great classes—

*Georgia Populist leader Thomas E. Watson (courtesy of Georgia Department of Archives and History)*

paupers and millionaires. . . . A vast conspiracy against mankind has been organized on two continents and is taking possession of the world. If not met and overthrown at once it forebodes terrible social convulsions, the destruction of civilization, or the establishment of an absolute despotism.[31]

Populist party builders would meet again, in July of 1892, to set their new People's party in motion. In July they adopted a platform with the principle that all wealth belongs to the workers and farmers who produced it—the maxim that "If any will not work, neither shall he eat." Policy planks demanded the nationalization of railroad, telephone, and telegraph services; civil service regulation of all federal bureaucrats; shorter work hours; a graduated income tax; equal rights for all men and women; the secret ballot; initiative and referendum; the direct election of U.S. Senators, the president, and the vice-president; and a subtreasury plan for currency distribution.

Throwing down the gauntlet to the gold standard Republican party and its hard-money position, this platform demanded the "free and unlimited coinage of silver." To many Populists, especially in the West, that was its most crucial plank. This would be the issue most substantially affecting later People's party history.

Iowa's James B. Weaver, that veteran of Greenback's 1880 presidential campaign, won the 1892 People's party presidential nomination. Weaver took 8.5 percent of the votes that Americans cast in 1892. He came in first in the popular votes of Colorado, Idaho, Kansas, Nevada, and North Dakota. Twenty-two of the nation's 444 electors voted for him.

Voters in ten of the eleven states that had seceded at the opening of the Civil War (all except Louisiana) had the option to vote for the People's party nominee. Weaver took over 15 percent of the popular votes cast in those ten states; in four of the ten, Weaver ran ahead of Benjamin Harrison, the Republican nominee.

Partisan Populism rose like a phoenix in the years just following the birth of the People's party. By the end of 1892, Populist state parties had achieved or nearly achieved major party status in Kansas, Nebraska, Colorado, and other midwestern and western states. By 1894 they were becoming major challengers, able to take on Democratic establishments, in North Carolina and Alabama. Nine Populist nominees won election to the U.S. House for the Fifty-fourth Congress (1895–1897). Six of these came from southern states, the other three from the Midwest and West. During the 1890s, Populists or Democratic-Populist fusion candidates won the governors' offices of Colorado, Idaho, Kansas, Minnesota, Montana, Nebraska, North Dakota, Oregon, South Dakota, Washington, and Wyoming.

There were 357 members of the U.S. House during the Fifty-fifth Congress (1897–1899); the twenty-two-member Populist delegation made up more than 6 percent of the chamber. Twelve of these twenty-two were from midwestern states, eight from the South, and two from the West. Five of the ninety U.S. Senators in the Fifty-fifth Congress were Populists. The Silver Republican and Nevada Silver parties, two silver coinage third parties that were based in the West and allied with the Populists, held another four House and seven Senate seats.

That was to be the most substantial presence Populists would ever hold in Congress. Those who revere numbers are in danger of drawing from those impressive figures the erroneous conclusion that, at the time of the 1896 elections, the condition of the People's party had been unreservedly healthy and good.

Those numbers masked two serious dilemmas confronting partisan Populism by that time. Each of these turned out to be a problem unresolvable, a factor that would lead Populism, as an independent partisan force, to begin its descent down a slippery slope to extinction. The Democratic party had some complicity in both. You may wish to keep in mind that image of a hungry-looking fish swimming at the tail of a smaller fish.

In the South, the interracial Populist movement suffered unrelenting, merciless race baiting from a conservative establishment that was desperate to defend its interests against Populist radicalism. Southern newspapers editorialized that Populism stood for rule by "ignorant Negroes and unscrupulous whites"; the Democratic party was portrayed as the singular agency for defending southern unity and autonomy and, above all, white supremacy. The word was passed that whites must support whatever was necessary to disenfranchise blacks. Some of these measures such as poll taxes and literacy tests bore a side effect of taking away the votes of many poor whites. All this went deeper than just the rhetoric of interparty competition. The lesson was that race was far more crucial than class, and that to preserve racial unity, white common folk must forget about whatever interests they might have thought they shared with poor people of color. It was the classic and finally successful game of divide and conquer.[32]

Already hemorrhaging from this southern race baiting, the People's party began to suffer a widening rift between its purists and pragmatists over party strategy and tactics. Purists in the People's party wanted, above all, to preserve their party's independence and principles. They were far less enthusiastic than were the party's pragmatists about searching for allies in other parties. The pragmatists wanted their party to give active encouragement to friendly forces outside the party, and to enter into fusion campaigns with other parties that were seeking some of the same goals that Populists sought. Midwestern and western Populists built many alliances with Democrats in their regions. U.S. Senator Marion Butler of North Carolina was one of a few southern Populists who built profitable ties with Republicans. But southern Populists were more likely than their comrades elsewhere to be purists.

**Cooptation** is the process whereby a major party appropriates the ideas of a third party and eventually absorbs the third party itself.

Cooptation was high among objectives of national Democratic strategists in 1896. Taking for themselves Populism's popular free silver issue, the Democrats in 1896 also endorsed People's party stands on income tax, railroad regulation, and other things. Democrats repudiated their own gold standard incumbent, Grover Cleveland, and gave their nomination to a Nebraska free silverite who had warm friendships with scores of western and midwestern Populists. This was William Jennings Bryan, the young, good-looking silver-tongued orator. In 1896 he would make the first of his three tries as the Democratic nominee for president.

As their convention closed, the Democrats publicly proclaimed to the nation's Populists that it was time now to unify around Bryan and his crusade, that the Populists must give up "selfish" devotion to party and dedicate themselves to "principle."[33] Bryan's belief in free silver and populism seems, like that of many of his Democratic followers, to have been genuine and true. Still, the big party's appeal to the smaller one to rise to principle did seem to smack of hypocrisy. It is always ironic when a major party preaches principle to a third-party audience.

That was the dilemma facing the Populists when they met for their own national convention in 1896. Despite warnings from its purist contingent that the Democrats were not to be trusted, Populism's fusionists carried the day. The People's party selected Democrat William Jennings Bryan to run on the Populist ticket too. As a sop to the purists, the party refused to endorse Arthur Sewall, Bryan's Democratic running mate. Tom Watson, an antifusion purist, ran a symbolic campaign as the People's party nominee for vice-president.[34]

The nominee of the Republicans, whose convention had preceded the Democrats' by a month, was Ohio Governor William McKinley. When the Republicans adopted a platform plank strongly backing the gold standard, a group of prosilver dissidents from western states walked out. They went on to found the National Silver Republican party. These Silver Republicans, like the Populists, gave their endorsement to William Jennings Bryan.[35]

McKinley, promising a "full dinner pail," outspent Bryan 7–1 in the first modern presidential campaign in history. McKinley drove home his claim that Bryan was a dangerous radical who wanted to destroy the free enterprise system. McKinley took 51.01 percent of the national popular vote, Bryan 46.73 percent.[36] Bryan's best regional results were in the Far West (where 64.4 percent of the voters cast ballots for him) and in the eleven southern states (where he took 62.9 percent). McKinley swept the Northeast and a lot of the urbanized parts of the Midwest. McKinley received 271 of the 447 electoral votes for president. Realignments during

1896 cast the GOP into the clear position of majority party in the nation. Republicans were to remain America's "natural governing party" until "Hoover's Depression" brought another realignment in the 1930s.

Democratic-Populist fusion, particularly the two parties' joint support of Bryan in 1896, opened the way for the Democratic party to destroy the People's party by devouring it. Populist representation in Congress tumbled precipitously from 1899 on; by 1903, there were no Populists left on Capitol Hill.

# The People's Party and the Wizard of Oz

The Populist cause had its effect on literature and popular culture. You may have grown up, as I did, loving the 1939 movie "The Wizard of Oz" and Lyman Frank Baum's 1900 book on which the movie was based, *The Wonderful Wizard of Oz.* I did not know until recently that this grand movie and book intentionally presented a political allegory of the Populist movement. As a South Dakota rural weekly newspaper editor, Baum held an ideal vantage for observing the course of Populism. Baum's Scarecrow stands for the farmer, the Tin Woodsman for the urban industrial worker. The Cowardly Lion is 1896 Democratic-Populist nominee Bryan, known for his roar but not much else. They are carried down the yellow brick road, the gold standard, which goes nowhere. Arriving in Emerald City, they seek favors from the Wizard of Oz, the president (Oz was an abbreviation for ounce, the standard measure for gold). Dorothy, symbolizing Everyman, went along with them. Dorothy is so naively innocent that she sees truth before the others. The Wicked Witch of the East, the banks, had kept the little Munchkins "in bondage for many years, making them work for her night and day" (Baum's words). The Wicked Witch of the West was Baum's symbol for large industrial corporations. Baum's message was that "the powers that be survive by deception. Only people's ignorance allows the powerful to manipulate and control them." I am indebted to Ms. Stephanie Beaty, a former student who, reversing roles, became my teacher by bringing me this insight.

**Sources:** Peter Drier, "The way it wOz and iz," *In These Times,* September 27–October 3, 1989; and Henry M. Littlefield, "The Wizard of Oz: Parable on Populism," *American Quarterly,* 16 (Summer, 1964), 47–58.

In 1900 the People's party "fusion faction," by then virtually absorbed into the Democratic party, went through the motions of endorsing William Jennings Bryan. Antifusion purists attending to the shell or remnant that the independent People's party organization had become nominated obscure Wharton Barker for president in 1900. Barker picked up one of every 300 votes cast. Tom Watson was the nominee in 1904 and 1908. Watson campaigned actively in 1904, in a failed effort to revive the party ghost. Watson took less than 1 percent in 1904, and a pitiful .19 percent in 1908.

As their party withered and died, surviving Populist leaders and activists took out in many different political directions. Newspaper editor J. A. Wayland aligned with the Socialist party. From his base in tiny Girard, Kansas, he edited *The Appeal to Reason* and distributed thousands of copies nationwide. The *Appeal* was to be American socialism's most influential newspaper ever.[37] Ex-Senator Marion Butler joined the Republicans and marched into obscurity with a North Carolina GOP relegated ever more to the margins by the march of the Solid South. Figuratively holding his nose, Tom Watson joined the Democrats, the party against which he had for so long waged war. He won election to the U.S. Senate in 1920. By the time of his 1922 death, he had garnered notoriety as a latter-day convert to vicious Negro baiting and anti-Semitism.[38] Watson's bitterness, demoralization, and demise seemed in a way to replay that of the Populist movement he had helped to nurture and tried to sustain.

But if you seek its legacy, look around. Many of Populism's stands—suffrage expansion, direct election of U.S. Senators, initiative and referendum, the graduated income tax, improvements in the condition of labor—long ago became integral features of national or state and local process and policy. Populism was America's first significant movement "to attack seriously the problems caused by industrialization," the first "to insist that the federal government had some responsibility for the common weal."[39] Many twentieth-century politicians have claimed the name populist. Some even deserved it.

## Notes

1. The two-party system was in transition in the 1850s, and some historians maintain that the GOP had not clearly achieved major party status by 1856. If this argument is valid, the Republican tally in 1856 (33.11% of the popular vote, 38.51% of the electoral vote) was an even more spectacular finish for a nonmajor

party than Theodore Roosevelt's in 1912. Party historian William B. Hesseltine wrote that "the Republicans were never a third party." Hesseltine, *Third-Party Movements in the United States* (Princeton, N.J.: D. Van Nostrand, 1962), 47.

2. See Alan R. Gitelson, *et al.*, *American Political Parties: Stability and Change* (Boston: Houghton Mifflin, 1984), 24-25 and 31-33.

3. Hesseltine, *Third-Party Movements*, 15-16.

4. *Ibid.*, 15-16; and Michael F. Holt, "The Antimasonic and Know Nothing Parties," in *History of U.S. Political Parties*, ed. Arthur M. Schlesinger, vol. 1 (New York: Chelsea House, 1973), 576-577.

5. See Kenneth C. Martis, *The Historical Atlas of Political Parties in the United States Congress 1789-1989* (New York: Macmillan, 1989). Another source lists their 1833-1835 House number as 53. *Members of Congress Since 1789*, 3d. ed. (Washington, D.C.: Congressional Quarterly, 1985), 183.

6. Holt, "The Antimasonic," in *History of U.S. Political Parties*, ed. Schlesinger, vol. 1, 592.

7. Richard H. Sewell, *Ballots for Freedom* (New York: W. W. Norton, 1975); and Frederick J. Blue, *The Free Soilers* (Urbana: University of Illinois Press, 1973).

8. Hesseltine, *Third-Party Movements*, 44-45.

9. Jay M. Shafritz, *The Dorsey Dictionary of American Government and Politics* (Chicago: Dorsey Press, 1988), 312.

10. Steven J. Rosenstone, *et al.*, *Third Parties in America* (Princeton, N.J.: Princeton University Press, 1984), 56-59.

11. Ray Allen Billington, *The Protestant Crusade, 1800-1860* (New York: Macmillan, 1933), 411.

12. Hesseltine, *Third-Party Movements*, 27-28.

13. Zachary Taylor's remains were disinterred in 1991 in search of evidence confirming or denying some American historians' speculation that Taylor might have been assassinated. Some television reports of the story conjectured that an ambitious Vice-President Fillmore might have effected his chief's demise. Medical experts who examined the body reported that Taylor's death was not the result of foul play.

14. Rosenstone, *et al.*, *Third Parties*, 58.

15. Glyndon G. Van Deusen, "The Whig Party," in *History of U.S. Political Parties*, ed. Schlesinger, vol. 1, 362.

16. Michael F. Holt, "The Democratic Party, 1828-1860," in *History of U.S. Political Parties*, ed. Schlesinger, vol. 1, 532-533.

17. Howard P. Nash, Jr., *Third Parties in American Politics* (Washington, D.C.: Public Affairs Press, 1959), 89.

18. *Ibid.*

19. David M. Potter, *The Impending Crisis, 1848-1861* (New York: Harper and Row, 1976), 443-445.

20. Rosenstone, *et al.*, *Third Parties*, 60-61.

21. Holt, "The Democratic Party," in *History of U.S. Political Parties*, ed. Schlesinger, vol. 1, 533-535.

22. Leon Friedman, "The Democratic Party, 1860–1884," in *History of U.S. Political Parties*, ed. Schlesinger, vol. 2, 900.

23. Hayes simultaneously announced education and transportation programs to benefit the South and that his cabinet would include at least one southern Democrat. C. Vann Woodward, *Reunion and Reaction: The Compromise of 1877 and the End of Reconstruction*, 2d. ed. (Garden City, N.Y.: Doubleday, 1956).

24. Wyoming Territory extended full voting rights to women in 1869. Neighboring Utah Territory did the same the next year. Of course, territorial residents did not have the franchise in presidential elections. In 1889 Wyoming became the first state to enter the Union under a constitution mandating full suffrage rights for women as well as men.

25. James L. Sundquist, *Dynamics of the Party System* (Washington, D.C.: Brookings Institution, 1973), 98.

26. Leonard Dinnerstein, "Election of 1880," in *History of American Presidential Elections*, ed. Arthur M. Schlesinger and Fred. L. Israel, vol. 2 (New York: McGraw-Hill, 1971), 1505.

27. See Lawrence Goodwyn, *Democratic Promise: The Populist Movement in America* (New York: Oxford University Press, 1976).

28. George B. Tindall, "The People's Party," in *History of U.S. Political Parties*, ed. Schlesinger, vol. 2, 1701.

29. See Rosenstone, *et al.*, *Third Parties*, 67–71.

30. John Hope Franklin, *From Slavery to Freedom*, 3d. ed. (New York: Alfred A. Knopf, 1967), 338–339.

31. See Hesseltine, *Third-Party Movements*, 57–58 and 148–151.

32. See V. O. Key, Jr., *Southern Politics in State and Nation* (New York: Vintage Books, 1949), esp. 7–9.

33. C. Vann Woodward, *Tom Watson: Agrarian Rebel* (New York: Macmillan Co., 1938), 293.

34. Tom Watson had served in the U.S. House from Georgia from 1891 until 1893. V. O. Key wrote in the 1940s that Watson may have been "the nation's ablest Populist leader. . . ." Key, *Southern Politics*, 118.

35. Betty Glad, *Key Pittman: The Tragedy of a Senate Insider* (New York: Columbia University Press, 1986), 9.

36. Bryan's popular vote total was 6,511,495. According to historian C. Vann Woodward, Populist vice-presidential nominee Watson received 217,000 votes in seventeen states where it was possible to designate one's vote specifically for him. Twenty-seven vice-presidential electoral votes went to Watson. Woodward, *Tom Watson*, 329.

37. See Elliott Shore, *Talkin' Socialism* (Lawrence: University Press of Kansas, 1988). Wayland's and his newspaper's ideological descendants today include the magazine *Mother Jones* and the independent socialist newspaper *In These Times*.

38. Goodwyn, *Democratic Promise*, 558–559.

39. Richard Hofstadter, *The Age of Reform* (New York: Vintage Books, 1955), 61.

# CHAPTER THREE

# Candles in the Wind:

## *Transient National Third Parties in the Twentieth Century*

*It seems to me you lived your life like a candle in the wind.*
—from "Candle in the Wind" ("Goodbye, Norma Jean")
by Elton John and Bernie Taupin

The golden age for national third parties of the transient, short-lived variety ended with the death of partisan Populism. Twentieth-century Americans have not experienced the ruptures in national two-party dominance that had offered hope to Antimasons, Know Nothings, and other nineteenth-century parties of cracking the ranks of the major parties in national politics. This is not to say that this century has been free of nationally significant short-lived parties. Theodore Roosevelt, running as a Bull Moose Progressive, took well over a quarter of the popular votes for president in 1912. Robert La Follette and George Wallace each won about a seventh of the votes in their 1924 and 1968 third-party quests for the presidency. Independent Ross Perot captured nearly one in every five popular votes cast in 1992. Transient parties won 1.5 percent of the 12,172 presidential electoral votes cast from 1904 through 1992.

But the cycles of life, especially the time of peak popular appeal, of our century's short-lived parties have tended to be even shorter than those of many of their forebears. The brevity of their existence has made it impossible for most of them to organize effectively down to the grassroots level. Thus, unlike either the continuing doctrinal parties (Chapter 5) or the non-national significant others (Chapter 6), most of this century's transient national parties have concentrated—and dissipated—their limited energies upon presidential campaigns. They have proven themselves unable to take their place in the ongoing governance of states and communities. Just one state governor, a Bull Moose Progressive, has won election on the ticket of a twentieth-century national short-lived party.

Voter support for some of these transient parties has been far more substantial than for the continuing doctrinal parties; but it also tends to be softer and more vulnerable to erosion as election day approaches. Popular enthusiasm brought about by the early media reports of a new insurgency from beyond the walls of the two major parties wanes as the Democrats and Republicans remind the electorate of its legitimate partisan loyalties, of wasted votes, of the quixotic hopelessness of a third-party cause.

In this century, seven independent or transient-party presidential candidates have scored more than 2 percent of the nation's popular vote for president. Public opinion polls of support for the latter six (scientific polling had not reached even its infancy by the time of the Bull Moose Progressives in 1912) reveal an average drop-off from peak (usually in late spring or summer) to just before the election of about 35 percent. Only the Dixiecrats, with their hard core southern base, experienced no significant drop-off. Legal barriers that excluded most of these parties from the ballots of at least a few states generally prevented their nominees from taking in the voting booths even that share to which they seemed entitled by the results of the last pre-election opinion polls.

There also is the weighty, ultimately insurmountable problem of financing an effective campaign. Although the most significant transient parties receive a lot more money than the continuing doctrinal parties do, their funds normally do not come close to those of the Republicans and Democrats. There should be little surprise that even the most important short-lived parties ended on the electoral periphery, finishing (except for Bull Moosers) behind both major parties in contests for the presidency.

## Third-Party Candles in Hostile Winds: 1912–1980

When V. O. Key characterized these parties as "recurring, short-lived . . . party eruptions," he left unclear what meaning he intended the word "recurring" to convey. Key meant at the least that these short-lasting parties come and go over the decades. Beyond that he may have wanted to suggest that ideological themes recur over time in a sequence of transient parties. There were ideological ties linking 1860 Southern Democrats with the 1948 Dixiecrats and, to some extent, with American Independents of 1968. On the left there were common values bonding Greenbackers and Populists. Links of ideology if not of mutual support in some sense tied the national Progressives of 1912 and 1924 and, more remotely, these two earlier parties with the 1948 Progressives. Twentieth-

**Table 3.1: Campaign Expenditures by Short-lived Parties Receiving over Two Percent of the Popular Vote for President, 1912–1980\***

| Party and Year | Party's Expenditure (in Dollars) | Average of Major Party Expenditures (in Dollars) | Third Party's Expenditure as Percentage of Major Party Average | Third Party's Vote as Percentage of Major Party Average |
|---|---|---|---|---|
| 1912 Progressive (Bull Moose) | 665,420 | 1,103,199 | 60.3 | 84.3 |
| 1924 Progressive | 236,963 | 2,564,659 | 9.2 | 40.0 |
| 1948 Progressive | 1,133,863 | 2,431,815 | 46.6 | 5.0 |
| 1948 Dixiecrat | 163,443 | 2,431,815 | 6.7 | 5.1 |
| 1968 American Independent | 7,223,000 | 18,498,000 | 39.0 | 31.4 |
| 1980 National Unity | 15,040,669 | 29,040,183 | 48.7 | 14.4 |

**Sources:** *Historical Statistics of the United States* (New York: Revisionist Press, 1984); Alexander Heard, *The Costs of Democracy* (Chapel Hill: University of North Carolina Press, 1960); *Presidential Elections Since 1789* (Washington, Congressional Quarterly, 1975); Rosenstone *et al.*, *Third Parties in America* (Princeton, Princeton University Press, 1984); and Federal Election Commission reports on financing in 1980.

*If they were available, figures from the nineteenth century might reveal comparable expenditure inequalities in that century. Spending necessities of course became increasingly onerous in the twentieth century "media age."

century Progressivism was in some sense an ideological heir of Greenbackers and Populists.

## Marching to a Leftist Drummer, 1912 and 1924

Arthur Schlesinger and other historians say that American history unfolds in cycles: periods of reform, change, progressivity eventually yield up to conservatism and rest, which in their turn then lose out to reform and change.[1] The 1930s were a time of movement and change. So were the 1960s; and this century's first fifteen or twenty years were the Progressive Era, which had run its course by the time of Republican Warren Harding's 1920 victory on a promise of returning the country to normalcy.

The movement of progressives in this century's earliest years drew from such radical nineteenth-century wells as the Populists and *Looking Backward*, Edward Bellamy's influential utopian novel published in 1888. There were radical strains in the progressive movement itself: socialists of various stripes, muckraking investigative reporters exposing America's seamy side in a range from filthy food processing to the destitution of life in the underclass, and others. But the real soul of the movement in this century's first fifteen years was middle class and liberal. Much of its energy went toward extending the participatory power of ordinary citizens, eradicating corruption, and building good government.

Sometimes it is said that the principal advantage of a federal system is that it provides states as experimental laboratories for policies which, if successful, may be enacted eventually in other states or even by the nation as a whole. Wisconsin progressives may give a little too much credit to their state when they claim that progressivism was "the Wisconsin Idea," that Wisconsin was the one important incubator for the liberal programs of both the Progressive and New Deal eras.[2] No one, however, will deny that Wisconsin and its Robert (Fighting Bob) La Follette very strongly influenced the nationwide progressive agenda and accomplishment during the earliest years of the twentieth century.

Elected governor in 1901, La Follette revamped his state's GOP into the progressive agency it was to be over the ensuing third of a century. From the state university in Madison, La Follette gathered a core of natural and social scientists into what today we would call a think tank. The professors did research and wrote treatises on progressive reforms and their likely results. La Follette thus brought the techniques of science to his program for change. Wisconsin under La Follette's influence pioneered in the use of primaries, initiative and referendum, as well as in advanced measures for conservation. In 1906 Fighting Bob went to the Senate where he remained until his 1925 death. During his Senate years La Follette devoted himself to sharing the "Wisconsin Idea" with the nation at large.[3]

Progressive Era pragmatists tended to believe more was possible inside than outside the national major party ranks. Both of the major parties had their progressive as well as conservative wings during this century's first twenty years, and both gave the nation a progressive president: Republican Theodore Roosevelt and Democrat Woodrow Wilson. Wilson's national self-determination and League of Nations objectives

*Robert La Follette campaigning, Cumberland, Wisconsin, 1897 (courtesy of the State Historical Society of Wisconsin)*

lent important if ultimately unsuccessful international dimensions to the progressive program.

Domestically the progressives accomplished a lot, with legislation against child labor and on behalf of workers' rights, the consumer, and the environment. Constitutional amendments adopted during the Progressive Era provided for woman suffrage, the direct election of U.S. Senators, and a graduated income tax. In their effort to democratize politics and to cleanse it of its seemingly endemic corruption, progressives initiated direct primaries, local nonpartisan elections, at-large arrangements for municipal councils, initiative, referendum, and recall in various parts of the nation. They brought some democratic reforms in the operation of the U.S. House. They also launched the commission and council-manager systems as alternatives to mayor-council city government.[4]

Today's liberals, painfully remembering George Bush's election-motivated 1988 assault on the "dreaded L word," may look back with nostalgia to the Progressive Era's peak years, 1911–1912. Progressive

Democratic and Republican Congressmen mowed down their parties' right wings and brought forth proposals, ratified by 1913, for a graduated income tax and for the direct election of U.S. Senators.[5] In the 1912 presidential election three-quarters of the electorate voted on the left: nearly 42 percent for winning Democrat Woodrow Wilson, almost six in a hundred for Socialist standardbearer Eugene V. Debs, and over 27 percent for the Bull Moose Progressive ticket of ex-President Theodore Roosevelt. Just 23 percent gave their vote to the conservative sitting president, Republican William Howard Taft.

It took some doing to push cautious and, for the most part, liberal people into stepping beyond the protective confines of the major parties and into the more radical strategy of building and feeding a third party. But Theodore Roosevelt persuaded his devotees to do just that in 1912. Roosevelt's Bull Moose army seceded from the GOP, thus splitting it and assuring its defeat that year. In 1922–1924, after the Progressive Era had run its course, Bob La Follette gathered up some of what was left of the movement and forged another Progressive party and a new third-party presidential bid.

**BULL MOOSE PROGRESSIVE** Roosevelt's Progressive (Bull Moose) party was a very personalistic undertaking; its very reason for being lay to a large extent in the appeal and ambition of TR himself. Roosevelt had won the vice-presidency in 1900. When President McKinley died of an assassin's bullet on September 14, 1901, Teddy Roosevelt became, at forty-two, the youngest man ever to be inaugurated president. The voters returned him to the presidency in 1904, then elected his protégé, William Howard Taft. The TR vigor and macho remained in 1912, and the man and his policies were enormously popular. Fathers still told their sons about TR and his Rough Riders' charge during the 1898 war with Spain.

Roosevelt and Taft drew much farther apart ideologically during the Taft years, and each blamed the other for the drift. Their friendship had long since ended by 1912. Roosevelt wanted to shake the presidency from Taft's clutches and retake it himself. Such a dream would be impossible today because of the **Twenty-second Amendment.** Even in TR's time a well-understood tradition set by Washington and Jefferson said "no more than two!" Roosevelt earlier had pledged his devotion to the two-term limit; but as 1912 approached, he revised his interpretation to read "no more than two consecutive terms."

After a big game African hunting safari and a European trip, TR returned to the States to prepare for the struggle. He set forth his campaign program as "The New Nationalism." In February 1912 he first threw his hat into the Republican ring. In his ten primary battles with Taft, TR won nine states. With popularity like that, a candidate would be well on the way to nomination today. But in 1912, indeed, as recently as 1968, the selection of most delegates (thus presidential nomination) remained in the hands of major party establishments. Taft was the establishment man. The GOP organization folks were determined to nominate him.[6]

The Republican convention was a raucous affair, and when the GOP nomination went to Taft, TR's supporters bolted and unanimously selected him for a third-party bid. Clearly, the Bull Moose Progressives began as a secessionist split-away from the GOP. Two months later at a convention in Chicago their new party officially came to life. The 2,000 delegates were a hodge-podge of "social workers, reformers, intellectuals, feminists, Republican insurgents, disgruntled politicians, and businessmen who favored the New Nationalism."[7] At Chicago they sang "Onward Christian Soldiers" and nominated TR for president. California Governor Hiram Johnson was named to the ticket for vice-president. The new party's platform demanded federal assistance to farmers, better working conditions, the prohibition of child labor, minimum wages for female employees, woman suffrage, direct election of U.S. Senators (to replace the old procedure in which each state's legislature selected the state's two senators), an income tax, conservation of natural resources, a federal agency for the regulation of trusts, and a plethora of other progressive reforms. The presidential candidate showed up to accept his nomination feeling, he said, "as fit as a bull moose"—hence the party's nickname and its symbol.

Although years would pass before scientific polling came into being, it was apparent from the beginning of the general election campaign that Taft had no prayer of winning reelection. Thus 1912 was unique in history in that the two major parties aimed their sharpest spears at a third-party campaign, that of the TR Progressives. The bad blood between former allies Roosevelt and Taft and Taft's deep resentment at Roosevelt's splitting the GOP (as standardbearer of the party that had enjoyed clear majority status in the electorate since 1896, Taft was entirely justified in laying his own imminent defeat right at the Bull Mooser's doorstep) led President Taft to particularly venomous attacks on his third-party opponent. It seems quite clear that Taft was gratified that the election went ultimately to Democrat Woodrow Wilson rather than TR.

In Milwaukee on October 14, 1912, a fanatic named John Shrank, raising some cry against a third-term presidency, brandished a gun and shot Roosevelt in the chest. Seriously though not permanently wounded, his shirt soaked in his own blood, TR insisted on going on with his speech.[8]

Roosevelt was the third and so far the last ex-president to seek reelection on a third-party ticket. His showing was better than either of the two preceding him. Roosevelt finished with eighty-eight electoral votes to Wilson's 435 and Taft's paltry eight. He took Michigan, Minnesota, Pennsylvania, South Dakota, and Washington. TR and his California running mate won a slight plurality and eleven of thirteen electors in the Golden State. The Progressives ran ahead of Taft in twenty-two of the other forty-two states.

Its November showing was indeed impressive. But the party itself had rather little impact on the legal enactment of the progressive agenda. Many of the proposals which were planks in the party platform already were well on their way to passage or ratification by the time of the party's birth. As an organization Bull Moose was fragile, especially weak and vulnerable at the grassroots. For viability the party required, but did not receive, the nurture and tender loving care of its very essence, TR. The party did enjoy one gubernatorial success. In 1914 California voters returned Hiram Johnson on the Progressive ticket. Johnson had taken his first gubernatorial victory there on the Republican line. The party held one U.S. Senate and nine House seats in the Sixty-third Congress (1913–1915) and it hung on to six in the House through the Sixty-fourth. But when the party approached TR about a 1916 rerun for the presidency, the man said no; thereupon, the Bull Moose party dropped and died.

**LA FOLLETTE PROGRESSIVE**    The 1912 returns from Wisconsin must have saddened TR; in that progressive heartland the Bull Mooser finished a poor third, twelve points below his national 27.39 percent average. Wisconsin voters were paying deference to their own "Mr. Progressive," Robert La Follette. Fighting Bob had sought the GOP's 1912 nomination, ending behind both Taft and TR. He would try again, unsuccessfully, in 1916 and 1920. La Follette was far from subtle in his sentiments about Roosevelt. TR, he said, was an opportunist manipulating and using the progressive program to further his own political ambitions. There was not much in the Bull Moose platform with which La Follette disagreed in principle. La Follette in fact had helped usher many of its issues into the mainstream. But when Roosevelt entered the third-party track, La Follette declined to endorse him or give any support.

La Follette also would come to be deeply disenchanted with Wilson. The Wisconsinite regarded America's 1917 entry into World War I as an act of profound presidential cynicism. After all, Wilson had won reelection in 1916 using the reminder that "he kept us out of war." By the close of this century's second decade, La Follette's views were shifting further to the left. Through his *La Follette's Magazine*, he produced and disseminated a comprehensive and rather radical perspective on events of the time:

> Big Business, operating through the "System," had permeated government in the United States. The people, operating through the progressives and . . . insurgents, had been on the verge of restoring government to the people. Skillfully, the managers of Big Business and the "System" . . . backed Theodore Roosevelt to crush progressivism, and elect Wilson. Then, partly to secure profits and partly to suppress progressive criticism, the forces of monopoly . . . combined with militarists and jingoes and corrupt politicians to bring American participation in the war. Wilson went to Paris, abandoned the idealism he had voiced in his Fourteen Points at the beginning of the war, and came back with a "League of Damnations"—a victor's vengeful peace which would make the world safe for American monopolists, imperialists, and militarists but not for democracy.[9]

La Follette followed with interest events of the Russian Bolshevik Revolution. Never an uncritical apologist for all actions taken in the name of Soviet power, he did applaud that new regime's dedication to modernization and redistribution. He condemned the various anti-Soviet ventures, including the military intervention undertaken by the United States and some other capitalist nations in support of the forces fighting the Bolsheviks during the Russian Civil War. He was, to this extent, a precursor of Henry Wallace and his 1948 Progressive party campaign against the Cold War with Russia.

By 1922 La Follette and his followers were seriously pondering whether to undertake a new third-party venture. These "La Follette radicals" were, and would remain, distinctly disinclined to give the party label to their anticipated course of action. In February 1922 representatives of many labor, farm, liberal Christian, and third party groups met in Chicago. The *Conference for Progressive Political Action* (CPPA), the name they gave to the movement launched there, did not even hint at the party essence of what they were doing. Voters in several states that November elected or returned a cadre of La Follette radicals to the Sixty-eighth Congress. These members of Congress were officially Republicans, Democrats, or (in a few cases) members of various third parties. Official records do not account for their affiliation with CPPA. Yet early in the Sixty-eighth Congress, they joined as a cohesive voting bloc. In substance though not name, the CPPA was informally taking its place as a party-in-government.

As late as 1924, La Follette made ont final bid for the Republican nomination. When the GOP rejected him again, the CPPA convened in Cleveland to select him as its own. The CPPA platform, which La Follette wrote himself, condemned monopolies and monopoly power; demanded radical executive branch reform, the election of federal judges and direct election of presidents, freer international trade, nationalization of the railroads, and the development of the federal electric power plant at Muscle Shoals, Alabama (a foreruner of FDR's socialistic TVA program); and roundly denounced imperialism, militarism, and war. For his running mate, La Follette chose Montana Democratic Senator Burton Wheeler, who had won fame for uncovering corruption in Republican President Harding's administration.

For the first and thus far the only time in its very long history, the Socialist party in 1924 joined in a presidential fusion campaign. The Socialists endorsed La Follette and his platform as their own. La Follette's name made it to the ballot of every state except Louisiana. In several states where ballot requirements proved difficult or impossible for the late-starting CPPA, La Follette ran instead on the Socialist line. CPPA-Socialist connections made the ticket vulnerable to a lot of **red baiting** during the campaign.

From its beginning the La Follette campaign was underfinanced, lonely, and quixotic and hopeless against the very popular incumbent Cal Coolidge. Harding had died in August 1923 and Silent Cal had succeeded to the White House untainted by any of the scandals of the Harding administration. Of a $3 million campaign war chest promised to La Follette by labor, less than 1 percent of the money ever materialized. Many of CPPA's affiliated groups, realizing that the campaign had not a ghost of a chance, sat on their hands throughout.

La Follette's most faithful campaign hands, as it turned out, were his own sons, Robert Jr. and Philip. A decade later these sons would go on to organize the Wisconsin Progressive Party in progressivism's heartland. The WPP was to come to spectacular achievement as that state's principal governing party until near the close of World War II.

Given the adversities, their dad's 1924 accomplishment was far from unimpressive. Fighting Bob took nearly 17 percent to Coolidge's 54 and 29 percent for darkhorse Democrat John Davis. He won his own state's thirteen electoral votes and ran second in the popular tallies of seven western and four midwestern states.

The CPPA died the next year. Its cause of death could be attributed to Robert La Follette's own death on June 18, 1925, but perhaps more so to the conservative temper of the times. La Follette progressivism was peripheral to the values of a decade devoted to "prohibition and bathtub gin," prosperity and profit, growth and speculation. Nationally the third-party impulse lay dormant in the late twenties.

Depression would be the stick to prod its reawakening. In Minnesota, Farmer-Labor became the key governing party in that state. Heirs of La Follette progressivism in neighboring Wisconsin recast their movement in third-party form in 1934. Given the radical impact of the Great Depression on Germany and other industrial nations, what seems surprising is that the reinvigoration of the third-party impulse was no stronger than it was in the United States during the 1930s. Some historians say it was because of a basic conviction by most Americans that their system, if not its policies, was legitimate. Others lay the decade's stability right at the doorstep of Franklin Roosevelt and his strong and assuring leadership.

### National Third Parties in the Depression Years

Miseries fostered by the Depression left some seeking radical solutions to the nation's and their own personal problems. The Communist party made its best presidential showing ever in 1932: 102,221 votes, more than one in every 400 cast. The Socialist party, another continuing doctrinal party, rebounded that year. Norman Thomas took nearly 900,000 votes, the third most impressive showing in history (excepting the 1924 fusion campaign) for a presidential nominee of the Socialist party.

The Socialist and Communist tallies dropped dramatically in 1936, and just one new 1930s national short-lived party, the Union party of 1936, was ever to claim a significant share of a presidential vote. By 1936 Franklin Roosevelt's pragmatism and his calm appeal to a distraught nation were weaning voters away from radical third-party prescriptions. FDR's liberal or progressive New Deal programs particularly decimated messages from the far left.

UNION PARTY    The 1936 Union party defied easy placement on a left-to-right ideological spectrum. Many of its symbolic attachments seemed to be with the left. Its presidential candidate, North Dakota Congressman William Lemke, was a nominal Republican. He had helped to found, and was still linked to, the leftist North Dakota Nonpartisan League. Physically unattractive—his head was bald and yellow-freckled, his face pitted from a bout with smallpox—he managed to take 1.96 percent of the nation's vote (13.4 percent in his home state) even though his party made the ballots of only thirty-five of the nation's forty-eight states.

Union's candidate seemed a weird duck to some voters. When his fans dubbed him Liberty Bill, foes quipped that "the Liberty Bill has cracked." His party's ethos actually was a curious, largely incomprehensible amalgam of left and right values, with the balance tilted to the right. To a lot of outsiders it must have seemed pure gobbledygook.

Union coalesced the remnants of Louisiana U.S. Senator Huey Long's "Share the Wealth, Soak the Rich" movement (Long was assassinated in 1935 and his movement's momentum died with him) and of Dr. Francis E. Townsend's "Share Our Wealth" campaign to force Washington to give all citizens over sixty years old $200 a month. Public pressure from the Townsend forces had helped push Congress to pass the Social Security Act of 1935.[10]

Union's ideological perspective really was the brainchild, not of its candidate, but of the party's founding father. Union's father was Father Charles E. Coughlin, a Roman Catholic priest. Of the many political demagogues swept into prominence by the Depression, Coughlin became one of the most powerful. His main access to influence was his weekly radio message which reached up to 40 million Americans through a nationwide hookup. He also spread his political message through his magazine *Social Justice* and activities of his National Union for Social Justice. One of his most ambitious and ill-fated moves to capture the nation's allegiance began when on June 19, 1936, Coughlin proclaimed to his large radio audience the birth of the Union party.[11]

Although anti-Communist in tone from the start ("choose God or Communism," he told his listeners), he seemed at first an apostle of the left. Coughlin inveighed against capitalism ("the enemy of civilization") and the "money-changing wolves of Wall Street" as passionately as against Marxism. In 1932 he lent his support to FDR ("Roosevelt or ruin"). During the early FDR years an appreciative president sometimes ate with him at the White House.

Long before 1936, Union's year, Coughlin broke with the New Deal and its "anti-God" president. Father Coughlin also veered to the hard right. By 1936 he was proclaiming that "I take the road of fascism." Coughlin's anti-Semitism was to become virulent and vulgar from 1936 on. Participants in pro-Nazi rallies in the late 1930s roared their enthusiasm when Coughlin's name was invoked. But his Union party died after the November 1936 election, and in the late 1930s Coughlin's influence upon mainstream America plummeted as well. Eventually he was silenced by a combination of popular demand, orders from his church, and the wartime censorship authorities of the government.[12]

## Left and Right in the 1948 Election

One of the most famous and poignant photographs in history shows a beaming and vindicated Harry Truman holding up an early day-after-election edition of the *Chicago Tribune*. Its bold but erroneous headline reads "DEWEY DEFEATS TRUMAN." Later returns from the previous day revealed that incumbent Democrat Truman took over 24 million votes to just under 22 million for his Republican challenger. Truman's share of all popular votes was a substantial plurality, but most 1948 voters (50.41 percent) voted for his Republican and third-party opponents. Later the electoral college would cast 303 for Truman, 189 for Dewey, and thirty-nine for Dixiecrat Strom Thurmond.

The two important transient parties of 1948, the *Progressive party* on the left and the *States' Rights Democratic party (Dixiecrats)* from the right, clearly did not determine who won, for initially they had jeopardized Truman's candidacy, not Dewey's. The third-party standard-bearers were disappointed with the results. Progressive Henry Wallace in particular seems to have entered the race really hoping to win. The thwarted Dixiecrats had aimed to deny Harry Truman a majority of electors, thus throwing the decision to the House where southern pressure might water down Democratic civil rights commitments. These two third-party campaigns were significant challengers anyway, together taking nearly 5 percent of the vote. Given the passing of World War II, the nation's return to prosperity, and the narrow range and inherent controversy of these two third parties' primary interests, their November showings were remarkable.

The Progressives mainly intended to nip the Cold War in the bud before it could proceed further. They were in fact the first third party ever organized to protest foreign policy.[13] Foreign policy as an issue is, except during war, almost always secondary, at most, in the voters' range of political interests. Dixiecrats had real concern about the liberal constituencies collected within the Democrats' New Deal coalition, about the prounion, anti-business drift of the national Democrats; but the Dixiecrats came to life as a party in protest of the national Democrats' developing commitments for civil rights. Dixiecrats proclaimed themselves to be the true Democrats, a corrective mechanism for the national major party far more than a deliberately created long-term third party. The essence of their insurgency—segregation, white supremacy, and states' rights—confined their appeal almost entirely to the South.

Henry Wallace gathered 2.38 percent of the national returns in the 45 states, all except Illinois, Nebraska, and Oklahoma, where his name appeared. In New York state, where he ran on the line of the locally

# The Political Odyssey of Lyndon La Rouche

History never fully repeats itself, of course; but there are some intriguing parallels between Father Coughlin and his closest followers and Lyndon La Rouche, Jr. (also known as Lyn Marcus) and his very secretive "La Rouchians." You are not likely to see much of La Rouche himself in the immediate future; as of this writing he is serving a fifteen-year term in federal prison for mail fraud and conspiracy to defraud the Internal Revenue Service (La Rouche's cellmate for a while was disgraced former televangelist Jim Bakker). You may remember La Rouche's paid television messages during recent presidential campaigns in which he set forth a strange tale of Queen Elizabeth's involvement with drugs, KGB links to Walter Mondale, and a 3,000-year-old global conspiracy, now led by Henry Kissinger, which could be undone only by the "neo-Platonic guardian" La Rouchians.

La Rouche began his political activism in the late 1940s as part of the Socialist Workers party, a Trotskyist Marxist-Leninist group. He had ties with various elements of the New Left in the 1960s. In 1976 he won 40,041 votes as nominee of his own nominally Marxist *U.S. Labor party.* That party made the ballot of twenty-four states plus the District of Columbia.

During the 1970s he rapidly swerved from far left to radical right. By 1978 he was saying that "it is not necessary to call oneself a fascist. It is simply necessary to be one." La Rouche and the La Rouchians became decidedly anti-Semitic in their rhetoric. They had been known to spy upon, and are said to have infiltrated and destabilized, many leftist groups. They were in close contact with certain people in the Pentagon and the National Security Council during the first Reagan term. A Pentagon official praised the La Rouchians as a "conservative group . . . very supportive of the [Reagan] administration."

During the 1980s La Rouche and his followers largely eschewed the third-party approach, finding it more profitable to enter state party primaries and to utilize the open and accessible presidential selection methods now used by Democrats (and Republicans), to penetrate the Democratic party. When in the 1986 Illinois Democratic primary two La Rouchians defeated party-endorsed "real Democrats" for lieutenant governor and secretary of state, Adlai Stevenson III, the Democratic gubernatorial nominee, felt impelled to distance himself from the La Rouchians by withdrawing from the Democratic line. Stevenson stood, unsuccessfully, as an independent. The GOP reaped the benefits from this Democratic debacle. La Rouchians were instrumental in convincing 2 million California voters to embrace an initiative proposition, ultimately defeated, for quarantining AIDS patients. La Rouche himself has collected millions in taxpayer-supplied federal matching funds in his campaigns for president.

La Rouche ran minor third-party or independent campaigns in 1988 and again (this time from his prison cell) in 1992.

**Sources:** Dennis King, *Lyndon La Rouche and the New American Fascism* (New York: Doubleday, 1988); David Corn, "Lyndon Who?" *The Nation*, 248 (June 26, 1989), 896–898; and Paul L. Montgomery, "One Man Leads U.S. Labor Party on its Erratic Path," *New York Times*, October 8, 1979.

influential American Labor party, Henry Wallace took 44 percent of all the votes he won in 1948.

The Dixiecrats took their 2.40 percent national share from just seventeen states. Nearly 99 percent of Thurmond's votes came from the eleven states that had joined the Confederacy during the Civil War. Unlike the more nationally based Progressives, the Dixiecrats' regional base yielded some electoral votes: the thirty-eight belonging to Alabama, Louisiana, Mississippi, and South Carolina plus the vote of one Democratic **faithless elector** from Tennessee. The Dixiecrats were the first and only third party since the Civil War to claim a bigger share of electoral than of popular votes. In much of the Deep South, sympathetic Democratic establishments arranged for Thurmond and his running mate, Mississippi Governor Fielding Wright, to run as Democrats rather than Dixiecrats in their states. Their victories in Alabama and Louisiana probably were due to their appearance on the Democratic line.[14] Despite the concerted effort of their populist Democratic Governor Jim Folsom, November voters in Alabama did not even have the Truman option. Alabamians could vote for Thurmond or Dewey, for Prohibition's Claude Watson or even Progressive nominee Henry Wallace. But there was no slate of Alabama electors pledged to the sitting president who won the nation that year.

It is quite possible that without the Wallace and Thurmond factors, Truman might have drubbed Dewey by 416 electoral votes to 115 rather than by the much smaller margin actually turned in by the 1948 electors. Had there been no Dixiecrat revolt, Truman probably would have taken those thirty-nine electors that cast for Thurmond. In New York, Michigan, and Maryland, states that collectively owned seventy-four electoral votes for president, Wallace's third-party tallies were larger than Republican Dewey's margin of victory over Truman. It cannot, of course, be proven that without Wallace enough of these votes would have been Truman's to give the three states to the Democrat; but many historians speculate that Dewey was indebted to Wallace for his victories in all three of these states.

**1948 PROGRESSIVE**   The Progressives of 1948 were, as many older Americans still recall, among the most controversial transient parties ever to surface in American politics. The writing of their history even now evokes a lot of passion. These Progressives, unlike their Dixiecrat counterparts, did not begin as a group in an act of secession from the national Democrats. They did share with the Dixiecrats an important taproot in the Democratic party. Henry Wallace himself had been a prominent Democratic New Dealer, the secretary of agriculture during FDR's first and second terms and vice-president during his third. Roosevelt replaced him with Truman on the 1944 ticket but then appointed Wallace secretary of commerce. Wallace broke with President Truman, who fired him at Commerce in 1946, and that December Wallace and others seeking the creation of a new third party set up the Progressive Citizens of America. The Progressives met for an important strategy session in Chicago in January of 1948, then formally launched their new Progressive party in Philadelphia in July. In Philadelphia Idaho Senator Glen Taylor took the Progressives' nomination for vice-president. Wallace's running mate had been, like the man at the ticket's top, prominent in national Democratic circles.

But there was something else about the personality of the 1948 Progressive party. That party was one of the last hurrahs for a global Communist strategy first laid out in 1935 by Moscow, by the international association of Soviet-directed Communist parties called the **Comintern,** and in the United States by the Communist Party-USA. The line of the Communist Party-USA historically followed directives or signals emanating from the Soviet capital. Communist Party-USA was a member of the Comintern until World War II, when in an act of felicity toward his bourgeois allies Stalin formally abolished the Comintern.

In 1935, with the Nazi suppression of German Communists and the dawn of German aggression in Europe, the Comintern line had shifted from fostering proletarian revolutions worldwide to the **Popular Front** (or United Front). Following the Popular Front strategy Communists around the world sought, with considerable success, to persuade other "progressive forces" (socialists, liberals, and others) to enter into coalitions with them against fascism and the Axis Powers, especially Germany, Japan, and Italy. In France, Spain, and other European countries Communists joined formal governing coalitions with such forces. For a time even the fiercely anti-Communist Chiang Kai-shek Nationalist regime found itself in tenuous alliance with Mao Zedong's Communists to resist Japanese aggression in China. Popular Front forces, including American Communists and their allied compatriots, fought unsuccessfully in the late 1930s to stop the Spanish fascist movement of Francisco Franco.

Communists terminated their Popular Front line after announcement of the Nazi-Soviet Nonaggression Pact, an August 23, 1939 marriage of convenience between bitter ideological adversaries. They restored it when Hitler on June 22, 1941, violated the pact by invading the Soviet Union. From 1935 to 1939 and later, from June 22, 1941, but especially after Pearl Harbor, American Communists billed themselves as FDR's staunchest supporters on the radical left. There was widespread sympathy by some progressive members and supporters of the Roosevelt administration, Henry Wallace among them, for the sacrifical and decisive role that the Soviet Union played from 1941 on in the defeat of Nazi Germany. Of course none of the positive feelings hurt American Communists at the time.

Fairness demands remembering that the World War II Grand Alliance (including the United States, the Soviet Union, Britain, and so many other nations joining to defeat the Germans, Japanese, and other Axis forces) was, at least from the perspective of Moscow and its friends, the Popular Front. Visions of postwar friendship between America and Russia were idealistic but not necessarily illogical or utopian. Nor was the resistance and resentment of many American progressives to the emerging Cold War, or even their charge that provocative acts by Truman and his advisors were primarily responsible for causing that Cold War. What most Americans today learn were decisive steps to rebuild Europe and to undergird freedom—the Marshall Plan, the Truman Doctrine ("containing Communism"), and others—many progressives of that time regarded as sinister efforts to protect illicit global interests of American capitalism and the military. Nor were the crimes of Stalin as widely and fully known to American friends of the Soviet Union, or for that matter even to Communism's staunchest American foes, as they are today.[15]

Not offering a presidential candidate under its own label in 1948, the Communist party and its cadres actively worked in the Wallace campaign and to influence—dominate—the organization of the Progressive party. How influential these Communists became is still debated.

Although it certainly was to become so later on, it seems an overstatement to say that in 1948 the Progressive party was a Communist front organization. Wallace himself expressed resentment at the more heavy-handed attempts of the Stalinists to dominate Progressive party affairs. In his acceptance speech at the national convention he spoke of his vision of "progressive capitalism." It is, however, not too much to say that throughout 1948 the Progressive party was a fellow traveler of world Communism. Progressive party delegates shouted down a blandly worded resolution proposed by a member of the Vermont delegation that the new party give no carte blanche support to any nation's foreign policy.[16] In so doing, they seemed to many Americans to be embracing Stalin's manipulation of events in Eastern Europe and elsewhere.

Communist party members and their allies were able to control the deliberations and product of the Progressive platform committee. The 1948 platform condemned "Big Business control of our economy and government," the two major parties ("both represent a single program—a program of monopoly profits through war preparation, lower living standards, and suppression of dissent"), efforts to outlaw the Communist party, and the activities of the House Committee on Un-American Activities. It also targeted racial Jim Crow and Taft-Hartley suppression of labor rights. It called for "a true American Commonwealth" and the nationalization of basic industries. Most fundamentally it demanded friendship and good relations between the United States and the Soviet Union.[17]

In truth the Progressives never came close to unifying all of the disparate elements of the American left, and many Americans holding leftist views either never found common ground with the American Stalinists or had severed what ties they had had before the Progressive party was born. The Socialist Workers party, a Trotskyist group that both hated and was hated by Communist Party-USA, ran its own candidate in 1948. So did the Socialist party. Black leaders almost without exception refused the temptation of the Progressives, going instead with Truman that year. Organized labor was beginning to root out its own internal Communist influences. In 1944 several prominent anti-Communist New York labor leaders, finding growing Communist influence in the New York American Labor party, withdrew to help found the Liberal party in that state. Others left ALP when that party endorsed Wallace for the presidency. Soon after and partly as a result of Wallace's announcement of his candidacy, the Congress of Industrial Organizations undertook a bitter purge of its Communist-led unions, almost wholly eliminating what had once been strong Communist influence in the CIO.

Other leftists were early supporters or activists in the Wallace campaign but withdrew, usually in favor of Truman, as Communist strength in the third-party movement became ever more evident to them. The Democratic party coopted much of the potential support for the Progressive ticket by its own appeal to leftists; the 1948 Democratic platform bore a forthright plank for civil rights, and Truman used some surprisingly leftist-sounding "give 'em hell" populist rhetoric early in his campaign. The steady withdrawal of non-Communists from the Progressives fed the party's domination by Communists, but of course also eroded what hope the Progressives had for a dramatic showing at election time. As the nation descended in the late forties and early fifties into the vicious red baiting of the McCarthy era, a non-Communist leftist's position on the Wallace campaign ("were you for Truman or for Wallace?") became one kind of litmus test to determine whether that person would be denounced as a fellow traveler or even as a Communist.

The Progressive party clung to life for one more presidential round. But the party's pro-Communist position on the Korean War cost it almost all of what was left of its seriously depleted non-Communist contingent. Vincent Hallinan, Progressive's 1952 nominee, took just 140,416 votes nationwide (less than one of every 400 cast), nearly half of them in New York on the American Labor Party line.

**DIXIECRAT** South Carolina Governor Strom Thurmond was Henry Wallace's 1948 Dixiecratic opposite bookend on the third-party right. The course of Thurmond's life has taken him to about as many places on the American party spectrum as it is possible for a mainstream politician to go. Born, like most native southerners of this century, into the Democratic party, he left it momentarily in 1948 to lead the third-party insurgency. Returning home to the Democrats, he nonetheless publicly backed Republican Eisenhower in 1952. In 1954 he won election to the U.S. Senate, the first and only candidate in American history to take a Senate seat on a write-in vote; 143,444 voters, nearly two-thirds of all who turned out, voted for Thurmond, whose name was not even on the ballot.[18] During the 1964 campaign of Republican Barry Goldwater, Thurmond bolted Democratic ranks to affiliate with an increasingly conservative GOP. He has remained a loyal and prominent Republican ever since. In 1968 he held South Carolina for Republican nominee Nixon. Everything else in the Deep South went that year to the Dixiecrats' ideological descendant, George Wallace and his American Independent party.

The 1948 Dixiecrat insurgency appears to have been the signal event in loosening the South's historic attachment to the Democrats. Thurmond's epic trek from 1948 to today has been seen by some historians and political scientists as a microcosmic symbol of the realignment of regional loyalties that now finds much, maybe most, of the white South in the Republican camp.

Thurmond's truest fans like to say that their man twice has come close to taking the presidency. In the early eighties Thurmond as Senate President pro tempore would have inherited that post had nuclear holocaust, bubonic plague, or some other catastrophe simultaneously wiped out Reagan, Bush, and House Speaker Tip O'Neill. This assumes of course Thurmond's survival of whatever mishap hit the nation's center of power. In 1948 he took thirty-nine electoral votes and would have become president with just 227 more. It is hard to say at which of these times he came closer. He was not very close either time.

South Carolina lore holds a lot of warmhearted humor about him. In 1968, years after his first wife's death, Thurmond, then sixty-five, took a twenty-two-year-old bride. Eyebrows were raised, many in his Bible-belt state observing that his attractive new wife was "young enough to be that man's granddaughter!" It certainly did not hurt the Senator's standing among constituents admiring virility and macho, especially not after the couple began to produce a family of four children. In 1991 the eighty-eight-year-old senator, victor again in a campaign for yet another six-year term, announced that he and his wife were separating. One of the popular down-home jokes features a lead-in for the late-night news: "Strom's Third Wife Born Yesterday! (Offspring at 11:00)."

Thurmond is a remarkable person. He is still one of the most conservative members of Congress. For his votes in the One Hundredth Congress, he received a ninety-two from the American Conservative Union, zero from the liberal Americans for Democratic Action. But the conservatism that he represents was mainstreamed during the Reagan era. Some of his leading critics on Senate legislation rank him and his staff at or near the top in constituency service. Thurmond led Capitol Hill southerners in the desegregation of staff. Many African-American as well as white students have served in his page and intern programs, the Senate's largest. The senator himself has mellowed ideologically. His rhetoric lacks almost all the stridency of (North Carolina) Senator Jesse Helms's. Some of Thurmond's Senate votes on civil rights measures in the eighties showed fundamental change in position on the rights of black Americans.

But the Dixiecratic insurgency that in 1948 collared Thurmond for the presidential race went out of the national mainstream, as far to the right, some scholars say, as that year's Progressives were to the left. That

*South Carolina's Governor J. Strom Thurmond speaking in Gainesville, Florida, during the States' Rights Presidential campaign, October 1948 (Strom Thurmond Collection, Photographs Series, Subseries A, General, Special Collections, Clemson University Libraries, Clemson University, Clemson, S.C.)*

is an interpretation of course, and certainly not the interpretation of that year's Dixiecrats. In their view it was the national Democrats who stepped out of bounds; Dixiecrats' solemn obligation was to bring the major party back.

The sequence of events strongly suggests in fact that had the Progressives not appeared as a party or had they not influenced the national Democratic course, Dixiecrats would not have seceded from the parent party to become what they officially called the States' Rights Democratic party. At the outset of the 1948 campaign, President Truman proposed a glittering array of liberal measures: national health insurance, slum clearance and low-income housing, federal assistance to education, and substantial increases in social security benefits and the minimum wage. On civil rights, the president called for a federal antilynching law, the abolition of poll taxes along with other steps to ensure black voting rights, the eradication of segregation in interstate travel and of job discrimination, and the creation of a Fair Employment Practices Commission. Enactment of many of these proposals would take years; some, like universal health insurance, have yet to become the law of the land. Clearly Truman intended in offering them to contain the hemorrhaging of his own campaign by coopting liberal would-be support for Wallace and the Progressives. The essence of his civil rights package came in the form of a February 2, 1948, message to Congress, just days after the January meeting of Progressives in Chicago.

At the July national convention where he took the Democratic nomination, Truman's plank on civil rights was replaced by one more liberal still in its support of the rights of African-Americans. One of this progressive plank's leaders on the convention floor, a young Minnesota politician named Hubert Humphrey, four years earlier had helped engineer the merger of his state's Democratic and Farmer-Labor parties. Truman's proposals and the Democratic platform did appropriate, as intended, much of the support that might otherwise have gone to Wallace. National Democrats apparently calculated little risk in their antagonism of conservative southerners. The Solid South, they felt, would not vote for the party of Lincoln and Reconstruction, and there simply was no other place for it to go.

The political minefields were not to be avoided that easily. In 1948 the South was still immune to the lure of Republicanism, but millions of southern whites were Dixiecrats at heart. It is worth remembering that those who founded the States' Rights Democratic party regarded themselves as the true holders and conduits of Democratic party tradition. Through their new party they would try to punish, thus correct. In so doing, they would build that place for disinherited southerners and other conservatives to go.

The Dixiecrats said they gave fair warning. A month after Truman's civil rights message to Congress, chief executives at the Southern Governors' Conference demanded of the South's Democratic convention delegates and presidential electors that they vote down Truman or any other candidate backing civil rights. Similar resolutions passed elsewhere, most notably at a May gathering of states' righters arranged in Jackson by Mississippi's Fielding Wright.

Threat became concrete reality in July at the Democratic convention. When the civil rights plank passed, all of the Mississippi delegates and half of Alabama's went for the door. Heckles and catcalls from some of the remaining delegates sounded their departure.

The new party took shape a week later at a hastily convened conference in Birmingham. Attending were "the big brass of the Democratic party in the Mississippi, . . . conservative leaders of Alabama, . . . Governor Thurmond of South Carolina and his entourage, and a miscellaneous assortment of persons of no particular importance from other states."[19] Thurmond's oratory during and after Birmingham spoke of states' rights, of Dixiecrat unhappiness with the Truman Democrats' civil rights package, of the urgent need to return to the South and to southerners (the Democratic party's staunchest loyalists) that region's prominent place in national politics. Fielding Wright, former Alabama Governor Frank Dixon, and other prominent Dixiecrats clung more than Thurmond to the vituperative language of white racism in their defense of segregation and white supremacy.

The issue-oriented States' Rights Democratic party never was exclusive property of Thurmond or any other indiviual who associated with it. Thurmond seems to have been its third choice for the presidency, the first two having declined the honor of nomination.[20] In their short platform the Dixiecrats repudiated "selfish appeals" by racial and religious minorities and praised the Constitution as a defending bulwark against the "chains of slavery" forged by "tyrannical majorities." The platform denounced the Democrats' civil rights plank and very strongly implied that the major parties, especially Truman's Democrats, were acting to create an American "totalitarian police state." It demanded Democrats' return to that party's states' rights traditions. Most notably, the platform writers put their new party on record as standing "for the segregation of the races and the racial integrity of each race; the constitutional right to choose one's associates; to accept private employment without governmental interference; and to earn one's living in any lawful way; . . . for home rule, local self-government, and a minimum of interference with individual rights."[21]

Electorally the Dixiecrats faced but never mastered a multitude of problems. The base of its appeal was southern and, as it turned out, primarily in the Deep South. Having liberated himself from most of the prospect of non-Communist defection to the Wallace movement, Truman felt free in the fall to move his oratory rightward, to coopt much of the potential support for the Dixiecrats. Democratic party establishments outside the Deep South remained loyal to Truman, who took Texas, Florida, even Georgia, and every southern state above South Carolina.

Unlike the 1948 Progressive party, the Dixiecrats proved unable to sustain themselves as a third party for another try in 1952. The States' Rights Democratic party died in 1951 when South Carolina's new governor, James F. Byrnes, declined an offer to lead it. The spirit did survive its flesh's demise. The Dixiecrat ethos prevailed in the Democratic Deep South establishments until at least the mid-1960s, when progressive winds from the new-mobilized and enfranchised southern black constituency began to bring southern Democracy more in tandem with national Democratic currents. As recently as 1960 all of Mississippi's Democratic electors and six of Alabama's, running without commitment to the Kennedy ticket, voted for conservative Virginian Harry F. Byrd rather than for Kennedy. Until 1965 the Democratic line on the Alabama ballot bore at its top the defiant slogan, "White Supremacy." A federal court order removed it.

## Peace and Freedom and
## George Wallace's American Independent

Some years are as bland as Melba toast. Others spark excitement, long after their passing, in the memories of those who lived them. Nineteen eighty-nine was the year when the Cold War ended (flag-waving apostles of Americanism, together with a lot of the nation's mass media, were quick to declare the Eagle's victory over the Bear), when the Berlin Wall came tumbling down, when popular revolt sparked by Soviet moves toward glasnost and perestroika brought democracy to Eastern Europe. In China, democracy was shortcircuited only by nasty, cynical, bloody repression.

Nineteen sixty-eight excites the memory of those who lived it, though many recall its torment far more than its triumphs. It was the year of Tet, a military setback but morale victory for Vietnamese Communists because it showed Americans that no light could be seen at the end of the tunnel; of My Lai, the most infamous mass atrocity that American forces ever were to commit in Vietnam. In China, the Cultural Revolution was at fever pitch in 1968. France went to the brink of revolution. Czechoslovakia's Prague Spring tragically ended by Soviet force of arms.

In the United States, attitudes bristled from long hot summers in which African-Americans, recoiling from the long years of racial injustice, burned down huge sections of America's northern ghettos. The social contract seemed direly threatened as Dr. Martin Luther King and Robert F. Kennedy were gunned down and killed, as Black Power and separatism replaced integration and reconciliation as core values of many of white racism's victims, as millions of young whites deserted liberal idealism ("Ask not what your country can do for you; ask what you can do for your country") to enlist in the New Left and the Counterculture. In 1968 a young man could be drafted to kill and die in Vietnam. But if under twenty-one, he was deemed too young in most states to be trusted with something as important as the vote.

The National Organization for Women celebrated its second birthday in 1968; another four years would pass before Congress would propose an Equal Rights Amendment, five before the Supreme Court would find a right to an abortion. Ronald Reagan served the second year of eight as California's governor in 1968, a dress rehearsal, as it turned out, for the presidency. Nineteen sixty-eight was the year when a wartime president, Lyndon Johnson, withdrew from his race for reelection after a poor showing in the New Hampshire primary against a peace candidate of his own party, Eugene McCarthy. It was the year of the Chicago Police Riot,[22] when Mayor Richard Daley's forces brutalized antiwar demonstrators in Chicago streets, when the mayor sought to rig the inner workings of the Democratic Convention, when Connecticut Senator Abraham Ribicoff denounced Daley's "Gestapo tactics" and Daley proved Ribicoff's point by silencing his microphone, when Walter Cronkite live on CBS admonished a roughed-up young floor reporter named Rather: "Get up, Dan. Nothing is at stake here but freedom of the press itself!" It was the last year when an establishment candidate, Vice-president Hubert Humphrey, could avoid submitting to the voters' voice in the primaries and still take his party's nomination. It was the year Richard Nixon first won the presidency.

**PEACE AND FREEDOM**   Nineteen sixty-eight was just the kind of year that gives life's breath to third parties. Leftist radicals had joined together in 1967 to found the Peace and Freedom party (PFP). There for the creation were 1960s-style white New Leftists, the Black Panther party, and other black nationalists. There also were some Old Left cadres, many of whom remembered their glory days in the 1948 Progressive campaign. Their infant party rejected the pragmatic 1968 methods of Democratic progressive doves Eugene McCarthy and Robert Kennedy, who wanted to seize the reins of the major party whose president had so vastly escalated the American war in Vietnam. Seeking to reach beyond America's small radical core to woo some people in the Democratic party's liberal wing, PFP produced a broad-ranging platform. It called for the immediate withdrawal from Vietnam, community control of schools and police, abortion rights, and environmental protection.[23]

PFP's most spectacular victory in the struggle for ballot access came in the Golden State. There Peace and Freedom mastered the draconian barriers of a state law under which a new party had to induce some 66,059 voters to register or reregister as its members. PFP produced 71,000 members.

The 1968 Peace and Freedom party nominee was Eldridge Cleaver. Then minister of information in the militant Oakland-based Black Panther party, Cleaver in 1968 published *Soul on Ice,* his best-selling but gritty and controversial autobiographical polemic on African-American life in racist America. At the time of his campaign he was on parole and also awaiting trial on an attempted murder charge. Soon after the election, he would go into hiding and skip the country. At thirty-three he was two years too young to meet the Constitution's age requirement for the presidency.[24] To many election officials countrywide those were three strikes that put Cleaver out. Some states did put Cleaver on the ballot; but California and others listed PFP without a designated nominee. Dick Gregory, a black humorist-social critic, broke with PFP and set up the Freedom and Peace Party with Gregory himself as nominee. Gregory's name appeared as PFP's offering on some states' ballots. In its Cleaver, Gregory, and no-name forms, the fractured movement took at least 84,756 votes in November in fifteen states.

Cleaver, in truth, turned out to be a most ineffectual campaigner. His speeches were incoherent, and it seemed to many that, despite the Black Panthers' antidrug bias, Cleaver usually was stoned on some controlled substance. The candidate's rhetoric focused on the Panther agenda with little attention to the broader issues that PFP wanted to sell to liberals. Throughout the campaign and until 1971 Panther leader Huey P. Newton sat behind bars for killing a cop in a 1967 police-provoked shoot-out. Cleaver's speech on the stump invariably featured the "Free Huey" demand. It was a call that could galvanize Panthers and also white New Leftists; but "Free Huey" meant little to most liberals that PFP wanted to reach.[25]

Peace and Freedom activists joined other antiwar radicals in creating the *Peoples party* in 1971. Benjamin Spock, the famed spare-the-rod baby doctor, ran in 1972 as Peoples party nominee for president. Spock won 78,751 votes in eleven states. Seventy percent of these came in California, where Spock's name appeared on the Peace and Freedom party line. This Peoples party's last presidential bid, in 1976, was a feeble one entirely overshadowed by another leftist challenge.

In 1976 *Eugene McCarthy,* venerated hero of the late sixties struggle to end the Vietnam War, ran an independent campaign for the presidency. Much of the support that PFP had taken in 1968 and the Peoples party in 1972 (and a lot of other votes too) went over to McCarthy in 1976. Though the war was now ended, candidate McCarthy still sharply criticized U.S. national security policy. He called for diplomatic ties with Cuba and Vietnam and for slashing $20 to $30 billion from the Pentagon budget.[26] On the homefront, McCarthy wanted a thirty-five hour work week and radical new measures to curb energy consumption. The candidate took 756,631 votes, nearly 1 percent of the nation's total, in thirty-two states. McCarthy's campaign had entered into an incredible eighteen lawsuits seeking ballot access. From the third-party perspective, that was its most shining legacy. Judicial decisions that year substantially diminished the barriers. Third-party and independent campaigns since 1976 owe Eugene McCarthy a considerable debt of gratitude.[27]

Since roughly the time of McCarthy's independent 1976 candidacy, the Peace and Freedom party has been changing its character in the firmamant of American third parties. A remnant of the national PFP does survive. But PFP is today mostly a non-national party operating within the borders of California, the place where the party always was most active. California's PFP expressly declared itself socialist in 1974.

Peace and Freedom, which claimed some 70,000 members, entered the 1990s as one of five political parties recognized by California as automatically entitled to ballot access. In the 1980s and since, the party has devoted its limited resources to networking among California leftists: independent socialists; veterans of Old Left and New Left organizations; activists in the feminist, peace, environmental, gay rights, Chicano, and African-American movements; and others. Included on the party's lengthy list of objectives and demands are a thirty-hour work week, with pay at a forty-hour rate; abolition of individual taxes and of the Central Intelligence Agency, and a 50 percent slash in Pentagon spending; job-creation programs and a legal guarantee of employment; a system of free and advanced socialized medicine; a reduction in the voting age to thirteen; and the free distribution of condoms to youths for disease control.[28]

PFP's conservative foes have been inclined to portray it as a body controlled by the Communist party for popular front purposes. Stephen Schwartz's 1989 characterization of Peace and Freedom as "CPUSA-dominated"[29] probably inflated reality; but it is undeniable that the Communist party has enjoyed some influence in PFP. In 1988 Eric Fried, a Communist, won 10 percent as PFP nominee in a three-way U.S. House race in Santa Rosa. Fried won the endorsement of five newspapers and the Sonoma County Organization of Public Employees, and he took 45–50 percent of the votes in three of the precincts. That year, PFP nominee Evelina Alarcon, who chaired the Los Angeles County Communist party, won 15.5 percent in a three-way state assembly race. Two years later Alarcon, running for secretary of state, won the endorsement of the Mexican-American Political Association. Alcaron's was the first official blessing in twenty years for a PFP candidate in a statewide election by California's largest Mexican-American association.

**AMERICAN INDEPENDENT**   Most non-Californians may never have heard of the Peace and Freedom party. That party is unfamiliar even to many who endured the tumult of 1968; but those who experienced 1968 will never forget the lightning bolt first irradiating southern skies as a signal of an impending national storm. That year Alabama's George C. Wallace set in motion through his new American Independent party a coast-to-coast movement of conservative whites who were itching to "send Washington a message" that the nation's blacks had pushed too far too fast, that wars worth fighting were worth winning, that it was time to suppress ghetto rioting and antiwar militancy and to return to law and order; in short, a crusade of folks wanting to send an antiestablishment message to the establishment that they were mad as hell with the very essence of what was happening in the sixties.

As American Independent nominee for the presidency that year, George Wallace came closer than any third-party candidate in a half-century to cracking the presidential ballot everywhere. Recruiting a team of four young lawyers—three Alabamians and a South Carolinian—to work on ballot access full time, the Wallace insurgents got their man's name on the ballots of all fifty states. The Ohio ballot turned out to be the toughest nut that was cracked. Wallace made Ohio's ballot only because the U.S. Supreme Court overruled a state access rule that had required, among other impossibilities, a petition signed by 15 percent of the number of Ohioans who voted in the most recent gubernatorial election.[30] Wallace wanted to appear everywhere under the AIP label. He eventually found himself listed, and fortunate at that, under one of six different tags. New York listed him as the Courage party candidate. Kansas put him on a Conservative line. Wallace's failure to crack the District of Columbia ballot was the only defeat of his ballot access campaign. Given the hostility to Wallace's message by the largely African-American constituency in the nation's capital, that closure meant little to the campaign. The authors of a major work on the 1968 presidential campaign point out the curious irony that in a year of New Left sloganeering for participatory democracy and "All Power to the People," it was the ballot access campaign of an ultra-conservative third-party insurgency that came closest to implementing those slogans: "The drive to get Wallace's name placed on the ballot of all fifty states . . . was perhaps the most remarkable triumph of participatory democracy at the grassroots in the campaign of 1968, not excluding the McCarthy campaign."[31]

Like most candidates of transient parties, Wallace's voter appeal peaked too soon—nearly a quarter of the electorate backed him in mid-September—and eroded badly as November approached. The major parties warned that a vote for Wallace was "a vote for Humphrey" (or was it for Nixon?), that the voters had better come home to Nixon (or to Humphrey?), who really could win. Nixon's handlers were launching one of the premier, and very successful, candidate packaging initiatives.[32] Central to their effort was adoption of a new **Southern Strategy** in which their candidate, coopting soft Wallace support, promised to go easy on school desegregation, to get tough on crime and on welfare cheats, to put southern conservative strict constructionists on the nation's highest court.

Wallace ended far this side of the White House. He also failed in his cherished goals of denying Nixon or Humphrey an electoral vote majority and thereafter striking a deal, pending House decision as to who would become president. He and retired Air Force General Curtis LeMay, the slash-and-burn hawk who ran with him, did remarkably well in spite of it all. Wallace took 13.53 percent of the national popular votes. His popular share ranged from 65.8 percent in sweet home Alabama down to 1.5 in distant Hawaii. Wallace won 4 percent or more of the votes cast in forty-five of the fifty states. Wallace took the fifth highest popular share that had ever been recorded for a third party in a presidential race. In raw vote tallies, Wallace's 9,901,151 placed him forty-two percent higher than any other third-party candidate up to that time. Since 1968 only Ross Perot among presidential candidates not running under a major party label has exceeded Wallace's popular tally and his vote share. The electors of Alabama, Arkansas, Georgia, Louisiana, and Mississippi and one North Carolina GOP faithless elector cast for Wallace. Third parties have done better than AIP's 8.55 percent share of electoral votes only three times in American history.

The Wallace factor took away from both major party nominees any hope of a majority mandate from the November voters. The Republican Richard Nixon's 43.42 percent share of the popular vote gave him a photo-finish victory over Democrat Hubert Humphrey, who won 42.75 percent. To this day scholars quarrel over who was hurt, or hurt more, by Wallace. It seems plausible that without Wallace, most of those who did vote AIP would have gravitated toward Nixon—the more conservative of the two major party candidates. On the other hand, Wallace's strongest inroads, and all his electoral votes, were in the southeast, traditionally the Democrats' most congenial turf. The solidity of the Solid South had been breaking down for some twenty years. Even so, had there been no AIP, southern whites and blacks well might have delivered substantial segments of their region to Humphrey in 1968.

*Governor George C. Wallace, 1968 candidate for president on the American Independent Party ticket (courtesy Alabama State Department of Archives and History)*

Whatever your conclusions, Table 3.2 suggests that the Wallace phenomenon may have affected the casting of up to 69 percent of the presidential electoral votes that year. Only in the states (with seventy-nine electoral votes) where Nixon won popular majorities, those (with thirty-nine) in which Humphrey took majorities, and in New York (with forty-three) where Wallace's tally was smaller than the difference between Humphrey's and Nixon's does it seem certain that Wallace had no effect on election outcomes.

The accomplishments of Wallace's third-party movement were remarkable indeed. Beyond the host of disabilities AIP endured in common with third parties throughout history, Wallace's organization suffered the slings and arrows of a national press that was almost unanimously opposed to Wallace's message and campaign. As if that were not enough, an internal problem, attributable in large part to party leader George Wallace himself, widened the barriers that separated AIP from the political mainstream. Never before in history had a significant national third party been organized so purely and exclusively as the personal vehicle of its top leader as AIP; not even the 1912 Teddy Roosevelt Bull Moosers.

George Wallace became a national figure in 1963. That was the year when, at his first inauguration as governor of Alabama, Wallace sounded the theme for his new adminstration: "Segregation now! Segregation tomorrow! Segregation forever!" It was the year when the new governor "stood in the schoolhouse door," symbolically defying the commitment of federal power to desegregating the University of Alabama. By early 1964 the third party-to-be already was a gleam in the governor's eye. First he would test the waters, to see if national fame could translate into voter support, by entering the 1964 Democratic primaries of Wisconsin, Indiana, and Maryland. Despite strong opposition from Democratic state establishments, he did very well in all three. As nearly everyone including Wallace knew, the incumbent, Lyndon Johnson, was not to be denied his party's nomination that year. Wallace pondered a third-party move even in 1964. But when the GOP nominated conservative Barry Goldwater (and Wallace's campaign war chest quickly dried up thereafter), Wallace decided to sit out 1964.

Although in the ensuing four years Wallace committed to a third-party course, his incipient third party remained unnamed until almost the last moment possible. The particular name might be unimportant, but a name it must have. Wallace first thought of Free American party, but he found "FAP" unappealing. Finally he came up with the American Independent party. AIP—both the name and the party—was Wallace's creation.[33]

Any party, however personalistic, requires activists to collect money, spread the word, and handle the campaign. Wallace's party did put together that able core of ballot crackers, and it assembled an effective fundraising operation which brought in millions, much of it in small amounts from loyal followers. Otherwise the AIP cadre mainly featured widely scattered pockets of true-believing volunteers nationwide. Except in those rare jurisdictions where a third party had to field candidates for lesser office in order to get its presidential nominee on the ballot, AIP did not bother to recruit politicians, prominent or obscure, to stand for election. Very few political figures enjoying wide name recognition joined Wallace in his third-party movement. There were some, almost

**Table 3.2: State-by-State Distribution of Support for Wallace (AIP), Nixon (R), and Humphrey (D)**

| Popular Vote Category | States | Electoral Votes | | |
| --- | --- | --- | --- | --- |
| | | Wallace | Nixon | Humphrey |
| Wallace majority; Humphrey #2 | Ala. Miss. | 17 | — | — |
| Wallace plurality; Nixon #2 | Ark. Ga. | 18 | — | — |
| Wallace plurality; Humphrey #2 | La. | 10 | — | — |
| Nixon plurality; Wallace #2 | N.C. Tenn. S.C. | 1* | 31 | — |
| Nixon plurality; Wallace tally larger than difference between Nixon & Humphrey | Alaska Nev. Calif. N.J. Del. Ohio Fla. Okla. Ill. Oreg. Ky. Va. Mo. Wis. | — | 191 | — |
| Humphrey plurality; Wallace tally larger than difference between Humphrey & Nixon | Conn. Tex. Md. Wash. Mich. W. Va. Pa. | — | — | 109 |
| Humphrey plurality; Wallace + other third-party tallies larger than difference between Humphrey & Nixon | N.Y. | — | — | 43 |
| Nixon majority | Ariz. N.H. Colo. N. Mex. Idaho N. Dak. Ind. S. Dak. Iowa Utah Kans. Vt. Mont. Wyom. Nebr. | — | 79 | — |
| Humphrey majority | D.C. Mass. Hawaii Minn. Maine R.I. | — | — | 39 |
| TOTALS | | 46 | 301 | 191 |

* One North Carolina Republican faithless elector, who cast for Wallace.

# George C. Wallace (1919–    )

George Wallace is one of the most interesting twentieth-century politicians this nation has seen. Clearly he has been among the most enigmatic. Observers have called him liberal, progressive, populist, demagogue, Napoleonic bantam rooster, know nothing, conservative, traditionalist, states' righter, segregationist, racist, even fascist. Events in his political career might vindicate many of these claims. Certainly Wallace's personality comes closer to Harold Lasswell's political agitator type than to the political administrator; almost everyone well acquainted with Wallace has said that for this man the real joy has been in the crusade, the campaign, not in the day-to-day routine of governing. Many have called him a fish out of water when not running.

Although born poor in rural southeastern Alabama (Wallace's hometown is tiny Clio), Wallace seems to have enjoyed a rather halcyon Huck Finn boyhood. He had a strong relationship with a loving and nurturing mother. His father was sickly and unsuccessful by the world's standards. The strongest male influence for much of Wallace's life was Billy Watson, a local kingmaker who for years was Wallace's political patron.

Short in physical stature (hence the Napoleonic dig from his detractors) but strong, he won the Alabama bantamweight boxing championship in 1936. Wallace was to take it again in 1937, the year he started his studies at the University of Alabama. By the end of 1942 he had a law degree and a wife, the former Lurleen Burns. George and Lurleen Wallace would have four children. (One of them, George Jr., was a bright young rising star in Alabama politics in the late 1980's and early 1990's. George Jr. impressed the state's liberal minority by what he did as Alabama's treasurer and by his desire to reform Alabama's regressive tax system. George Jr. won one of Alabama's seats in the U. S. House in 1992).

As stepping stones to the governor's office and to national fame (or infamy), the senior George Wallace twice won election to the legislature and then election to an Alabama circuit judgeship. In the legislature, especially his first term during which Jim Folsom was governor, Wallace was closely associated with, was indeed a legislative leader of, Folsom populism and interracialism. In his first bid for the governorship in 1958, Wallace denounced the Ku Klux Klan and won endorsements from the NAACP and from the state's small but signficiant Jewish community. But he lost in the then-all-important Democratic primaries—specifically in the run-off primary, a southern electoral tradition—to a race baiting segregationist named John Patterson. When the returns were in, the defeated candidate told some friends that he had been "out-niggered" by Patterson. He vowed that no one ever would "out-nigger" him again.

Wallace won the governor's office in a landslide election in 1962. When race is factored out, Wallace's first gubernatorial term looks to have been one of the most liberal in that state's history. True to his populist roots, he undertook ambitious programs for industrial growth (thus creating jobs that were to benefit African-American as well as white Alabamians), educational reforms (especially the beginnings of a system of vocational and post-secondary technical education), the construction of nursing homes and medical clinics, and conservation. Wallace raised taxes and incurred short-term debt to pay for these things. Even his sharpest critics often praise him for his educational and growth policies of that time.

Tragically, Wallace during this term remembered his vow not to be "out-niggered." In rhetoric and action, the governor appealed to some of the basest instincts in a country long beset by racism. At his 1963 inauguration he said that

> This nation was never meant to be a unit of one, but a unit of the many . . . and so it was meant in our racial lives. . . . If we amalgamate into the one unit as advocated by the Communist philosopher, then the enrichment of our lives, the freedom for our development is gone forever. We become, therefore, a mongrel unit of one under a single all-powerful government . . . Today I have stood where Jefferson Davis stood, and took an oath to my people. It is very appropriate then that from this Cradle of the Confederacy, this very heart of the great Anglo-Saxon Southland, that today we sound the drum of freedom. . . . In the name of the greatest people that have ever trod this earth, I draw the line in the dust and toss the gauntlet before the feet of tyranny. And I say, "Segregation now! Segregation tomorrow! Segregation forever!"

A few months later Wallace, rejecting a fervent plea from President Kennedy (delivered in person to the governor's office by Attorney General Robert Kennedy), "stood in the schoolhouse door"

at his alma mater and delivered a states' rights speech verbally defying federal power. Symbolism done, he then stepped aside, in
effect allowing the admission to the University of African-American
students Vivian Malone and James Hood under a federal court order.
Psychohistorians have said that southerners, the only Americans who
(until Vietnam) clearly had lost a war, often show a quixotic affection
for lost causes. Non-southerners, seeing that the governor so obviously lost the real battle that day, may not have understood the
importance of Wallace's symbolic victory or even that Wallace had
scored it.

Alabama's constitution barred the governor from reelection in
1966, and Wallace's desperate (and heavy-handed) attempt to amend
it failed. So that year Wallace ran his wife Lurleen. During Lurleen
Wallace's tenure, George was governor in all except name. He served,
it was said, as "prime minister," with Lurleen acting as ceremonial
chief of state. Lurleen died of cancer in 1968, the year that her
husband ran for the presidency on the American Independent party
ticket. (Wallace would twice marry again, his second and third mar-
riages ending in divorce.) The state eventually changed its basic law
for the benefit of George Wallace. Although his national political
preoccupation sapped some of his popularity down home (he barely
managed to survive a very strong challenge in the 1970 Democratic
gubernatorial primaries), Wallace went on to reclaim his state's governorship in 1970, again in 1974, and for one final time in 1982. No
other Alabamian has come even close to the Wallace tenure in the
governor's mansion.

Non-Alabamians most remember him as the man who claimed
to speak for the nation's hardhats and cops and dime store clerks
and other "decent, tax-paying, Godfearing, law-abiding" common
folk and who waged verbal war on black militants and "welfare
cheats," hippies and antiwar demonstrators, "pointy-headed
pseudo-intellectuals" and "briefcase toting federal bureaucrats." In
1968 he took a larger share of the vote than any third-party presidential candidate in the forty-four years that had passed since the
campaign of candidate Fighting Bob La Follette. But Wallace actually
was a national figure long before 1968. By 1963 he was making the
speakers' circuit to northern campuses, often encountering either
heckling or stony silence.

In 1964 Wallace briefly tried his hand for the Democratic presidential nomination. That year, with $700 to spend and opposition

from the Catholic Church, the liberal Protestant establishment, organized labor, and the Wisconsin Democratic party, Wallace took more than a third of the votes in the presidential primary of progressivism's old heartland, Wisconsin. Wallace won 30 percent in Indiana and nearly 45 percent in Maryland.

Wallace's state departed in November 1964 from its long traditional loyalty to the Democratic party. Together with four other deep southern states plus Arizona (Goldwater's home), Alabama voted for conservative Barry Goldwater, the Republican nominee for president. In the Senate that year, Goldwater had voted against the 1964 Civil Rights Act.

In 1972, after his momentary venture into third-party waters, Wallace sought again the Democratic nomination for president. On the day after he was shot while on the campaign trail in Maryland, Wallace took 51 percent in the Michigan primary to McGovern's 27 percent and Humphrey's 16. But the would-be assassin's gun really ended his national career. He has lived since then as a paraplegic, and he is said to suffer constant, searing pain. Complications very nearly killed him in 1992.

I lived in Alabama during most of the 1970's. In 1973 I went to hear the governor speak. They rolled him in in a wheel chair. When the introducer called on Wallace's large and friendly audience to "stand up for the man who stood up for Alabama," the response was thunderous and emotional. Remembering Wallace's race baiting days, I (like a few others) held to my seat. I still have some regret about my momentary lapse of civility.

In the years following the 1965 Voting Rights Act, when massive voter registration drives were transforming black Alabamians in effect from subjects to influential citizen-participants, Wallace mellowed a lot in his public stands on race. Three of my university students decided in 1974 to do a study of the KKK and the relationship Wallace had had with the Klan during his first administration. They arranged to interview Robert Shelton, at the time one of the most prominent Klan figures in America, at his home near Tuscaloosa. They saw on the wall of Shelton's home a large portrait of Wallace. When asked for his opinion of the man, Shelton replied that "Wallace isn't as white as he used to be."

During his third and fourth administrations, Governor Wallace poured in large infusions of state and federal funds to towns, like Tuskegee, that were electing African-American candidates to their mayoralties and councils. Many of these black local officials responded with gracious words of reconciliation, even praise, for the governor. Black voter support played a substantial role in Wallace's fourth gubernatorial election in 1982. Wallace went on to appoint two African-Americans to major cabinet posts in his last administration.

Many people believe to this day that the "real George Wallace" showed through in the racist rhetoric of his first inaugural and his stand in the schoolhouse door. Others, perhaps remembering a line—"you don't need a weatherman to know which way the wind blows"—from an old Bob Dylan song, see him as a political opportunist willing to say and do whatever seemed necessary at the time to achieve his goals.

Wallace himself, in his entreaty for rehabilitation of image and place in history, presents a third, very different, perspective. Long ago he went public with the admission that *Brown* v. *Board of Education,* the pivotal 1954 school desegregation decision, was necessary and just and that southern traditionalists had been wrong to resist it. He admits to serious error in his racial rhetoric and says that the schoolhouse door stand was wrong, at least from a public relations point of view. But he says that he has been misunderstood, that his real objective always was the defense of states' rights far more than of segregation. He maintains that through his own rhetoric of defiance he intended to deflect, and did deflect, what otherwise might have been far more violent resistance from the good ol' boy types.

Muting physical violence may have been one of his objectives. When he says that that was also a result of his actions, he is unconvincing. Of twenty-nine people killed during the modern civil rights struggle, ten were slain in Alabama during Wallace's first term. There were four African-American children killed by a 1963 Birmingham bomb at black Sixteenth Street Baptist Church. There was Viola Liuzzo, a northern white civil rights worker felled by a Klansman during the 1965 Selma, Alabama, march for voting rights.

Whatever conclusions you draw about "the essential George Wallace," the man's impact and legacy are beyond dispute. The Wallace factor conditioned the law and order platform of Richard Nixon, Republican victor of the contest in which Wallace ran as an American Independent, and it set the Southern Strategy which Nixon's handlers developed and which the GOP has followed ever since. Wallace thus had something to do with the 1980 victory of conservative Republican Ronald Reagan and with the course on which

Reagan took the country. He also helped paved the way for a fellow deep southerner, Jimmy Carter—a progressive co-regionist shorn of his region's racial stain—to the helm of the nation.

**Principal Sources:** Marshall Frady, *Wallace* (New York: World Publishing Co., 1968); and Jack Bass, "How History Will See Wallace," *The State* (Columbia, S.C.), April 9, 1989. Also forthcoming Wallace biographies by Steve Lesher and Dan Carter.

all rough-hewn segregationist types, people like Louisiana's Leander Perez and Georgia's Lester Maddox.

Strom Thurmond did not enlist, despite the ideological overlap between Thurmond's 1948 campaign and Wallace's twenty years later. In 1948 George Wallace, alongside Alabama's populist Democratic Governor Jim Folsom, had declined the long walk with Dixiecrats, sticking instead with the party of Truman. What went around came around two decades hence. In 1968 Thurmond honored his still-new attachment to the Republicans and backed Nixon to the hilt. Thurmond's interventions delivered South Carolina as Nixon's only win in the Deep South, and Thurmond contributed to the Nixon triumphs in North Carolina and other states in the region. South Carolina's Harry Dent, a longtime Thurmond associate, then took assignment in the Nixon administration. As deputy counsel, Dent was to see to it that the new Southern Strategy won implementation at the policy level, that in other words southerners stayed happy, for the future electoral benefit of Nixon and of Republicans to come.

Weak therefore in its structure, George Wallace's AIP also said precious little about what it would specifically do should the voters sweep its man into the presidency. AIP's lengthy platform, which (like all American party statements of principle) went mainly unread, even by supporters, was filled with the mad as hell sentiments bonding Wallace with his flock. It inveighed against a national establishment unwilling or unable to deal with "riots, minority group rebellions, domestic disorders, student protests, spiraling living costs, soaring interest rates, a frightening increase in the crime rate, war abroad and a loss of personal liberty at home." It found

> cities . . . in decay and turmoil; . . . local schools and other institutions . . . stripped of their rightful authority; law enforcement

agencies and officers . . . hampered by arbitrary and unreasonable restrictions imposed by a beguiled judiciary; crime [run-
ning] rampant through the nation; . . . unreasonable government
[farm] subsidies; welfare rolls and costs [soaring] to astronomical
heights; our great American institutions of learning in chaos;
living costs [and taxes] [rising] ever higher; interest rates . . .
reaching new heights; disciples of dissent and disorder [being]
rewarded for their disruptive actions at the expense of our law-
abiding, God-fearing, hard-working citizenry.

The platform condemned the "so-called 'Civil-Rights Acts,' particularly
the one adopted in 1964, which have set race against race and class
against class." It opposed all federal gun control efforts.

Its indictment vituperative and full, the platform's prescriptions were
mostly glittering generality. It called for law and order, states' rights,
cutting off foreign aid to critics of U.S. actions in Vietnam, "freedom
from interference and harassment from and by the government at all
levels." One of the platform's most specific demands was for a constitutional amendment for periodic elections or referenda on federal district
judges and "reconfirmation" of higher federal judges at "reasonable
intervals."[34]

Far more central to the Wallace outreach were the "Wallacisms,"
those pithy short phrases (today we would call them sound bites) that
the candidate used to reach his folk in person and via television. Some
borrowed, most were Wallace originals. A few still creep into the rhetoric
of candidates since Wallace. Many stick in the memories of people who
recall 1968:

Law and order

(Tweedle-dee, tweedle-dum,) there's not a dime's worth of difference
    (between Democrats and Republicans)

Pointy-headed pseudo-intellectuals

Brief-case toting (pointy-headed federal) bureaucrats

If I were president the streets of Washington would be safe (even if
    I had to station troops every 20 feet).

Besides their man, people made the AIP the formidable force it became. Wallace billed himself, thought of himself, and to some extent was
a populist in the style both of the old People's party and of latter-day
voices of "people power" like Wallace's early mentor, Jim Folsom. Wallace
called his people "cops, dime store workers, and hardhats, and other
God-fearing, taxpaying, law-abiding" good folk. His critics saw them
as rubes, rednecks, and as right-wing racist ruffians. Survey research

was sophisticated and scientific enough by 1968 to give a coherent profile of the Wallace voter. The person most likely to vote AIP that year was a white unskilled worker under thirty years old, who lacked a high school diploma, and had little or no self-identity as a Democrat or Republican. Those most prone to join the Alabama governor's camp opposed school integration, wanted to suppress urban violence by whatever force necessary, and thought the federal government was too powerful.[35]

Nineteen sixty-eight was to be AIP's one and only glory year. The party after that descended on a slippery slope toward oblivion following the long-recognizable pattern of America's most significant national third parties. It must have occurred to AIP loyalists in the years after 1968 that their party was a deflating balloon, its leakage uncontained by the hand of its unfaithful master.

In 1972 George Wallace, his national hand strengthened by his showing four years before, filed his candidacy in presidential primaries of the Democratic party. The results, from Florida on, were astounding. Democratic powers began to take Wallace seriously. Yet he remained every bit the anti-establishment outsider seeking to open the door via the pressure of people power. After its Chicago debacle and November defeat in 1968, the Democratic party had democratized its presidential nominating process. The obstacles to an outsider, like Wallace, taking the Democratic prize were, though formidable still, no longer impenetrable. Now it was not unreasonable for the Alabama rebel to hope. Wallace no doubt suspected that the Democratic establishment, despite all, might find some way to deny him the presidential nod. Wallace's 1972 position was curiously analogous to that of Jesse Jackson in the 1980s. Maybe a vice-presidential nomination would have mollified the Alabamian. Anticipating the prospect of closure from either spot on the Democratic ticket, Wallace kept open his option to return to the third party for the presidential run.

Late night news on Tuesday, May 16, noted clear Wallace victories in the Michigan and Maryland Democratic primaries. It was all so anticlimactic to the previous night's lead story. Fanatical twenty-one-year-old Arthur Bremer had pulled out a pistol on Monday at a Wallace campaign stop in a Laurel, Maryland, shopping center. Bremer would receive a sixty-three year sentence for the shots felling George Wallace and three bystanders. The bullet that paralyzed Wallace removed the Alabamian forever as a serious presidential challenger.[36]

Wallace loyalists still tried to get him to make a third-party run. But when Wallace in a telephone hookup from his Birmingham hospital bed declined its nomination, the third party at a Louisville convention picked California Republican U.S. Representative John Schmitz for the presidency. A congressman from conservative Orange County, Schmitz held membership in the John Birch Society. Under his leadership the third party veered away from Wallace pragmatism toward hard-right purism. Schmitz filled his oratory with Birchite conspiracy theory. As strongly as libel law would take him, he implied Democratic and Republican involvement in the global designs of international Communism.

All things considered, Schmitz's total was far from unimpressive. Schmitz made the ballots of thirty-seven states and took 1,090,673 votes, 1.4 percent of the nation's total. Schmitz ran better outside the South than in the region where the party was born. Schmitz's best tally, 9.3 percent, came in Idaho. Most Americans who had voted for Wallace in 1968 backed Nixon's reelection in 1972.

Without Wallace at its helm, AIP was factionalizing by 1972. One group held to the old American Independent party label. Another rechristened itself the American party (AP). Somehow the glue stayed stuck for Schmitz that year. When November passed, the two groups split apart. In 1976 AIP ran Lester Maddox, the ax handle-wielding, Bible-thumping segregationist former restauranteur who had served as Georgia's governor. AP selected right-wing farm magazine publisher Thomas Anderson, who had been Schmitz's 1972 running mate. One voter in 500 voted for Maddox and one in 500 for Anderson in 1976.

The 1980s emptied these parties' already thinning ranks. Some former loyalists enlisted enthusiastically in the Republican-centered Reagan Revolution. Others took out for places in the hard radical right. Both parties did offer candidates for the presidency in 1980. AIP's 1980 standardbearer, former Louisiana U.S. Representative John Rarick, took just 41,172 votes. Percy Greaves, a retired New York economics professor, won only 6,539 votes on the American party ticket that year. Delmar Dennis was the AP nominee in 1984 and 1988. Dennis took 3,456 votes in 1988; his 1988 AIP counterpart, an unknown named James Griffin, received 27,818.

Last rites would have been in order for Wallace's party at about the time its founder left it. Like so many other significant national third parties, Wallace's proved transitory. Like the People's party of the last century, the brevity of American Independent's life is in large part attributable to AIP's success in mainstreaming its ideas and demands. In its legacy, then, Wallace's party survived. For the quarter-century preceding the 1992 Clinton victory, Wallace and his AIP saga bore considerable weight upon the character of U.S. politics. Because of the depth and continuity of its impact upon the course of the Republican party, and thus upon the relative fortunes of the two major parties and the direction of American public policy, George Wallace's 1968 insurgency has been the most important national third-party movement to be born up to now in the last half of the twentieth century.

The strength of Wallace's appeal in 1968 went beyond white backlash. Wallace defined a new right-wing populism, capitalizing on voter reaction to the emergence of racial, cultural, and moral liberalism. Wallace demonized an elite Democratic establishment, providing a desperately sought-after moral justification to those whites who saw themselves as victimized and displaced by the black struggle for civil rights and by broader social change.[37]

The Republican party really has been remolded, transformed some would say, largely due to lessons learned at Wallace's knee. Consider for illustration HR-1, a civil rights bill passed by the U.S. House in 1991. What was remarkable was not that the House approved it; it was that the division over passage came so close to a party line. Democrats favored the bill by 250–15. Just twenty-two Republicans joined those 250 Democrats (and the one independent, Vermont's Bernard Sanders) in voting yes; 143 House members of the party of Lincoln voted against the measure. President Bush had clearly warned that he would veto. It mattered not that its sponsors wrote in language specifically banning quotas; this was, the president said, a quota bill.

As the nineties began, the Republican party had held the keys to the White House for all but four of the years since Wallace's third-party insurgency in 1968. Party self-identification by survey respondents revealed that the GOP had not yet completed its cherished goal of becoming the nation's majority party; but those findings seemed somehow irrelevant. In its presidential election appeal, the Republican party had long since attained what was, in effect, majority status. Justices chosen by Republican presidents from Richard Nixon on were, by the 1980s or early 1990s, demolishing liberal Supreme Court precedents on issues ranging from privacy to affirmative action to procedural due process.

Many factors figured into both the ascendancy and the rightward course of the Republicans from the 1960s on; but as Thomas Edsall and Mary Edsall clearly document in their 1991 treatise on the contemporary politics of race, core lessons learned by the GOP were the teachings of George Wallace:

> The sea change in American presidential politics—the replacement of a liberal majority with a conservative majority—

involved the conversion of a relatively small proportion of voters: the roughly five to ten percent of the electorate, made up primarily of white working class voters, empowered to give majority status to either political party. Alabama Governor George C. Wallace was the politician who showed the Republicans how to seize lower-income white voters. Running as a third-party candidate in 1968, Wallace capitalized on the huge defection of white Democrats, particularly in the South, as the Democratic Party formally repudiated segregation. He won just under 14 percent of the vote. Wallace and Nixon together that year won 57 percent of the vote, however, establishing what would become the conservative presidential majority. This majority carried every presidential election but one over the next twenty years— the one exception being Southern Baptist Jimmy Carter's victory in the wake of Watergate, the worst Republican scandal in history.[38]

### The National Unity Campaign and Other Third Parties in 1980

Nineteen eighty was to be something of a third-party banner year. Eugene McCarthy's independent candidacy of 1976 had drawn over three-quarters of a million voters; but that did not come close to 1980, when 823 voters in 10,000 (8.23 percent) cast ballots for presidential nominees other than Ronald Reagan and Jimmy Carter.

No truly riveting issue tempted most of these defectors from two-party turf. Carter and Reagan were themselves the principal reason for many of the departures. President Carter was an unpopular incumbent carrying the onus of perceived failure, especially to "kick the asses" of those hostage-holding Teheran "bandits." Americans also felt inclined to punish the president for an economy that was in poorer shape than in any presidential election season since the Great Depression. A lot of voters saw Ronald Reagan as a tottering old Yesterday's Man with ideas that, while pleasing to the Archie Bunkers, were out of touch with the times. Reagan's economic proposals had drawn ridicule as "voodoo economics" from a Reagan opponent in the Republican primaries—from George Bush, the man who eventually would become Reagan's running mate in the 1980 general election campaign.[39]

The most lustrous by far of the 1980 third-party payoffs, 6.61 percent of all votes cast, went to John Anderson and his National Unity Campaign. Anderson's 5,719,437 gave him the second highest third-party raw vote tally recorded up to that time. Nineteen eighty was the best year yet, and would have been better still, except for the "Anderson factor," for the Libertarian party. Ed Clark as nominee of that continuing doctrinal party (see chapter 5) took 920,859 (1.07 percent). The Anderson and Clark campaigns, 1980 beneficiaries of recent George Wallace and Eugene McCarthy ballot access spadework, still needed extraordinary finesse to accomplish what they did; Clark and Anderson clawed their way to the ballots of the national capital and of every state. It was the first time in sixty-four years that even one third-party candidate's name had appeared every place where people cast presidential votes.

Farther back in the pack, Barry Commoner and his new Citizens party took 230,377 votes in the twenty-nine states where his name made the 1980 ballot. Another 227,401 gave their ballots to sixteen tiny, inconsequential campaigns.

**NATIONAL UNITY CAMPAIGN**   John Anderson, the candidate of the new National Unity Campaign, was white-haired, dignified, and intelligent, and to lots of folks he "looked presidential." Anderson was serving his tenth U.S. House term, with nearly twenty years' experience, as representative of a district in Illinois. Even so, he entered 1980 as an obscure Republican backbencher with little fame or name recognition beyond Illinois.

Anderson in 1978 had been marked for political death by the emerging New Right crowd in his own major party. Although he had survived that challenge and gone on to reclaim his seat that year, he expected real trouble in 1980 as the Republican party's center of gravity shifted steadily rightward. Anderson seems never to have harbored hopes of really taking the presidency by means of his 1980 campaign. He did not, of course, go out of his way to bring that bad news to his supporters at the time. It is very likely that Anderson saw defeat in his cards for 1980 and opted for the dignity of losing his bid for the highest office in the land rather than the ignominy of losing his rather lowly seat in the House.

Anderson began 1980 seeking the nomination of his Republican party for president. He did quite well in some early races in Vermont and Massachusetts. His campaign suffered the fatal wounds of a second-place showing in home state Illinois (Reagan came in first there), then a third-place finish two weeks later in nearby Wisconsin. Before April ended he was moving very strongly toward a third-party track; but not until June 8, quite late in the game, did he formalize his candidacy as the National Unity Campaign.

Anderson declared it an independent, not a third-party, candidacy. But Anderson's bid, like Eugene McCarthy's in 1976, differed in almost no material way from George Wallace's or other recent campaigns of transient parties. It may have occurred to some of Anderson's staff that

During the next few months you may well have the first opportunity in years to see the election of a candidate for President chosen by the people, not by the political experts.

See what some concerned citizens have to say about John Anderson...

John Anderson, presidential candidate of the National Unity Campaign, 1980 (National Unity Campaign brochure)

an "independent" campaign might be more appealing at a time when millions of Americans were calling themselves independents and expressing deep disaffection for political parties. The National Unity Campaign's independent status was, however, out of necessity more than of conscious, deliberate symbolism. By June 8, the books were closing in many states for new parties seeking November ballot access; but in some of these, there still was time to qualify as an independent. In a few jurisdictions, where it was easier for late-starting third parties then for independents to qualify, Anderson's campaign billed itself as a party.

It seemed to some observers strange that the New Right had marked him, for as an Illinois Congressman, Anderson had carefully garnered the reputation as a straight-arrow conservative. In his presidential campaign, however, Anderson clearly staked out progressive ground. His National Unity Campaign reached out overtly to those Republicans who objected to their party's rightward drift toward Reaganism. The Anderson people wanted to build a coalition of progressives—Democrats, Republicans, and independents—who could not support the Reagan campaign, but who also were disinclined to embrace the reelection of "failed" President Jimmy Carter.

Anderson came to be known as a courageous, no-nonsense campaigner, one willing to suffer the fury of those who, not liking the message, might slay the messenger. He laid out the essence of his gun control program—handgun registration, a waiting period for purchase, a ban on Saturday night specials, mandatory prison for those using guns in commission of crimes—amid the hoots and heckles of the convention audience at the New Hampshire Gun Owners Association.

The National Unity program called for a gasoline tax of 50 cents per gallon for conservation and energy independence, and a compensatory 50 percent cut in Social Security taxes. In the aftermath of the disaster at Three Mile Island, Anderson said that there should be no new nuclear power plant start-ups and that measures must be passed to ensure the safety of those nuclear plants already existing. He demanded ratification of the Equal Rights Amendment and supported the pro-choice position on abortion. Anderson called for Social Security for homemakers and federally funded child care; he rejected President Carter's resurrection of draft registration as well as such Pentagon big ticket items as the MX missile and B-1 bomber.

Because John Anderson appealed to progressive voters, his campaign burdened Jimmy Carter's reelection efforts and thus benefitted Ronald Reagan. Anderson did not, however, cost Carter the election. Reagan's 8,417,813 vote margin over Carter was much bigger than Anderson's 5,719,437 total. Reagan's lead over Carter was even larger in the electoral college: 489 to 49. If, in the absence of an Anderson campaign, Carter had taken every Anderson popular vote in the fifteen Reagan states where Anderson's tallies were larger than the difference between Reagan's and

Carter's, Reagan still would have won in the electoral college by a margin of at least 104 votes.

Anderson drew his support mainly from upscale people. He scored best in high-income families and among professionals and managers. Anderson's supporters were considerably younger on average than either Carter's or Reagan's. Jews liked him far more than Protestants or Catholics did. He did much better in the Far West and the East, especially New England (where his share was twice that of his national average), than in the conservative South. Voters who thought of themselves as independents were twice as likely as Democrats and three times as likely as Republicans to vote for the National Unity ticket.

Adding to the burden of his own early obscurity and his pressing need for name recognition was the fact that Anderson found it impossible to tempt any nationally famous political figure to make the race with him. Former Wisconsin Governor Patrick Lucey, who finally entered as Anderson's running mate in August, was as unknown to the nation at large as Anderson had been at the beginning of 1988. The National Unity Campaign faced the gamut of other problems that have confronted "also rans" throughout third-party history. The campaign's popular appeal peaked too soon, at about 23 percent, in the summer before the crucial November vote.

Given the fact that Anderson more directly threatened Carter, Reagan could afford to play nice guy. The Carter campaign strongly signaled that an Anderson vote would be, in effect, a vote for Reagan, the most conservative major party nominee in a half-century. Carter's campaign also made Anderson's road to ballot access as tough and difficult as possible; frustrated ultimately in their objective to keep Anderson off some ballots, the Carter folks did force Anderson and his fragile organization to expend precious time and money on access battles.

Because Anderson's standing in the opinion polls was still strong in September, the League of Women Voters invited Anderson to participate in the first nationally televised debate of the fall general election season. Jimmy Carter's campaign handlers did not want their man to do anything that might validate Anderson's quest for the presidency. Carter thus refused to participate in the debate. Reagan and Anderson battled it out alone. By the time of the second debate, October 28, Anderson's standings had slipped so badly that the league did not invite him. Reagan and Carter received millions of Federal Election Campaign Act dollars to use in their outreach to voters. Anderson, who received nothing from the Federal Election Commission to wage his general election campaign, was compelled to use a lot of his precious time for fundraising rather than for reaching ordinary voters.

Given all this, the accomplishments of Anderson and his National Unity Campaign seem remarkable. Anderson won an extraordinary amount of free press—not, of course, nearly as much as that going to the major parties—a lot of it sympathetic if condescending in treating Anderson's "noble but hopeless" campaign. Gary Trudeau virtually endorsed him in the *Doonesbury* cartoon, and Anderson made a guest appearance on "Saturday Night Live."[40] Anderson (and the Libertarians) continued the movement toward opening ballot requirements that Wallace began in 1968 and McCarthy continued in 1976. Later third-party campaigns and the American electorate generally have reaped the benefits. Anderson was the first third-party candidate ever invited to a nationally televised debate with even one major party presidential candidate. He was the first third-party or independent candidate to qualify, by virtue of his November vote share, for after-election funds under provisions of the 1974 Federal Election Campaign Act. Just nine non-major-party candidates preceding him and one since have taken vote shares larger than Anderson's in presidential campaigns.

CITIZENS PARTY   The unenthusiastic response of many voters to the Democratic and Republican nominees of 1980 benefitted third parties; but the Citizens party was hamstrung by Anderson in reaching disaffected voters. The Citizens party clearly was antiestablishment. A reporter called that party "an anti-business amalgam of environmentalists, consumerists, anti-nuclear activists, and minority rights advocates."[41] Their party was launched by 262 delegates who showed up for a mid-April 1980 organizing conference in Cleveland.

As third parties go, it was not a bad start. Barry Commoner, the Citizens party's sixty-two-year-old driving force, received its presidential nomination. A biologist by training and university-connected, Commoner was very well known as "Dr. Ecology" to the nation's environmentalists. Commoner had been one of the principal parents of the modern ecology movement. A widely acclaimed author before and since his 1980 foray into the presidential politics, he had a 1971 best-seller, *The Closing Circle*, that had become one of the manifestoes of American environmentalists. La Donna Harris, Commoner's running mate, was a committed and most impressive Comanche Indian activist in the movement of Native Americans.[42]

Their party was a frothy, left-wing blend of populism and democratic socialism. For public appeal purposes, the party avoided using the word socialism; it referred instead to "economic democracy," to "rational planning," sometimes to "social governance." Blaming big business greed and lazy governmental incompetence for many of the nation's ills, the Citizens party demanded public control of key industries—especially energy—and citizen representation on corporate boards. The party called for terminating nuclear power plants and for a radical shift to solar power. It stood for massive military cutbacks, price controls to curb inflation, and firm new public policy commitments to human rights, minority rights, and feminism. The party voiced support for the family farm and for small business. It especially favored local, grassroots citizen initiatives to reclaim power and to restore and reinvigorate the nation.

Most short-lived parties, concentrating their limited resources and energies upon the presidential campaign, have been weakest, most fragile and vulnerable, at their local grassroots core. The Citizens party reversed this pattern. Never amounting to much as a national organization, the party was a lot stronger in some localities. The Citizens party was, unlike the Republicans and Democrats, a formal membership association. At its peak when 5,000 people were on its membership roster, the party had active locals in many places across the country. Throughout their party's existence, the members quarreled over strategy and tactics. There were the nationalists who wanted, through mass media coverage of the Commoner-Harris campaign, to appeal to the public nationwide. It was free media coverage that the nationalists coveted; their infant party's entire budget for national media was a mere $5,429.[43] The localists said, on the other hand, that the party should focus on building at the grass-roots and on local election campaigns. Some of the localists opposed even nominating candidates for president and vice-president.

In 1980 the Citizens party nominated three candidates for U.S. Senate, eleven for the House, and eight for state legislative seats. Vermont was the state friendliest to the Citizens party. Its Vermont U.S. House nominee won one vote in eight, and two Citizens party candidates for the Vermont legislature earned 20 percent of the votes in their districts. Nineteen eighty-one brought the party its only win in a contested race; voters in Burlington, Vermont, sent a Citizens party nominee to its board of aldermen with a 52 percent share of the vote.

Citizens party people were in agreement on two basic points. First, they knew that their party stood no chance of winning the presidency in 1980. They believed, however, that 1980 was just the beginning for a party destined to be around for a long, long time. They were right, of course, on the first point. The Commoner-Harris ticket took just one vote in 400. Their second prediction turned out to be wrong. Nationally at least, little was left of the party four years after its birth; the tally for Sonia Johnson, the radical feminist nominated to run in 1984, was less than a third the size of the 1980 Commoner-Harris return. After the 1984 campaign, the Citizens party just disappeared. Many of its activists went on to nourish local Greens groups dedicated to environmental, antinuclear, and other issues. Some Citizens party veterans dropped out of politics or departed for different places in the democratic left.

## H. Ross Perot and the Nineties

Third-party presidential campaigns for the rest of the 1980s brought meager results. In 1984, seventy-seven voters in 10,000 stepped beyond the two-party confines. One in a hundred did so in 1988. Right-wing national third parties in particular shriveled up; much of their appeal was being coopted by conservative Republicans.

Something quite remarkable was about to happen in 1992. Accounts of that year's politics would feature three headlines. Clinton's victory turned out an incumbent and restored Democratic control of the presidency after twelve continuous Republican years. At least fifty-five of every one hundred voting-age Americans voted, the highest percentage in twenty-four years. Ross Perot, a political novice and the richest man in Texas, a state known for its people of wealth, ran as an independent for the presidency and took nearly 19 percent of the national vote. It is too early to tell the relative importance of each of these events. Each certainly related to the others. The significance of the Perot movement well may lie in what it indicates about the vulnerability of the major parties to a future outsider challenge, by Perot or someone else.

Ross Perot's was the third largest share of votes ever taken by a presidential candidate not running as nominee of a major party. Millard Fillmore and Teddy Roosevelt, the previous candidates whose third-party accomplishments outpaced Perot's, were former presidents, flush with national fame, who had been seeking to return to the White House.

Although well-recognized in many quarters of the U.S. business community, Perot was unknown to most Americans at the beginning of 1992. Accepting an invitation to appear February 20 on CNN's "Larry King Live" call-in show, Perot used that forum to announce that if the people wanted him to run and if they would secure his place on the ballot of every state, he would enter the presidential race and give it his very best shot.[44]

There were scoffers aplenty, and they said that Perot was being both arrogant and naive. In his sixties (he was born in 1930), five-feet-six-

*Ross Perot in Dallas during the 1992 presidential campaign (AP/Wide World Photos).*

inches tall, with big ears, a high-pitched nasal voice, and a distinctively Texas-southwestern manner of speaking, Perot seemed lacking in the charisma that some say is vital to reaching people's hearts. So said the naysayers anyway. But beginning that night on "Larry King Live" Perot and a growing legion of supporters put together one of the most remarkable populist crusades ever. Experts and pundits still debate the authenticity of Perot's populist credentials. Those who enlisted came without doubts.

To many, Perot embodies the American dream. Born middle-class, Perot is a billionaire two or three times over. What got him there, besides hard work, a lot of luck, and willingness to cut corners, was Perot's exceptional endowment in the can-do entrepreneurial spirit. Unlike many other third-party candidates, whose long suit is vision, Perot's life experience leads him to believe, and to convey to his followers, that problems some say are intractable are surely solvable and solvable *now*.

An IBM salesman years ago, Perot was frustrated by his employer's indifference to his idea for custom-designed computer systems. Thus began Electronic Data Systems, which Perot started in 1962. Building from ground up, in EDS he erected the U.S. leader in information services. A graduate of the Naval Academy, Perot has been known to transfer his can-do spirit and take-charge style to hostile locations beyond the United States. During the Vietnam War he tried his best to effect air delivery of twenty-six tons of food to American POWs in the Communist capital, Hanoi. A decade later he engineered a daring commando raid that rescued two EDS employees imprisoned in Iran. That episode was the subject of Ken Follett's popular 1983 book *On Wings of Angels*. There were lots of people early in 1992 who knew of Perot only because they had watched a television miniseries based on Follett's book.

From the time of his February 20 CNN appearance on, Perot seemed to sense instinctively that television would be his good and vital friend. Promising a campaign of substance, not sound-bite, Perot proved himself a world-champion sound-biter. That was because Perot's sounded so innocent and unjaded, so unmanipulative. Ingeniously synthesizing two Bush bites, Perot proclaimed that the nation was "in deep voodoo." "When the rubber hits the road" and "we can fix anything" captured the spirit of Perot as can-do problem solver. Tapping into the throw-out-the-rascals sentiment of voters in 1992, Perot publicly devoted his insurgent movement "to clean out the barn." Perot spoke sometimes of "taking back America," more elegantly framing that populist-outsider theme.

Perot reached out to people through interview programs, spot ads, and paid "infotainment" specials (sometimes seemingly amateurish ones featuring the candidate with graphs and charts), and in the fall through televised candidate debates. Perot was especially intrigued by electronic town hall meetings. He seemed to see in them a lot of potential for resurrecting the spirit of participatory democracy, and he promised that they would be a feature of the Perot presidency-to-come.

The power and effect of Perot's outreach to people astounded nearly everyone except maybe Perot. A Harris poll taken the second week in June gave Perot 37 percent to 33 percent for the sitting president and just 25 percent for Clinton. Other surveys were showing about the same. People were seriously wondering now whether 1992 was the year when a non-major-party outsider insurgency really might take the presidency.

A few weeks later things were souring in the Perot camp. Perot began to take mass-media jabs, like those Clinton and Bush had to endure. That was one kind of compliment, sure recognition that the media too were beginning to take Perot seriously. But media talk about his personality quirks (the word "bizarre" began to appear in some characterizations of the independent candidate) was sure to take some toll. Whatever the reason, Perot's numbers began dipping in the opinion polls.

Perot seemed even more inclined than most politicians to foot-in-mouth disease. A speech to the NAACP convention during which Perot condescendingly addressed his listeners as "you people" offended many African-Americans. Perot seemed unable too to decide whether to go with media handlers or to continue instead to count on "the volunteers and I" populist trademark style that his movement had come to assume. Early in June he had commissioned Ed Rollins and Hamilton Jordan, renowned wizards of past major-party campaigns. Before long he gave them both their walking papers.

With Perot's campaign tattered and Clinton about to accept the Democratic nomination, Perot announced on July 16 that he was withdrawing from a race that he had not yet even formally entered. The ensuing week's *Newsweek* cover featured, not Clinton, but a picture of Perot under the caption "THE QUITTER." In his own legions's ranks, Perot's surprise bombshell brought outrage and cries of "Benedict Arnold!" People departed in droves, though a substantial core (many of them furious too) resolved to stay on, to continue the petition drives, and ultimately to convince (or force) their man to make the run after all. When Perot announced on October 1 that he was returning to the race millions of former loyalists forgave all and returned to him. Millions of others did not.

One of the mysteries of 1992 is why Perot made his temporary departure from the race. Articles in U.S. newspapers bore details of Perot's life history and proclaimed, *after* the fact, that the withdrawal was all predictable "vintage Perot."[45] A theory kinder to him is that Perot never *really* withdrew at all. People who believe this point out that in every state Perot kept in place an organizational core, often with even a paid "volunteer" or two, and that the petition drives continued.

They view Perot as a wily fox, crafty enough to duck while Bush and Clinton savaged each other and were devoured by a hungry press.

At the time he pulled out, Perot declared that he hoped it would save his nation from the likely constitutional-political crisis of an electoral college paralyzed and unable to give the necessary majority to any one presidential candidate. Perot's tune had changed by the time of an October 25 interview with "Sixty Minutes": Republican dirty tricksters were the real reason he had gotten out; they had been harassing one of his daughters (Carolyn), Perot now was saying (they allegedly doctored a picture to make her appear a lesbian), and they intended to disrupt her upcoming wedding.

Some media people had another story of strange events, with Perot himself as culprit. An article in the October issue of *Vanity Fair* expressed what had been rumored for months: that using electronic surveillance, Perot allegedly had spied on the intimate lives of his daughter Nancy and her boyfriend, who happened to be Jewish and a professor at Vanderbilt University. Perot withdrew, it was said, because media revelation of his spying might feed the widespread feelings that Perot was bizarre and authoritarian and certainly would lead some to charge him with being anti-Semitic too.[46]

Perot dropped temporarily from sight, but not from the minds of media people, of Bush and Clinton, or of anyone working in the Democratic and Republican campaigns. Reports contined about the Perot petition drives and that Perot and others were working on a platform for the campaign that he had officially deserted.

Just as he had with the timing of his withdrawal announcement, Perot again stole major-party thunder. His platform, *United We Stand: How We Can Take Back Our Country*, appeared in the nation's bookstores the very week the Republicans were in convention at Houston. Soon it would rise to the best-seller lists. Perot had long ago made some policy commitments. He was for abortion choice, gun control, the line item veto, and some entitlements cuts. But his strong suit before *United We Stand* had been his populist can-do outsider style. That would not change with the book's publication. Perot still would be vulnerable to charges that he spoke in glittering generalities and that the holes and gaps in his policy agenda were large enough to berth middle-sized battleships. But his platform did bring some clarity to his stands on the issues, especially in matters of the economy.[47]

Perot demanded immediate and substantial moves toward deficit reduction, and he bravely promised that a Perot presidency would deliver higher taxes (a higher maximum income tax rate, a fifty-cent-per-gallon increase in gasoline tax over a five-year period, and higher taxes on Social Security benefits) and substantial cuts in military spending as well as in expenditures for Medicare and other social programs. Some of his followers may have seen this in something other than purely material terms. To them it symbolized Perot's resolve to clean up the mess that the insiders had produced. Thus it enabled them to vote in protest to the way things were. Had there been a chance that Perot could win and thus be empowered to impose such discipline and austerity, many of these people might not have given him their vote.

By late September strong indications were surfacing that Perot was about to reenter the race. Perot arranged for representatives of the Bush and Clinton campaigns to confer with Perot's state-organizational leaders. Then, after he polled these leaders as to what they wanted him to do, Perot announced October 1 that he was back in the race to stay. Perot said that his supporters wanted a world-class campaign, and a world-class campaign was what he would give them.

Perot mainly used television in his "new" five-week campaign. He appeared on interview and call-in shows and bought time in blocks ranging from seconds to half-hours. The debates proved to be one of the most important ways of showcasing Perot. By invitation of the bipartisan commission that now manages such matters, Perot took part in all three presidential debates. Performance assessments gave Perot high marks in them all.

Few if any observers gave ratings like that to James Stockdale, the snowy-haired sixty-eight-year-old retired Navy vice-admiral whom Perot had chosen as his running mate. A combat pilot in Vietnam, Stockdale had spent more than seven years as a POW. Stockdale's credentials as scholar and teacher are impressive. But his single encounter with Al Gore and Dan Quayle left many wondering about Perot's judgment and the seriousness of Perot's quest for the White House.

The two major-party presidential candidates used kid gloves in handling Perot, and reserved their bare-knuckle hits for each other. This was strategy carefully designed to woo soft Perot support through kindness. Perot himself normally jabbed much harder at Bush than at Clinton. Sometimes Perot seemed to set out deliberately to take the edge off Bush's sharpest attacks on Clinton. But Perot's rhetoric in the campaign's closing days became more like Bush's in questioning the relevance of Clinton's experience as Arkansas governor and the value of all those "chicken-pluckers'" jobs that Clinton had produced.

Perot and Stockdale failed to take any state's popular plurality and thus a share of electoral votes. But as Table 3.3 indicates, the Perot constituency was truly nationwide and very diverse demographically. The "typical," most characteristic Perotista (Perot voter) was a young western white male, a non-partisan, who felt that his family situation had worsened with George Bush on watch. But millions of those who voted Perot bore none of those qualities at all.

Post-election partisan bickering did nothing to explain what impact the Perot vote had had on the central contest between Clinton and Bush. To Bush spin-doctors' contention that Clinton's 43 percent plurality was not any mandate, Clinton people answered that nearly two-thirds of the voters had voted for change, mostly casting ballots for Clinton. Without Perot, they seemed to be saying, Clinton would have taken a substantial majority of the popular vote.

Some Republicans have argued conversely that without Perot Bush might have won reelection. Self-identified Republicans in the electorate were far more inclined to bolt to Perot than were their Democratic counterparts: 18 percent of the Republicans did, but just 13 percent of the Democrats. The enormous size of Perot's state-by-state constituency deprived both major-party candidates of popular majorities almost everywhere. In not one state did the sitting president take an absolute majority of popular votes. Although Bill Clinton won overwhelmingly in Washington, D.C., his very own Arkansas was the only *state* that gave him a popular majority. Thus it was at least arguable that Perot's returns could have determined the results in states casting up to 529 of the nation's 538 electoral votes.

Clinton, the candidate who took the popular plurality (and a substantial majority of electoral votes), clearly won title to the presidency. But he was the only person ever to win that office without taking a majority in any state other than his own. Clinton's popular plurality was smaller than that of any other winner since 1912.[48] That had been another important third-party year, the year of the Bull Moose Progressives.

After November 3, 1992, Perot and some of his hard-core followers resolved that somehow they would stick together for political battles to come. They adopted the phrase *United We Stand America* to label what they hope to carry on; but they seemed unsure of what form their movement should take. Some talked about a loosely structured grassroots movement. Others spoke of a public lobby. There were those with the audacity to say they wanted a brand new party. Many of Perot's followers clearly are hoping to convince him to offer himself again in 1996.

Lessons learned in 1992 carry a lot of irony. Perot's phenomenal showing clearly indicates that public disaffection for the two major

**Table 3.3: Demographic Dispositions for and against Ross Perot**

| *Percentages Given to Perot by Groups Giving Perot at Least 22 Percent of Their Votes* | | *Percentages Given to Perot by Groups Giving Perot No More Than 16 Percent of Their Votes* | |
|---|---|---|---|
| Independents (Non-Partisans) | 30 | Blacks | 7 |
| Family worse off financially | 25 | Jews | 10 |
| First-time voters | 23 | Age 60 and over | 12 |
| Age 18–29 | 22 | Democrats | 13 |
| Veterans | 22 | Retired | 13 |
| Westerners | 22 | Hispanics | 14 |
| White Men | 22 | Gays/Lesbians/Bisexuals | 14 |
| | | Post-graduate education | 15 |
| | | White born-again Christians | 15 |
| | | Southerners | 16 |
| | | Over $75,000 family income | 16 |

*Perot's Percentage of Popular Votes, State-by-State*

| | | | | | | | |
|---|---|---|---|---|---|---|---|
| Maine | 30 | Colo. | 23 | Ohio | 21 | Md. | 14 |
| Alaska | 27 | Mass. | 23 | Del. | 20 | N.Y. | 14 |
| Idaho | 27 | N.H. | 23 | Fla. | 20 | N.C. | 14 |
| Kans. | 27 | N. Dak. | 23 | Ind. | 20 | Va. | 14 |
| Utah | 27 | Okla. | 23 | Iowa | 19 | Ga. | 13 |
| Mont. | 26 | R.I. | 23 | Mich. | 19 | La. | 12 |
| Nev. | 26 | Conn. | 22 | Pa. | 18 | S.C. | 12 |
| Wyom. | 26 | Mo. | 22 | Ill. | 17 | Ala. | 11 |
| Oreg. | 25 | S. Dak. | 22 | N.J. | 16 | Ark. | 10 |
| Ariz. | 24 | Tex. | 22 | N. Mex. | 16 | Tenn. | 10 |
| Minn. | 24 | Vt. | 22 | W. Va. | 16 | Miss. | 9 |
| Nebr. | 24 | Wisc. | 22 | Hawaii | 14 | D.C. | 4 |
| Wash. | 24 | Calif. | 21 | Ky. | 14 | | |

**Sources:** Voter Research and Surveys, ABC; *New York Times*, November 5, 1992; and *USA Today*, November 5, 1992. Reports by these different sources on a few demographic groups varied by one percentage point.

parties, if not for the two-party system itself, is broad and deep. Both major parties surely must feel vulnerable now to some new independent or third-party challenge. They would be far *more* vulnerable than they are were it not for the Federal Election Campaign Act, the "major-party protection act"[49] that every four years bestows millions of federal dollars to the Republican and Democratic presidential general election campaigns. Severely limiting the size of private donations, FECA thus further enfeebles third-party efforts to make up for what they do not receive from the government.

One thing that FECA does *not* impose is expenditure limits on campaigns that do not receive the federal money. Media reports say that Ross Perot spent at least $60 million, maybe a lot more, on his "world-class" 1992 presidential campaign. If that is true, it is because he was rich enough to spend at a level that very well may rival the expenditures by Clinton or by Bush of those FECA "public" funds. The irony is that the success of some future populist third-party or independent campaign, maybe in 1996 or in the year 2000, will likely depend on its selection as standardbearer someone who, like Perot, is very, very rich.

## Notes

1. Arthur M. Schlesinger, Jr., *The Cycles of American History* (Boston: Houghton Mifflin, 1986).

2. Charles McCarthy, *The Wisconsin Idea* (New York: Macmillan, 1912).

3. William B. Hesseltine, *Third-Party Movements in the United States* (Princeton, N.J.: D. Van Nostrand, 1962), 68–71.

4. Lewis F. Gould, ed., *The Progressive Era* (Syracuse, N.Y.: Syracuse University Press, 1974).

5. George E. Mowry, "Election of 1912," in *History of American Presidential Elections, 1789–1968,* ed. Arthur M. Schlesinger and Fred L. Israel, vol. 3 (New York: McGraw-Hill, 1971), 2137.

6. Paul F. Boller, Jr., *Presidential Campaigns* (New York: Oxford University Press, 1985), 191–192.

7. *Ibid.,* 192.

8. *Ibid.,* 195.

9. La Follette's perspective as presented by Hesseltine, *Third-Party Movements,* 83.

10. William E. Leuchtenburg, "Election of 1936," in *History of American Presidential Elections,* ed. Schlesinger and Israel, vol. 3, 2822–2823.

11. "Charles Coughlin, 30's 'Radio Priest,' Dies," *New York Times,* October 28, 1979.

12. *Ibid.*

13. Steven J. Rosenstone, *et al., Third Parties in America* (Princeton, N.J.: Princeton University Press, 1984), 106.

14. V. O. Key, *Southern Politics in State and Nation* (New York: Random House, 1949), 342.

15. For a critical and incisive account of the links of some American progressives to the world Communist movement and to the Communist Party-USA

in the 1940s and 1950s, see William L. O'Neill, *A Better World* (New York: Simon and Schuster, 1982).

16. *Ibid.*, 148–149.

17. "Progressive Party Platform, 1948," text in Hesseltine, *Third-Party Movements*, 180–185.

18. Alberta Lachicotte, *Rebel Senator: Strom Thurmond of South Carolina* (New York: Devon-Adair Co., 1966), 101–102.

19. Key, *Southern Politics*, 335.

20. See William D. Bernard, *Dixiecrats and Democrats* (Tuscaloosa: University of Alabama Press, 1974), 115; and Lachicotte, *Rebel Senator*, 43.

21. "States' Rights Platform of 1948," text in *History of U.S. Political Parties*, ed. Arthur M. Schlesinger, vol. 4 (New York: Chelsea House, 1973), 3422–3425.

22. *Rights in Conflict: "The Chicago Police Riot"* (The Official Report to the National Commission on the Causes and Prevention of Violence), report submitted by Daniel Walker (New York: New American Library, 1968).

23. Lawrence Lader, *Power on the Left: American Radical Movements Since 1946* (New York: W. W. Norton, 1979), 246–247.

24. Lewis Chester, *et al.*, *An American Melodrama: The Presidential Campaign of 1968* (New York: Viking Press, 1969), 739.

25. Lader, *Power on the Left*, 248.

26. Ted Vaden, "New Congress Faces Familiar Issues," *Congressional Quarterly Weekly Report*, 35 (January 1, 1977), 17.

27. Rosenstone, *et. al.*, *Third Parties*, 115–116.

28. *Encyclopedia of Associations*, 23d ed. (1989) (Detroit, Mich.: Gale Research Inc., 1989), 1459–1460. See John Trinkl, "California Peace Party Alive and Well," *Guardian*, September 8, 1982.

29. Stephen Schwartz, "United States of America," *Yearbook on International Communist Affairs, 1989*, ed. Richard Staar (Stanford, Ca.: Hoover Institution Press, 1989), 148. See Joelle Fishman, "Impact of the 'Independent Plus' in the Election of '88," *Political Affairs*, 68 (January 1989), 12–19; and Rosalino Munoz, "Building People's Political Power," *People's Daily World*, May 10, 1990.

30. *Williams* v. *Rhodes*, 393 U.S. 23 (1968).

31. Chester, *et al.*, *An American Melodrama*, 284–285.

32. See Joe McGinniss, *The Selling of the President 1968* (New York: Pocket Books, 1969).

33. Marshall Frady, "The American Independent Party," in *History of U.S. Political Parties*, ed. Schlesinger, vol. 4, 3436.

34. "American Independent Party Platform of 1968," *Ibid.*, 3447–3474.

35. American Institute of Public Opinion surveys, nos. 771 and 772; Center for Political Studies (University of Michigan) 1968 National Election Study.

36. Frady, "The American Independent Party," in *History of U.S. Political Parties*, ed. Schlesinger, vol. 4, 3443.

37. Thomas Byrne Edsall and Mary D. Edsall, "Race," *Atlantic Monthly*, 267 (May 1991), 62–63.

38. *Ibid.*, 53–81; quote on 62.

39. Rosenstone, *et al.*, *Third Parties*, 117.

40. *Ibid.*, 118.

41. Allan J. Mayer, *et al.*, "Dr. Ecology for President," *Newsweek*, 95 (April 21, 1980), 48.

42. Fred Harris, La Donna Harris's spouse and a populist Democrat, actively supported the Citizens party and its Commoner-Harris ticket. Four years earlier, Fred Harris had run unsuccessfully for the presidential nomination of his major party. He also had served as a U.S. Senator for Oklahoma (1964–1973) and as chairman of the Democratic National Committee (1969–1970).

43. Richard J. Walton, "Citizens Party," *The Nation*, 232 (May 16, 1981), 589.

44. Tony Chiu, *Ross Perot: In His Own Words* (New York: Warner Books, 1992), x.

45. For example, Jim Nesbitt of Newhouse News Service, whose article appeared in the July 19, 1992, edition of *The State* (Columbia, S.C.) as "Pullout Was Vintage Perot."

46. Marie Brenner, "Perot's Final Days," *Vanity Fair*, 55 (October 1992), 74ff.

47. Ross Perot, *United We Stand* (New York: Hyperion, 1992). Perot favored investment tax breaks and other incentives for creating jobs. He opposed the new free trade agreement with Mexico. On health insurance he never moved out of those vague generalities.

48. Unpublished November 20, 1992, "Memorandum to Interested Parties" from Democratic strategist Harrison Hickman.

49. Rosenstone, *et. al.*, *Third Parties*, 26.

# CHAPTER FOUR

# Not Whistling Dixie:

## *Women, African-Americans,*

## *and the Third-Party Course*

*In Dixie Land I'll take my stand.*
—line from "Dixie"

Harold Lasswell gave politics one of its best-known definitions, certainly its pithiest. Politics, Lasswell said, is "who gets what, when, and how." There is a lot of value there. That definition teaches or reminds us, among other things, that politics, bloody or peaceful, gentle or mean, always involves dividing lines, figurative or literal barricades separating adversaries in the political struggle. The pragmatic style of American mainstream politics normally obscures those lines of battle. Successful politicians learn that in America the rewards of cooptation far surpass those of confrontation. Marxists lament the proven capacity of American capitalist politics to blur popular consciousness of the one true divider, that class barricade separating haves from have-nots. They see it all as a grim Faustian game; working Americans, Marxists say, all too frequently sell their souls and birthright for empty promises from the powers that be.

People, Marxist and otherwise, who feel the compulsion to craft third parties often insist that in America there are not really two major parties but just one powerfully coopting party with two almost identical branches. Although the life of their fragile creation may be snuffed out eventually by the American mainstream's enormous cooptive power, third-party builders seem to be unusually aware of the barricades or dividing lines in politics.

For some third-party architects class has been the only divider worth a fight. Others have gone to the barricades over different matters: over race or gender issues. Late nineteenth-century radical agrarianism

140

produced a southern political disposition that was remarkably progressive on many matters through at least the period of Franklin Roosevelt's presidency.[1] But the South would continue during the twentieth century to be a traditionalist bastion on race and gender issues.[2] It was the region that spawned both the Dixiecrat and the American Independent party movements. Southern segregationism, the disenfranchisement of black southerners (men and women) well into the 1960s, and southern hostility to the civil rights movement are, of course, confirmed facts of American history.

By early 1920, eleven western states plus New York had granted women full suffrage rights. Twenty-three states had some limited suffrage provisions for females. Of the other thirteen, which had failed to move at all toward woman suffrage, eight were in the South and three were border states. Thereafter required by the Nineteenth Amendment to extend the vote to women, some southern states did not give their own seal of approval by formally ratifying that amendment until the 1960s or 1970s.

The **Equal Rights Amendment** (ERA), proposed by Congress in 1972, fell three votes short of the thirty-eight needed to make it the law of the land. Just two of the eleven states that had joined the Confederacy during the Civil War were ever to ratify ERA; both of these later tried without success to rescind their ratifications.

Southern whites point out that prejudice never was a peculiarly southern problem. There always have been scores of race and gender traditionalists born and raised far north of the Mason-Dixon line and without any southern ties or contact. Today, as traditionalism fades in its southern heartland, the South gradually is ceasing to bear a differentiating value system.

The focus of this chapter is upon the parties built by activists for woman suffrage, by feminists, and by African-Americans. The values and demands these parties conveyed particularly confounded the race and gender views of scores of people in the American South. But those who associated with parties like these suffered and endured the animus and resistance of traditionalists throughout this nation.

# Third Party Ventures in the Women Suffrage and Feminist Movements

The National Organization for Women (NOW), this nation's largest feminist association today, began in 1988 to do some serious third-party thinking. The 2,500 people who showed up for NOW's 1990 San Francisco convention endorsed pro-choice candidates of the major parties, mainly Democrats. But they also crafted a blueprint for a potential new third party. According to one of NOW's leading advocates of the third-party course, "we are not talking about a women's party. We're talking about (a party to promote) women's rights, lesbian and gay . . . rights, environmentalism, disarmament, and civil rights."[3] This NOW-initiated new party was formally launched at a Philadelphia meeting in August 1992. They named it the 21st Century party.

NOW's third-party venture constitutes but the latest in a tradition of third-party initiatives dating back to the old Equal Rights party of the 1880s and continuing in the National Woman's party (NWP). Beginning in 1913 as the Congressonal Union for Woman Suffrage, the National Woman's party gave itself the NWP name in 1916. With 35,000 activitists as members, NWP was in its prime the militant wing of the suffrage movement. That was in the half-decade before passage of the woman suffrage Nineteenth Amendment. Now shorn of the assertive force of those early years, NWP lives on today at its headquarters in Washington, D.C.

It became conventional wisdom among social scientists during the decades preceding the 1980s that, anatomical differences aside, there were no politically significant variances between men and women as to either values or voting dispositions. The 1980s either brought or revealed a now well-documented **gender gap.** Women have shown themselves to be considerably less inclined than men to vote Republican in presidential elections. Some commentaries have placed more emphasis upon the gender gap than the statistical figures seem to warrant; but most opinion studies do reveal somewhat more liberal attitudes among women than men on many public policy issues, especially in areas of war and peace and social welfare. Feminist scholars attribute some of this to economics pure and simple. Many women today are single parents heading single-income households, and a massive gender-based income gap remains in America. Women are far more likely than men to reside in families with incomes falling below the national average.

Feminism is a term of twentieth-century vintage, reaching back only as far as 1912–1913.[4] Though warmly accepted by National Woman's party activists, the word was spurned by most other organizations in the woman suffrage movement. Widely used in today's political lexicon, feminism defies easy definition. Whatever the benchmark for measuring feminist commitment, be it support for resurrecting the defeated Equal Rights Amendment, a pro-choice position on the abortion issue, or self-

**Table 4.1: Differences in Presidential Voting Patterns Among Men and Women**

| | | *1980* | | *1984* | | *1988* | | *1992* | | |
| | Reagan (R) | Carter (D) | Anderson (NU)* | Reagan (R) | Mondale (D) | Bush (R) | Dukakis (D) | Bush (R) | Clinton (D) | Perot (Ind.) |
|---|---|---|---|---|---|---|---|---|---|---|
| Men | 55 | 36 | 7 | 62 | 37 | 57 | 41 | 38 | 41 | 21 |
| Women | 47 | 45 | 7 | 56 | 44 | 50 | 49 | 37 | 46 | 17 |

*Percentages*

**Sources:** Various *New York Times*/CBS News exit polls, as reported by Gerald Pomper and colleagues, *The Election of 1984* (Chatham, N.J.: Chatham House Publishers, Inc., 1985) or Michael Nelson *et al.*, *The Elections of 1988* (Washington: CQ Press, 1989). Voter Research and Surveys, 1992.

* National Unity Campaign.

identification as a feminist, gender differences offer no safe prediction of an individual's views. On the issue of feminism in general, the dividing line cuts across the two gender groups.

The same cannot be said of the division of opinion about suffrage during the first women's movement, the campaign culminating in the 1920 ratification of the woman suffrage Nineteenth Amendment. The roots of that movement reach at least as far back as the early decades of the nineteenth century. Some say it began with Abigail Adams, who packed off husband John to the constitutional convention with her admonition to "remember the ladies." (He promptly forgot.) Scientific opinion surveying did not begin before our century; but it seems a sure bet that well into the second decade of the twentieth century most American males harbored condescending contempt for a movement they regarded either as silly or dangerous.

Suffragist activism normally institutionalized itself in interest group form, in associations like the National American Woman Suffrage Association (NAWSA). The party path seemed self-defeating for a movement that, though articulating in theory the interests of the majority, was speaking for a disenfranchised majority that could not deliver the votes. Still there were rare times when suffragists charted a third-party course.

**EQUAL RIGHTS** The Equal Rights party bade for the presidency in 1884 and 1888. It received just 4,149 votes, all from men, in 1884 and even fewer than that four years later. If judged only by those meager poll returns, the party did not amount to much. Equal Rights was not the first to advocate the vote for women; Prohibition had broken that ground in its 1872 platform. But Equal Rights was the premier party whose heart and soul was woman suffrage. It was the first with a female nominee who earnestly campaigned for the presidency. Belva Lockwood, a schoolteacher-turned-lawyer who was the first woman ever to argue before the U.S. Supreme Court, was the party's nominee in 1884 and 1888.

### National Woman's Party

The National Woman's party revered the memory of its old Equal Rights forebear.[5] Drawing instruction perhaps from the Equal Rights party's paltry electoral returns in the 1880s, NWP eschewed the method of nominating candidates for office. But in 1914, the activists of the Congressional Union for Woman Suffrage (CU), the organization that would recast itself as NWP two years hence, were cheered by the participation of eighty-three-year-old Belva Lockwood in one of their demonstrations on Capitol Hill.

From its earliest days, when it called itself Congressional Union, NWP embraced the indirect pressure tactics of picketing and demonstration to draw media and public attention to the suffrage cause. NWP also showed itself willing to use **direct action**—nonviolent methods of public protest that, at least in the context in which they take place, are illegal. (That it was so very successful at capturing media coverage and readers' awareness makes it intriguing to ponder what NWP might have accomplished in the "television era.")

Even though it did not formally nominate candidates, the National Woman's party took a strong interest in election outcomes. NWP enrollees or women closely allied with NWP and its founder, Alice Paul, sometimes presented themselves as candidates. One of these was Anne Martin, who ran in 1918 as an independent for a vacant Nevada U.S. Senate seat. Martin finished in third place with 4,603 votes. Democrat Charles Henderson won that set with 12,197 votes.[6]

The National Woman's party worked to defeat male candidates for office. NWP targeted presidential and congressional Democrats, even those who were sympathetic to the suffrage cause. This was because during the Woodrow Wilson era the Democrats were seen as the party in power. According to NWP's way of thinking, the Democrats had to give a full accounting for the failure to pass the woman suffrage amendment. NWP worked assiduously to defeat Wilson's 1916 reelection bid even after Wilson registered strong support for woman suffrage in an address to the convention of the National American Woman Suffrage Association (NAWSA) that year.

# Belva Ann Lockwood (1830–1917)

Belva Ann Bennett was born a child of farmers in Niagara County, New York. In 1868, the thirty-eight-year-old woman married sixty-five-year-old Ezekiel Lockwood, a dentist/Baptist preacher who was a Union veteran of the Civil War. (It was her second marriage. She had a daughter, Lura, by her first husband, a young farmer who died in 1852.)

Belva Lockwood possessed strong ambition and a desire for personal recognition and success—attributes associated in past and even contemporary American culture with men far more than women. Finding nearly every door closed to her because of her sex, Lockwood, using her brain and a gritty resolve, knocked a lot of them down. In clearing away barriers for herself, Lockwood also opened passages for other women.

Although Lockwood would become a lawyer later on, her first profession was teaching. Graduating at fourteen from a one-room school, she took a job (at $5-a-month plus board) teaching children in that very same place. At twenty-two, she entered Genessee College, an institution where doors had just opened to female students. Three years later, with a B.A. in hand, she won appointment as principal of Lockport (New York) Union School. Her salary, $400 a year, was just two-thirds the size of those of her best-paid male assistants.

For three years she owned and ran a women's seminary—finishing school—in Oswego, New York. Lockwood made a profitable transaction in selling that school, and in 1866 she took off for Washington, D.C. There she established one of the capital city's very first coeducational schools. But already tiring of being an educator, she was becoming convinced that the path to the top lay in the study and practice of law.

Most law schools then were all-male bastions. The forty-year-old Belva Lockwood did manage to secure for herself a place in the first batch of women (fifteen in all) ever admitted to any entering class of the National University Law School. Lockwood (along with just one other of those female cohorts) stuck it out to earn her degree.

Because of the objections of male chauvanists in her graduating class, National University's administration and trustees initially declined to grant Lockwood her diploma and thus her admission to the D.C. bar. Lockwood took these valued objects (title, in effect, to practice before the District of Columbia Supreme Court, the forerunner of today's D.C. Court of Appeals) only after a pressure campaign she led for herself. Fueled by her indignation at the injustice of it all, she had fired off a rude, uncivil (and effective) letter to U.S. President Ulysses S. Grant, the nominal head of National University.

Lockwood thereafter built up a thriving law practice. It was profitable too, earning her the impressive income of about $300 monthly. Lockwood's actions in one noteworthy case brought $5 million to settle a Native American (Cherokee) claim on the federal government. Lockwood began to speak out for women's rights. She opened her law offices to meetings of suffragists and other liberal activists.

Of the two greatest milestones in Belva Lockwood's life—her most substantial accomplishments in the movement of American women—the first and perhaps the more important came in March 1879. That was when Belva Ann Lockwood became the first woman in history admitted to practice before the U.S. Supreme Court. Finding no precedents in English common law for the admission of women to the bar, all but two of the justices declared that a congressional statute would be necessary for admitting Lockwood.

Massachusetts U.S. Representative Benjamin Butler, a Republican who soon would switch to the Greenback party, was known for his support of women's rights. Butler sponsored a private bill for Lockwood's admission to the Supreme Court bar. Its passage in Congress was due to Lockwood's own intense lobbying on Capitol Hill and the support of some sympathetic newspapers. One of Lockwood's earliest actions as a new member of the Supreme Court bar was to sponsor the petition of Samuel R. Lowery, the fourth African-American (the first from the South) to win admission to that bar.

The second milestone, in 1884, was Belva Lockwood's first third-party campaign for the American presidency. Far from something she had actively sought, her nomination by the California-based *National Equal Rights Party of the Pacific Slope* came to her as surprising news in a letter mailed from the Golden State. Marietta Stow, editor of *The Woman's Herald of Industry,* had helped engineer Lockwood's selection. Stow ran as Lockwood's vice-presidential running mate.

Feeling the need for a platform on which she and her campaign could stand, Lockwood penned one herself. That progressive document pledged the nominee and party to justice and equality for people irrespective of race, sex, or nationality (with a specific inclusive reference to Native Americans), world peace, economic development, civil service reform, and prohibition.

Like history's other serious but futile third-party campaigns, Lockwood's bore more than its share of ironies. The novelty of this first serious bid by a woman for the presidency brought Lockwood's campaign much media attention. Some of the coverage was sympathetic, but most was insultingly condescending. Her own hometown's Lockport *Daily Journal* cooked up a ditty, with Lockwood as brunt, for its readers' amusement: "My soul is tired of politics/its vicious ways, its knavish tricks/I will not vote for any man/But whoop it up for Belva Ann." Although some suffragists backed Lockwood, others cast their lot with Greenback nominee Ben Butler. Some of the movement's best-known leaders seemed to think that embracing any third party would be the functional equivalent of spitting into a heavy wind. Elizabeth Cady Stanton and Susan B. Anthony gave their support to Republican nominee James G. Blaine. (Anthony went out of her way to publicly criticize the Lockwood campaign.) It would take the Republican party thirty-two years to reciprocate; the 1916 GOP platform finally endorsed national woman suffrage.

The supreme irony was that even though Lockwood met all of the Constitution's qualifications for the presidency and could offer her candidacy to the nation's voters, neither she nor any woman in America could vote for Lockwood (or for any of Lockwood's presidential opponents). Thus, every one of the 4,149 votes she took in the six states where her ballots were distributed was cast by a man. Wyoming, where women already could vote in territorial and local elections, soon would become the first state to enter under a constitution mandating woman suffrage even in presidential and congressional elections. That would be in 1889, one year after Lockwood's second and final quixotic quest as Equal Rights nominee for the presidency.

Over more than a quarter century beginning in 1880, Lockwood served in delegations attending peace conferences in France, Britain, Switzerland, and Italy. She fruitfully worked for better remuneration for sailors and marines and successfully lobbied for a congressional act requiring equal pay for equal work for male and female government workers. She even had some hand in pushing Congress to pass the Sherman Act. She was in wide demand as a public lecturer on current events. Syracuse University gave her an honorary LL.D. (Doctor of Laws) degree.

**Principal Source:** Julia Davis, "A Feisty Schoolmarm Made the Lawyers Sit Up and Take Notice," *Smithsonian Magazine,* 11 (March 1981), 133+.

Several of the NWP leaders, Alice Paul included, had lived some years in England. In charting their tactic of punishing American Democrats as the party in power, these leaders drew on experiences they had had in British politics. NWP's critics in other branches of the suffrage movement branded it naive for NWP to transfer British practice into the American process. These critics had a point. In America then, as America today, presidential and congressional elections were separate affairs. Moveover, the relative lack of congressional party discipline made it impossible for major parties to work as cohesive units either favoring or opposing woman suffrage.

All of these tactics alienated NWP from the National American Woman Suffrage Association, from which Congressional Union (thus NWP) had sprung. NAWSA, 2 million members strong, held moderate views and endorsed more "respectable" methods than those of CU and NWP. But it was the latter's militancy that revived and mobilized a movement that had grown dormant by the beginning of this century's second decade. Thus CU and NWP seem to have played the decisive role in the final passage of the Nineteenth Amendment.

This radical new force received support from some of the best-known suffragists of the time, from the likes of Crystal Eastman (the driving charge behind the Woman's Peace party of World War I) and of Mary Ritter Beard. But the very soul and breath of CU and NWP was their founder and leader, the young woman named Alice Paul (1885–1977).

Paul was born in Moorestown, New Jersey. She earned her B.A. from Swarthmore in 1905. Quaker by faith, social worker by profession, Bohemian in spirit, Paul lived in various American and British intentional communities, those utopian experiments of the time, during her first four years after Swarthmore. A brilliant scholar (she was inducted into Phi Beta Kappa), she did graduate work at the New York School of Social Work before earning her M.A. and Ph.D. at the elite ivy University of Pennsylvania. In the 1920s, after the passage of woman suffrage gave her time to do so, Paul received two law degrees. She was admitted by the District of Columbia bar to practice in 1928.

Paul spent most of the years 1907–1910 in England. She actively worked in Britain's radical suffragist and working class political movements while pursuing graduate study. England turned out to be Paul's principal training for the role she was to play in leading the militant wing of the suffrage movement back home. In England she met Lucy Burns, an American compatriot who would become Paul's closest friend. Paul and Burns were jailed for their movement work. They took part

*Alice Paul, founder of the National Woman's party (courtesy of the National Woman's party)*

in prison hunger strikes and watched intently the media's interest in such things.

In January 1913 Paul and Burns found themselves in command of NAWSA's Congressional Committee. That was a scant two months after the impressive second-place showing of Bull Moose Progressive Teddy Roosevelt (the Progressive platform had endorsed woman suffrage and Jane Addams had seconded Roosevelt's nomination), and just two months before Woodrow Wilson's first inauguration as president. In some sense the forerunner of CU and NWP, the Congressional Committee was

NAWSA's arm to lobby for a national woman suffrage amendment. But until Paul's arrival as Congressional Committee's chair (Burns was vice-chair), that lobbying arm was a paper tiger indeed. NAWSA's total allocation to Paul's Congressional Committee predecessor for the year 1912 had been an incredibly puny ten dollars!

The new regime of Congressional Committee quickly turned things around by moving the focus from lobbying to publicity-grabbing demonstrations and other in-the-street kinds of political action. This shift flowed naturally from Paul's British experience. Mary Ritter Beard gave its best theoretical formulation: large but powerless groups can develop their own power by becoming visible and conscious to themselves and others. It was a lesson learned by Paul's forces and well learned decades later, during the television era, by civil rights and a host of other movements.

Paul's most memorable demonstration came at the beginning of her movement: a march up Washington's Pennsylvania Avenue on the day before Wilson's first presidential inauguration. Although historians differ on the number who walked (estimates range from 5,000 to 10,000), the numbers were by any accounting staggering for such an event at that time. A parade permit fully authorized the march; but from the beginning, the walkers were beset by hostile onlookers who harassed, jeered, and blocked the women. Media reports were priceless even if faintly condescending, and much of the public seems to have sympathized with the committed marchers. Baltimore papers reported this way:

> Five thousand women, marching in the woman suffrage pageant today, practically fought their way foot by foot up Pennsylvania Avenue, through a surging throng that completely defied Washington police, swamped marchers, and broke their procession into little companies. The women, trudging stoutly along under great difficulties, were able to complete their march only when troops of cavalry from Fort Myers were rushed into Washington to take charge of Pennsylvania Avenue. No inauguration has ever produced such scenes, which in many instances amounted to nothing less than riots.[7]
>
> The women had to fight their way from the start and took more than one hour in making the first ten blocks. Many of the women were in tears under the jibes and insults of those who lined the route. At Fourth Street progress was impossible. Commissioner Johnson called upon some members of a Massachusetts National Guard regiment to help clear the way. Some laughed,

and one assured the Commissioner they had no orders to act as an escort. At Fifth Street the crowd again pressed in and progress was impossible. The Thirteenth Regiment, Pennsylvania National Guard, was appealed to and agreed to do police duty. . . . Very effective assistance was rendered by the students of the Maryland Agricultural College, in guarding the women marchers. It was where Sixth Street crosses the avenue that police protection gave way entirely and the two solid masses of spectators on either side came so close together that three women could not march abreast. It was here that the Maryland boys formed in single file on each side of the [women] and became a protecting wall. In front a squad of boys locked arms and formed a crowd-breaking vanguard. Several of the "war correspondents" were forced to use their fists in fighting back the crowd. . . . The parade itself, in spite of the delays, was a great success. Passing through two walls of antagonistic humanity, the marchers, for the most part, kept their tempers. They suffered insult, and closed their ears to the jibes and jeers. Few faltered, though some of the older women were forced to drop out from time to time.[8]

A month after this march, Paul set up the Congressional Union. By December 1913, CU had enough backing to start a weekly paper to publicize the cause. In 1914, NAWSA fired her for insubordination from her place of leadership in the Congressional Committee. From then on, Paul and CU, reconstituted NWP in 1916, charted their own independent course. Through it all, Paul and her forces held to those in-the-street kinds of political methods. They frequently suffered beatings from male chauvinists. After America entered World War I in 1917, NWP activists were arrested and jailed. Forced feedings sometimes broke their prison hunger strikes. Television cameras did not exist to document their demonstrations and their suffering. But media reported, and these activists would have appreciated the 1960s chant: "The whole world is watching! The whole world is watching!"

By 1916 the suffrage movement had won for women the right to vote for president in twelve states. Montana Republican Jeannette Rankin that year became the first woman ever to win a seat in the U.S. House. Six more states, New York included, extended some suffrage rights to women in 1917, and even in the resisting southern region, Arkansas women won the right to participate in the then all-important Democratic primaries. By the beginning of 1918, women could vote in states holding 45 percent of the nation's electoral votes.

Alice Paul chaired NWP from its founding until 1921, the year after passage of the national woman suffrage amendment. She remained on its executive committee for many years thereafter. NWP's numbers naturally began dissipating when the Nineteenth Amendment, the party's central political objective, entered the Constitution. But Paul and NWP had one more fight to make. Proclaiming that woman suffrage was but "a tiny step" toward the full liberation of women, Paul and her party began to press state-by-state for equal rights bills and upon Congress for a national Equal Rights Amendment. NWP agitation procured the first congressional hearings for ERA in 1923.

Opposed from the right, this new party initiative also brought criticism from other women's organizations. The new League of Women Voters, along with some of the long-established suffrage groups, came out opposed to ERA. They feared, they said, that an amendment like that would wipe out protective legislation beneficial to women. Alice Paul gave an acrid retort. So-called "protective legislation," she said, was false "recognition of the inferiority of women."

Far from faultless, NWP deserved some of the criticism it got. Radicals though they were, NWP enrollees always had come mainly from the professional classes. They too quickly spurned protective legislation that was more likely to benefit working-class women. In their single-minded devotion to ERA, they may have neglected other issues legitimately concerning American women. An entreaty from African-American women for an NWP campaign against the continued disenfranchisement of black women (along with black men) in the Jim Crow South brought Alice Paul's reply that this was a "race issue," not a "woman's issue."[9]

Even so, NWP earned a lot of praise from feminists of the latter day, and not just for its instrumental role in passing the Nineteenth Amendment. The League's position on ERA changed eventually to one of support, and new feminist groups like NOW put ERA high on their lists of national objectives. But for years NWP, its members aging, its numbers diminishing through mortality, nearly alone continued the drumbeat for ERA. In 1972 at last, Congress proposed it; it went down to defeat three states shy of the thirty-eight needed to add it to the Constitution.

NWP also had something to do with the 1964 Civil Rights Act provision that bans employment discrimination based on sex. As originally drafted, Title VII applied just to "race, creed, and national origin." A delegation of NWPers, constituents of Virginia's Howard Smith, lobbied their congressman to broaden the wording to include sex. Although he was a longstanding ERA supporter, Smith's segregationist views and his desire to kill the 1964 Act were likely foremost in his support for sponsoring the broadened language. The Act passed, to the surprise of many, "sex" and all.[10]

## African-Americans and the Third Party Course

New York City is headquarters for the *National Black Independent Political party*. Though it is largely powerless, NBIPP's very existence gives testimony that African-Americans look sometimes at the third-party option for political action.

The calculus black third parties have faced presents a different and less hopeful reality than the one confronted by would-be architects of women's or feminist parties. The United States is, after all, majority white, and African-Americans are but one racial minority of many. For many blacks (and a lot of whites) race seems a less meaningful and legitimate line dividing "us" from "them" than is class or ideology. Jesse Jackson's Rainbow Coalition strategy straddles the racial divider, presenting itself as a progressive movement of African-Americans, Hispanics, women, gays, homeless people, environmentalists, peace activists, and others to seize the Democratic party reins from the powerful who have held them for so long. If such ideological-class logic were to hold, many middle-class blacks satisfied with the status quo might opt, against Jackson, for the campaign of a conservative black or white candidate. For these reasons and others, most partisan African-Americans have, like their white counterparts, focused their loyalties unswervedly upon the major parties. Interest groups like the National Association for the Advancement of Colored People, Southern Christian Leadership Conference, Congress of Racial Equality, and Student Nonviolent Coordinating Committee proved to be effective conduits for African-Americans' demands on the system.

Over the years some African-Americans do leave interest groups and the major parties and go on to found, support, or become active in independent black political parties. Sometimes the appeal is black nationalism. Demands for inclusion, for an equitable share in the American dream, also have generated black third parties.

Most partisan black Americans retained their loyalty to the Republican "party of Lincoln" into the early 1930s. But the GOP seemed already to be turning its back on the aspirations of African-Americans by 1877, when it consented to the termination of Reconstruction in a still-unreconstructed South. During the Democratic Solid South era southern Republican state organizations split into lily white party establishments and the *Black and Tan GOPs*. Some Black and Tans lasted from soon after the Civil War until the 1960s. Others came as twentieth-century reactions to the exclusion of blacks from GOP state organizations in many parts of the South. In effect if not intent Black and Tans were virtual third parties, loyal to Lincoln's memory but unable either to secure from the national GOP any relief from their ostracism or to receive, along with their white counterparts, many of the benefits of federal patronage when Republicans controlled the White House. But there were times during the Democrats' Solid South monopoly when the Black and Tans furnished a southern state's only elected Republican officials. These were typically municipal, ward, county, or school district office holders in majority black places where African-Americans somehow managed to hang onto the franchise.[11]

If, as historians have charged, white Republicans lost their "soul," white Democrats were remarkably slow in developing theirs. African-Americans substantially realigned with the Democratic party in the 1930s. Today, as the century draws to an end, blacks are among that party's most devoted demographic groups. But in the South, Democratic leaders retained a markedly segregationist Dixiecrat bent into the 1960s. As recently as the late 1940s, a white state Democratic establishment managed to exclude from the franchise ninety-nine adult black Alabamians out of a hundred. Many Deep South blacks remained disenfranchised through the first half of the sixties.

A Democratic saga reminiscent of the GOP's Black and Tans came in 1964, when the black *Mississippi Freedom Democratic party* (MFDP) challenged that state's lily white party establishment by demanding Mississippi's place at the national convention. MFDP justifiably claimed itself to be the voice for 850,000 voteless Mississippians. With the earthy eloquence of leader Fannie Lou Hamer, it won the sympathetic support of some elements of the national Democratic power structure and from a huge segment of the mass media; journalist Richard Rovere wrote for *The New Yorker* that Mississippi's white regulars that MFDP wanted to replace had about as much right to seating as would "a delegation of Republicans, Communists, or Prohibitionists." MFDP sent a biracial delegation, four whites along with sixty-three blacks. But the national Democratic party offered MFDP just two seats at large. That was a compromise offer that MFDP found easy to refuse.[12]

The last legal barriers to black voter participation came down in the sixties. Years earlier the Supreme Court had invalidated two disingenuous disqualifying strategies: grandfather clauses went by the boards in 1915 and whites-only southern Democratic party primaries in 1944.

But only with passage of the 1965 Voting Rights Act did it become illegal for most deep southern counties and states to impose literacy tests. Many of these tests had been designed, not to measure literacy, but for the more sinister purpose of disqualifying even well-educated blacks while passing almost all whites. That 1965 law also allowed federal officials to be present at places where there was prima facie evidence of racial bias in registration or balloting, to see to it that things went fairly. Poll taxes went into history's great ashcan through the Twenty-fourth Amendment (1964) and the Voting Rights Act of 1970.

Massive voter registraton drives engineered in the early-to-mid-sixties by young militants of the Student Nonviolent Coordinating Committee (SNCC) brought the names of hundreds of thousands of African-Americans to voter rolls for the first time. By the end of the sixties, hundreds of blacks, many running as Democrats, were winning local offices in all the southern states.

Almost from its beginning long before the modern civil rights movement, the African-American struggle for freedom has encountered a "(black) **nationalist-integrationist duality**"—competing perspectives on ends and means.[13] In its infancy in the very early 1960s, SNCC was an integral part of the movement, led by Martin Luther King Jr., and others, for black entry into the mainstream. Some of its activists already had earned their stripes in the early sit-ins, beginning in Greensboro in 1960, and SNCC itself was present for the famed Freedom Rides of 1961. But SNCC activists generally were younger than those either of NAACP or of King's Southern Christian Leadership Conference (SCLC), and many in SNCC had "grown up hard" in working-class or underclass families. Before the mid-sixties, SNCC already was detaching itself from the integrationist view and embracing black nationalism. Its slogan became a defiant "Black Power!". It would change its name to Student National Coordinating Committee to underscore its new repudiation of the dictates of nonviolence. This transformed SNCC expelled white activists from its leadership ranks. (Many white SNCC veterans went on to activity in various militant New Left organizations of the late 1960s.) Eventually SNCC would dissociate entirely from groups wanting integration. Driving much of the change was Stokely Carmichael, SNCC's chairman for a time and a leading force in its southern voter registration drives.[14]

Interest group in essence, SNCC did occasionally trek, party style, into electoral waters. In 1965 SNCC and its Stokely Carmichael worked with local African-Americans to set up in Alabama the *Lowndes County Freedom Organization.* Overwhelmingly black and one of the nation's poorest counties, Lowndes was the place where a white racist's gun

# La Raza Unida Party

In the United States, most politically active Latinos, except for those in the Cuban-American community, tilt toward the Democratic party. Third-party ventures undertaken by Hispanics have been far rarer than those of African-Americans. La Raza Unida ("la raza" means in Spanish what "the people" means in English) was set up early in the 1970s as the organized partisan expression of a militant Chicano movement bearing the same name. La Raza Unida party has local organizations in some 100 communities, primarily in the Southwest. This left-leaning party proclaims its devotion to the interests of Mexican-Americans and of Mexicans in the United States, specifically those of the working class. La Raza seeks to empower Chicanos through the electoral system and to educate working class Chicanos for more effective exercise of political power.

**Principal Source:** *Encyclopedia of Associations,* 23d ed., ed. Karin E. Koek, *et al.,* vol. 1 (Detroit: Gale Research, 1989), 1458.

brought down white civil rights worker Viola Liuzzo. Black maid and farm hand wages there ranged from three to six dollars a day. Lowndes schools remained rigidly segregated more than a decade after *Brown* v. *Board of Education* and the typical African-American child left school in the sixth grade. As of March 1965 not one citizen in its black majority had managed to register to vote.[15]

Adopting the black panther for its symbol, Lowndes's Freedom Organization earned its common name, *the Black Panther party.* Its seven candidates for county office carried guns throughout the campaign.[16] Despite intimidation and the constant threats of economic reprisal and with almost no support from the Johnson adminstration in Washington, Carmichael and the Panthers managed by the November 1966 election to register 2,758 of Lowndes' 13,000 voting-age blacks. But white voters still outnumbered blacks by election time; through election fraud 2,823 white names appeared from a potential pool of 1,900! County government raised filing fees from $50 to $900. Democratic party ads on local radio told new black voters the lie that their vote would not count if not cast on the Democratic line. The local (African-American) Baptist Alliance, along with the integrationist SCLC, publicly opposed the

Panthers as extremists. Despite everything, Panther's candidates all polled nearly 42 percent of the county vote.[17]

## The Oakland-based Black Panthers

Lowndes's events drew little attention from the American people at large. But young militants in the bleak ghettos of far-off Oakland, California, were watching closely. About 50 percent of Oakland's half-million were minority people, and the city's white-dominated police had a sorry record of harassment and brutality. Many African-Americans felt, as did a lot of Mexicans and Chinese, that Oakland cops worked under a deliberate plan to keep them subjected.

In 1966 Huey Newton and Bobby Seale set up in Oakland the *Black Panther Party for Self-Defense*. Borrowing the popular name for Lowndes's Freedom Organization, these Oakland Panthers also drew on its symbolism. Their banner showed a scowling panther ready to do in its enemy.

Symbolism was central to that new Panther organization. So was life-style. Newton and Seale insisted that Panther cadres be role models for young blacks in the struggle for liberation. Panthers always were to refrain from drugs, and they were not to use alcohol while on party duty. Remembering Mao Zedong's words that "power grows out of the barrel of a gun," Panthers were to carry weapons, make them visible to all, and keep them loaded for use. Wherever they found police harassing people Panthers were to confront the cops militantly and aggressively. Panther words and slogans—All Power to the People, Pig (police or more generally the white power structure), Off the Pig, and others— found their way into the decade's vocabulary, especially in New Left and counterculture rhetoric.[18]

There was power as well in the symbolism of Panther uniforms. As Panther fever gripped young ghetto blacks nationwide and as the Panther movement captured the imagination and support of young white leftists, Panther poster art went like hotcakes in African-American neighborhoods and university enclaves. One most memorable pose featured a stern Huey Newton, dressed in Panther pressed shirt, black leather jacket and beret, and sitting in a wicker chair. His hair, though closely cropped, showed the Afro style. Newton held in one hand a high-powered rifle, in the other a spear.

Panther ideology, articulated in the party's "Ten Points" platform and elsewhere, embraced and synthesized black nationalism and Marxism-Leninism. Nationalism and Marxism-Leninism bear mutually competitive principles. Articulated purely, they seem mutually exclusive. International in vision, Marxism-Leninism has presumed to speak for the working class and more generally for the world's downtrodden. Nationalism bears the aspirations of a people sharing ethnic/racial and historical-cultural bonds.

The Panthers were ideological pragmatists, not purists. Black nationalists they were, and the leadership positions they set up for the party seemed a prototype for new government. Newton was the party's first Chairman, Seale the Minister of Defense, Eldridge Cleaver the Minister of Information (sometimes called Minister of Education). At a time when it appeared that SNCC would merge with the Panthers (the merger never came), Newton named Stokely Carmichael as Panther Prime Minister and SNCC's James Forman as Minister of Foreign Affairs. Panthers saw African-Americans as colonial subjects suffering the same injustices borne by Third World peoples of color in Africa and Asia. But Panthers rejected the emphasis that black cultural nationalists of the time placed upon African dress, language, and customs. Panthers also declared impracticable some nationalists' vision of an independent black nation in the American Southeast. The Panthers wanted a community's residents to have full control of the police, schools, and other institutions as they operated within the community.

As Marxist-Leninists, the Panthers said they spoke for the *lumpenproletariat*, the hardcore underclass toward which Karl Marx had shown suspicion, not affection. Panthers felt far more inspired by Third World communist movements, in China but especially in Cuba, than by regimes in the Soviet Union and Eastern Europe. The Panthers saw themselves as a Leninist "vanguard party." Hence their emphasis on internal discipline and their lack of concern that formal membership at their party's peak was just 5,000. Their class analysis led them to reject the bias of other black nationalists against whites in general and to seek (and find) white allies in the 1960s leftist movements.

Most white New Leftists were enraptured by the Black Panthers. White radicals were taken in particular by the militant style with which the Panthers confronted the American ruling class. As the New Left itself radicalized in the late sixties, many young white radicals would look to the Panthers as the vanguard in revolutionary struggle.

As a disciplined party, Panthers found far more common ground with New Left groups like Students for a Democratic Society (SDS) than with the psychedelic hippies and Yippies of the Counterculture. But bridges were built with the Counterculture too; Eldridge Cleaver's 1968 running mate on the Peace and Freedom ticket was Youth International party (Yippie) leader Jerry Rubin.

The very heart of Black Panther thinking, the party's soul or essence, came right out of the pages of *Wretched of the Earth*, the powerful writing of Frantz Fanon. A black psychiatrist from French Martinique, Fanon had worked in a French Algerian hospital while secretly giving aid and comfort to the Algerian revolutionaries. In his book Fanon embraced violent struggle, not just for its efficacy in bringing liberation but also for what it gives to the psyches of the oppressed: "At the level of individuals, violence is a cleansing force. It frees the native from his inferiority complex and from his self-despair and inaction; it makes him fearless and restores his self-respect."[19]

Black Panthers, "the living incarnation of . . . Fanon's 'revolutionary native' for whom the acceptance of violence was a purifying step toward self-respect,"[20] offered themselves as examples to young blacks everywhere. Far-flung America first tuned into the Panthers when, brandishing their guns, they muscled their way to the floor of the California Assembly to protest a soon-to-be-passed 1967 bill that prohibited carrying loaded weapons in California's incorporated areas. Panther publications broadened public awareness of the party. A "Black Panther Coloring Book," its graphic drawings each captioned with assertive and violent Panther language, reached thousands of young hands around the country.

*Black Panther*, the party newspaper, found an audience growing eventually to 200,000. But the Panthers' most effective work came in community organizing. They set up free clinics, ambulance services, legal aid, schools, and free clothing stores. Their crowning achievement was a free breakfast program that eventually came to feed tens of thousands of ghetto children in many parts of the country. From their Oakland base they built Panther chapters in forty cities, and prison inmates organized Panther units. Supporters turned out in the thousands for some Panther rallies. Public opinion polls revealed that the party at its popular peak garnered the strong respect of a quarter of all African-Americans and of 43 percent of blacks under twenty-one. Marlon Brando and other prominent whites contributed to the party. Leonard Bernstein raised a stir among conservatives when he gave a Panther fundraiser in his New York penthouse.[21]

Their rhetoric was revolutionary, their philosophy and style violent. But the Panthers did enter into electoral politics, at least in their Oakland-Berkeley base across the bay from San Francisco. Panthers won a seat on the Alameda county school board and four on the Berkeley community development council. Bobby Seale took over 35 percent in his 1973 bid for Oakland's mayoralty. Panther support helped elect Oakland's first black mayor in 1977. That was the year that Panther Elaine Brown very nearly won an Oakland city council seat.[22]

Newton was just twenty-four, Seale thirty, when they set up the party. Panthers were young, from their late teens to early thirties, in the Panther heyday, and unlike SNCC, their party was born on the nationalist side of the "nationalist-integrationist duality." That party produced several of the best-known radicals in a decade known by its fascinating people. Much of their fame, a kind of Robin Hood allure, they owed to police attacks and shoot-outs with police, whose hatred for the Panthers equalled the Panthers' for them.

Huey Newton, a founder of the Panthers, was born in Louisiana, the son of a railroad worker/Baptist preacher. His paternal grandfather, Newton said, had been a "white rapist." In the Oakland to which Huey Newton moved with his family, he studied Chinese philosophy, attended junior college, even took a year of law school. He became a follower of Malcolm X, the Black Muslim leader slain in 1965.[23]

In October 1967, a year after co-founding the party, Newton was arrested for killing a policeman. The police apparently knew that Newton was driving the car they stopped that day, and they stopped him just to make life difficult. Newton himself took five bullets in the shoot-out that followed. For the policeman who fell dead in that shooting, Newton spent nine months in jail awaiting trial. A conviction came for voluntary manslaughter, but it was reversed because of the trial judge's errors. Two later trials brought hung juries, and Newton won release in 1971 after some three years in prison.[24]

In 1974 Newton was picked up again and charged with another shooting. Jumping bail, he spent three years in exile in Castro's Cuba. This case ended in mistrial in 1979, the trial jury splitting 10-2 in favor of acquittal. Newton's life ended violently in 1989, years after his Panther days had drawn to a close. A young tough gunned him down in the same mean Oakland streets where Newton had organized his Black Panthers twenty-three years earlier.

The Panthers also had their Seale and their Cleaver. Bobby Seale and Huey Newton had been friends for a year by the time they started their Black Panther party. Seale previously had served a four-year stint in the American military, the last six months in stockade for displaying a bad attitude in protesting a racial incident. When Newton was imprisoned for shooting a policeman, the Panther chairmanship went to Seale.

During the turbulent 1968 Democratic Convention in Chicago, Seale flew to the Windy City to throw Panther support behind the huge antiwar, anti-establishment demonstrations there. There for just hours, he gave only two speeches. But Seale's message was full of the standard and violent Panther rhetoric: "roast the pigs," "barbecue some pork," "send the cops to the morgue slab."

Seale's Chicago trip made him a defendant in the infamous "Chicago Eight Conspiracy Trial." Seale's seven co-defendants had been leaders of the Chicago demonstrations. Among those standing trial with Seale were New Left antiwar activists Tom Hayden, Rennie Davis, and Dave Dellinger and Yippie leaders Abbie Hoffman and Jerry Rubin. Even though Seale had never met or talked with most of the seven, he was also charged with the federal offense of "conspiring to travel interstate for the purpose of fomenting a public disturbance." Seale in court demanded his constitutional right to a lawyer of his choosing and, because the lawyer he wanted was ill, a delay of trial. Judge Julius Hoffman denied both these demands as well as Seale's follow-up entreaty that he be allowed to defend himself. Thereupon Seale denounced the judge in his court as a "racist, fascist pig," and Judge Hoffman ordered Seale gagged and chained hand-and-foot to his courtroom chair. The ghastly spectacle of a black militant champion of liberation in chains made worldwide headlines. The judge soon declared a mistrial on Seale's conspiracy charges, and in a new trial Seale won release from Judge Hoffman's contempt citations.[25]

Eldridge Cleaver's *Soul On Ice* lent early fame to the Panthers, and the party welcomed its author for the star quality he brought with him. Arkansas-born, Cleaver had moved as a youth with his folks to Los Angeles. As a teenager in the early 1950s he hustled pot and got into scrapes with the law.

Athletic and appealing, Cleaver had countless relationships with women, many of them white. In 1957, when he was twenty-two, Cleaver was picked up and charged with rape and assault. Cleaver's nine-year imprisonment gave him time to compose a lot of the essays that make up *Soul on Ice*.

Cleaver wrote of his passion for Beverly Axelrod, the white female lawyer who championed his release. He incisively analyzed racial stereotypes in American culture—the Omnipotent Administrator (white males), Supermasculine Menial (black males), Ultrafeminine (white females), and the self-reliant Amazon (black females)—and their devastating impact upon African-Americans' self-image. He traced out and praised Malcolm X's repudiation of black racism, a latter-day conversion costing Malcolm his life, and he celebrated white young people's commitment to the sixties liberation struggles. But Cleaver also declared black-on-white rape an insurrectionary, political act, deserved retribution for the centuries-long assault on black America.[26] That was Cleaver's most inflaming point. Today, in the century's last decade, *Soul on Ice* remains on many libraries' list of banned books. The censors most often raise Cleaver's rape declaration to justify their trespass on the First Amendment.

Cleaver ran as Peace and Freedom nominee for the presidency in 1968. On April 6 the Oakland police approached Cleaver, who had just parked his car. Cleaver had reason to feel skittish; it had been just two days since King's Memphis assassination, and racial tensions were near flashpoint everywhere. Cleaver and 17-year-old Panther Bobby Hutton retreated to a nearby basement when, Cleaver said, the cops opened fire. Deciding on surrender, Cleaver stripped nude to show the police he had no concealed weapons. As Cleaver and Sutton walked toward their floodlights, the police began shooting. Cleaver took a hit in the leg, Sutton falling dead from five police bullets. Cleaver was charged for attempted murder. He ran his presidential campaign on bond pending trial.[27] He also began teaching a Berkeley course. In September the university regents, feeling pressure from Governor Ronald Reagan, denied academic credit to those who were taking it.

Just weeks after the November election Cleaver jumped his $50,000 bail and went underground. He made his way to Cuba, then Algeria and France, before returning to America in 1975. Cleaver's break with the Panthers was already underway by 1969, when Panther units swearing fealty to Cleaver began to challenge the Newton-Seale led Panther regulars. His mid-seventies return to the States brought a visibly changed man. A professed born-again Christian, he would write *Soul on Fire* in testimony to his new love affair with Jesus and America. Texas fundamentalists helped Cleaver to work through the legal problems facing him from the 1968 events. Cleaver bought a home in a prosperous section of California's Los Altos. For a time he would seek a white market for tight-fitting codpants, Cleaver's dream for personal profit in the free enterprise system.

Given their macho image and style, it may be unsurprising that the Panthers were slow in accepting the feminist struggle. They outraged almost everyone else at the 1969 Students for a Democratic Society convention when Panther's spokesman gave the demeaning "Pussy Power" label to the women's liberation movement. But there were women in the Black Panthers, and some would come eventually to positions of party leadership. Angela Davis briefly crossed Panther turf on her trek from SNCC to the Communist party.[28] Huey Newton appointed women to the Panther central committee in 1970. Around 1974, when Newton went underground and headed for Cuba, Bobby Seale left the Panthers for good.[29] In 1974 Elaine Brown assumed the party chair, and over the next few years she and Ericka Huggins held the party's top two leadership posts.

Today a tiny Black Panther core holds on in Oakland. But their party, as Newton and Seale built it, virtually has ceased to exist. The Panthers found themselves both constrained by and locked into that macho-militant image which they had cultivated and which the mass media, in bringing fame to the Panthers, had been instrumental in setting in place. By the mid-1970s, sixties-style radicalism was waning, the stage being set for the conservative Reagan Revolution. Had nature taken its course, the Panthers still might have gone by now into history's ashcan. But nature's course never was allowed. The historical record gives one unequivocal answer to explain the Panthers' demise: the FBI and local law enforcement exterminated the Black Panther party.

Director J. Edgar Hoover launched his FBI's secret COINTELPRO operation in 1967. In a private memo to the Albany office, Hoover said COINTELPRO's objective was "to expose, disrupt, misdirect, discredit, or otherwise neutralize the activities of black nationalist, hate-type organizations and groupings, their leadership, spokesmen, membership and supporters."[30] Hoover's racial attitudes, his attacks even on Dr. King and the integrationists, and his hostility toward all left-wing things are fully documented.[31] In Hoover's mind, and in the thinking of Alameda County (Oakland) District Attorney Ed Meese (who later would serve President Reagan as Attorney General) and of other agents of "law and order," the Communist party no longer was the principal menace to safety and national security. The Black Panthers had become Public Enemy Number One. COINTELPRO's anti-Panther operation amounted to war:

The creation and distribution of misinformation, sometimes of straight-out lies. For example, letters to Panther members purporting their leaders' theft of party money, Swiss bank accounts, sexual rendezvous with white women. Materials manufactured by the FBI but attributed to the Panthers and to the rival cultural nationalist US Organization of Ron Karenga; they were fashioned to promote violent warfare between the two groups.

Tapping of Panther phones, monitoring shipments of the *Black Panther*, surveillance of Panther meetings and rallies, and infiltration of the Panther organization by paid FBI informants.

FBI and FBI-investigated or encouraged police raids of Panther offices. There were twenty-one such raids in eleven states in a single year, 1969. Arrangement for the assassination/murder of

Panther activists. Sometimes operating indirectly, by fomenting inter-group warfare, the FBI at other times worked directly through death squad-type raids. One notorious example: the Illinois State's Attorney-directed (and FBI-instigated) predawn December 4, 1969, raid killing Chicago Panthers Fred Hampton and Mark Clark. It was a unilateral police barrage, with just one shot returned by the Panthers. An FBI infiltrator had supplied the floor plan, and most of the attack unit's bullets aimed for the bedrooms.

The suppression of defense evidence, sometimes even infiltration of the defense, and manufacture of prosecution evidence in Panther trials.

Think what you will about the Panthers themselves. Whatever you decide, our government's war on the Black Panthers (and other groups) violated the human rights and pluralism for which we have demanded respect by governments beyond America's boundaries. At the dawn of the nineties at least fifteen ex-Panthers still were serving time for events of their Panther days. Julia Cade of the American Civil Liberties Union's National Prison Project declared all of them "political prisoners." Given the official record of vicious assault on their party, she makes a very strong point.[32]

## The Civil Rights and Feminist Communities: Party Options in the Nineties

Now, near the end of a century, many African-Americans are finding in the Democratic party a more congenial welcome than the party gave before. Jesse Jackson's 1980s campaigns for the Democratic party presidential nomination won serious attention from white Democratic leaders. (Some of their reactions bore far more the character of fear and consternation than of warm enthusiasm.) After the 1988 presidential election, Ron Brown came to chair the Democratic party. Brown was the first black ever to head a national major party. African-American Democrats won the mayoralty of America's largest city, the Virginia governorship, and the right to face ultraconservative North Carolina Republican U.S. Senator Jesse Helms. Helms won in a close election attracting worldwide attention.

Even so, the early 1990s brought charges that the Democratic party is taking for granted the support it receives from African-Americans and from feminists, environmentalists, and others who have been disaffected by the rightward shift of the GOP. Suspicions circulate that the Democrats' top goal now is to woo back southern (and other) conservative whites who have been deserting to the Republicans, and that key white Democrats want to purge their party's public image as the party of minorities. The Democratic Leadership Conference (DLC), a group of moderate, mainly southern, Democratic leaders, worked diligently in the early 1990s to wrest any remaining power from the party's liberal wing so that the party might present a centrist face and a "winnable" presidential candidate to the electorate. The 1992 election of Bill Clinton, a DLC mover and shaker, validated for many Democrats what DLC had set out to do. But there also were worries that alienated progressives might leave the Democrats to help craft some new left-liberal party.

**NEW ALLIANCE**   The Bronx was the birthplace for the New Alliance party (NAP) in 1979. NAP bills itself as a "black-led, multi-racial coalition of progressive people."[33] During the 1980s it worked alongside many groups opposed to Democratic Mayor Ed Koch and his "anti-black, reactionary" policies. NAP stood shoulder-to-shoulder with the Reverend Al Sharpton when Sharpton pressed black Tawana Brawley's claim, later discredited, that a white gang had abducted and raped her in suburban Dutchess County. The party takes anti-Zionist positions (associating, for example, with the Palestinian cause), but it strongly denies charges that it is anti-Semitic. NAP identifies itself with the struggle of lesbians and gay men. NAP's supporters claim that theirs is America's fourth largest party (just behind the Libertarians) and that it is moving up fast. It got that way, they say, because it did what the Democratic party would not do: it developed and pushed a genuinely progressive agenda.

Historians someday may recall that New Alliance was an organization offering itself in good faith as left-wing corrective or replacement for the Democrats. But there are observers now who charge that NAP's true identity is something other than what it claims. An investigative report in *The Nation* suggested that NAP's guiding light (and a prime reason for the party's considerable wealth) is one Fred Newman. Newman, who is white, is the founder and eminence in a neo-Marxist strain of psychotherapy known as social therapy.[34] The independent radical leftist *Guardian* newspaper has characterized NAP as "a cultlike organization once linked to right-wing Lyndon La Rouche" that seeks to infiltrate genuinely left-wing associations.[35] Stephen Schwartz, writing for the conservative Hoover Institution, called the party "a strange group of Black nationalists influenced by psychoanalysis (who) broke away from the La Rouche movement."[36]

*The New Alliance party's Lenora Fulani (center) leads a gay pride march, New York, 1988 (photograph by Bill Edwards, courtesy of the New Alliance party)*

"Two roads are better than one" is a prominent NAP slogan. That means in practice that NAP backs Democrats who accept its endorsement but that NAP also runs its own candidates for office. In 1988 NAP supported, or claimed to support, Jesse Jackson's quest for the presidency. But with Jackson cast aside, NAP ran its own candidate for the nation's top office. NAP's standardbearer, New York African-American psychologist Lenora Fulani, qualified for and took federal matching funds. She used them for seeking ballot access and for advertising her third-party campaign. To the surprise of nearly everyone outside NAP, Fulani made the November ballot of all fifty states and Washington, D.C. NAP's Fulani took 225,934 votes, one of every 400 cast. In the early 1992 presidential primaries NAP backed former Irvine Mayor Larry Agran, who made a quixotic run for the Democratic nomination.

Fulani would stand again as NAP's presidential nominee in 1992. The party remained electorally active in the years intervening. Herb Silverman, an atheist, ran a write-in campaign for governor of South Carolina in 1990. Silverman ran as nominee of the United Citizens party, the tiny party on whose ballot line Lenora Fulani had run in 1988 (and would run again in 1992) in South Carolina. Silverman's unfulfilled quest was to challenge a state constitutional provision banning nonbelievers from gubernatorial office. In California a NAP-backed candidate won a contested primary to become the Peace and Freedom party's 1990 nominee for governor. NAP offered congressional and local candidates in Massachusetts, New York, and other states in 1990 and 1992.

NAP's electoral glow has been too dim so far to bring sleeplessness to the Democratic party. Fulani appeared on only forty of the fifty-one presidential ballots in 1992, and her popular tally was less than that of 1988.

Democrats do worry about declining voter turn-out by African-Americans and others whose votes, when they do vote, tend to be Democratic. The 1992 election brought millions back to the polling booths, at least temporarily reversing a long decline. But Americans are still less inclined to vote than a quarter-century ago, and apathy more often than alienation keeps people home on election day. Some nonvoters do vote with their feet, deliberately sending a message to the major parties that something is wrong. When blacks or feminists vote with their feet, most are addressing their message in effect to the Democrats.

Lee Atwater (now deceased), the Republicans' national chairman in the earliest part of the George Bush years, tried new outreach strategies to recruit African-Americans for the GOP. Atwater also counseled his party to be a big tent welcoming pro-choice voters, even pro-choice candidates, who might favor Republican positions on issues other than abortion. Efforts like those seemed unlikely to win much support from African-Americans or from people in the women's movement. At most, they could soften further the support for the Democratic party.

Those concerned about the future of the Democratic party do have reason to fear that Democratic efforts to win back conservative whites may precipitate the withdrawal of large numbers of party liberals into a new third-party venture. Words used by Jesse Jackson on the occasion of the June 1991 meeting of Rainbow Coalition had an eerie reminiscence to those of George Wallace twenty-three years before. There are few if any differences that really matter between the two major parties, Jackson said as he announced that he was seriously thinking about launching a new party dedicated to progressive goals.[37] Jackson's threat seemed particularly poignant, coming alongside news that NOW activists would be initiating their new 21st Century party.

Others too were trying to build a broad new third-party coalition of environmentalists, feminists, unionists, minority activists, lesbians and gays, and people in general who were fed up with things. One group, based in New Jersey, called itself the New party. Another was set up by Ron Daniels. Daniels, who had served as Jesse Jackson's deputy campaign manager in 1988, christened his new movement the Campaign for a New Tomorrow. Daniels's name appeared on nine of the fifty-one presidential ballots in 1992. In some places he ran on the Peace and Freedom party line.[38]

Like much of the left, Jesse Jackson in 1992 played faithful Democrat actively working for the election of Clinton-Gore. It remained to be seen whether a Clinton-led Democratic party would resist liberal pressures so as to root itself firmly in the center, and whether, if so, left-liberal disenchantment might take a substantial third-party course.

## Notes

1. See Everett Carll Ladd, Jr., and Charles D. Hadley, *Transformations of the American Party System* (New York: W. W. Norton, 1975), esp. 129–177.

2. See Daniel J. Elazar, *American Federalism: A View From the States*, 2d. ed. (New York: Thomas Y. Crowell, 1972), esp. 84–126.

3. NOW Executive Vice-President Patricia Ireland, quoted by Eleanor Bader, "Both Sides Now: In and Out of Two-Party System," *Guardian*, July 18, 1990.

4. Sara M. Evans, *Born for Liberty: A History of Women in America* (New York: Free Press, 1989,), 167.

5. This account of the National Woman's Party is indebted to Eleanor Flexner, *Century of Struggle: The Woman's Rights Movement in the United States*, revised ed. (Cambridge, Mass.: Belknap Press, 1975); Dale Spender, *Women of Ideas* (London: Routledge and Kegan Paul, 1982); Louise M. Young, *In the Public Interest: The League of Women Voters, 1920–1970* (New York: Greenwood Press, 1989); and Evans, *Born for Liberty*.

6. Betty Glad, *Key Pittman: The Tragedy of a Senate Insider* (New York: Columbia University Press, 1986), 53–54.

7. *Baltimore American*, March 4, 1913.

8. *Baltimore Sun*, March 4, 1913.

9. Paula Giddings, *When and Where I Enter: The Impact of Black Women on Race and Sex in America* (New York: William Morrow, 1984), 166–169.

10. Evans, *Born for Liberty*, 276.

11. See Hanes Walton, Jr., *Black Republicans: The Politics of the Black and Tans* (Metuchen, N.J.: Scarecrow Press, 1975).

12. David Harris, *Dreams Die Hard* (New York: St. Martin's, 1982), 60–89; and Lawrence Lader, *Power on the Left: American Radical Movements Since 1946* (New York: W. W. Norton, 1979), 164–165.

13. Lader, *Power on the Left*, 110.

14. Carmichael alienated many women from SNCC and from the nationalist movement in general when word passed of this demeaning macho Stokely utterance: "The only position for women in SNCC is prone." Sara Evans, *Personal Politics: The Roots of Women's Liberation in the Civil Rights Movement and the New Left* (New York: Vintage Books, 1979), 87.

15. Lader, *Power on the Left*, 187, 191.

16. Milton Viorst, *Fire in the Streets* (New York: Simon and Schuster, 1979), esp. 367–369 and 486.

17. Lader, *Power on the Left*, 193.

18. The Youth International party (Yippies), a counterculture association that was more tongue-in-cheek than genuine third party, in 1968 nominated a pig named Pigasus for U.S. president. As an act it was part guerrilla theater, or theater of the absurd, and part humorous fun. Pigasus made no state's ballot, but did pick up some write-ins in November.

19. Frantz Fanon, *The Wretched of the Earth* (New York: Grove Press, Inc., 1963), 73.

20. Tom Hayden, *Reunion: A Memoir* (New York: Random House, 1988), 308; also see 164.

21. Lader, *Power on the Left*, 268–269.

22. *Ibid.*, 335.

23. *Ibid.*, 217.

24. Todd Gitlin, *The Sixties: Years of Hope, Days of Rage* (New York: Bantam Books, 1989), 348.

25. See especially Hayden, *Reunion*, 339–412.

26. Eldridge Cleaver, *Soul On Ice* (New York: Dell Publishing, 1968).

27. Lader, *Power on the Left*, 246–247.

28. Davis and George Jackson, a Panther prison inmate, would later fall deeply in love. Jackson's 1970 *Soledad Brother* had made him one of the most famous prisoners in America. Jackson was shot and killed by a guard at San Quentin on August 21, 1971.

29. Early in the 1990s, Bobby Seale was serving on the Temple University faculty.

30. Quoted in "The Fate of the Panthers," *The Nation*, 251 (July 2, 1990), 6.

31. For example, David J. Garrow, *The FBI and Martin Luther King, Jr.* (New York: W. W. Norton and CO., 1981).

32. For details of the campaign to destroy the Black Panther party, see Frank Donner, *The Age of Surveillance* (New York: Alfred A. Knopf, 1980); Nelson Blackstock, *COINTELPRO* (New York: Anchor Foundation, 1988); Kenneth O'Reilly, *Racial Matters* (New York: Free Press, 1989); and "The Fate of the Panthers," *The Nation*, 6–7.

33. November 1, 1988 telephone interview with New Alliance party press secretary Annie Roboff. See *When Democracy Is On the Job, America Works* (1992 Fulani for President campaign booklet available from New Alliance party).

34. Bruce Shapiro, "The New Alliance Party: Dr. Fulani's Snake Oil Show," *The Nation*, 254 (May 4, 1992), 585–594.

35. Vanessa Tait, "California Elections Depress Progressives," *Guardian*, June 27, 1990, 7.

36. Stephen Schwartz, "United States of America," *Yearbook on International Communist Affairs, 1989*, ed. Richard Staar (Stanford, Ca.: Hoover Institution Press, 1989), 152.

37. "Jackson Hints at Third-Party Bid," *The Charlotte Observer*, June 6, 1991.

38. Kim O'Donnel and Steven Wishnia, "Can We Have a Party This Year?" *Guardian*, June 24, 1992.

# Sustained by Faith:

## *Doctrinal Parties*

> *Throughout the centuries there were men*
> *who took first steps down new roads*
> *armed with nothing but their own vision.*
> —Ayn Rand

> *If a man plant himself on his own convictions and*
> *there abide, the huge world will come round to him.*
> —epitaph on the grave of Allard K. Lowenstein

Distant corners of American politics—sometimes obscure, always fascinating—are piled high with doctrinal parties and their true believers. These loyalists' fidelity to creed has sustained some of their parties for decades. Communists, Socialists, and Prohibitionists managed on occasion to exert some influence upon the political mainstream. The doctrine of Libertarians today is an almost anarchistic reverence for individual freedom. Justifiable optimism underlies Libertarian aspirations to have an impact now.

Among the doctrinal parties, there are some so extreme that Libertarians, or, for that matter, members of the Communist Party-USA, seem moderate by comparison. The most radical, the tiniest, the otherwise most inconsequential party sect sometimes bears the potential to capture the nation's headlines, even (rarely) to affect the character of public policy. Consider for illustration two events, one taking place in 1979, the other nearly a decade later.

*Greensboro, North Carolina. Saturday, November 3, 1979.* Soon after 11:20 a.m., Ku Klux Klansmen and Nazis shot up a "Death to the Klan" rally just commencing at the poor and African-American Morningside Homes housing project.[1] That rally had attracted around fifty demonstrators, along with curious observers from the neighborhood. Planning the rally and directing as it got under way were cadres of the

*Communist Workers party* (CWP), a Maoist association with an anti-Soviet outlook.

Greensboro officials had given a permit authorizing the rally. The demonstrators died unarmed because their permit stipulated no guns. The raiders did not shoot randomly. No ordinary bystander was slain. It was more like a carefully preplanned surgical strike. The raiders spent their deadly force on the leading demonstrators and CWP cadres at the scene. Eight lay wounded, one of them severely paralyzed from a head wound. Five others died in the momentary gunfire: a well-known Durham pediatrician, another physician who had left his practice to do union organizing (at the time of his death he was president of a textile workers' local), an African-American nurse who had done advocacy work for cotton mill victims of brown lung disease, a union activist with a Harvard divinity degree, and a Duke honor graduate.

Some of the forty or so raiders were local people. Most, however, came in from a North Carolina textile belt many miles to the west of Greensboro. They were truck drivers, longtime workers in the region's cotton mills, and other blue-collar folk. Along with the Klansmen in this raiding force, there were members of the Tarheel branch of the *National Socialist Party of America* (NSPA). NSPA already was known for its Nazi rebel-rousing in the Chicago area, where the party had its national headquarters.

This was not the first trouble between CWP and the raiding groups. In July, CWP activists invading a Klan rally at tiny China Grove, North Carolina, had burned a Confederate flag. In a public letter that it sent in October, the Communist Workers party denounced the Klan as "one of the most treacherous scum elements produced by the dying system of capitalism." That letter dared the Klansmen to show up for this Greensboro "Death to the Klan" event.

National news reports of the Greensboro violence evoked memories of street fighting between German Nazis and Communists in the years just before the Third Reich. Greensboro demonstrators used their fists and placard sticks to pelt arriving Klan and Nazi cars. The two sides then began stick-fighting just before the first shots rang out. In this Greensboro war, only one side held all the guns.

Greensboro police had a paid informer, Edward Dawson, planted inside the raiders. Dawson worked both sides of the street. He told the police that Klansmen and Nazis would show up, armed to the gills. Dawson assured the raiders that the anti-Klan demonstrators would come without guns. The Klansmen and Nazis also knew exactly where the rally was to begin. Weeks before the Greensboro massacre, photographs of the intended human targets had been passed among the raiders hand-to-hand.

Dawson arrived in the vehicle at the head of the nine-car caravan from out of town. The police showed up too late to provide security for the demonstrators, even though an unmarked cruiser had followed the Klan-Nazi procession into the demonstration neighborhood. Greensboro cops arrested sixteen.

The state would demur from prosecuting for conspiracy; thus, all of the raiders brought to trial—four Klansmen, two Nazis—were charged with pulling triggers. (Edward Dawson was not in the defendants' rack, and the prosecution agreed not to call him to testify in court.) Videotaped evidence viewed by the all-white, Christian jury positively identified five of the defendants as having done some shooting; but this jury in North Carolina's lengthiest trial up to that time accepted the defendants' claim of self-defense and exonerated them all. A civil rights case initiated later on in federal court brought a six-month sentence, to be served on work release, for the Klansman who had fired the very first shot and acquittals for the other defendants.

*Washington, D.C., June 21, 1989.* On this day, the United States Supreme Court invalidated a Texas law. That law had banned the desecration of the American or Texas flag. The high court also set aside both the conviction and sentence—one year in prison and a $2,000 fine—of one Gregory Lee (Joey) Johnson.

Back in the summer of 1984, Johnson and his comrades in the Youth Brigade of the Maoist *Revolutionary Communist party* had stolen and besieged an American flag. Johnson doused the cloth in kerosene and set it ablaze. As the flag disintegrated, Johnson's group chanted "America, red, white, and blue, we spit on you." They carefully planned their demonstration to capture the news. The Revolutionary Communist Youth Brigade chose Dallas at the time that Texas city was hosting the Republican national convention.

The Supreme Court in 1989 found flag-burning to be a constitutionally protected First Amendment right of symbolic speech. In overruling this statute from the Lone Star State, it effectively abrogated similar laws of many other states too. The justices divided 5-4. The slim majority cut across ideological lines: two Reagan-appointed conservatives, Kennedy and Scalia, joined liberals Brennan, Marshall, and Blackmun in rising to the defense of the First Amendment.[2]

Newspaper columnists went on to warn against defending the cloth in a way that would abridge the very freedoms that the cloth represents. But much of the public, along with President Bush, demanded action.

Many on Capitol Hill said they wanted a flag protection amendment in the U.S. Constitution. What Congress enacted instead was a statute akin to the state laws that the Court had overruled. In 1990 the Supreme Court invalidated that brand new congressional act.[3]

Much of this chapter focuses upon the almost bewildering array of third parties on the doctrinal left and right in America. But first we take up the Libertarian party, the most visible national doctrinal party today. Libertarian tenets do not lend themselves to neat classification according to the normal typology of left-to-right.

## The Libertarian Party and Its Doctrine of Freedom

It was on C-Span, not NBC. Even so, Libertarians must have savored the feeling that their twenty-year-old party finally was rising to a new plateau. The 1991 Libertarian party (LP) national convention, at Chicago's Marriott Hotel, was there for observation by viewers around the country who happened upon it on their channel-changers.

Libertarian conventions are known for the exotic things missing from the wimpy affairs the Democrats and Republicans give. In LP's infant days, its meetings brought together tie-dye hippie life-style radicals, along with fashionplate free market disciples of the gospel of Adam Smith and Ayn Rand. The hottest things the vendors could sell at the 1983 LP convention were T-shirts with slogans honoring the memory of left-anarchist Emma Goldman and that of Gordon Kahl, a martyred leader of the right-radical tax resistance Posse Comitatus group.[4]

C-Span watchers at the time of the 1991 convention could observe about 500 of the most freethinking political activists in America. Delegates at this Chicago meeting would select Andre Marrou, the last of three Libertarians who won election to the Alaska legislature in the eighties, as LP's nominee for the 1992 presidential campaign. At the time of his selection, Marrou was working as a Las Vegas real estate broker. Right away, Marrou sounded what was to be his campaign's major theme: End the Federal Income Tax! Abolish the Internal Revenue Service!

Dick Boddie, who took the second highest share of delegate votes in a field of eight candidates, is an African-American veteran of 1960s New Left struggles. Several letters from readers in the May 1991 issue of *Libertarian Party News* had favored Boddie's candidacy over Marrou's only because a black nominee would attract for LP more free media coverage. Attitudes like that seem quirky or cynical to some folks outside the Libertarian fold.

Marrou may have found his Chicago victory gratifying; but his Libertarian comrades, following usual course, gave their loudest applause when None of the Above was placed in nomination. Some of the anarchists of this nearly anarchist party voted for None of the Above.

LP is a doctrinal party. Libertarian party identity, unlike those of the major parties, is largely defined in terms of the body of ideas that are dear to party identifiers. But Libertarian ideas are for disassembling, not erecting, barriers to individual sovereignty of mind, expression, and action. This is the reason why LP has not suffered the problem of splintering and sectarianism that so often plagues doctrinal parties of the left and right. LP does have its "purist" and "pragmatic" wings; but Libertarians of both varieties cling to a doctrine of freedom, radically construed. Libertarians proclaim that their philosophy entirely transcends the left-to-right spectrum others use to locate ideological perspectives; Libertarian thinking shares conservative commitments to economic freedom but the liberals' devotion to personal freedom.[5]

The party venerates early libertarian prophets, people like Adam Smith and Thomas Jefferson. Contemporary Libertarian thought is deeply rooted as well in Ayn Rand (especially *Atlas Shrugged*, her 1957 novel) and in Murray N. Rothbard's *For a New Liberty* (1973). Some of the party's most distinctive ideas have come from the Cato Institute, a libertarian public policy think tank with financial benefactors who have been known to make generous contributions to LP.[6]

Libertarian perspectives, borne in the party's platforms, testify that freedom remains a radical idea even in the third century of the American polity. LP's 1990 platform demands the termination of all restrictions (including prescription requirements) on the production, sale, possession, and use of drugs and (including age requirements) of alcohol; the repeal of all limitations on consensual sexual activities; the revocation of all laws limiting firearm possession and use; the elimination of all restrictions on immigration; and the repeal of legislation which may either limit the abortion right or provide public funds for abortion.

This platform commits LP to work for the abolition of individual and corporate income taxes, the eventual repeal of all taxes. Libertarian platform goals include: revocation of the Federal Election Campaign Act; ultimate termination of the Social Security system and of all federal crop-support programs; and elimination of the Federal Reserve System, Immigration and Naturalization Service, Environmental Protection Agency, and many other agencies. The party demands abrogation of compulsory school attendance laws and the eventual privatization of the entire educational process in the United States. In its platform planks on foreign affairs, LP expresses support for the world movement for human rights, opposes American interventionism and foreign aid, and calls for U.S. withdrawal from the United Nations.

Libertarian activists bear and often seem to enjoy the stereotype that they are upscale nonconformists. Political scientists John C. Green and James L. Guth randomly selected 100 people whose names appeared on public records of the Federal Election Commission as contributors to the Libertarian National Committee. Green and Guth secured, from sixty-seven of those selected, responses to an extensive 350-item questionnaire. The results of their study reveal that there is a lot of truth in those stereotypes.[7]

Fifty-three percent of the respondents ranged from twenty-five to thrity-nine years of age. A majority of their fathers had been professionals, businessmen, or managers. Eighty-four percent of the respondents were college graduates, and three out of four were employed in computer or engineering fields or were scientists, technicians, managers, small business owners, lawyers, or medical professionals. Forty-eight percent identified themselves as former Republicans, only 7 percent as previous Democrats. Nearly twice as many had been conservative as had been liberal before "seeing the light" and becoming Libertarians. Fifty-eight percent claimed no religious identification at all. (Written statements volunteered by some of the respondents indicated some deep hostility toward religion.) In responding to an array of value affirmations, 97 percent identified as very important the "freedom to do what I want to do." Forty-seven percent found it very important to "follow a strict moral code." These Libertarians expressed considerable alienation from national government. When asked "how much of the time do you think you can trust the government in Washington to do what is right?", 60 percent replied "only some of the time," 40 percent "seldom" or "never."

LP has contested every presidential election since 1972, when the token candidacy of John Hospers, a philosophy professor at the University of Southern California, made the ballots of four states. People of distinction they may be; but in the crucial game of political name recognition, all of LP's presidential nominees have fallen short. Only Ron Paul, the party's 1988 nominee, ever held an important national office; in 1976–1977 and again from 1979 until 1985, Paul had served a Houston district as a Republican member of the U.S. House. There is some irony here. Substantial political visibility, valuable to any candidate hoping for votes, may raise Libertarians' suspicion that the contender's

**Table 5.1: Libertarian Party Presidential Campaigns (1972–1988)**

| Year | Presidential Nominee | Nominee's Age on Election Day | Nominee's Occupation | Number of Ballots Bearing Nominee's Name | Number of Popular Votes Nominee Received | Nominee's Percent of all Popular Votes Cast |
|------|---------------------|-------------------------------|---------------------|------------------------------------------|------------------------------------------|---------------------------------------------|
| 1972 | John Hospers | 54 | Philosophy professor | 4 | 3,671 | — |
| 1976 | Roger MacBride | 47 | Corporate law/ business | 32 | 173,019 | .2 |
| 1980 | Edward Clark | 50 | Corporate Law | 51 | 920,859 | 1.1 |
| 1984 | David Bergland | 49 | Law | 40 | 227,204 | .2 |
| 1988 | Ronald Paul | 53 | Physician; former Republican member of U.S. House | 47 | 421,720 | .5 |

**Sources:** *Presidential Elections Since 1789* (Washington, Congressional Quarterly, Inc., 1975), 107; and Federal Election Commission reports on results of 1976, 1980, 1984, and 1988 elections.

soul has been sold off to the political establishment. National political fame thus may disqualify one from LP nomination.

LP named lawyers to lead its 1976, 1980, and 1984 presidential campaigns. Reward may have motivated the party to nominate Roger MacBride for 1976. A Virginia Republican elector in 1972, MacBride had cast his electoral votes for John Hospers and for Hospers' Libertarian running mate, Tonie Nathan. Nathan thereby became the first woman ever to appear in the tallies of electoral votes. Ed Clark, LP's nominee for 1980, was a lawyer for Atlantic Richfield. One of the party's ablest speakers, Clark had taken more than 5 percent of the California vote in a 1978 race for governor. Heavily bankrolled by David Koch, his wealthy vice-presidential running mate (Koch had been nominated because of a promise to be very generous), Clark's 1980 candidacy made its way to the ballots of every state and the District of Columbia. Clark won nearly a million votes. David Bergland, the presidential nominee for 1984, was strongly identified with the LP's purist wing. Like Andre Marrou two campaigns later, Bergland was a party insider whose nomination recognized years of faithful service.

Libertarians have some backing for the claim that theirs is the third party in America. In the early 1990s, just under 10,000 people held national LP membership through payment of the annual dues of at least twenty-five dollars. The party pointed with pride to its 200,000 registrations in the fifteen states that allowed voters to register as Libertarians. Activists recalled 1986, when 200 Libertarian nominees in statewide races amassed nearly 3 million votes. For years, LP has fielded candidates for Congress. More than 100 Libertarians were holding elective offices, mainly local ones, in twenty-two states early in the 1990s.[8] Three New Hampshire state legislators won or retained their seats as Libertarians in the November 1992 elections. LP is the most effectively organized national doctrinal party today, the only one now set up and really functioning in every state.

Libertarian optimism for the long term thus may not be ill-advised. But if anything seems certain, it is that LP is not now at the threshold of achieving the status of a major party or even of unambiguous entry into the political mainstream. Soon after Andre Marrou's selection to run for the presidency, Joseph Sobran, senior editor of the *The National Review*, wrote an essay virtually endorsing the Libertarian nominee. Far from the optimism normally expressed on such occasions, Sobran's was a grim discourse on what should but would not be. Sobran fully availed himself of the opportunity to fault the mainstream, the media most especially, for its preoccupation with major party minutiae, its neglect of the important offerings of Libertarians:

> The most important result of the 1992 Presidential election is now clear: George Bush will beat Andre Marrou. . . . [To] be the candidate of the Libertarian Party these days is to be deprived of even the fifteen minutes of fame that Andy Warhol taught us is every American's birthright. The media regard the two-party system as sacred, though the Constitution says nothing about it. In fact it has dwindled to a one-party system. . . . After all, Mr. Bush has no fundamental differences with the Democrats. . . . The Libertarians do. . . . Marrou wants to restore our freedom. This is why he will be consigned to the oblivion of a minor candidate. After all, you can't be a major candidate unless you stick to minor issues.[9]

Marrou joined Clinton, Bush, and Perot on the ballots of fifty states and Washington, D.C. Unlike Perot, the Libertarian was excluded from the fall debates, largely ignored by the media, and doomed to obscurity. Despite all, nearly 300,000 Americans gave him their votes for president.

# "The Joy of Sects": Parties of the Socialist and Communist Left

In anticipation of this book, I spent a week in New York City interviewing leaders and activists in third parties headquartered there.[10] For several frustrating hours, I stood outside and then inside national Communist Party-USA headquarters in Manhattan seeking a conversation with a representative of that party. Like many other visitors there, I suspected that I would appear in candid photos in an FBI file as a result of my approach to that building. If so, I hope that I smiled prettily at the appropriate moments.

Frustration eventually yielded to success. I was invited to travel to the Brooklyn home of Si and Sophie Gerson. The Gersons, longterm party comrades, celebrated their sixtieth wedding anniversary in 1991. Si Gerson ran for a New York city council seat in the late 1940s as a Communist. He has been a member of the CPUSA Central Committee, and for many years he was associated with the party's newspaper and other Communist publication activities.

I confess that I brought many stereotypes with me when I visited the Gersons in 1981. Most of them evaporated during my two hours in their pleasant middle-class home. I was surprised for instance that their social drink of choice seemed to be Scotch rather than Russian vodka. We talked about their party's vision for America, Si Gerson's arrest during the McCarthy era, the party's relationship with Moscow, the labor and civil rights movements, and about Communist political activity.

We discussed the American left in general. About the strong disposition of left radicals to divide over issues both incomprehensible and irrelevant to mainstream folks, the Gersons heartily agreed with my observation that sometimes the left is its own worst enemy. We facetiously paralleled the situation to a bit of Jonathan Swift satire (apparently directed at British Catholics and Protestants) featuring bitter warfare between Big Endians and Little Endians over whether an egg should be cracked on its large or small end. Si Gerson thought there should be a book on the divided American left and that it should be titled either *The Joy of Sects* or *Let Dogma Eat Dogma*. I trust that he would not be unhappy at my appropriating one of these as this section's title.[11]

## "Mainline Denominations" in a Sectarian World

The radical left has never come close to the influence of Christianity on American life and culture. Even so, the division and strife besetting the socialist and communist left may remind you of the denominational-sectarian condition of organized Christianity. Dozens of very small socialist and communist sects—no one knows just how many—exist on the distant periphery at any single point in time. Four continuing doctrinal parties—the mainline denominations of the radical left—partially ascended out of the utter obscurity of the smaller sects. Sustained in part by their differentiating ideological niches—their articles of faith—these four still live on at ages now ranging from more than fifty years to well over a century.

The *Socialist Labor party* (SLP), originating in 1876–1877, venerates the memory of Karl Marx (1818–1883) and identifies itself as Marxist. It rejects Leninism, the body of thought associated with V. I. Lenin (1870–1924), the principal founder of the Soviet state. For more than a century, SLP has been strongly attuned to the thought of Daniel De Leon (1852–1914), who enrolled in the party in 1890.

Dating from 1901, the *Socialist party* (SP) is, as it has been, a pluralistic, multi-tendency party committed to socialist transformation but also to democracy and social reform.

The *Communist Party-USA* (CPUSA), like Communist parties in many countries, was born in the world socialist schism that was occasioned by the Russian Bolshevik Revolution. Ever since its inception in 1919, CPUSA has dedicated itself to Marxist-Leninist principles. CPUSA members have thought of themselves as cadres in a vanguard party organized to operate along the authoritarian lines Leninists know as democratic centralism. CPUSA long maintained a fraternal relationship with the Soviet Communist party, and recognition by the Soviet party of CPUSA's place in the world Communist movement.

The *Socialist Workers party* (SWP) was an outgrowth of the 1920s struggle between Joseph Stalin (1879–1953) and Leon Trotsky (1879–1940) for succession to Lenin's leadership in the Soviet Union. SWP was founded in 1938 by Trotskyist dissidents, many of whom had left or been expelled from CPUSA. Defeated, displaced, and eventually murdered by an agent of Stalin in Mexico, Trotsky characterized the Soviet Union under Stalin's iron rule as a "degenerate workers' state." Trotskyists believe themselves to be the true disciples of Leninist thought.

**SOCIALIST LABOR**  The Workingmen's party, born in 1876, was reconstituted and given its new name a year later. Of all political parties operating in the United States today, only the Democratic, Republican, and Prohibition parties outrank the Socialist Labor party in longevity. Today's SLP members trace the real history of their party back as far as 1890, when Daniel De Leon joined.[12]

**Table 5.2 Presidential Campaigns of Socialist and Communist Continuing Parties, 1892–1992**

|  | Socialist Labor | Socialist* | Communist | Socialist Workers |
|---|---|---|---|---|
| Number and dates of presidential campaigns | 22 | 18 | 10 | 12 |
|  | 1892–1976 | 1900–1920 1928–1956 1976–1980 1988–1992 | 1924–1940 1968–1984 | 1948–1992 |
| Presidential elections (number/years) in which party nominee received over 2% | 0 | 6 1904, 1908, 1912, 1916, 1920, 1932 | 0 | 0 |
| Presidential elections contested by party in which nominee received under 0.10% | 73% | 33% | 60% | 92%** |
| Highest vote tally/year/ candidate | 53,811 (1972) Louis Fisher | 913,664 (1920) Eugene V. Debs | 102,221 (1936) William Z. Foster | 91,310** (1976) Peter Camejo |
| Highest percentage of all votes cast/year/ candidate | 0.29% (1900) Joseph Malloney | 5.99% (1912) Eugene V. Debs | 0.26% (1936) William Z. Foster | 0.11%** (1976) Peter Camejo |

Data compiled from *Presidential Elections Since 1789* (Washington D.C.: Congressional Quarterly, Inc., 1975); and 1976–1992 reports of Federal Election Commission.

* Socialist party data include 1900 candidacy of Eugene V. Debs as nominee of Socialist party's immediate precursor, the Social Democratic party. SP data exclude 1924, when the party gave its support to the Progressive nominee.

** Socialist Workers party data are subject to dispute. SWP claimed 94,415 votes in 1972, when Linda Jenness ran. This is, at face value, the largest presidential tally and the largest percentage (0.12%) of all votes cast in a presidential election in SWP history. However, nearly one-third of these votes apparently resulted from an unintentional irregularity of voting procedure in a part of Arizona. The data reported in the SWP column above assume a real 1972 SWP presidential tally of about 65,000.

Curaçao-born, De Leon took two university degrees at the University of Leiden in the Netherlands. Not yet twenty when he arrived in the States, De Leon studied law and then won a coveted faculty position at Columbia University as lecturer in international law. He certainly was brilliant, but also rigid and authoritarian. Soon after joining SLP, De Leon dominated it. He even edited *The People,* the party's official weekly and later daily newspaper.

Syndicalism, a current originating in France, influenced De Leon's thinking. Syndicalists wanted to build revolutionary industrial unions. They believed that these new syndicates would prepare the workers for, then lead them through, the epochal revolutionary act, which might take the form of a general strike. As syndicalists foresaw things, the syndicates would become thereafter the organizational structures for the new socialist order arising from the ruins of capitalism. The Wobblies—the Industrial Workers of the World, with leaders like Big Bill Haywood and "Mother" Mary Jones—were to be the ringing example of militant syndicalism in the United States. But because syndicalist ideas captured part of the mind of De Leon, they found their way into SLP too.

Under De Leon's sway, SLP created the Socialist Trade and Labor Alliance (STLA). STLA was to bear the militant character of a labor organization constructed along industrial rather than craft lines. The De Leonists agitated, mostly without success, to convince workers to leave the comparatively moderate Knights of Labor and American Federation of Labor and to join together in STLA. STLA soon ceased to exist and was absorbed eventually by the Industrial Workers of the World.

Far outlasting De Leon (who died in 1914) in possessing the party, De Leonist principles have remained SLP's articles of faith throughout this century. De Leon shared Marx's conviction that meaningful change is transforming and revolutionary. Revisionist social democrats may fall for the shams of reform and evolution, De Leon said, but SLP must devote itself faithfully to Socialism. De Leonists envision, as syndicalists did, a proletarian state organized on industrial union lines. De Leon and his disciples have shared some of the syndicalists' excitement about industrial unions as the locomotive designed to drive the revolution too. But while purists in the syndicalist movement scorned elections as an effete paper tiger, De Leon and his SLP declared elections important, at least for educative/propaganda purposes.

Socialist Labor, from 1892 on, contested twenty-two consecutive presidential elections. Never did an SLP presidential nominee poll more than three votes in a thousand. Usually the party's returns were far less that that. SLP finally withdrew from presidential politics after 1976.

The party lives on today at its headquarters in Palo Alto and in its local sections around the country. It publishes and still offers, to those who are interested, works of patron saint Daniel De Leon. *The People*, SLP's longstanding newspaper, still carries on. The party faithful manage to get their paper out just once every other week now.

The sectarian malady has been known to afflict the SLP body, as those of other leftist parties. In 1881, even before De Leon arrived to insist upon the straight and narrow path, key SLP activists withdrew to found the transient Revolutionary Socialist party. Twentieth-century De Leonist big endians and little endians have functioned inside SLP but also in outside dissident groups—the Daniel De Leon League, League of Socialist Reconstruction, the Industrial Union party, and others.

SLP's most life-threatening hemorrhage, and as it has turned out the split most seriously and permanently diminishing SLP's position on the left and in the political system, was the 1899 withdrawal of the party's anti-De Leon faction led by Morris Hillquit. Hillquit and many of those leaving with him joined forces with Eugene V. Debs and others in creating the Socialist party.

**SOCIALIST**   The Socialist party was born at an Indianapolis convention late in July 1901. Its genesis was the final merger of two associations: the Social Democratic party, founded in 1898 and led by Debs and Victor L. Berger, and the Hillquit-led SLP moderate wing. On their way to merger, these two groups in 1900 had joined together in offering Debs as their candidate for president. It was the first of five Debs campaigns, the four later ones coming under the banner of the Socialist party.[13]

Eleven years after its birth, SP was soaring as high as it ever would go. At its peak in 1912, SP counted 118,045 formally enrolled members. More than 300 party-affiliated English- and foreign-language publications were reaching readers numbering over 2,000,000. *The Appeal to Reason*, SP's most important newspaper, claimed a weekly circulation of more than three-quarters of a million. Debs took 900,369 votes in 1912. That was 5.99 percent, the highest percentage ever taken in a presidential race by any continuing doctrinal party running alone (without fusion with another party). Debs won over 16 percent in Nevada and Oklahoma, and more than one vote in ten in five other states, all in the West. Socialist Victor Berger represented Milwaukee in the House for the Sixty-second Congress (1911–1913). In 1912, twenty Socialists sat in the legislatures of California, New York, Oklahoma, Pennsylvania, Rhode Island, and Wisconsin. (Socialist state legislators two years later numbered thirty-one.) Socialists held 1,200 offices in 340 cities in 1912; among them

*American Socialist leader Eugene V. Debs (courtesy of the Eugene V. Debs Foundation, Terre Haute, Indiana)*

were the mayors of Schenectady and seventy-eight other communities of twenty-four states.[14]

The years succeeding 1912 must have left the party faithful wondering what they or their leaders had done to deserve the misfortunes visited upon their recently robust party. There appeared a bitter breach between the Socialist party and Industrial Workers of the World, a basic conflict over ends and means that proved finally irreparable. SP's antiwar militancy met sharp, damaging official repression following U.S. entry into

*Debs (back row, with child in his arms) and the Red Special Band, 1908 (courtesy of the Eugene V. Debs Foundation, Terre Haute, Indiana)*

the Great War in 1917. Undoubtedly a prisoner of conscience (though the nation often denies that it takes political prisoners), Eugene Debs ran his 1920 presidential campaign as an inmate of Atlanta Federal Penitentiary. Although Milwaukee voters elected in 1918 and again in 1920 to return Victor Berger to Congress, Berger's House colleagues both times denied that antiwar Socialist his seat. (Berger was sentenced to prison in 1919 because he had expressed his sentiments against the war.)

SP's most substantial and sustained loss was the 1919 departure of its communist left wing to take part in the new American bolshevism. The conservatization of the nation, even of labor, in the 1920s further diminished SP energies. It was a substantially weakened Socialist party that in 1924 joined in support of Robert La Follette's Progressive campaign.

There were some bright spots to mitigate party gloom. Meyer London, a Socialist, held a New York City seat in the U.S. House for 1915–1919 and 1921–1923, and Victor Berger finally returned to the House to represent Milwaukee from 1923 until 1929. The party retained for a while some important centers of local power in places like Bridgeport and Reading.

Milwaukee was Socialism's largest "pink city." The party remained

# "Human Resources" in the Socialist Party

The Socialist Party, like most other left-doctrinal parties, organized itself on a dues-paying formal membership basis. In its glory days, SP attracted into its rank and file many distinguished and talented people from nearly every field—people like Carl Sandburg, John Dewey, Jack London, Helen Keller, Upton Sinclair, Charles Beard, Margaret Sanger, Thorstein Veblen, and Walter Lippmann.

In its flush years, sometimes in lean ones too, SP has had sensitive, able, even charismatic leaders.

*Eugene V. Debs* (1855–1926) stood head and shoulders above all others in a party known for its strong leadership. Intelligent though he was, Debs was neither an intellectual nor a professional politician. (For two terms the city clerk of his native Terre Haute, Debs then won election in 1885 as a Democrat in the Indiana legislature. Those were the only government posts he would ever attain.) Yet Debs is well known in American labor history and is one of the most famous of all third-party figures. People who knew him personally said that Debs's strength lay in his personality, a deep social consciousness rooted in his own life experience, and a strong disposition to say what he believed.

Debs was the fifth child of French-Alsatian immigrants who had arrived, nearly penniless, in America six years before his birth. At fourteen, he quit school to work for the railroad. His first job, a gritty nasty one for which he earned fifty cents a day, was to scrape grease from steam engines. He rose to become a locomotive fireman within eighteen months, and by the time he was twenty Debs already was involved in union activity.

Debs became president of the American Railway Union (ARU) in 1893. He led its successful 1894 strike against Great Northern. Brand new, ARU was organized, not as craft unions were, but on the more militant lines of industrial unions. In 1894 ARU supported the strike of Pullman Car Company workers by refusing to handle Pullman rolling stock. In an intervention clearly favoring the corporate side, President Grover Cleveland, a Democrat, dispatched troops to the strike scene. A federal court in Chicago issued an antistrike injunction, and Debs found himself sentenced to a half-year in prison.

This jail time was critical in Debs's life. Debs's incarceration made his name known in households all over America. During his imprisonment, Debs picked up and read Marx's writings. When freed from prison, Debs became briefly involved with Populism, then landed for good in the Socialist movement. In on the 1898 founding of the Social Democratic party, Debs was one of the primary figures who launched the Socialist Party of America in 1901. Debs also was one of those who created the Industrial Workers of the World in 1905, but he left it later, when he thought it too radical.

Debs ran for the presidency in 1900, 1904, 1908, 1912, and 1920. He declined to run in 1916. The trademark of the Debs campaign style came to be the Red Special. Debs used this whistle stopping train to reach voters around the country.

Although 1912 brought his most spectacular presidential share of the vote, Debs actually took a higher vote tally—913,664—in 1920, his last contest for the office. (It came out to 3.42 percent; woman suffrage had vastly expanded the total size of the electorate.) That was remarkable—incredible, some say—because on election day Debs was in federal prison (he already had served more than a year and a half of a ten-year sentence). Debs had been arrested after giving an antiwar speech in Canton, Ohio. His agitation against U.S. participation in the war brought a conviction for violating the Espionage Act. President Warren Harding finally released Debs in December 1921, but even then did not restore the citizenship which had been taken from him.

*Norman Thomas* (1884–1968) was a powerful voice in the SP during the Depression, World War II, and for more than a decade of the Cold War. Thomas was his party's most persistent candidate, running once for governor of New York, twice for mayor of New York City, and six times (1928–1948) for president. He was very involved in other organizations too. He briefly headed the Fellowship of Reconciliation, then was an editor at *The Nation,* a venerable independent-left magazine. For years he co-directed the League for Industrial Democracy, an organization born early in this century as the American version of the British Fabian Society. (The influential Fabian Society was founded in Britain in 1883–1884 with the objective of fostering a new democratic socialist order. It gave birth to the Labour party early in this century.) Thomas was one of the founders of the American Civil Liberties Union.

Thomas's first approach to socialism was through the Christian church. Ordained, like his father, as a Presbyterian minister, he for a time pastored a Harlem church and served an inner city settlement house. World War I made him a pacifist and carried him to membership in the SP.

The Depression era brought influence to Thomas and the SP as a kind of left-wing conscience for the Democratic party and the Franklin Roosevelt administration. It was not a comfortable role for the third party to play; Socialist radicals, in particular, wanted their party, far more than reforming society, to be the cutting edge for transforming it. But SP, in its demands, for example, for public works programs and for unemployment insurance, had a considerable effect upon the creation of New Deal programs.

*Michael Harrington* (1928–1989) experienced first hand the realities of poverty in affluent America when he worked in the radical Catholic Worker movement. A Trotskyist in some of his early days, Harrington joined SP in 1953 and served as its national chairman from 1968 until 1972.

Democratic Socialists of America (DSA), founded by Harrington, is a nonparty group working in the left wing of the Democratic party. Affiliated with the Socialist International, a global cooperative association of parties and groups, DSA is the most influential avowedly democratic socialist organization in the United States today.

Harrington died of cancer in 1989. A professor and prolific author, Harrington was widely known, and is remembered today for *The Other America,* his book that sparked the 1960s War on Poverty.

**Principal Sources:** Nick Salvatore, *Eugene V. Debs: Citizen and Socialist* (Champaign: University of Illinois Press, 1982); *Letters of Eugene V. Debs: 1874–1926,* ed. J. Robert Constantine, 3 vols. (Champaign: University of Illinois Press, 1990); Eugene V. Debs, *Walls and Bars* (Montclair, N.J.: Smith, Patterson Publishing Corp., 1973); Theodore Debs, *Sidelights: Incidents in the Life of Eugene V. Debs* (Chicago: Charles H. Kerr Publishing Co., 1980); Bernard J. Brommel, *Eugene V. Debs: Spokesman for Labor and Socialism* (Chicago: Charles H. Kerr Publishing Co., 1978); James C. Duram, "Norman Thomas as Presidential Conscience," *Presidential Studies Quarterly,* 20 (Summer 1990), 581–589; James C. Duram, *et al., Norman Thomas* (New York: Irvington Publishers, 1974); Murray B. Seidler, *Norman Thomas: Respectable Rebel,* 2d. ed. (Syracuse, N.Y.: Syracuse University Press, 1967); Michael Harrington, *Socialism: Past and Future* (New York: Arcade Publishing, Inc., 1989); Michael Harrington, *The Other America* (New York: Penguin Books, 1971); Harry W. Laidler, *History of Socialism* (New York: Thomas Y. Crowell Co., 1968); and Sidney Lens, *The Labor Wars* (Garden City, N.Y.: Anchor Press/Doubleday, 1974).

a power in that city through the years of the mythical Laverne and Shirley. Milwaukee's last Socialist mayor, Frank Zeidler, left office in 1960 after three terms. He and the Milwaukee Socialists preceding him had run virtually corruption-free local administrations, and they had provided city services of exceptional quality. Ironically, older Milwaukee residents remember the Socialists as fiscal conservatives who somehow balanced the city's books.

SP has never returned to the vigor of its 1912–1914 period. But the radical lessons that Americans learned from the Great Depression and the party's strong second-generation leadership by Norman Thomas restored some of SP's stature and strength in the thirties. Thomas took 883,990 presidential votes in 1932, the year that liberal Democrat Franklin Roosevelt first won the White House. That was to be Thomas's best presidential showing in six attempts. Thomas's 2.22 percent share in 1932 was, except for La Follette's 1924 fusion race, the best return by far for any SP presidential nominee since Debs.

Unfortunately for the party, most of SP's rekindled energies were to be decimated by bitter internal struggles over ideas. In 1936 a party in need of members took in several hundred Trotskyists looking for a home; they soon were expelled by SP for disloyalty and disruption. Although SP never capitulated to external pressures to respond affirmatively to the Popular Front outreach of CPUSA and the world communist movement, there were many in SP who wanted their party and the Communists to reconcile.

Many of the party's internal problems grew out of the dilemma that Roosevelt era New Deal liberalism posed for Socialists. The political climate of the 1930s was far more conducive to socialist ideas than that of the preceding decade. SP-articulated platform positions on social security, public ownership of electric power, trade union rights and collective bargaining, and public housing found their way into Roosevelt-proposed New Deal legislation in the 1930s; cause-and-effect was far more likely than coincidence in these connections between Socialist planks and public policy.

The threat or danger in all this was cooptation. By the late 1950s, the party would belong to social reform and to nothing more radical than a mixed economy. But in the headier days of the thirties, a large part of SP's soul still rested with the dream of social transformation. SP radicals feared that their party might inadvertently save capitalism by reforming it. That concern prompted them to push through a 1934 change in the party's declaration of principles; these radicals dedicated the party to "organizing and maintaining a government under the workers' rule."

Party moderates roundly denounced that provocative but toothless proviso as communistic.

Many in the party seemed to fear that, beyond coopting SP ideas, the Democrats would eventually devour the independent party itself. Those who thought estimations of that threat to be overblown were reminded of a true story, then just forty years old, of Populists gobbled up by Democrats. Norman Thomas contributed a lot toward containing the danger; Thomas offered, through his own presidential candidacies, at least token opposition to FDR and the president's party. But a substantial group, with vital leaders like Bridgeport, Connecticut, mayor Jasper McLevy, left SP in 1936 to found the Social Democratic Federation (SDF). Most SDF'ers supported Roosevelt's reelection campaigns rather than Thomas. (SP and SDF finally re-joined in 1968.)

SP's position within post-World War II American politics has been so marginal that it seems remarkable that the party carries on today. Even though thousands, some as prominent as Victor and Walter Reuther, kept their emotional attachments to the party, most of them did not bother to formally join or support their party with dues.[15] SP was not one of the primary targets of the McCarthy-era witch-hunt; but it was weakened by the national fear of and animus toward all left-wing things. As states made third-party access to their ballots ever more difficult in the forties and fifties, Socialists' earlier hope and pride over their party's returns were replaced by frustration and embarrassment. After 1956, SP withdrew from electoral politics at the presidential level. Not until 1976 did the party resume the practice of nominating for president.

Like most other old left elements, SP was denied substantial influence upon New Left currents in the sixties. Michael Harrington, then a socialist leader both inside and outside SP, did appear at Port Huron, Michigan, for some of the earliest deliberations preceding the Port Huron Statement. That was the 1962 manifesto of Students for a Democratic Society (SDS). Harrington went officially as representative, not of SP, but of the League for Industrial Democracy (LID), a nonparty group seeking to foster democratic socialism in America. (SDS in its early days was tied financially to labor organizations—the setting for that Port Huron conference was an AFL-CIO retreat—and SDS at the time considered itself to be LID's ideological-organizational offspring.) Tom Hayden, the principal author of the Port Huron Statement, and others present for the conference remember that Harrington came in a truculent mood, intent mainly upon the unreachable objective of convincing the SDS'ers to adopt an anti-Communist stance.[16]

If anything, SDS and the New Left in general further marginalized and weakened SP as an organization. The Young People's Socialist League, SP's longstanding youth group, formally dissolved itself in 1964. It had become irrelevant, its young activists said. Many of them were already deeply involved in SDS.

From the time in the late 1950s of SP withdrawal from contesting for the presidency, the party split over the most fundamental of issues: what was the role and future of the party? The majority faction (the "Realignment caucus") adopted the position that what America needed was not a third party but a meaningful (ideologically altered) second party. The majority faction also said that since SP had failed in previous decades to win over labor, it had become crucial for Socialists to go to where labor was; that is, into the Democratic party. The minority faction ("Debs caucus") insisted that, despite all difficulties, Socialists must maintain their faithful devotion to building and strengthening the third party.

In December 1972, the Realignment caucus took the momentous step of changing SP's name to Social Democrats, USA, thus enabling the organization and its members to enter into work within the Democratic party. For five months thereafter, SP technically did not exist; but in May 1973, Debs caucus people, laying claim as heirs of the venerable old party, reconstituted it as Socialist Party, USA.[17]

Social Democrats, USA split again later in 1973. The more left-leaning of its remaining members followed Michael Harrington into creation of Democratic Socialist Organizing Committee, later renamed Democratic Socialists of America. Social Democrats, USA and Democratic Socialists of America are both nonparty groups working within the Democratic party.

Today Socialist Party, USA maintains its national headquarters in New York City. In 1976, SP ran Frank Zeidler, a Socialist ex-mayor of Milwaukee. David McReynolds, a long-term Socialist, antiwar, and gay rights activist, was the 1980 presidential standardbearer. Diane Drufenbrock, a Catholic nun, stood as McReynolds's vice-presidential running mate. Willa Kenoyer, SP's 1988 presidential candidate, received 3,788 votes. J. Quinn Brisben ran in 1992. Not once since the party's return to presidential politics has SP managed to win even 7,000 votes.

**COMMUNIST** You may remember the chaotic scene, in the Hollywood film *Reds*, in which the left-wingers stormed off the floor of the 1919 SP convention, loudly signing the "Internationale" as they went. They were on their way to taking part in the first wave of American participation in the brand new international communist movement. Their departure was technically an expulsion rather than secession; but it was

*Poster in support of Willa Kenoyer's 1988 bid for the presidency as the candidate of Socialist Party, USA. Ron Ehrenreich was her running mate (courtesy Socialist Party, USA).*

a moment forced by SP's communist wing, which had determined to seize SP or, failing that, to desert it.

Already by the time of this withdrawal, American communism was torn by sectarian division. Two new parties each claimed the exclusive right to organize the communist movement in America. They both would be appealing for recognition by the Communist International, or Comintern, the new Soviet-maniuplated association of Communist parties.

The Communist Party of America was organized, led by, and identified with ethnic Russians, many of whom were immigrants with almost no fluency in English. They were bold enough to claim the American franchise for a movement so driven by events in Russia.

The Communist Labor party, led by Benjamin Gitlow and John Reed, sought a more distinctly American identity suitable for reaching the nation's laboring masses. Gitlow's name would come to be associated with an important 1925 Supreme Court case, *Gitlow v. New York*. Reed had written *Ten Days That Shook the World*, a laudatory account of the Bolshevik Revolution, which he had observed. (On his death in 1920, Reed was honored by burial in the Heroes' Grave in Red Square, with a plaque on the Kremlin wall. The 1981 film *Reds* commemorates Reed's life and that of American radical Louise Bryant. Reed and Bryant married in 1917.)

Federal policy in the First Red Scare (after World War I) was set out to destroy both of these new communist parties. The highly controversial 1920 Palmer Raids (named for Attorney-General A. Mitchell Palmer) produced the arrests of 10,000 and drove both parties underground for a while.

The Communist Party of America and Communist Labor party merged in 1921, apparently because they were directed by the Comintern to do so. Using various names (including Workers party, a legal cover under which the party contested for the presidency in 1924 and 1928), the party finally settled on *Communist Party of the USA* (CPUSA) in 1929.[18]

CPUSA's influence on mainstream America never has been stronger than during the Great Depression and World War II. From a party enrollment of under 10,000 in 1929 (membership having been decimated by the expulsion first of Trotskyists, then of a group accused of social democratic revisionism), CPUSA membership grew by 1944 to a record high of 80,000. The party's best tally for president came in 1932, when nominee William Z. Foster took 102,221 votes in thirty-eight states.

Under a borough-based Proportional Representation system approved in 1936 (it was abandoned in 1947, an apparent casualty of the Cold War), New York City voters elected two Communist candidates to their city council. Peter V. Cacchione won a seat from Brooklyn in 1941, and he was reelected in 1943 and 1945. Black Harlemite Benjamin J. Davis won one of Manhattan's seats in 1943 and 1945.[19]

Substantial sectors of the trade union movement, especially unions affiliated with the Congress of Industrial Organizations, came to be influenced by the party. For years, CPUSA was able to control the

National Maritime Union, the International Longshoremen's and Ware-housemen's Union, the United Electrical Workers' Union, the National Union of Marine Cooks and Stewards, and the International Union of Mine, Mill, and Smelter Workers, among others. The party influenced a bitter 1929 Gastonia, North Carolina, textile workers' strike which was believed then (and sometimes has been recalled) to be the determining struggle over whether southern labor would be unionized or instead remain (as it has) largely unorganized.

In its lean years as in its relatively prosperous ones, CPUSA has attracted some support in an African-American community that has suffered both racial discrimination and, as an outgrowth of racism, economic deprivation. In the early 1930s, the party was calling for black self-determination in areas in the South where African-Americans made up a majority of the population. CPUSA nominated a black candidate, James W. Ford, for the vice-presidency in 1932, 1936, and 1940. Black Americans as distinguished as Paul Robeson and W.E.B. DuBois affiliated with CPUSA. Angela Davis, the African-American scholar-social activist, has been one of the nation's most famous figures enrolled in CPUSA late in the twentieth century. By count of the party statisticians themselves, 21 percent of the 400 delegates attending CPUSA's Twenty-fourth National Convention in 1987 were African-American.[20]

The Communist party's critics and foes have favored the metaphor of Soviet puppeteer and CPUSA marionette in characterizing CPUSA history. Party leaders claim this grossly inflates the slavishness of CPUSA devotion to Moscow's lead. But clearly the party, especially in the period before Mikhail Gorbachev's mid-1980s rise in the U.S.S.R., was very attuned and responsive to Soviet signal-calling.

Under the leadership of Earl Browder through most of the 1930s and early 1940s, the party's line closely followed Moscow's. Deserting its radical inveighing about proletarian revolution, CPUSA in 1935 embraced the Popular Front. The party threw support to the Roosevelt administration and its New Deal programs. CPUSA also cultivated ties with Minnesota's Farmer-Labor party, the American Labor party of New York, and other progressive or antifascist forces. "Communism is twentieth-century Americanism" became CPUSA's public slogan in the late 1930s. Meetings of CP locals began with the same ritualistic pledge of allegiance that preceded gatherings of Boy Scouts or Rotarians.

CPUSA support for the administration abruptly terminated after Hitler and Stalin signed their Nonaggression Pact on August 23, 1939. When, on June 22, 1941, Nazi Germany invaded the Soviet Union, the Communist party began its public demand for American entry as an ally of Moscow (and London). CPUSA support for the administration resumed in force when the Pearl Harbor attack brought the United States formally into the war. After Stalin terminated the Comintern in deference to his capitalist allies, CPUSA rechristened itself the Communist Political Association and declared that it was no longer a political party.

The Progressive party campaign was, from the perspective of these American Communists, the last hurrah for the war era Popular Front. The party, which had been resurrected as CPUSA in 1945, strongly supported and substantially influenced that 1948 campaign. But by that time, the Cold War already was well under way. As early as 1946, Earl Browder, accused of "deserting to the side of the class enemy,"[21] had been purged from the party.

The bleakest period of anti-CPUSA repression, the first decade and a half after World War II, also may well have been the sorriest era in the history of personal freedom in the United States. A party submissively following the line of America's erstwhile ally, later redefined as superpower enemy number one, was vulnerable to the anti-Communist hysteria which was political collateral highly valued by Joseph McCarthy (elected to the Senate in 1946), by members of the House Committee on UnAmerican Activities (HUAC), and by all too many other major party witch-hunters. Vulnerable too were all members of CPUSA and of other left-radical parties or groups (despite the constitutional principle of no guilt by association) as well as thousands more who would be accused or merely suspected of "fellow traveling" with Communists.

On the homefront of this Cold War, the political theme of an era was set, not by statement or slogan, but by a question: "Are you now, or have you ever been, a member of the Communist party?" Large numbers of teachers were dismissed, professors denied tenure, government employees fired, often for nothing more radical than their refusal on principle to sign a loyalty oath. The purges tangibly damaged the national interest; for example, the loss of most of the State Department's China experts, whose right-wing critics somehow managed to burden them with losing China to the Chinese Communists. Ubiquitous blacklisting remolded Hollywood films, radio, and television into dull, soft, gutless media and kept many of the most creative writers and performers out of their crafts for years.

Government repression during this Second Red Scare very nearly destroyed the Communist party. (To the professional anti-Communists, that was justification enough for the witch-hunt, despite its more general assault on personal freedom in America.) In 1940 CPUSA had managed to sidestep the Voorhis Act, a law passed that year making it illegal for an American party to be affiliated with an international organization. The party circumvented that act by formally disavowing its connection with the Comintern. But another 1940 act seriously ensnared CPUSA nine years later.

In 1949, CPUSA General Secretary Eugene Dennis and other leaders of the party were tried and convicted of violating the Smith Act. It was draconian legislation that had made it a crime (punishable by up to ten years; raised to twenty in 1956) to teach or advocate the violent overthrow of American government; to organize for the purpose of such teaching and advocacy; to communicate with such an organization; or to conspire to do any of these things. In the 1949 case, the Communist leaders were charged only with conspiracy. In 1951, the Supreme Court, over the vigorous dissents of civil libertarian justices Hugo Black and William Douglas, sustained both the conviction and the Smith Act on which the conviction was based.[22]

In 1950 Congress passed the Internal Security Act. Also known as the McCarran Act, this legislation required all communist and "communist front" organizations to register, and mandated the registration of all of their members, with the United States Justice Department. McCarran also legalized the internment of subversives in circumstances of war or insurrection. Newly passed sedition laws in many states declared even membership in CPUSA to be an offense mandating imprisonment of twenty years. Legislation proclaimed unions "infiltrated" by Communists to be illegal.

CPUSA fortunes were combing new depths by 1956–1958. Proclaiming America's inexorable descent into fascist dictatorship (a very reasonable observation, if inaccurate in prediction), the CPUSA leadership in the early 1950s had directed a segment of the party cadre to withdraw from the official organization in order to build an underground structure capable of functioning under a fascist regime. Hounded by a decade of government repression, CPUSA was further demoralized by Soviet events in 1956. That was when Nikita Khrushchev (selectively) chronicled and denounced the crimes of Joseph Stalin. It was the year that Khrushchev blemished his own more liberal reputation by his bloody destruction of an anti-Soviet revolution in Hungary. By 1958, CPUSA, its membership down to 7,000, was on the brink of extinction.

Gus Hall, born in 1910, knows that the U.S. does not always mean it when it says it never takes political prisoners. Hall spent years in jail as a "Smith Act Communist" during the McCarthy era. Hall rose to become CPUSA's General Secretary in 1959. Still leading the party at the opening of the 1990s, Hall had by then joined Kim Il-Sung of North

Korea and Cuba's Fidel Castro as seniors without peer among world communist leaders. Hall's roots were in the Finnish working class milieu on the Iron Range of Minnesota's far north. Hall became a popular leader among the party rank and file.

Assisted by Earl Warren era Supreme Court decisions that, among other things, legalized party membership and invalidated registration requirements, Hall initiated a slow party rebuilding phase. Soviet events, like the crude suppression of Czechoslovak freedom in 1968, sometimes temporarily set back CPUSA's regeneration.

Still nursing its wounds from the 1950s, the party managed to exert very little influence on the New Left in the sixties. Despite the W.E.B. DuBois Clubs, CPUSA's most notable but rather feeble 1960s outreach to youth, the party's 1960s successes in recruiting the young were confined mainly to the "red diaper" crowd—daughters and sons of old communists.

More substantial party growth from the late 1970s on brought CPUSA an enrollment estimated at 15,000 by the latter years of the 1980s. There were reports of new building or reactivation of party locals in various parts of the country. The Young Communist League, CPUSA's youth group, seemed more vigorous. The party also was working through front groups—the U.S. Peace Council, National Council of American-Soviet Friendship, National Alliance Against Racist and Political Repression, and the Labor Research Association.

*The Daily World*, the New York-based party paper which descended from *The Worker* of an earlier era, regularly reached the hands of thousands of readers. (*The Daily World* merged in 1986 with *People's World*, CPUSA's West Coast weekly, to become *People's Daily World*.) The party's other publication activities have included books and the journal *Political Affairs.*

CPUSA reacted with ambivalence to changes of the Gorbachev era. Hall and other old party leaders had assumed the style of post-Stalin liberal reformers (hence the charge of revisionism leveled at them by some other American communist groups), but on a more limited scale than that of a Boris Yeltsin or even of someone like Gorbachev. Ideologically, CPUSA never really embraced Eurocommunism, the trek of some West European communist parties sharply away from Leninism toward social democracy. Lenin's vision and his idea of a vanguard party were far from junk to a small body living in the belly of the beast; that is, to CPUSA, trying to operate within the anti-Communist, anti-Soviet superpower. Always rumored to be heavily dependent upon Moscow's funding, CPUSA found, as did the Castro regime in Cuba, that the

Gorbachev government was a lot stingier than its predecessors. That may be why around 1990 *People's Daily World* became *People's Weekly World.* CPUSA discomfort rose even higher in 1991, as power passing away from the Soviet center and the Communist party of the Soviet Union rapidly devolved upon the republics and upon the likes of Russia's Boris Yeltsin.

Most organizations of the American left lined up in righteous indignation over the August 1991 Soviet coup by Stalinist hardliners. CPUSA was notably slow in joining this queue. On the coup's first day, Gus Hall produced a tape and sent it out to the party locals. In it, Hall condemned Gorbachev's last pre-coup speech as "anti-socialist," averred that Gorbachev's removal was justified, and warned his comrades against criticizing the coup. Days later, Hall was scrambling to change that position for the public record. But Hall's intial support may have split the party. Gil Green, a liberal member of CPUSA's National Committee, said that most of the party's rank and file, though not a majority of the leaders, opposed the coup from the beginning. "Hall's time," Green observed, "is very short."[23]

The ending of the Cold War brought both opportunities and dilemmas to CPUSA. Warming Washington-Moscow relations, approaching *de facto* alliance if not real intimacy, knocked out all that had propped up Americans' hysterical anti-Communism of the previous four and a half decades. (Some diehards remained, insisting that everything that had happened, even the reunification of Germany, was all fraudulent delusion. Empirical evidence sometimes seems irrelevant in matters of faith—anti-Communist, Communist, or otherwise.) With Gorbachev and Reagan—and later Bush and Yeltsin—becoming partners, CPUSA found fewer powerful domestic enemies seeking to keep it quarantined from the mainstream.

In what amounted to a resurrected popular front, CPUSA participated in the Citizens' Alliance, the governing coalition of Berkeley, California. It supported Harold Washington for the Chicago mayoralty and enjoyed some limited influence in his administration. The party also claimed a share of the credit for the election of Carrie Saxon-Perry, the first African-American woman ever to take the mayoralty of Hartford, Connecticut. As the last decade of the century began, CPUSA was holding some considerable power in California's Peace and Freedom party. A CPUSA-endorsed "independent" candidate for a Massachusetts U.S. House seat won nearly 30 percent of all votes cast in the district in 1988. The same year, a Clevelander running as a Communist for a district seat in the Ohio state legislature won 6 percent of the vote.

Although CPUSA ran its own presidential campaigns from 1968 through 1984, it sat out 1988, apparently because it wanted to demonstrate its support for Jesse Jackson's quest for the Democratic nomination.[24]

The dilemmas the party faced were matters of soul and spirit. No longer so isolated, CPUSA was losing its attractive aura as forbidden fruit for young radicals seeking self-release from the bonds of society's authority. More important still, communism as a belief system was collapsing around the world, even in the Soviet Union. That must have devastated morale within CPUSA, and it would make extremely difficult the party's crucial task of attracting new members.

**SOCIALIST WORKERS**   V. I. Lenin, the founder of the Soviet state, died in 1924. The 1920s brought a bitter successon struggle between Leon Trotsky and Joseph Stalin. A brilliant intellectual and Marxist theorist, Trotsky had lived for a short time in the United States before arriving back in Russia in time to participate in the Bolshevik Revolution. Trotsky then built up the Red Army, enabling it to defeat the anti-Soviet forces in the civil war.

Stalin had risen in pre-revolution Bolshevik ranks doing much of the movement's needed dirty work; by robbing banks, for example, for party revenue. Distinctly gifted at boring his way into positions of leadership, Stalin was firmly in control of the Soviet regime by 1927–1928.

Expelled from the Soviet Union in 1929, Trotsky was stripped of his citizenship in 1932 and in 1940 murdered, apparently at Stalin's behest. (In a document somehow kept secret until 1956, a dying Lenin had seemed to oppose Stalin's succession. "Stalin," Lenin had declared, "is too rude".)

In the United States, CPUSA purged itself of its Trotskyists late in the 1920s. The Socialist Workers party, handiwork of American Trotskyists (many of them had joined together earlier in an organization called the Communist League of America—Opposition), was founded in 1938.[25] Also born in 1938 was the Fourth International, an association of Trotskyist communist parties in which SWP provided some of the strongest early leadership.[26]

Cut off from political power, the Trotskyist movement seemed a dead letter from the start in most parts of the world. But in the U.S., organized Trotskyism commanded some support, especially among leftist intellectuals who found Stalinism stagnant and stultifying.

The early SWP was blessed by able leaders—James P. Cannon and Max Schachtman among them. SWP gained some toehold within organized labor, for several years actually controlling the Teamsters Union. At the time, the party also was the leading section of the Fourth International. To comply with the federal Voorhis Act, the SWP formally withdrew from the Fourth International in 1940; but the party sustained its "fraternal" connection to that Trotskyist network.

Like CPUSA, its longstanding, bitter adversary on the left, SWP was for years the target of overt and covert hostile action by American government. In 1941 Cannon and seventeen other SWP leaders were convicted and imprisoned. It was the first Smith Act prosecution, eight years before Dennis and his fellow Communists were hauled into court. CPUSA actually pushed for conviction of the rival Trotskyists in 1941.[27] Weakened by the lockup of so many of its leaders, SWP yielded its hold on the Teamsters. That tangibly worsened the union's internal conditions; organized crime, stepping right away into the vacuum, substantially influenced the Teamsters over the years since.[28]

In 1986 Federal District Judge Thomas Griesa awarded $264,000 in damages in a suit SWP had filed thirteen years before. According to SWP's claim back in 1973, the FBI, through the COINTELPRO program, had been breaking law, systematically harassing and disrupting the party. A 1987 injunction by Judge Griesa barred the government from using any information about the party that it had collected in that context.[29]

SWP's imprint upon the 1960s New Left was greater by far than the Socialists' or Communists'. That may be why J. Edgar Hoover had so fervently desired to make life difficult for the Trotskyist party. SWP's Young Socialist Alliance (YSA) was organized and active on many university campuses in the sixties. YSA members passed into other students' hands copies of *The Militant* (the party newspaper), periodicals and other SWP materials, and books printed by SWP's Pathfinder Press. YSA'ers were deeply involved in the anti-Vietnam and other sixties mass movements.

The extent to which the party should take part in such movements or in other ways participate in mainstream politics has provoked internal controversy over the years. SWP has been more loosely organized than CPUSA, with internal splintering endemic to party life. For years SWP has endured what seems to an outsider to be the most fickle membership on the radical left. Leaving at as rapid a rate as they came (in the 1980s and since at a far more rapid rate), SWP veterans have gone on to nurture and feed rival Trotskyist groups or other leftist associations or have landed in organizations firmly and permanently anchored in the mainstream. A few, like Lyndon La Rouche, trekked the full ideological distance from left end of the spectrum to right. Even so, it is SWP's self-image that it is a dedicated Leninist revolutionary vanguard party. The party has availed itself of every chance to condemn CPUSA for its

Popular Front and other "revisionist, soul-selling" Communist party accomodations with the mainstream.

SWP refrained from electoral politics in its early years; but it has never failed, since 1948, to offer a candidate for the presidency. The party also has contested hundreds of other races for Congress and for state and local offices.

SWP's internal strength peaked in the mid-1970s. Young Socialist Alliance membership stood at 5- to 10,000 at the close of the sixties. YSA began feeding substantial numbers into its parent party a few years later. Presidential nominee Peter Camejo took nearly a tenth of a million votes in 1976. Formal membership in his party then stood at some 2,500; several times that many were attached in spirit and supportive. Late-1970s SWP national conventions could bring out almost 2,000 people, most of them under thirty years old.

From the early 1980s on, SWP deserted its strident, polemic anti-Soviet rhetoric and began to adopt a critical support stance toward the U.S.S.R. (SWP hostility toward CPUSA continued on largely unabated). SWP became downright glowing in its treatment of socialist regimes in the developing states: Nicaragua's Sandinista government, for instance, or Castro's Cuba.

The party fell on hard times in the 1980s. SWP leaders were forced to make an embarrassing admission late in that decade: departures from SWP were so outpacing the volume of entries that the party had shrunk to half the size it had been just ten years before.[30] Outside commentary about the party early in the 1990s often began with the adjective "fading." From its national headquarters in lower Manhattan, SWP was holding on to its newspaper and book publishing operations, still maintaining a network of some thirty-five bookstores that also served as meeting places for party locals.

### Other Left-Doctrinal Party Sects

The world Trotskyist movement always has been riven by sectarian division. Trotskyists argue over issues that seem esoteric or meaningless to folks outside the Trotskyist faith. Back in his succession struggle with Trotsky, Stalin had declared that Soviet and world communist resources should be devoted first to building socialism in the Soviet Union. Vigorously disagreeing, Trotsky said the first focus must be on instigating and supporting communist revolutions worldwide. Some Trotskyists inferred therefrom an obligation to be redder, more thoroughly communist, than the Stalinists. Other Trotskyists, revulsed by the brutal totalitarianism of Stalin's regime, took their distance from Stalin on the less radical, more social democratic, side.

Trotskyists also questioned what to make of their master's observation that under Stalin the Soviet Union was a degenerate workers' state. Some of them became nearly as critical of the Soviet Union and of the Soviet bloc of nations as of the United States and the rest of the capitalist world. But others, lacking their own real world socialist models, would give a kind of critical support to the U.S.S.R.; even more, to socialist nations in the developing world—Cuba under Fidel Castro, for example—despite these countries' close attachments to the Soviet Union.

A myriad of Trotskyist parties and associations, frequently led by people expelled from or who left SWP, has grown up in the United States.[31] One of the oldest existing ones, other than SWP itself, is the *Workers World party*, founded in 1959. Stephen Schwartz, an unsympathetic observer of American communist organizations, characterizes the Workers World ideological perspective as "a bizarre mixture of Trotskyism and Maoism." Workers World response to the August 1991 Soviet hardliners' coup was, like CPUSA's, an exception to the general chorus of condemnation heard on the U.S. left. Workers World continued in fact to give its verbal support even after the coup's total failure. This party has run presidential candidates since 1980. Its best return ever was in 1984 with 17,893 votes.

The secretive Spartacist League was founded in 1964. Workers League, another sect, ran for the presidency in 1984, 1988, and 1992. Other groups populate the Trotskyist section of the radical left too: Socialist Action, North Star Network, Fourth International Tendency, and others.

Maoism, or Mao Zedong thought, has been the ideological niche for still other Leninist sects in America. Mao Zedong (1893–1976) led the Chinese Communist movement in the years before liberation in 1949 and then the People's Republic for much of its first seventeen years.

Mao's objectives and theories were, like Lenin's, strategic and tactical. Mao combined communism with what was, in effect, Chinese nationalism. He envisioned a socialist (eventually communist) order entirely free of the external clutches of capitalist imperialism. Understanding the preponderantly peasant-rural reality of even twentieth-century China, Mao rooted the Chinese Communist movement firmly in the peasantry, allied with the small urban proletarian class. Sometimes he called for a tactical alliance among peasants, proletarians, petty bourgeoisie, and national bourgeoisie to rid China of external capitalist-imperialist manipulation. Mao emphasized military force ("power," he said, "grows out of the barrel of a gun") and the importance of solidarity and interaction (the "mass line") between liberation forces and the people. He brilliantly articulated the strategy and tactics of guerrilla warfare. Mao's methodology of liberation was the reverse of Marx's urban revolution. In Mao's country or rural strategy, China's large coastal cities would be the movement's very final targets.

It is significant that the American Maoist movement, and many of the Maoist party sects, grew up in the late 1960s and early 1970s. That was a period remembered for its radicalism in the United States. It was the time, in the People's Republic, of the Cultural Revolution, the reddest period of Mao's tenure as China's great helmsman. Many of these American Maoist sects initially billed themselves as pro-Chinese only to become bitter critics of the new Chinese leadership after 1976. After Mao's death in 1976, Chinese leaders blamed the ultra-leftist Gang of Four for all of the excesses that had occurred in the Cultural Revolution. Jiang Qing, Mao's wife, was one of the Gang of Four. Thus, in China blaming the Gang became a discreet way of posthumously censuring even Mao himself. (Some of the most radical of American communists then reached out for other real world models to emulate; for example, the Marxist-Leninist party of the USA for years followed Albania's lead.)

The *Progressive Labor party* (PLP) was founded in 1962 by Milton Rosen and Mort Scheer, two communists of long standing who had been expelled from CPUSA in 1961. Rosen and Scheer had had the audacity to say that revisionism had supplanted true communist thinking in CPUSA, which (as they saw it) had become nothing more than the left wing of the movement for liberal reform. Soon Rosen, Scheer, and their new party were looking to China under Mao's leadership as the alternative to revisionism. PLP doctrine was that capitalism, far from being improvable, would inevitably descend into fascism; the only remedy, therefore, was violent revolution.

PLP was alive for some thirty years. It reached its prime in the late 1960s. PLP's own membership may have been no larger than 350 then. But through the May 2 Movement, its youth wing, PLP came by the end of that decade virtually to dominate Students for a Democratic Society.

I interviewed Mort Scheer in a Brooklyn coffee shop on June 3, 1981. Scheer told me that PLP's only substantial challenger in SDS at the close of the sixties had been the Weathermen, a group that soon changed its name to Weather Underground and went into activities some would identify as those of a terrorist organization. For a while in the 1960s,

PLP claimed a fraternal relationship with the Chinese Communist party, one that Scheer compared in our interview with CPUSA's ties to the Communist party of the Soviet Union. PLP at the time was regularly publishing *Challenge-Desafío*, its English-Spanish bilingual newspaper.

One of PLP's sources of strength was that, in its self-perception as the revolutionary vanguard, the party insisted on internal discipline as it influenced a New Left movement touched by factions, and flower children, and other such things. Committed Marxists, PLPers believed that workers, not students, were the potential primary agents of revolution. Students' role, the party said, was to help build a communist revolutionary base among the toiling masses.

Rejecting CPUSA revisionism, PLP also condemned the (black) nationalism of the Black Panther party. Though PLPers celebrated the Cultural Revolution, there were faults they found even in their beloved China. PLP criticized in particular the nationalist element in Mao Zedong thought.

In 1967 Berkeley radical Bob Avakian founded the Bay Area Revolutionary Union, the group renamed *Revolutionary Communist party* (RCP) in 1975. Avakian's group exerted some influence upon Vietnam Veterans Against the War late in the war in Southeast Asia. RCP had some 2,000 members and the apparent endorsement that the Chinese party previously had bestowed upon PLP.

RCP broke apart in 1978, most of its members leaving (or purged) over the refusal of Avakian and other leaders to countenance the denunciation in China of the Gang of Four. Thereupon, the much smaller RCP, its Beijing franchise snatched away, did outrageous things to demonstrate its fidelity to Mao's memory.

RCP characterized Chinese reform leader Deng Xiaoping as a "posturing, boot-licking, sawed-off pimp." In 1979, 400 party members protesting Deng's visit to Washington battled police in Lafayette Park. There were fifty injuries, sixty-nine arrests, and felony charges against Avakian and sixteen others. Avakian left for France to avoid a long probable prison term.

In 1980 three RCP members at the Alamo hauled down the Texas flag and hoisted a red banner in its place. Two others threw red paint on the Soviet and American ambassadors at the United Nations.

It was a 1984 demonstration by RCP's Youth Brigade and its Gregory Johnson that led the Supreme Court to conclude, in *Texas* v. *Johnson* (1989), that flag-burning is a constitutionally protected First Amendment right. Johnson also was involved in the litigation in which the high court, in 1990, invalidated a flag protection act of Congress.

*Defendants, members of the Revolutionary Communist Party Youth Brigade, and their lawyers celebrate outside the Supreme Court, May 14, 1990, after the high court's ruling in U.S. v. Eichman invalidated a Congressional flag protection act. At far left in second row is Gregory Johnson, national spokesperson of the Revolutionary Communist Party Youth Brigade (courtesy of the Revolutionary Communist Party).*

Most U.S. communist groups were profoundly demoralized by the collapse of Soviet and East European communism. The Revolutionary Communist party was an exception. RCP developed very close ties with Shining Path, a violent Peruvian Maoist movement that has seemed likely to seize power in that Latin American state. As Shining Path's leading North American champion, RCP has been able to recruit new members, especially young Latinos. RCP's *Revolutionary Worker* newspaper appears in both English-language and Spanish-language editions.[32]

The Communist Party (Marxist-Leninist), the American third party receiving Beijing's favor in the late 1970s, disbanded in 1982. It was succeeded by the League of Revolutionary Struggle. There also was the Frontline Political Organization, previously known as Line of March.

The *Communist Workers party* (CWP) was completely unknown to most Americans until the 1979 Greensboro incident, when five CWP members died in Klan-Nazi gunfire. CWP, most of the members of which were Chinese-Americans, deserted its violent Maoist rhetoric in the early 1980s. In 1985, it changed its name to the New Democratic Movement. Henceforth, both directly and through a front group called Asian-Americans for Equality, it would try to work within, or infiltrate, the

Democratic party. By 1987 one of their own was serving on the New York State Democratic Committee, and the New Democratic Movement was influencing a well-known Democratic political club in New York City.

## The White Supremacist and Neo-Nazi Far Right

Individuals and organizations of the American far right regard themselves as bitter adversaries of those on the left.[33] Even so, there is a curious symmetry in the situations faced respectively by the radical left and the radical right in confronting the political mainstream.

Shared ideas as well as descent in a common tradition define and, to an extent, bond the elements of the far right, just as people and organizations on the far left share in a very different tradition and hold certain beliefs in common. The lineage of the contemporary radical right extends as far back as the first Ku Klux Klan, born after the Civil War. This tradition carried on in the very substantial revival of the Klan after World War I, and in the pro-Nazi, anti-Semitic Silver Shirts and German-American Bund of the 1930s.

The American radical right holds antiblack, white supremacist views. By the time the 1980s ended, cable customers in at least fifty big city markets had access to "Race and Reason," a white supremacist talk show hosted by Tom Metzger. "Mud people" was becoming by then a part of the linguistic currency used by many far right people in communicating with each other; as the line went, people with "blood in the face"— "Aryans" whose racial purity enable them to blush—could count on an earth someday purged of its nonwhite "inferior, pre-Adamic mud people."[34] That idea originated as a quasi-theological prophecy of Christian Identity, one of the central components of the contemporary ultraright. Just about every far right activist today has read *The Turner Diaries*, William Pierce's 1978 novel about a band of white racists who launch a full-scale race war resulting, by the 1990s, in a system of white supremacy. The Order, a secretive paramilitary group responsible in the 1980s for many violent and malevolent acts, was the creation of people who saw Pierce's book as the blueprint for a glorious future racial order.

The American radical right speaks with special clarity in its condemnation of Israel. Beyond this shared anti-Zionism, most of the disparate ultraright elements also are overtly, even crudely, anti-Semitic. ZOG is another of those terms in the far right lexicon. An acronym for Zionist Occupation Government, ZOG is what ultrarightist folk call government in the United States. Like some of their leftist counterparts, people on the far right are fond of spinning conspiracy theories. These rightist formulations most often feature "crafty, scheming Jews," who, it is said, have come to control the mass media, Federal Reserve Board, and just about everything else one could imagine. *The Spotlight*, with a weekly circulation of 100,000, is the most widely read national far right newspaper. Its founder, Willis Carto, also started the Institute for Historical Review. The Institute was a revisionist association known for its barbed and provocative challenges to the authenticity of the Holocaust.

The far right, like its leftist counterpart, has endured harsh repression from lawmakers, acting out of repugnance or fear, and from administrative actions taken in response to perceptions of endangerment to people's safety or national security. Governmental suppression of the pro-Nazi right during World War II was nearly comparable in ferocity to the assault on antiwar and pro-Bolshevik leftist activity during and just after World War I. The primary targets of the FBI's COINTELPRO operation launched in the late 1960s were organizations of the old and new left; but COINTELPRO agents infiltrated and sometimes undertook to manipulate and weaken Klan and Nazi associations too.

Far right influence is limited, like that of the far left, by the very small number of identifiers. The radical right also suffers sectarian strife comparable to the divisions endured on the far left. Elinor Langer, who has painstakingly studied the far right, estimated in 1990 that there were 10 to 20 thousand members of the principal component organizations of what Langer termed the "American neo-Nazi movement."[35] These include the various Klan associations and splinter groups; all of the elements of the Christian Identity movement; Posse Comitatus; Youth of Hitler, Confederate Hammerskins, American Front, and other radical right skinhead groups; and avowedly Nazi groups, many of which descend from the American Nazi party of George Lincoln Rockwell. As many as 200,000 more, Langer estimates, passively support these and other white supremacist associations of the radical right.

## Parties of the Far Right

One issue dividing the hard racist right is how to respond to the avowals and symbols of Nazism. Though often quite willing to work in concert with professed Nazis, many Klan and other radical right groups are themselves indisposed to adopting the outward forms of a movement inspired by a regime against which the United States shed its blood and treasure during World War II. Public relations, along with patriotism, explain such groups' reserve. After all, it would be hard to motivate, in any but the most hard-core racist, an enthusiasm for a movement that carries the moral baggage of the Holocaust.

**NATIONAL STATES' RIGHTS**  The National States' Rights party (NSRP)—not to be confused with the States' Rights Democratic party of 1948—was one of those far right groups that stopped just short of avowing Nazism. NSRP adopted its name to appeal to southern racial traditionalists; but NSRP chose as its symbol one very familiar in Nazi Germany—the thunderbolt. The party drew up its official platform in 1958, and adhered to it without revision for the nearly three decades of NSRP's active life. That statement of party principles demanded a "White Folk Community," whites-only government, complete racial separation, laws banning racial intermarriage, and the voluntary repatriation of blacks to Africa.

At its peak, NSRP claimed 12,000 members. Party leaders boasted that theirs was the largest party on the radical right. Observers outside the party estimated NSRP membership at 1,500.[36]

J. B. Stoner, NSRP's national chairman, achieved notoriety for the crude and corrosive racial rhetoric used in his many unsuccessful Georgia electoral campaigns. A veteran Klan activist, Stoner was convicted in 1980 for the 1985 bombing of an African-American church in Birmingham.[37] In 1990 Stoner lost his Georgia primary race for the Democratic nomination for lieutenant governor.

*The Thunderbolt*, NSRP's monthly paper, was edited for years by Dr. Edward R. Fields, a well-known Georgia racist. The paper occasionally pictured NSRP rallies at which white South African neo-Nazis delivered fraternal speeches, or party conferences attended by anti-Semitic refugees from communist eastern Europe. It carried articles with titles like "Pro-Jew Ministers Changing Christianity into Materialist-Atheist Judaism" (April 1980) and "Is Carter Illegitimate Brother of Kennedys?" (September 1976). In the years after NSRP ceased activity as a party, Fields continued to edit his paper, which he renamed *Truth at Last*.

**ROCKWELL PARTY LEGACY**  George Lincoln Rockwell (1918–1967), "fabled founder of the *American Nazi party*,"[38] was the creator of the post-World War II avowed Nazi movement in the United States. In his careful study of the American far right, James Ridgeway refers to Rockwell as Hitler's Lenin. Radical right activists—non-Nazis as well as avowed Nazis—today recall Rockwell as "a seminal figure in the Aryan movement."[39] Rockwell's larger than life aura no doubt is due in part to his assassination in 1967.

Son of a vaudeville comedian, Rockwell studied at Hebron Academy and at Brown University. The United States entered World War II just as Rockwell was about to undertake a career as an advertising illustrator.

Thereupon, he enlisted in the Navy and became a pilot so that he could (as he would later say with considerable irony) "go fight Hitler." Rockwell was recalled into service during the Korean War.

A supporter of early 1950s McCarthyite anti-Communism, Rockwell moved on to the racist right after reading Hitler's *Mein Kampf* and hearing the speech of a veteran leader of the 1930s Silver Shirts. In 1959 he set up the American Nazi party and installed its headquarters at his home in Arlington, Virginia. Years later, an activist in Rockwell's party would romanticize this act of creation: "Commander Rockwell," he said, had chosen Arlington because it was just a heartbeat—"striking distance"—from the center of national power. Rockwell knew that National Socialism's enemies used "Nazi" as a pejorative, comparable to the term "commie" used by Communism's foes; nevertheless, Rockwell dubbed his new party "Nazi" because that would assure it torrents of free publicity.[40]

The World Union of National Socialists, an international Nazi body with affiliated national groups, had its American headquarters at the Arlington home of the American Nazi party. Its European office was in Denmark.

The American Nazi party never had, even by the most generous estimates, more than a few thousand members;[41] but the party, under the leadership of the always flamboyant Rockwell, was showered by mass media attention. Millions of young *Playboy* readers became conscious of Rockwell and his party when *Playboy* ran an interview in which African-American writer Alex Haley questioned the Nazi leader. Publicly forecasting that they would come to power by electoral means in 1972, these American Nazis developed a disquieting slogan: "The Jews are Through in '72." Rockwell and his followers were pelted by eggs and rocks while picketing a Boston theater showing *Exodus*. The party members traveled the South in a "hate bus" with an affixed banner reading "We Hate Jew Communists." Seeking to carry his message to other "Aryan peoples," Rockwell was denied entry into Australia and expelled by the United Kingdom. Rockwell once suggested, probably not very seriously, that his American Nazis were willing to enter into a tactical alliance with a secondary enemy, the Black Muslims, against their common foe, the Jews.[42]

On August 25, 1967, Rockwell was shot dead outside a laundromat in Arlington. Rockwell's murderer, John Patsilos, had adopted the name Patler because it sounded more like Hitler. Patler had been closely associated at times with the American Nazi leader; but three times Rockwell had purged the mentally unstable Patler from his party, the

*NSWPP brochure*

last time permanently.[43] Overcoming determined resistance from many quarters, Rockwell's followers secured burial with military honors for their slain leader.

In the years following Rockwell's death, and partly because of it, the Nazi movement in the United States began to shatter like a shotgun shell. One Nazi remnant, led by Matt Koehl, named itself the *National Socialist White People's party* (NSWPP).NSWPP considered itself to be Rockwell's party in its second generation, not merely a party descendant.

There was some justification for this claim, in part because NSWPP held on to the keys of the Arlington headquarters of the old American Nazi party. NSWPP also maintained the place the American Nazi party had held in World Union of National Socialists.

According to the NSWPP line, the task of the first generation had been to grab and exploit free publicity so as to build popular consciousness of the Nazi movement; now it was time, after Rockwell's death, to build a small and disciplined cadre of racial idealists committed to building the Aryan New Order. NSWPP nurtured locals, particularly in midwestern cities. The party ran mayoralty, city council, and school board candidates, in places like Baltimore, Milwaukee, San Francisco, and St. Louis. Local elections like these often are officially nonpartisan; but NSWPP candidates wore swastikas and revealed their affiliations in other ways while campaigning. They normally took 5 to 10 percent, sometimes as much as 20 percent, of the vote.[44]

A spokesman for NSWPP announced late in 1982 that the party would be moving its national headquarters away from Arlington to a location in the American Midwest. The party's name was to change to the *New Order*.[45] The third generation was beginning, this spokesman was taking pains to say. By 1987, the New Order had established its new national office just outside Milwaukee, Commander Matt Koehl's hometown. No longer would it seem quite so credible for party activists to claim an unbroken line as "the party of Rockwell."

Many of the leading hard right luminaries, or rogues, of the 1980s and since had cut their political teeth in Rockwell's party. William Pierce, an erstwhile Oregon physics professor, trekked through the American Nazi party, then went on to write *The Turner Diaries*. Robert Forbes, a former American Nazi, ran for lieutenant governor of Arkansas in 1990. Forbes won 46 percent in the first round of Republican primary voting before being beaten by a black Republican in the runoff. David Duke, known for his Klan organizing and for building the National Association for the Advancement of White People, earlier had had a brief connection with the Arlington Nazis. Duke ran in 1988 as the presidential nominee of the new far right Populist party. In 1989 he won election to the Louisiana House of Representatives as a Republican. Despite rather systematic shunning from the national GOP establishment, Duke in 1990 unsuccessfully sought a U.S. Senate seat. In 1991, Duke contended, again as a Republican, for the Louisiana governorship. Duke, who took more votes than incumbent Governor Buddy Roemer in Louisiana's unique wide open primary, lost the general election to former governor Edwin Edwards, a Democrat.

# An Interview with Martin Kerr

I was in the Washington, D.C., area interviewing leaders of various third parties when the time came to travel down to the Arlington national headquarters of the NSWPP for a prearranged interview with Martin Kerr. Not knowing the way, I mustered up the moxie to summon a taxi and ask the driver to take me to National Socialist White People's party headquarters. The cabby glanced at me in the back seat with the disdainful look of someone who has just detected the aroma of rotten fish; but he agreed to take me there. On the way over, he made a point of telling me that he had been one of the American soldiers who in 1945 had gone in to liberate the notorious Dachau Concentration Camp near Munich. He shared every gory detail of what he had seen, and told me how much he hated Nazis. I found myself repeating over and over that my mission that evening was scholarship, that I was not in sympathy with those Nazis in Arlington.

The German swastika banner flew alongside the American flag at the entrance to the two story brick headquarters building. After paying (and generously tipping) the cabby, I was greeted by three young men who wore brown shirts and swastika armbands. They showed me inside to a tiny bookstore, where *Mein Kampf, The Eternal Jew,* and a few other selections were on display.

Martin Kerr, whom I had never seen before, was rather short, but otherwise unexceptional in appearance. He had a mustache—a big, bushy one, not the Hitler cutoff kind. He directed me to a second-floor conference room, and we seated ourselves across from each other at a table. A large portrait of Hitler and a swastika banner adorned the walls. For the next hour and a half, I questioned and he answered. Everything was taped by me on a portable recorder sitting on the table. You will be reading only a few of the exchanges between us.

One remark at the outset: Efforts, such as Mr. Kerr's, to trivialize the Holocaust may be more immoral than the blanket claims of some other radical rightists that there never was such a thing. This is because gullible minds are more likely to believe the former than the latter.

**JDG:** Please state your name, your position with the party, and tell me about your background and what brought you to the party.

**MK:** I am Martin Kerr. I am the party's National Organizer and head of the Editorial Department, which produces *White Power* (the party paper) and other written materials.

I am twenty-nine years old. I grew up in the state of New Jersey, in suburbs of New York City. My father was in business with a Jew. My parents were moderate moderates. To them, Gerald Ford was the epitome of wise statesmanship. They were aghast when I became a National Socialist. Maybe it was not too surprising; that was in the 1960s, when kids were breaking away from what the old folks believed.

I owe my conversion to Hugh Hefner, and to Alex Haley's *Playboy* interview with George Lincoln Rockwell. I had started reading and thinking early. Everywhere I turned, there were platitudes: equality, peace, love. "Red and yellow, black and white, they are precious in his sight." I saw the same theme, with just a little different packaging, in Christianity, in Socialism, and in Communism.

Obviously, it was untrue. People were machine-gunning each other, blacks were being hosed, dogs being unleashed on them.

One day I picked up my dad's *Playboy*. I came to the Rockwell interview, and thought "this will be good for a few laughs." But I was amazed. For the first time, I actually read someone who didn't skirt the issue—blacks and whites are not equal, for example. I wrote his party, got information, studied it, and eventually joined up.

I went to Hofstra University. It was in the publicity-grabbing days of the party, and I was good at it. I worked in organizing and other party activities.

The Jewish Defense League marked me for death. The JDL blew up my father's home and also the home of a party supporter, because it thought I was in one of those places. It nearly killed my parents. It also fundamentally changed their attitudes toward Jews. My parents and I later reconciled. My father is now deceased.

**JDG:** What makes you think that America, right now, is fertile ground for a movement like yours?

**MK:** Actually, I'd have to agree with the implication of your question. America is not fertile ground for a National Socialist mass movement right now. We're not a mass movement. Here's the thing—we're a revolutionary organization in very stable, pre-revolutionary times. So we're biding our time for now, preparatory to building a National Socialist mass movement.

There are many Jews in America, and they are extremely wealthy, powerful, and well-organized. Because they control the media,

Americans have been brainwashed against National Socialism. There are stupid shows like "Hogan's Heroes" and "The Holocaust" on TV. So in most people's minds, "Nazi" is synonymous with evil. The educational establishment and media nurture this.

But as Adolf Hitler said, just because a movement is out of synch with public opinion doesn't mean it is doomed—it just means that when victory comes, it will be more of a triumph!

As long as the situation remains moderate, people will turn to moderate leaders. But when the situation becomes extreme, they will turn to extreme leaders. If we have an economic collapse, with massive social upheaval, the people will turn away from the Jimmy Carters and Ronald Reagans—the kinds of leaders who got us into this mess. They will turn instead to extreme leaders, of the left or right. The country is in decline right now, and already we are seeing growing polarization. The traditional minority groups will gravitate toward left organizations that have upheld their special needs and interests. Whites, on the other hand, will gravitate toward right groups, and eventually to extreme groups—Klan outfits and the National Socialist White People's party—that truly uphold their racial interests. We will surely see a radicalization of the white masses in America!

One of our worst problems right now is our media image. All that the white masses know is what National Socialism's enemies have told them. They're told that National Socialists are murderers, haters who kill babies and put people in ovens.

Because people believe this, individuals with personality defects—sadists, jerks, losers—are attracted to the party in numbers disproportionate to their percentage in the population. A large percentage of people who show up downstairs say "I'm here, I want to be a Nazi. I want to kill niggers, I want to gas Jews!"

We don't want them in NSWPP. It's as simple as that. They have only a Hollywood image of Nazis. In the past, unfortunately, our party (and some National Socialist splinter groups continue to do this today) let these people in, thinking they could be used, then thrown out later. That doesn't work. If you let them in, then when the rare decent person comes by who's psychologically balanced, he encounters these cretins talking about torturing Jews and blowing up places—and it drives the decent person away.

One thing that has hurt the National Socialist movement tremendously is that many would-be National Socialists think that the goal of the party should be to establish a carbon copy of the Third Reich here on American soil—the uniforms, the symbols, the salute, and all. But that's inorganic; it won't work.

Adolf Hitler had only six years to build a new society before war was forced upon him. The Third Reich, then, should not be equated with the Aryan "New Order," National Socialists' perfect vision. The National Socialist world view is a totalitarian one; therefore, any state built on National Socialists principles would be totalitarian in scope. Liberals [liberal democrats] think of the state, any state, as a malevolent force. We agree with them about the American state today; it is bad, and we don't revere that state at all. But we know that the power of the National Socialist state would be benevolent. We confidently predict that freedoms like those in the First Amendment (speech, press, and others like that) would be preserved in a National Socialist state.

It is on the precept of race that we base our vision of the future. Our immediate goal is the creation of a White People's Republic on the North American continent. Never in history has there been a successful multi-racial society. Either one race has subjugated and enslaved the other, or the state and society have broken down into chaos and race war.

Here we will see the same. The federal system will break up. Mexicans will colonize the southwestern part of the United States, and Mexico will eventually take it over. Some parts of North America, probably in the Southeast, will be taken over by blacks. When this collapse comes, we want a significant place for the North American white republic, not necessarily the whole continent, but a goodly section—probably toward the present U.S. and Canadian Midwest.

Many people ask: "What will you do to the blacks and the Jews?" We'll not do anything to them. Simply put, we will separate ourselves from them. The repatriation of blacks to Africa, which was U.S. policy until Abraham Lincoln was assassinated, may or may not be workable today. A black people's republic may be a more likely possibility now.

Our bottom line, though, is a white people's state. Jews will not be a part of it. As for the Jews, we're not fortune tellers. We do know that we won't gas or otherwise kill people. Our party has no projection about the Jews. But I personally think that if the Jews see National Socialists about to take power, many will emigrate; they will choose to pack and leave. They will not stay around to find out if these are "nice Nazis" or not.

We are not out to hurt other races. But just as Communists believe that history progresses through class struggle, we believe changes come through race struggle.

**JDG:** A recent issue of your *White Power* newspaper carried an article headlined "There Was No Holocaust!" Given the abundance of pictorial and documentary evidence affirming the authenticity of the Holocaust, would you please comment? Was there a Holocaust or not?

**MK:** I'd say that, as it has been presented to the American people, the Holocaust story is so inaccurate, with so many distortions, that it bears no relation to actual events.

Certainly the Jews were put in camps, and they were not handled with kid gloves. SS guards were not pro-Jewish! I've heard some people say that no one was killed, that they served ice cream to the Jews, and that sort of thing. Well, that isn't true either. These were concentration camps, and it was pretty bad, in all of them.

But certainly there was no program to systematically exterminate the Jews. I think that probably what happened was that, especially near the war's end, certain camp commanders, without sufficient food or medical supplies, undertook to exterminate or to murder a certain percent of the camps' populations. And I think there were some organized exterminations early on on the Eastern Front, especially of Jews who were in partisan groups.

I'd say that the total number of Jews killed in the war, including those killed by Allied bombs was a million, not the 6 million you usually hear about. Auschwitz was bombed by the Allies!

I'd say that Hitler did not know about the Holocaust. When Himmler learned about it, he ordered it stopped. An SS attorney named Karl Morgan was commissioned to wipe out corruption in the SS. Based on his investigations, some SS guards, even some camp commanders, were transferred to penal battalions or executed for mistreating prisoners. Killing prisoners went against SS policy and the policy of National Socialist Germany.

So I'd say it is a question of degree, not one of whether there was or wasn't a Holocaust. If you mean a deliberate, systematic attempt to exterminate all of Europe's Jews, the answer is no, there was no Holocaust. But if you mean were there Jews killed and mis-treated, the answer is yes, there was a Holocaust.

These things must be seen in the light of Allied war crimes as well; the greatest single war crime in human history was the Allied bombing of Dresden, Germany, in which 400,000 people died in a twenty-four-hour period. People were never brought to justice for this, or for Hiroshima, Nagasaki, or Hamburg. In comparison to Dresden, the largest number ever killed by German bombs at a single time during the Battle of Britain was 800.

In war, no one is truly a civilian—everyone is a combatant. Bad things happen. People are killed. The fact that many Vietnamese civilians died at My Lai by official action of the U.S. Army does not mean that mass extermination was U.S. public policy. It means only that low level field commanders undertook to do this. This is what happened in Europe, both in the camps and on the Eastern Front.

There were no extermination camps in wartime Europe. There were concentration camps. The United States also had concentration camps, which it used for Japanese people in America.

**Source:** Author's interview with Martin Kerr, June 30, 1981, National Socialist White People's party Headquarters, Arlington, Virginia.

Glenn Miller was a veteran both of the Green Berets and of Rockwell's party. He went on thereafter to Klan work. Calling himself "ultra right plus a million miles," Miller drew on his Klan and Nazi connections to set up the *White Patriot party* in the early 1980s. The White Patriots' goal, they said, was an independent white nation in the South. Organized like a military unit, the White Patriot party expended more energy in paramilitary training than in waging political campaigns; Miller did, however, take some 5,000 votes in North Carolina's 1984 gubernatorial race.

The *National Socialist Party of America* (NSPA) has been one of the many groups claiming lineage to George Lincoln Rockwell. Frank Collin founded NSPA after being expelled from the National Socialist White People's party in 1970. The Nazis who participated, alongside Klansmen, in the November 3, 1979, Greensboro shootout were members of the North Carolina branch of NSPA. After John Hinckley's 1981 attempt on the life of President Reagan, NSPA claimed that Hinckley was an expelled former party member.

The tiny NSPA band was, if anything, even more extreme and provocative than the National Socialist White People's party, which NSPA regarded as its bitter rival. Frank Collin, NSPA's leader, was fond of making crude jokes in public about his party as the "final solution." Ironically, Chicago columnist Mike Royko alleged that Collin was half-Jewish, and that his father had survived the notorious Dachau camp.[46] Evidence supporting Royko is so substantial that almost everyone (except for Collin and his NSPA loyalists) who commented on the issue accepted the claim either as probable or as a fact. Collin thus may have provided one of the purest examples of what scholars observe as the self-hate often associated with a prejudiced personality.[47] Collin would lose his position as NSPA leader following a 1980 conviction for child sexual abuse.[48] But he still was firmly at the party's helm at the time of the Skokie controversy.

Most of the inhabitants of Skokie, a Chicago suburb, are Jewish; many of them survived the Holocaust. Because of that community's ethnic composition, NSPA targeted Skokie as a site where it wanted to demonstrate. In state and federal cases decided in 1978, the party took its most valued trophy ever: recognition of its First Amendment right to march even in hostile Skokie. David Goldberger, an attorney with the Illinois branch of the American Civil Liberties Union, represented Collin and his Nazi band in court. For Goldberger, a Jew, the issue was freedom.[49] NSPA bluster going into the case was supplemented by seeming timidity coming out. Faced with the promise of hostile response, from the Jewish Defense League in particular, NSPA decided against marching in Skokie; it demonstrated instead, under heavy police protection, in nearby Chicago.

**THE NEW "POPULISTS"** Far right activism, and the construction of nonparty groups, flourished in the conservative national environment of the 1980s. But the Reagan Revolution enervated the third party-building impulse on the right, because Reagan's initiatives commanded the energetic support of many right radicals as well as conservatives. The Reagan decade would encounter just one hard right achievement of note in fashioning a national electoral third party. Various Klan and Christian Identity groups, collaborating with remnants of the old George Wallace movement, did launch in the early eighties a new creation; with some audacity, they named it the *Populist party*.

The Populist party was Willis Carto's brainchild and creation. A former John Bircher and veteran of the Goldwater and George Wallace campaigns, Carto already enjoyed renown in right-wing circles as founder, in 1957, of the Liberty Lobby. *The Spotlight*, a weekly tabloid published by Liberty Lobby since 1975, is filled with allegations of conspiracy, corruption, and dictatorial design; with tips on how either to resist or to manipulate and use the mainstream's rules and policies; with far right perspectives, along with guarded coverage and selected praise of current events on the right. *The Spotlight* was what guided the Populist party's principles and course during the party's early years.

This new party movement would try to reach some of the same kinds of ordinary folk whose nineteenth century ancestors had been Populists. Bob Richards, an Olympic star, ran in 1984 as the new Populist party's first presidential candidate. Voters in midwestern and southern Farm Belt states, in rural Idaho, and in California (where Richards appeared on the American Independent party line) gave him almost all of his national tally of 66,241.

But Populist party principles—its ideological soul—would be very different from those of the old People's party. Robert Weems, the Populist party's first national chairman, was a Klan activist in Mississippi. The party's mainstream heroes—Senator Jesse Helms and others like him—resided invariably in the right wing of the Republican party. George Hansen's stock with these antiestablishment Populists rose dramatically after that Idaho ex-Congressman's conviction for income tax violations. Hansen gave one of two principal speeches at an important 1987 party conference. The other was delivered by David Duke, one of the best-known figures in the white racial hard right.[50]

This new organized Populism cared not at all about including, or appealing to, African-Americans; white racial feelings were among the principal reasons why it came to life. The party's nomination for the 1988 presidential race went to David Duke, who took 45,869 votes in twelve states. From its early days, the party was riven by sectarian strife. There was the embarrassing spectacle of mutual excommunications by Willis Carto and by California American Independent leader Bill Shearer, two of the leading Populist movers; each registered his own separate Populist party with the Federal Election Commission.[51] Litigation involving the two factions made relationships even more corrosive.

Even so, as the nation entered this century's last decade there were signs that the Populist party still had some vigor. Two of its nominees, one in Kentucky, the other in New Jersey, took an eighth of their districts' votes in 1990 elections for the U.S. House.

James "Bo" Gritz was tapped by the Populists for the 1992 presidential contest. On the ballot in eighteen states, Gritz took more votes than either Richards or Duke before him. It was not the first charge

Gritz had taken up, and it was far from the most glamorous. Years ago Gritz led a Rambo-type raid into Laos to seek and liberate POWs.

## Conclusion

The lives of doctrinal parties are sustained, if for a long time, by their supporters' faithful devotion to party vision and principle. Viewed from the perspective of the pragmatists dominating the political mainstream, the doctrinal parties reside on the other side of an unscalable mountain. The very nourishment of these parties lies in their commitment to creed. But the doctrine itself—its radicalism, the fear and loathing that it summons forth, its seeming irrelevance to what motivates mainstream people, or the purity (dogmatism) of the true believers' doctrinal attachments—has a lot to do with isolating these doctrinal parties. They are, as V. O. Key observed, "in a sense outside the system."[52] Some readers thus will dismiss them as irrelevant, of interest only (if interesting at all) because of their exotic qualities.

Thus, it is worth remembering that doctrinal parties sometimes have influenced mainstream politics. The Prohibition party made its mark on political currents (and in the enactment of the Eighteenth Amendment) during the Progressive Era early in this century.

Consider too the rather congenial years for American Socialists and Communists. The Socialist party had a formidable presence in local government and even some clout in national politics in the years preceding World War I. SP would influence New Deal policies two decades later. CPUSA influenced minority, labor, and intellectual communities in America during the Depression and into World War II.

By the early 1990s, even "mainline denominations" of U.S. socialism and communism had withered down to little more than tiny party sects. CPUSA seemed a partial exception. But the ending of the Cold War and disarray of world Communism exacerbated already-serious recruitment, financial, unity, and morale problems within the ranks of CPUSA. Alexander A. Drosdov, editor of the newspaper *Rossiya*, has revealed that in 1990 a disintegrating Soviet Communist party cut itself loose from its financial commitments to "fraternal" parties—outlays that had totaled $4 billion in the eighties. CPUSA, a needy supplicant, suddenly found itself without its annual grants of at least $2 million.[53] A non-Communist journalist's report on the condition of CPUSA after the failed August 1991 Soviet hardliners' coup estimated party membership at only 2,000–5,000, mostly "elderly Jewish socialists, sixties' peace activists, and disaffected minorities."[54]

CPUSA held its 1991 convention in Cleveland, in an atmosphere of secrecy unparalleled since the passing of the McCarthy era. The time was December, when American newspaper headlines were featuring the collapse of the Soviet Union. CP by then was bitterly divided between orthodox Leninists and liberals, nearly a thousand of whom (maybe a third of the party) had signed a dissident manifesto demanding both party democracy and CPUSA support for building a movement for genuinely democratic and humane socialism. The hardliners, led by Gus Hall (he was holding by then the title National Chair), allowed the liberals one chance to speak: a rousing, impassioned call by historian Herbert Aptheker (a party veteran of fifty-four years' duration) for party reform and renewal. But the hardline group had the power to declare the party's articles of faith: Leninism, centralism, the revolutionary role of the proletariat, and the vanguard party. Hall's group denounced the liberals as a faction (ominous in the Leninist lexicon) and reduced the convention delegations (sometimes refusing to seat anyone) from districts where party liberals were very influential. In what seemed the early stages of purge, the majority removed from party leadership the liberal editor and associate editor of *People's Weekly World* and some of CPUSA's most famous folks, Charlene Mitchell (the African-American who chaired the National Alliance Against Racist and Political Repression) and Angela Davis among them. The Cleveland bloodletting may have prolonged the life of the beleaguered party, but it surely furthered CPUSA's distance from mainstream America. About the convention, one dissident remarked that "Gus Hall and his group turned the CP into a sect. Some people might have thought it was a sect already; there were hundreds of us who didn't think so."[55]

Disturbing signs were arising, meanwhile, that the hard racist right was finding things more congenial in mainstream America. In the eighties and nineties, mainstream Republicans were playing "the race card" with a lot of finesse. The hard right surely watched as the Bush campaign used "Willie Horton" to beat up Dukakis. It saw the visual effect of a black hand in a Jesse Helms ad taking the job "to which you" (presumably a white) "were entitled." David Duke, the former Nazi-Klansman-right-wing Populist, was just one of many hard right folks emboldened to think they might find a home in what once had been the party of Abraham Lincoln.

Of all contemporary hopes in the doctrinal parties, the most defensible (if not wholly reasonable) may well be those of Libertarians. Like many third-party people, Libertarians harbor a real dislike of both major parties. Most Libertarians express particular animosity toward the GOP, the party from which many of them came. This may be because the Republican party makes political capital of many of the antistatist sentiments that are the Libertarian party's raison d'être. Some Libertarians candidly reveal that their dream is someday to replace the GOP in a revamped two-party system in which the Democratic Party might live on.

# Notes

1. This account of the Greensboro massacre and follow-up events is indebted to Wyn Craig Wade, *The Fiery Cross* (New York: Simon and Schuster, 1987), esp. 379–382 and 398–399; and Elizabeth Wheaton, *Codename Greenkill: 1979 Greensboro Killings* (Athens, Ga.: University of Georgia Press, 1987).

2. *Texas* v. *Johnson*, 491 U.S. 397 (1989).

3. *United States* v. *Eichman*, 496 U.S. 310 (1990).

4. Anne Groer, "Libertarian Lark," *The New Republic*, 189 (October 3, 1983), 15–17.

5. "Not Left, Not Right, Not Center," *Liberty Today*, undated tabloid advertisement from Libertarian party.

6. Frank Smallwood, *The Other Candidates: Third Parties in Presidential Elections* (Hanover, N.H.: University Press of New England, 1983), 173–174.

7. John C. Green and James L. Guth, "The Socialization of a Third Party Elite: the Case of the Libertarians," paper presented at annual meeting of South Carolina Political Science Association, Charleston, April 2, 1983.

8. "What is the Libertarian Party?", undated information sheet produced and periodically revised by the Libertarian National Committee.

9. Joseph Sobran, "Andre Marrou: A Man of Ideas," *The State* (Columbia, S.C.), September 7, 1991.

10. On parties of the Socialist and Communist Left, see Harvey Klehr, *Far Left of Center: The American Radical Left Today* (New Brunswick, N.J.: Transaction Books, 1988).

11. June 3, 1981 interview with Simon Gerson and Sophie Gerson, Brooklyn, N.Y.

12. This account of the Socialist Labor party is indebted to Harry W. Laidler, *History of Socialism* (New York: Thomas Y. Crowell Co., 1968).

13. This account of the Socialist party is indebted to *ibid.*

14. Michael Bassett, "The Socialist Party Dilemma, 1912–1914," *Political Parties in American History*, vol. III, ed. Paul L. Murphy (New York: G. P. Putnam's Sons, 1974), 1021–1034; James Weinstein, *The Decline of Socialism in America* (New York: Monthly Review Press, 1967), 27, 84–85, 93, 103, 115; and Christopher Lasch, *The Agony of the American Left* (New York: Vintage Books, 1968), 35.

15. See Smallwood, *The Other Candidates*, 58.

16. See Tom Hayden, *Reunion: A Memoir* (New York: Random House, 1988), 73–102; and Todd Gitlin, *The Sixties: Years of Hope, Days of Rage* (New York: Bantam Books, 1989), esp. 109–126.

17. Kenrick G. Kissell, an undated, untitled letter on the recent history of the Socialist party, available from Socialist Party, USA.

18. See *Highlights of a Fighting History: Sixty Years of the Communist Party, USA*, ed. Philip Bart (New York: International Publishers, 1979), 3–52. Much has been written about the Communist Party-USA. For example, Roger Keeran, *The Communist Party and the Auto Workers' Union* (New York: International Publishers, 1986); Mark Naison, *Communists in Harlem During the Depression* (New York: Grove/Weidenfeld, 1985); Joseph R. Starobin, *American Communism in Crisis, 1943 to 1957* (Berkeley: University of California Press, 1975); Irving Howe and Lewis Coser, *The American Communist Party: A Critical History* (New York: De Capo Press, 1974); James Rorty, *McCarthy and the Communists* (Westport, Conn.: Greenwood Publishing Group, 1972); Max M. Kampelman, *Communist Party v. the CIO: A Study in Power Politics* (Salem, N.H.: Ayer Co. Publishers, 1971); and Robin D. Kelley, *Hammer and Hoe: Alabama Communists During the Great Depression* (Chapel Hill: University of North Carolina Press, 1990).

19. See Simon W. Gerson, *Pete* (New York: International Publishers, 1976).

20. See Stephen Schwartz, "United States of America," *Yearbook on International Communist Affairs, 1990*, ed. Richard Staar (Stanford, Ca.: Hoover Institution Press, 1990), 141. According to these figures, 43% of the delegates were women. 4% were Chicano, 2% Puerto Rican. 60% were under the age of 45, and 40% had been party members for under a decade. One-third of the delegates were members of labor unions.

21. Charles Hobday, *Communist and Marxist Parties of the World* (Santa Barbara, Ca.: ABC-CLIO, 1986), 307.

22. *Dennis* v. *United States*, 341 U.S. 494 (1951).

23. Ann Wagoner, "If You Liked Tiananmen Square, You'll Love This," *Guardian*, September 11, 1991; and Andrea Stone, "Communists in USA Shaken," *USA Today*, August 30, 1991.

24. Schwartz, *Yearbook, 1989*, 148–149.

25. See *The Founding of the Socialist Workers Party*, ed. George Breitman (New York: Anchor Foundation, 1982); James P. Cannon, *History of American Trotskyism* (New York: Pathfinder Press, 1972); Constance A. Myers, *The Prophet's Army: Trotskyism in America: 1928–1941* (Westport, Conn.: Greenwood Publishing Group, 1977); and *The FBI on Trial: Victory of the Socialist Workers Party Against Government Spying*, ed. Margaret Jayko (New York: Pathfinder Press, 1988).

26. The International Working Men's Association, remembered as First International, was founded by Karl Marx and others in 1864 and lasted until 1876. The Socialist International (Second International) was born in 1889, snuffed out by World War I, revived in 1923 as Labor and Socialist International, smothered

in the march toward World War II, and reborn as Socialist International in 1951. The Cominterm, or Third International, was founded in 1919 and formally liquidated by Stalin in 1943.

27. Lawrence Lader, *Power on the Left: American Radical Movements Since 1946* (New York: W. W. Norton and Co., 1979), 71.

28. See Schwartz, *Yearbook, 1989,* 152.

29. John E. Haynes, *Yearbook, 1988,* 128–129.

30. *Ibid.,* 129.

31. This account of other left-doctrinal sects is indebted to Smallwood, *The Other Candidates;* Hobday, *Communist and Marxist Parties;* M. P., *Yearbook, 1970,* 485–489; Harvey Klehr, *Yearbook, 1977,* 501; Klehr, *Yearbook, 1978,* 419–420; Joseph Shattan, *Yearbook, 1981,* 108; Haynes, *Yearbook, 1988,* 129; and Schwartz, *Yearbook, 1989,* 146–53.

32. Simon Strong, "Where the Shining Path Leads," *New York Times Magazine* (May 24, 1992), 12–17, 35; and "Shining Path Winds Its Way Into America," reprinted from *Washington Post* in *The State* (Columbia, S.C.), November 26, 1992.

33. The section on the radical right is indebted to Elinor Langer, "The American Neo-Nazi Movement Today," *The Nation,* 251 (July 16/23, 1990), 82–107; and James Ridgeway, *Blood in the Face* (New York: Thunder's Mouth Press, 1990). Also author's August 5, 1991, telephone interview with Joe Roy, Chief Investigator, Klanwatch Project of Southern Poverty Law Center, Montgomery, Ala.

34. Langer, "The American Neo-Nazi Movement Today," 83; and Ridgeway, *Blood in the Face,* 17.

35. Langer, "The American Neo-Nazi Movement Today," esp. 85. Langer's labeling presents some difficulty, as she concedes; some of the organizations designated "neo-Nazi" by Langer do not identify themselves as such.

36. Ciaran O. Maolain, *The Radical Right: A World Dictionary* (Santa Barbara, Ca.: ABC-CLIO, 1987), 388.

37. Wade, *The Fiery Cross,* 325.

38. Donald A. Downs, *Nazis in Skokie* (Notre Dame, In.: Notre Dame University Press, 1985), 31.

39. Ridgeway, *Blood in the Face,* 66.

40. Author's June 30, 1981, interview with Martin Kerr, *White Power* editor, Arlington, Va.

41. Ridgeway, *Blood in the Face,* 66. Even that figure may be wildly grandiose and inflated. John Rees, the editor of a newsletter on fringe groups, estimated that the American Nazi Party at its peak had some 50 to 60 active members.

42. Dennis King, *Lyndon La Rouche and the New American Fascism* (New York: Doubleday, 1989), 37. Rockwell's group received the legal assistance of the Illinois branch of the American Civil Liberties Union in a 1966 case. *Jewish War Veterans* v. *American Nazi Party,* 260 F. Supp. 452 (1966). A Jewish lawyer secured for Rockwell an acquittal on a disorderly conduct charge in a case in

which the presiding judge was an African-American. Ridgeway, *Blood in the Fact*, 68.

43. Author's June 30, 1981, interview with Martin Kerr.

44. *Ibid.*

45. "Nazi Leader Says Office to Move," *Greenville News*, (S.C.) December 28, 1982.

46. Mike Royko, "'Ol' Daddy o' Mine' isn't a Nazi Favorite," *Chicago Daily News*, June 23, 1977.

47. See Gordon Allport, *The Nature of Prejudice* (Reading, Mass.: Addison-Wesley, 1954).

48. Maolain, *The Radical Right*, 386.

49. *Village of Skokie* v. *NSPA*, 51 Ill. App. 3d. 279; 366 N.E. 2d. 347 (1977); and *Collin* v. *Smith*, 447 F. Supp. 676 (1978). See Downs, *Nazis in Skokie*.

50. Ridgeway, *Blood in the Face*, esp. 129, 131.

51. *Ibid.*, 131.

52. V. O. Key, Jr., *Politics, Parties, and Pressure Groups*, 5th. ed. (New York: Thomas Y. Crowell, 1964), 255.

53. "U.S. Communists Got Soviet Aid," *The State*, (Columbia, S.C.) December 1, 1991.

54. Stone, "Communists in USA Shaken."

55. Statement of "Geoffrey," quoted by Max Elbaum, "Death or Rebirth at Communist Convention?" *Guardian*, December 18, 1991. Also see Carl Bloice, "I Would Call What Happened a Quasi-Purge," *Guardian*, December 18, 1991. Many of the dissidents would withdraw from the Communist party and regroup as the Committees of Correspondence. They worked to form a coalition of radicals on the democratic left.

# Non-National

# Significant Others:

## *Important State and*
## *Community Parties*

*The People's Republic of Burlington*
—caption on a Vermont bumper sticker

Given the conservatism that seemed to characterize the American political mood in the 1980s, the story of Burlington may be startling. Tucked
away in Vermont's northwest corner, Burlington with its 40,000 is by
far the largest city in America's most rural state. Burlington's mayor
during almost all the 1980s was Bernard (Bernie) Sanders. Sanders's rise
contradicted stereotypes about Vermont parochialism. Jewish and with
Brooklyn roots, Sanders also held ideological proclivities one does not
expect to find in rural places like Vermont. Sanders, like many late
twentieth-century politicians, preferred a label other than liberal for
himself. But Burlington's mayor was no conservative. The tag he proudly
and publicly wore was socialist. Friends and enemies alike decorated
their car bumpers with stickers proclaiming the "People's Republic of
Burlington." The mayor preferred symbolism of a different sort: during
Sanders's tenure, the wall of the chief executive's office bore the weight
of a large portrait of Eugene V. Debs, the patron saint of this century's
American socialists.

A new local lexicon reflected Burlingtonians' awareness of their may-
or's uniqueness. Municipal employees often greeted each other as "com-
rade."[1] Locals dubbed Sanders's supporters on the Board of Aldermen
"Sandernistas."[2] Remarks like those, when made by friends, came with
a lot of tongue-in-cheek. Sanders believed in a democratic form of

socialism, and in any case the limited place of local governments in the constitutional scheme of things denied him the authority to create a socialist utopia in northwest Vermont.

More to the point, the mayor always had to contend with Burlington's Republicans and Democrats. In his first successful bid for the mayoralty in March 1981, Sanders ran as an independent. He then joined with other Burlington leftists in constructing a local third party, the *Progressive Coalition* (PC). The PC gathered some support from students and faculty of the University of Vermont and other Burlington colleges and a little from the brie and Beemer liberal yuppie types; but the bulk of its votes came from the elderly, tenants, and working people of the city. PC's successful intrusion into the local mainstream bought for Burlington a status unique in the 1980s: "The only three-party city in America."[3]

In 1988 Mayor Sanders and his PC held six of thirteen seats on the city's Board of Aldermen. The other seven were occupied by Republicans and Democrats. The mayor and his followers sometimes spoke of their opposition as Republicrats or even as the Regressive Coalition. On key votes Republicrat aldermen often combined against Sanders and the Progressives. An anti-Sanders candidate jointly endorsed by Republicans and Democrats won 45 percent of the votes in the March 1987 mayoralty election.[4]

Traditional local power-holders—Democratic and Republican politicians, business people, the utilities, administrators at the University of Vermont and at Medical Center Hospital, and others—bitterly resented Sanders's resort to what they saw as the rhetoric of class warfare. This polemic written by Sanders for the *New York Times* is an example:

> The United States has the lowest turnout of any industrialized nation.... [T]he main reason is that Democratic and Republican candidates have little or nothing to say to tens of millions— mostly the poor, working people, and youth. Both major parties, dominated by wealthy individuals and corporate interests, are deeply out of touch with these citizens.
>
> The two major parties not only fail to provide serious solutions to the enormous problems facing our society but, in many instances, don't even discuss the issues. Given the level of the current political debate, the interesting question is not why half the people don't vote but why half the people do.
>
> The richest 1 percent ... now owns more than half the nation's wealth. While we had a doubling of billionaires within

the last two years, close to three million Americans now sleep out on the streets.[5]

Sanders and the Progressives occasionally managed to tilt local policy in directions more favorable to low and moderate income Burlingtonians. Sanders's city brought about progressive tax reform. It won federal grants for 200 housing units (an accomplishment during an era of funds-slashing and scandalous corruption in Reagan's Department of Housing and Urban Development) and also established a municipal land trust that sells houses but retains ownership of lots. Two emergency shelters with eighty beds for homeless people attracted the attention of national news and talk shows. Major steps came in areas ranging from environmental protection, downtown beautification, and enhanced police protection to women's rights and child care. Burlington infused new life into its neighborhood planning groups, thus encouraging wider citizen participation in local decision making. The size of the voting electorate doubled in the 1980s, testimony perhaps to the excitement generated by the "Sanders factor." *U.S. News and World Report*, arguably America's most conservative major newsweekly, in December 1987 recognized Sanders as one of the nation's twenty best mayors.[6]

Sanders, the PC, and Burlington laid at least one other claim to uniqueness. Burlington in the 1980s was, as *Burlington Free Press* editor James Welch saw it, "the only city in America with its own foreign policy."[7] Mayor Sanders repeatedly spoke out against Washington's support for the Nicaraguan Contras. Under his leadership the city set up "sister" relationships with Yaroslavl in the U.S.S.R. and with Puerto Cabezas, Nicaragua.

Sanders left office in April 1989 on completion of four consecutive two-year terms. His ideological opposite, America's most conservative president in a half-century, had departed Washington three months earlier. Sanders had decided in 1988 that it was time to take his message statewide. Announcing that he would not stand for election to another mayoral term, he ran instead as an independent for Vermont's lone U.S. House seat. October 1988 polls showed him in second place, behind the Republican nominee but ahead of the Democrat. November 8 vote tallies confirmed these surveys' accuracy. Sanders ended with 90,836 votes to 98,653 for Republican Peter Smith and only 45,242 for Democrat Paul Poirier. Sanders's supporters faced the dilemma generally burdening third parties and their followers in America's single member district plurality elections: that their vote might help elect the most ideologically incompatible contestant. A national newspaper referred to Sanders "siphoning votes from the left" and concluded that "Smith probably has a socialist to thank for his elevation to Congress."[8]

Although Smith's plurality was enough for election, a substantial majority of voting Vermonters cast ballots for his socialist and Democratic opponents. But an interpretation more favorable to Sanders than the newspaper's would be that Poirier's supporters not only helped elect Smith but also deprived Sanders's followers of the opportunity, almost unprecedented in the last four decades, to send a socialist voice to Congress. Californian Ronald Dellums has served in the U.S. House since his first election in 1970. Dellums is linked to a non-party group called Democratic Socialists of America; but he runs on the Democratic ticket. A 1988 Sanders victory would have brought the first independent or third-party socialist to Congress since New York American Laborite Vito Marcantonio left that body in 1951.

Sanders's near-miss in the statewide race was, like his four mayoralty victories, remarkable. Leftist intellectuals like Noam Chomsky said that it repudiated observations that America had "moved right." Sanders kindled hopes for a significant partisan third force on the left as America began its approach to the twenty-first century.[9]

As visionary as that dream may seem even now, Vermont returns two Novembers later fanned and fed with some empirical evidence what before had seemed just wishful thinking. In 1990 Vermont voters gave independent congressional candidate Bernie Sanders 117,522 votes. Smith, his incumbent Republican foe, retired from office with just 82,938. Somehow the Democratic candidacy of Delores Sandoval never left ground; Sandoval ended with a pitiful 6,315. The candidate of the tiny Liberty Union party drew 1,965. Sanders had taken 56.3 percent.

Vermont's new House member moved quickly toward alignment with liberal forces on the Hill. The House's lone independent joined 182 of his chamber colleagues (179 Democrats, three Republicans) in saying no to a resolution authorizing President Bush to use military force against Iraq. Whatever they may have thought about Sanders's Desert Storm vote, Vermonters liked their new House member. The voters gave him a landslide 60 percent in 1992, returning him for two more years.

A Vermont editorialist attributed Sanders's voter appeal in Burlington and throughout the state to "charisma and bold convictions." Many Vermonters, it would appear, admired Sanders's fidelity to principle even when they personally disagreed with his perspective on things.[10]

Sanders and the most ideological of his followers must have seen some gathering clouds during the course of the mayor's 1988 House campaign. In October the PC, overriding Sanders' objections, adopted a new rule allowing its future mayoralty nominees to seek endorsement, though not formal nomination, by one or both traditional major parties. A local newspaper columnist chronicled this decision as "pragmatism over political purity."[11] Cooptation, the process by which major parties gobble up third-party ideas and eventually a third party itself, may have begun to work its way through the politics of Burlington, Vermont.

For the March 1989 mayoralty campaign, the Progressives faced a more immediate challenge: Nancy Chioffi, running on a ticket jointly endorsed by Democrats and Republicans, was waging a formidable campaign against PC nominee Peter Clavelle. Moreover, Sandra Baird, nominee of the local Greens party, threatened to take vital votes from Clavelle's leftist base;[12] but Clavelle, lacking Sanders's charisma and name recognition, beat back his Republicrat and Greens challengers, keeping the mayoralty in PC hands. Mayor Clavelle won reelection virtually unopposed in 1991. His PC comrades held their own on the Board of Aldermen. PC also possessed several seats in the Vermont House during the early 1990s.

Although it has the nation's only true three-party system today, Burlington is just one of many cases late in this century in which a significant third force has influenced local politics. A party known as People for Change holds a share of Hartford, Connecticut, city council seats. If you were to visit Santa Monica, Berkeley, or Irvine, you might find that posters proclaim those California cities to be "People's Republics." The radical Berkeley Citizens' Alliance and the Santa Monica branch of the Campaign for Economic Democracy have had considerable community influence or power.

You should take careful note of what Bernie Sanders and other Vermont Progressives have achieved by way of third-party construction but also of what has eluded them, at least for now. The PC is a major force in the politics of a single city which, though Vermont's Big Apple, is small to middle-sized by national standards. The Progressives would like to extend their party organization statewide and even into turf far beyond tiny Vermont. They may even succeed in this. In 1990 Burlington's local PC merged with the Vermont Rainbow Coalition, the statewide remnant of Jesse Jackson's two 1980s presidential bids; together they set up the *Progressive Vermont Alliance*. It was a deliberate, conscious move toward forging a powerful new statewide party.

The national visions of Vermont Progressives still seem grandiose and unlikely for now. In his various campaigns for Congress political circumstances led Bernie Sanders down the path of an independent rather than that of third-party standardbearer. The safest prediction is that

# Hartford's People for Change

A law in Connecticut reserves a third of the seats on city council for independents and minority parties. Through most of the 1980s, Republicans held virtually by default the three "minority" seats on the council of heavily Democratic Hartford.

Things would change in 1987. That was the year that dissatisfied workers and labor organizers, people from Hartford's Puerto Rican and African-American communities, lesbian and gay rights activists, and other left-progressive folks joined to create People for Change. This new party's platforms demand jobs, housing, and decent health care. Its candidates frankly call for redistributing wealth and power. A 1989 People for Change nominee was Hartford's first openly gay council candidate.

The party offers at election time a black, a white, and a Puerto Rican candidate for the city's three minority seats. People for Change took two of these seats in 1987 and again in 1989. It won all three in 1991.

**Source:** Louise Simmons, a University of Connecticut faculty member who is author of several published works on the topic as well as a forthcoming (Temple University Press) book. A political activist, Simmons won election in 1991 as a People for Change council nominee.

future historians will remember the PC and maybe the Progressive Vermont Alliance too as examples, potent ones to be sure, of the non-national significant other third-party type.

Parties of this type are, by definition, important political actors within their own turf. In many places in the last century but mainly in New York state and Connecticut today, some of them have joined with major parties in fusion electoral campaigns. Sometimes contributing the margin of victory in such races, they thus have proved to a major party the importance of its alliance with the third party and the need to defer to policy and patronage demands that their partisan junior partner makes. Occasionally they have induced a major party to nominate as its own the standardbearer of the third party, vastly increasing thereby the likelihood of third-party victory at the polls. Cases of electoral independence, when the third party runs on its own without fusion with a major party, sometimes have brought victory to the third party and thus seats on city councils, in state legislatures, even in Congress. Usually the seats a third party wins, if any at all, leave the party at a distant tertiary level of power and influence far below that of the major parties. There have been occasions when third-party seats were enough for a balancing role in which the party and its officeholders could determine which major party won in legislative voting.

In rare circumstances non-national significant others themselves have become major, even governing, parties in the politics of communities, as with Burlington's PC, or of entire states. Third parties of this particular type have won fifteen state gubernatorial elections, six in the last century, nine in this, in campaigns in which they ran without fusion with one of the national major parties.

But such parties remain electorally confined, also by definition, to the territory of a particular community or set of communities or to the boundaries of a single state. Some non-national significant others begin and end their existence within a specific locality. There are also those that start in a single location, spread to different locations within the state, and may even penetrate structures of state power at the capital. Some have organized statewide from the outset. But whether the result is of choice by the party and its followers or because of external circumstances beyond the party's control, the non-national significant other does not extend its electoral organization beyond the bonds of the particular state which gave it life. Except for those rather unusual cases when a party of this type sends its candidates to Congress, non-national significant others do not extend whatever presence they may have in government to national policy-making councils in Washington.

## Nineteenth-Century Non-National Significant Others

Given the localism or decentralization in American politics of the last century, especially before the Civil War, it is not surprising that the nineteenth century produced many non-national significant others. The earliest of these locally important third-parties were contemporaries of the short-lived Antimasonic party, America's premier national third party. Parties of workers or the underclass sprouted, flourished, and then quickly died in various northern cities before the Civil War: the Workingmen's party in Philadelphia and other Pennsylvania communities in the late 1820s and very early 1830s, New York's State Guardianship party of that same time, and the Antirent party in the New York City of 1839–1845. Because newspapers of the time focused so little on local events outside the area of their own readership, most Americans living then may not have known that these parties even existed.

But as Table 6.1 illustrates, the last century must have brought national fame to several non-national significant others which, despite their territorial confinement, passed at least one of two benchmark tests of political potency: (1) the elevation of one or more of their enrollees to the office of governor in a state, (2) the taking of one or more seats belonging to their state in Congress. These include the Nullifiers, two Conservative parties and the Readjuster party in Virginia, the Law and Order and Union parties of Rhode Island, various state Labor parties in the century's two waning decades, and the Silver party in sparsely settled Nevada. Purists would quarrel with treating the Nullifiers as a single-state party. Pro-nullification sentiment existed in many parts of the South during the 1830s; indeed one Nullifier held a U.S. House seat for Alabama from 1833 to 1837; but the Nullifiers were essentially a South Carolina political party following the leadership of prominent South Carolinian John C. Calhoun.

These important non-national parties of the last century settled at various points on the ideological spectrum. Nullifiers and the pre-Civil War Virginia Conservatives were among the South's agencies defending states' rights and the southern way of life, including its peculiar institution—slavery. The Law and Order party stood for a time in conservative challenge to a state insurgency aimed at reformulating the constitutional foundations and democratizing the political life of Rhode Island. Rhode Island's Union party, like the second Virginia Conservatives, rose in opposition to the power and radicalism of the Republican party. There also were those parties firmly attached to the late nineteenth-century left: the reform-minded Virginia Readjusters; social democratic state Labor parties; and Nevada Silver, with bonds of sentiment and support for the national Populism of the time.

## Non-national Parties in the Twentieth Century

There were times in the nineteenth century—the 1820s, the 1850s, and very nearly in the 1890s—when the national two-party fabric became tattered or wore out entirely. Opportunities thus opened for short-lived national parties and for non-national third parties too to surge toward the mainstream. In the twentieth century, by contrast, the garment generally has held. Transient national third parties have arisen and some brought in impressive returns at the polls. Popular passion for Perot's 1992 independent challenge attests to a substantial loss of public affection

# The Locofoco Party

Locofocos began as a radical faction in the New York Democratic party. They wanted pro-labor legislation, official recognition of trade union rights, property redistribution, and a far more egalitarian condition of property relationships. Their name, ascribed mainly by outsiders, derived from the October 29, 1835 meeting at Tammany Hall during which these radicals broke with the Democratic regulars. Symbolizing this separation, they lit candles using matches known at the time as "locofocos." Having left the Democrats, the Locofoco movement reconstituted itself the Equal Rights party. By the end of 1837, the Democratic party had largely coopted, or gobbled up, this fledgling third party. Locofocos did influence the New York and even the national Democratic party, driving home especially the importance of bringing labor into future Democratic coalition-building strategies. The Whigs derisively tried and partially succeeded in ascribing Locofoco to Democrats and their party nationwide.

**Principal Source:** Hans Sperber and Travis Trittschuh, *American Political Terms* (Detroit, Mich.: Wayne State University Press, 1962), 245–247.

for the Republican and Democratic parties. Even so, these major parties have dominated national electoral politics almost unrelentingly throughout this century. Twentieth-century third-party representation in the U.S. Congress has not come even close to that of nineteenth-century third parties. Never at any one time since 1900 have third parties held more than 3.1 percent of the seats in either Senate or House. Usually the numbers have been far less; third parties were entirely shut out of twenty-one of the forty-six Congresses from the Fifty-seventh (1901–1903) through the One-hundred and Second (1991–1993).[13]

But if the major parties' corner on the national electoral market is a problem for all twentieth-century electoral third parties, it has proven a problem far more costly to the short-lived national parties than to non-national significant others. When transient national parties (or independents) concentrate upon a presidential campaign, they dare enter a domain that the major parties regard as theirs alone. By contrast, presidential contests tend to be of secondary interest, if of interest at

**Table 6.1 Nineteenth-Century Single-State Third Parties Winning Seats in Congress and/or Popular Election of State Governor**

| Party | Time | Location | Party Program | Relations with other Parties | Congressional and/or Gubernatorial Representation |
|---|---|---|---|---|---|
| Nullifiers (mainly S.C.) | 1830s | Major party statewide. Mainly in SC, but nullification sentiment elsewhere in South. One Nullifier elected to House from Ala., 1833 and 1835. | States' rights; support for John C. Calhoun, his "doctrine of concurrent majorities," and his advocacy of state nullification of undesirable federal acts. | Split-away from Democrats | 1831–1833: Senate, 2 seats House, 4 seats 1833–1835: Senate, 2 seats House, 9 seats 1835–1837: Senate, 2 seats House, 8 seats 1837–1839: House, 6 seats States' Rights Democrats sympathetic to Nullifiers selected by legislature for governor: 1830, 1832, 1834, 1836, 1838, and 1840. |
| Conservatives (Va.) | 1837–1841 | Mainly western and northwestern Va. | States' rights; opposition to Martin van Buren | Splinter from Democrats. | 1839–1841: House, 2 seats |

**Table 6.1**—continued

| Party | Time | Location | Party Program | Relations with other Parties | Congressional and/or Gubernatorial Representation |
|---|---|---|---|---|---|
| Law and Order Party (R.I.) | 1842–c.1845 | Major party statewide. | Landowner opposition to democratic Dorr Rebellion and to its Suffrage party. | Some preference for Whigs over Democrats. | 1843–1845: House, 2 seats James Fenner elected governor on Law and Order ticket, 1843, 1844. |
| Union party (R.I.) | 1861–1863 | Significant temporary coalition statewide. | Conservative opposition to GOP "radicalism." | Conservatives from other parties participated. | 1861–1863: House, 2 seats William Sprague elected governor on Democratic-Union fusion ticket, 1861 |
| Conservative party (Va.) | 1869–mid 1870s | Major party statewide. | Opposition to GOP "radicals" and to Radical Reconstruction. | Conservatives from various party backgrounds participated. Eventually coopted by Democrats. | 1869–1871: House, 5 seats Conservative nominee Gilbert C. Walker won governorship, 1869 |

| Party | Years | Area | Program | Notes | Results |
|---|---|---|---|---|---|
| Readjuster party (Va.) | 1879–1884 | Major party statewide. | Reformist; especially readjustment of state debt and of tax system for benefit of yeoman farmers. Interracialist, including blacks. | Participation by (former) Democrats, Republicans, others. Some links to Greenbackers in other states. Eventually merged with GOP. | 1881–1883: Senate, 1 seat; House, 2 seats. 1883–1885: Senate, 2 seats; House, 4 seats. Readjuster William E. Cameron elected governor, 1881. |
| Independent state Labor parties: | | | | | |
| Va. | 1887–1889 | Southwest Va. | Social democracy and workers' rights. | | 1887–1889: House, 1 seat |
| Wis. | 1887–1889 | Milwaukee area. | | | 1887–1889: House, 1 seat |
| Ark. | 1891–1893 | East and northeast Ark. | | | 1891–1893: House, 1 seat |

**Table 6.1**—*continued*

| Party | Time | Location | Party Program | Relations with other Parties | Congressional and/or Gubernatorial Representation |
|---|---|---|---|---|---|
| Silver party (Nev.) | 1893–1901 | Major party statewide. | Bi-metalism; free coinage of silver and many People's party issues. | Links to national People's party and to Silver Republicans of other states. Various factions eventually absorbed by Democrats and Republicans. | 1893–1895: Senate, 1 seat House, 1 seat 1895–1897: Senate, 2 seats House, 1 seat 1897–1899: Senate, 2 seats House, 1 seat 1899–1901: Senate, 2 seats House, 1 seat Silverites John E. Jones and Reinhold E. Sadler won gubernatorial election in 1894 and 1898 respectively. |

**Sources:** Kenneth C. Martis, *The Historical Atlas of Political Parties in the United States Congress 1789–1989* (New York: Macmillan, 1989); and Joseph E. Kallenbach and Jessamine S. Kallenbach, *American State Governors, 1776–1976* (Dobbs Ferry, N.Y.: Oceana Publications, 1977).

all, to parties organized only within the boundaries of single states or communities. Those parties' prime electoral targets are offices back home or, at the most, seats in Congress. Many of this century's most noteworthy non-national significant others have been what historian William Hesseltine called **satellite parties**—associations "exercising local power while still revolving in the orbit" of one or the other of the two nationally acknowledged major parties.[14] Symbiotic relationships often arise between a major party and its satellite. The smaller party may endorse its ally's presidential candidate and receive in return the major party's patrongae or its blessing for races back home.

Thus for many non-national parties, this century has afforded opportunities to depart the periphery, to come into—or close to—the mainstream. Look for example at the non-national parties' share of all third-party U.S. congressional seats. Of the 113 Senate and House seats[15] held by third parties during the Congresses from 1901 through 1992, 68 percent belonged to non-national significant others. Twenty-three percent went to transient national and just 9 percent to continuing doctrinal third parties. During the seventy-one-year period beginning in 1921, non-national parties held an astounding 95 percent of all third-party congressional seats. Single-state parties have won nine gubernatorial elections in this century, three more than parties of that type took in the nineteenth century.

## Significant Single-State Third Parties in the Great Plains and Wisconsin

If someone were to ask you to draw up a list of America's best-known twentieth-century leftist political figures, you might be surprised how many names appeared from the upper Midwest. Your list certainly would include Hubert Humphrey and George McGovern, Robert La Follette, Eugene McCarthy, and Walter Mondale. No one's leftist list ever would include Wisconsin's Joseph McCarthy; even so, you might quickly conclude that the upper midwestern political mainstream has rested several degrees to the left of American mainstream politics elsewhere. Coincidentally or not, Wisconsin and the midwestern Great Plains states enjoy a reputation for perhaps the cleanest, most corruption-free politics anywhere in the country.

Political scientist Daniel Elazar is well known for observing and identifying in America three regionally based political cultures. Traditionalism, in the past at least, affected values in most parts of the South.

**Table 6.2 Twentieth-Century Single-State Third Parties Winning Seats in Congress and/or Popular Election of State Governor**

| Gubernatorial Election | | | | Seats in Congress | | |
|---|---|---|---|---|---|---|
| Party | Year | Candidate | Percent of Popular Vote | Year | Senate | House |
| Union Labor (Minn.) | | | | 1919–1921 | | 1 |
| Farmer-Labor (Minn.) | | | | 1923–1925 | 1 | 2 |
| | | | | 1925–1927 | 1 | 3 |
| | | | | 1927–1929 | 1 | 2 |
| | | | | 1929–1931 | 1 | 1 |
| | 1930 | Floyd B. Olson | 59.30 | 1931–1933 | 1 | 1 |
| | 1932 | Floyd B. Olson | 50.57 | 1933–1935 | 1 | 5 |
| | 1934 | Floyd B. Olson | 44.61 | 1935–1937 | 1 | 3 |
| | 1936 | Elmer A. Benson | 60.74 | 1937–1939 | 2 | 5 |
| | | | | 1939–1941 | 2 | 1 |
| | | | | 1941–1943 | | 1 |
| | | | | 1943–1945 | | 1 |
| American Labor (N.Y.)* | | | | 1925–1927 | | 1 |
| Progressive (Wis.) | 1934 | Philip F. La Follette | 39.12 | 1935–1937 | 1 | 7 |
| | 1936 | Philip F. La Follette | 46.38 | 1937–1939 | 1 | 8 |
| | | | | 1939–1941 | 1 | 2 |
| | | | | 1941–1943 | 1 | 3 |
| | 1942** | Orland S. Loomis | 49.67 | 1943–1945 | 1 | 2 |
| | | | | 1945–1947 | 1 | 1 |
| American Labor (N.Y.) | | | | 1939–1941 | | 1 |
| | | | | 1941–1943 | | 1 |
| | | | | 1943–1945 | | 1 |
| | | | | 1945–1947 | | 1 |
| | | | | 1947–1949 | | 2 |
| | | | | 1949–1951 | | 1 |
| Conservative (N.Y.) | | | | 1971–1973 | 1 | |
| | | | | 1973–1975 | 1 | |
| | | | | 1975–1977 | 1 | |
| Alaska Independence | 1990 | Walter J. Hickel | 38.95 | | | |
| A Connecticut | 1990 | Lowell P. Weicker | 40.36 | | | |

**Sources:** Kenneth C. Martis, *The Historical Atlas of Political Parties in the United States Congress 1789–1989* (New York: Macmillan, 1989); and Joseph E. Kallenbach and Jessamine S. Kallenbach, *American State Governors, 1776–1976* (Dobbs Ferry, N.Y.: Oceana Publications, 1977).

* Organizationally unlinked to the later and more formidable New York American Labor party.

** Loomis died before inauguration day. Position went to Republican lieutenant governor-elect.

Individualism pervades the political life of most of the urban Northeast, Midwest, and Far West. Moralism is alive in rural New England pockets, but it reigns supreme in the rural and mixed rural and urban states of the upper Midwest. Traditionalists see political participation as a privilege and believe the political payoffs should go to the privileged. Individualists emphasize a right of participation; they contend that the rewards belong to those who exercise that right. Elazar's Moralism is the most progressive and visionary of the three cultures, conveying as it does the idea that government is to serve the common weal or the public good. This lofty objective implies active government intervention into the economy. It also directs moralists to see participation as the central duty of good citizenship. Midwesterners were among the earliest to adopt such participatory devices as open primaries, initiative, referendum, and recall. For years upper midwestern voter turn-out has been among the best in the country.[16]

The liberalism inherent in the political culture of the region helped launch midwestern excursions into leftist politics during the first four decades of this century. There also were other stimulants for radical movements in the region. In the Dakotas, Iowa, Kansas, Nebraska, and the rural areas of Minnesota and Wisconsin many farmers recognized themselves as have-nots, victimized by grain elevator operators, railroads, bankers, and the other interests. Workers in Milwaukee, Minneapolis, St. Paul, and other cities likewise had grievances against these powerful interests, and the overlapping concerns sometimes led to united farmer and worker political action.

There was an ethnic base for some of the movements. Twentieth-century Wisconsin saw two important leftist movements, Socialism and Progressivism. Its Socialism lay confined mainly to its base in polyglot but predominantly German Milwaukee.[17] Progressivism, centered in the capital city, Madison, appealed across ethnic lines and throughout Wisconsin; but it drew much of its strength from voters of German heritage. The Minnesota Farmer-Labor party appealed in the Twin Cities and Duluth areas to workers and miners irrespective of their national origins. That party's farmer contingent was mainly Scandinavian. Farmer-Labor was weakest in the fertile Anglo lands of southern Minnesota, much stronger in western and northern areas settled by Swedes, Norwegians, Danes, and Finns. Many of these Scandinavian emigrants had brought with them to Minnesota experiences in the social democratic movements of their native countries.

Midwestern leftists adopted various institutional forms, only one of which was the third party. North Dakota radicals, especially William

Lemke and Socialist party activist Arthur C. Townley, adopted for that state a strategy of infiltrating and dominating the ruling state GOP. In 1915 they organized the Farmers' Nonpartisan Political League which, through its control of the state Republican organization, dominated North Dakota politics from 1917 until 1921. The primary institutional voice for Minnesota radicalism was a third party called Farmer-Labor. Farmer-Labor by the mid-1920s had superseded the Democrats as the principal opposition to the ruling Republicans, and in the 1930s Farmer-Labor was the main governing party in Minnesota. Wisconsin progressivism was more ambivalent than either Farmer-Labor or the Nonpartisan League toward the third-party strategy. Under the aegis and later the memory of their patron saint Robert M. La Follette, Wisconsin progressives long worked, like Nonpartisan Leaguers, within their state's dominant GOP. But Bob La Follette showed some disposition toward the third party approach when in 1924 he left the Republicans and ran a significant race as Progressive party presidential nominee. In 1934 La Follette's progressive heirs organized a state party called Progressive. Wisconsin's third-party Progressives enjoyed a decade as one of the leading parties in Wisconsin politics.

### Nonpartisan League (North Dakota)

Purists may deem it inappropriate to treat the Nonpartisan League as if it were a third party. Although technically an interest group, it successfully employed a party strategy: penetration of the state Republican party and, through mastery of that party, the control of North Dakota politics and policy making. North Dakota's GOP was ripe for the plucking, for it was the dominant party in a state where parties were vulnerable to takeovers through open primaries and the absence of voter registration requirements.[18] Clearly the league was an important third force, indeed the dominant force, in North Dakota politics for a half-decade.

There is no doubt that the league was radical. Whether it should be remembered as socialist depends upon whether you are thinking of Arthur Townley and its other socialist founders and leaders or its largely non-socialist farmer rank and file. Much of the league's platform called for policies or programs easily seen as socialist: state-owned banking, hail insurance, mill and grain elevator operations. One account of Nonpartisan League history dramatically refers to the "red glow on the northern horizon."[19]

Townley seems to have harbored a condescending attitude toward

*Automobile displaying Farmer-Labor poster, circa 1925 (courtesy of the Minnesota Historical Society)*

the league's farmer followers. One of his cohorts remembered Townley's advice to

> make the rubes pay their god-damn money to join and they'll stick—stick 'til hell freezes.... Find out the damn fool's hobby and then talk it. If he likes religion, talk Jesus Christ; if he is against the government, damn the Democrats; if he is afraid of whiskey, preach prohibition; if he wants to talk hogs, talk hogs— talk anything he'll listen to, but talk, talk, until you get his god-damn John Hancock to a check for six dollars.[20]

Despite such demagoguery, the league served its farmer constituents and in some ways the public good as well. Nonpartisan League Republican Lynn J. Frazier was governor from 1917 until 1921. Just before the close of this century's second decade a league-dominated state legislature approved a state elevator, mill, and bank, and a public hail-insurance corporation; established a department of weights and measures and state grain-grading standards; partially exempted farm improvements from taxation; substantially raised the assessed valuation for tax purposes of railroad, electric utility, and bank properties; banned railroads' discrimination in supplying boxcars to cooperative elevators; passed forward-looking labor legislation; extended suffrage to women;

raised the minimum age for leaving school to seventeen; began the consolidation of schools that would eventually eliminate one-room schoolhouses; and initiated a program of adult education in the state.[21]

The league early was subject to ferocious red-baiting attacks from powerful North Dakota economic interests, which found their first really galvanizing issue in the Nonpartisan League's lack of enthusiasm for America's 1917 entry into World War I. Marx had said "the working man has no country." The Socialist party, drawing from Marx and other sources, opposed U.S. participation in the war. League leaders, though pragmatic men, took their cues from that party's position. Eventually offering some tepid support for the nation in arms, they invariably coupled it with slogans like "we will consent to the conscription of our men if you will agree to the conscription of your wealth." That was no music to the patriot's ear.

Eventually weathering that storm, the league was in its prime during the five years beginning in 1917. It lasted, sometimes showing its political muscle, for decades after that. Governor Bill Langer (later he went to the U.S. Senate), a North Dakota populist of the Depression era, was a Nonpartisan Leaguer. Quentin Burdick, elected to the U.S. Senate in 1960 and still there at the time of his death in 1992, learned his politics from a father who spent two decades as a leaguer in the U.S. House. Normally the league ran its candidates as Republicans; but sometimes it was willing to back a Democrat in the general election. In 1956, the league formally switched to the Democrats; but by then it had long since yielded the place it once held as the primary force in North Dakota politics. The league lost its monopoly on October 21, 1921. That was the day when the voters removed Governor Frazier and Attorney General William Lemke in the first statewide recall election America had ever seen. During the recall campaign, the league's adversaries, failing to produce any evidence of criminal acts, were forced to focus upon "mismanagement and poor judgment." Ironically, in 1920 a legislature still controlled by the Nonpartisan League had laid in place the machinery for statewide recall.[22]

### Farmer-Labor (Minnesota)

The league's founders harbored a dream of extending their organization as a national farmers' political movement. Although the league won converts and even enjoyed some influence for a time in South Dakota, Nebraska, Wisconsin, Montana, Idaho, Colorado, and the state of Washington, their dream largely failed. The major exception was in Minnesota where the movement took a very different institutional form, an independent third party named Farmer-Labor.[23] Leaguers initially saw in Minnesota's dominant Republican party and that state's open partic- ipation procedures an opportunity to duplicate the penetration strategy they had used so effectively in North Dakota. But Minnesota, unlike the Dakotas, was urban as well as rural. Minnesotans included a large class of urban workers who, like their country cousins, nursed many legitimate grievances against the corporate interests then prevailing in Minnesota politics. Minnesota-born Arthur Townley and other leaguers ably assisted in Farmer-Labor's creation, and from the beginning farmers' support was as important as workers' to the party. But it was labor leadership that persuaded its league counterpart to accept the third party approach for Minnesota. The Farmer-Labor party first appeared on that state's ballot in 1918, but its full development as an organized coalition of farmers and workers was not complete until 1924. Principal credit for the party's birth and development belonged to William Mahoney, who edited the *St. Paul Union Advocate.*

The party was in some sense the culmination of a long Minnesota tradition of radical protest against exorbitant railroad rates, corrupt grain elevator operators, United States Steel, wealthy ogres, and hard times in general. It was an extraordinary achievement in a country in which radicals, especially socialists, usually have been left in the cold. Americans often are said to be ideological innocents who lack a class consciousness. Farmer-Labor was deliberately class-based, successfully appealing to workers and farmers despite their partially conflicting in- terests. It also received and welcomed support from professionals as well as from some small merchants (petty captialists) insofar as they held interests at odds with big business. Most of Farmer-Labor's founders, however, and many of its leaders were avowed socialists who sometimes articulated its program in unabashedly democratic socialist terms. The most famed and controversial example was in the party's 1934 platform which openly proclaimed the Farmer-Labor vision of a "cooperative commonwealth" for Minnesota and the nation.

Rejecting the cadre organization used by the national major parties, Farmer-Laborites borrowed from European social democrats and created a mass membership organization. Members of trade unions, coopera- tives, and farm groups affiliated with Farmer-Labor were automatically members of the party, their dues paid by the affiliated organization. Other Minnesotans became Farmer-Labor members by joining a ward or township club and paying annual party dues. The party was in several senses radical: frequently in rhetoric, often in style and policy, always in the nature of its organization, and occasionally in its articulated vision of the good society. Most significantly, the party succeeded electorally while most other radical class-based American parties have failed.

A lot of people, both in and outside of Minnesota, dreamed of building a major national party merging agricultural and labor interests. A Farmer-Labor presidential ticket made the ballots of nineteen states in 1920. Parley P. Christensen of Utah, the Farmer-Labor nominee, took nearly one percent of all presidential votes cast that year. This, like all later attempts to forge the national party, finally failed. Thus, Minnesota's independent Farmer-Labor party should be remembered as a third party. But it became a major party in that state, more powerful than the Democrats and eventually overtaking the GOP as well.

In 1922 Minnesotans elected Farmer-Laborite Henrik Shipstead to the U.S. Senate. The party retained that seat until 1940. Two other party nominees won election to the Senate, Magnus Johnson to fill a vacancy in 1923 and Ernest Lundeen in 1936. Twelve won election to the U.S. House, the first two in 1922. In 1932 and again in 1936, Farmer-Laborites won the majority of the states' seats in the U.S. House. Floyd B. Olson, the party's ablest leader, won consecutive gubernatorial elections in 1930, 1932, and 1934. Farmer-Laborite Hjalmar Petersen completed the last months of the deceased Olson's last term, and the party's Elmer A. Benson won that office in 1936. Minnesota's early twentieth-century practice of electing state legislators on a nonpartisan ballot makes estimates of the party's strength in the legislature imprecise. Legislators friendly to the party held lower chamber majorities during some of the 1930s but never in the upper chamber. Farmer-Laborites also held for a time such significant local posts as the Minneapolis mayoralty.[24]

An important Minneapolis thoroughfare bearing his name as well as other memorials remind today's Minnesotans of Floyd Olson's ranking among their state's gubernatorial greats. Olson showed particular concern for poor farmers and workers, who were the core of his party's constituency. Olson's administration initiated several actions to protect desperate farmers from mortgage foreclosures. He, like Governor Benson later on, also intervened in labor strikes. Olson and Benson were extraordinary in that their interventions usually were for the support of the strikers. The Olson administration likewise took action against chain stores, which were encroaching upon small merchants in Minnesota.

In some sense Olson fell within the tradition of American pragmatism. Holding a genuine affection for Franklin Roosevelt, Olson gave little more than lip service to others' efforts to build a national Farmer-Labor party. Olson's Minnesota party tended to keep to the orbit of the national Democrats.[25] For his gubernatorial bids, he formed an All-Party

Group through which Minnesota Democrats and Republicans so wishing might offer their support. Some of these non-Farmer-Laborites found rewards in appointive posts in Olson administrations.

His pragmatism tempered but never neutralized the radical element in Olson. Though delivered at a time when the Depression was convincing many that capitalism was bankrupt, the words in Olson's speech to his party's 1934 convention were even then some of his most controversial. "When the final clash comes between Americanism and Fascism, we will find the so-called Red as the defender of democracy and the super-patriot and captain of industry on the side of mass slavery." Of himself, he said in the speech, "I enjoy working on a common basis with liberals . . . , but I am not a liberal. I am what I want to be—I am a radical." In widely publicized remarks to demonstrators a year earlier, Minnesota's governor had said that if capitalism proved unable to prevent a recurrence of depression conditions, "I hope the present system of government goes right to hell, where it belongs."[26]

Hjalmar Petersen, Olson's unelected interim term successor in 1936 and the party's unsuccessful 1940 and 1942 gubernatorial nominee, was a leader of Farmer-Labor's non-socialist, anti-Communist right wing. But the 1936 election brought to the governor's office Elmer Benson, one of the party's best-known leftists.[27] Benson is remembered as a doctrinaire socialist lacking Olson's tempering pragmatism. Benson's rhetoric and style resembled Olson's most radical. A 1936 radio speech from Chicago had Benson serving "a frightening warning on the capitalistic war lords that if they involve this country in war they must subject their wealth to conscription." The next year the governor told militants of the "People's Lobby" who had stormed through a locked door and were forcibly occupying a committee room at the capital in St. Paul that "it is all right to be a little rough once in a while."[28] In a 1938 campaign speech Benson linked the Chamber of Commerce and National Association of Manufacturers with various fascist associations as "among groups which seek to destroy American democracy."[29]

Farmer-Labor radicalism showed itself as well in official party pronouncements, particularly in the dark Depression days of the early 1930s. The commitment of many of its leaders to a socialist vision won its clearest public expression in the famous or, depending upon your viewpoint, infamous 1934 "Cooperative Commonwealth" platform of the party. That platform well may have been the most radical ever presented by an American party holding statewide major party status. It began with an allusion to the abundant resources, advanced technology, and farm and labor skills which the nation had available to it and to the

# Floyd B. Olson (1891–1936)

Though possessing style remembered as "sometimes coarse and ribald," Floyd B. Olson was a charismatic, riveting speaker, a persuasive champion of the underdog. Olson's calls for change reminded many of an evangelist working the crowd at a revival meeting. He evoked in Minnesotans strong emotions of love or hate. The governor experienced much pain and suffering during his last months, and his death from cancer at the height of his political career brought to his memory a legendary quality not unlike that of the slain President John Kennedy. Yet Olson remains to this day a controversial figure.

Though American-born, Olson was a son of Scandinavia. His mother was Swedish, his father Norwegian. He grew up in the north Minneapolis slums under circumstances conditioning his lifelong self-identification with the underclass. As a young man he was something of a rolling stone. He worked in various jobs in Alaska and in the Pacific coast states. He returned home and put himself through the University of Minnesota law school.

Olson served as County Attorney of Hennepin County (Minneapolis), where he came to be known as a fierce foe of political corruption but as compassionate toward petty offenders. He ran unsuccessfully in 1924 as the Farmer-Labor nominee for governor. That was the contest in which he first discovered his vulnerability to opponents' accusations that he was in league with Communists. By the end of the 1920s the stock market had crashed and the nation was suffering its worst depression. Olson in 1930 became Farmer-Labor's first to win the governorship.

In personality he tended toward Harold Lasswell's political agitator type. Olson described himself as a radical, but his biographer characterized him as more rebel than radical. Yet he also showed some of the pragmatism of Lasswell's political administrator. His doctrinaire followers occasionally criticized him for his accommodations, as in his search for middle ground in the violent 1934 truckers' strike and his failure to push vigorously his party's radical 1934 platform. But it may have been his pragmatism that won for him and his party their statutory achievements in a legislature controlled or partly controlled by conservative opponents.

Under Olson's leadership the legislature in 1933 enacted a graduated state income tax that sharply reduced state reliance upon the regressive propery tax. Olson also led the state to acts banning yellow dog (anti-union) contracts and antistrike injunctions and postponing farm mortgage foreclosures. No other Farmer-Labor leader accomplished as much as he.

**Principal sources:** William E. Lass, *Minnesota* (New York: W. W. Norton, 1977) and George H. Mayer, *The Political Career of Floyd B. Olson* (Minneapolis: University of Minnesota Press, 1951).

ironic situation in which millions found themselves unemployed, degraded, and in want—conditions which the party held to be inherent in the system itself:

> Palliative measures will continue to fail. Only a complete reorganization of our social structure into a cooperative commonwealth will bring economic security and prevent a prolonged period of further suffering .... We therefore declare that capitalism has failed and that immediate steps must be taken by the people to abolish capitalism in a peaceful and lawful manner and that a new, sane, and just society must be established; a system where all the natural resources, machinery of production, transportation, and communication shall be owned by the Government and operated democratically for the benefit of all the people and not for the benefit of the few.[30]

By congressional action the farmer was to have secure tenure, or greater security at any rate, to his land. Banking was to be nationalized and lending was to become a government monopoly operated on a nonprofit basis. Public utilities, water power, transportation and communication, mines, packing plants, and factories, with the exception of genuinely cooperative enterprises, were to be publicly owned by state or federal government. Idle factories were to be seized by government and operated for the benefit of the needy. In Minnesota insurance was to become an exclusive function of the state, which would provide nonprofit programs of employment, retirement, health and maternity, natural disaster, and life insurance. The redistribution of wealth was to come through heavily graduated taxes on incomes, gifts, inheritances. Consumers were to be free to establish cooperatives. Minnesota voters were to have the opportunity, through amending their constitution, to establish a public electric power system. School textbooks were to be publicly printed and freely distributed to Minnesota's children.

Few of these proposals ever made the statute books. Most were calls for made-in-Washington national policies, and despite the Depression neither the national environment nor the Roosevelt administration was disposed to changes so drastic. In Minnesota itself the platform was roundly condemned, even by rightists within the party, and Farmer-Labor suffered sharp red-baiting attacks from outside. Although the party did not repudiate its 1934 platform, it issued a lengthy explanation that its intent only had been to propose what Scandinavians know as the "Middle Way"—a socialized economy but democratic polity.[31]

Minnesota voters punished the party by handing defeats to many of its 1934 candidates. Olson won reelection, but his plurality was smaller than the combined totals for his Republican and Democratic opponents. By 1936 Farmer-Labor had recouped its losses; Minnesotans elected Benson to the governorship and Farmer-Laborites to a majority of the state's U.S. House seats. But in 1937 Benson gave his sympathetic and impolitic speech to the People's Lobby and his party went into a tailspin from which it never really recovered.

Farmer-Labor lost the gubernatorial elections of 1938, 1940, and 1942. Farmer-Labor relations with the national Democrats and Franklin Roosevelt had ranged from businesslike to cordial, and many Farmer-Labor leaders considered themselves to be left-New Dealers. The 1940s brought sentiments among leaders both of Farmer-Labor and of Minnesota's Democrats for merger, sentiments substantial enough by 1944 to carry the day.[32] The two parties became the Democratic-Farmer-Labor party, a marriage that by 1948 was for all intents and purposes irrevocable. From 1944 to this very day, Minnesota voters have found the DFL on their ballot as the major opposition to the state Republican Party. Democratic presidential nominees run in Minnesota as DFL'ers.

Cooptation seems an inescapable ingredient in the story of this merger. Throughout the FDR era Farmer-Labor revolved in the national Democratic orbit and that may have been only one step removed from the eventual full integration into the Democrats' national machinery. But it would be grossly inaccurate to infer that Minnesota's Democratic party was the principal coopting agency. Until its very end as an independent party, Farmer-Labor appealed to many more Minnesota voters than did the Democrats. Farmer-Laborite Petersen in 1942 won 299,917 gubernatorial votes, compared to 409,800 for a popular incumbent Republican but only 75,151 for the Democratic nominee. Historians say that even at the time of merger the state Democratic party was little more than an organizational funnel for national Democratic patronage.

The story of Farmer-Labor's relations with national and state Democrats to its right makes for interesting reading, but no more interesting and perhaps no more important than that of its relationship to organizations to its left. From 1925 on Farmer-Labor's constitution bore a provision barring from membership any person or oganization "advocating political or economic change by means of force . . . or revolution or advocating any other than a representative form of government." It is clear that this provision was intended mainly to mute charges of bolshevist influence in the party. The party used no special vigor in its enforcement. The stipulation did symbolize Farmer-Labor commitment to evolutionary change and a democratic system.

Various groups of Trotskyists made several largely unsuccessful attempts in the 1930s to influence Farmer-Labor politics. Historians who today specialize on Farmer-Labor history divide, not on the influence of these Trotskyists, but on the extent to which Stalinists of the Communist Party-USA were able to penetrate Farmer-Labor and, through it, to affect Minnesota politics for a time.

In the early 1920s American Communists worked to penetrate and influence Farmer-Labor. But in 1924 the Comintern endorsed a new line, the proletarian revolutionary strategy. What this meant for Farmer-Labor from 1924 until 1935, when the line changed again, was unyielding hostility from the Communist party. Indeed one reason why in the long run Olson contained the political fallout from the 1934 platform disaster was that he was able to cite chapter and verse the many sharp criticisms that the Communists had leveled against him and his party.

The Comintern line shifted in 1935, this time to a popular front by Communists with liberals, progressives, and socialists interested in, or who might be persuaded to become interested in, a world defense against fascism. In Minnesota itself the first enunciation by Communists of the popular front line virtually coincided with the 1936 victory of the Farmer-Labor left wing in the person of Elmer Benson. Though no Communist himself, Benson was far from reluctant to work with Communists in what he considered to be a common cause. Some Communists held appointive posts in state government during the two Benson years. Even a rather sappy biography of the governor concurs that "the term 'red' when applied to anyone fighting on his side aroused . . . [Benson's] passionate soul to deep and bitter indignation. . . . Nor did he think it improper to accept support of so-called 'reds' or to use their talents to advantage in government jobs."[33]

So what is to be made of the allegations of Communist influence, even control, of Farmer-Labor? Scholars are really divided on this issue. Those who embrace the Communist thesis stress the 1930s ascendancy in Minnesota and elsewhere of the Congress of Industrial Organizations with Communists prominent in its leadership and the withdrawal of many farmers and of some of the American Federation of Labor contingent from Farmer-Labor participation at the very time of increasing CIO activity in the party. They also point to strong Communist support in the 1936 election to Congress of Farmer-Laborite John T. Bernard, a militant ex-miner. Bernard was the only member of Congress to vote against American neutrality in the Spanish Civil War, a war in which Soviet Russia was deeply engaged. The most convincing exponent of this Communist thesis may be Arthur Naftalin, a Minnesota historian who also was a Democratic activist at the time of the Democratic-Farmer-Labor merger. After the birth of DFL he served various state and local posts, four terms as Minneapolis mayor among them. Naftalin contends that by the time of the merger, Farmer-Labor had become "in terms of its controlling elements virtually a Communist front organization." He suggests indeed that Farmer-Labor willingness to merge may be explained by Communist hope, ultimately thwarted, to penetrate the state and national apparatus of the Democratic party.[34]

There are others who maintain that the question is irrelevant and warn against resurrecting the red baiting spirit of McCarthyism. Still others concur that the question is pertinent but contend that those such as Naftalin substantially overstate Communist strength in Farmer-Labor. James M. Youngdale, for instance, agrees that "Communists . . . came to have some influence" in the party, but he says that the extent of that influence has been "overdramatized." For Youngdale and others of his persuasion Democratic desire to coopt goes much further than Communist hopes for influence in explaining the 1944 merger of Democrats and Farmer-Laborites.[35] It may be a fact of no little importance that Farmer-Labor's last gubernatorial nominee, Petersen, was prominent in his party's right wing. This strongly suggests that until the very end of Farmer-Labor's independent existence its base, many times larger than that of Minnesota Democrats, was essentially non-Communist and perhaps even anti-Communist.

### Progressive Party (Wisconsin)

The leaders of Wisconsin's Progressive Party had their ties with Minnesota Farmer-Laborites. Progressive Governor Philip La Follette gave the oration at the 1936 public funeral of Floyd Olson in Minneapolis, and Progressives participated alongside Farmer-Laborites and others in late 1930s conferences exploring the possibility of creating a significant national party on the left. They also built bridges to Milwaukee Socialists and other radicals in and out of Wisconsin. In common with these other third parties, Wisconsin's Progressives found themselves victimized by charges from conservatives that they were reds or at least fellow-travelers.[36] Such rhetoric was particularly overblown and inaccurate when it came to the Wisconsin Progressive party. Unlike most other significant midwestern third party movements before the close of World War II, the Wisconsin Progressives should be remembered as liberals far more than as radicals. Admittedly, leaving the protective confines of the two-party system always requires something of a radical spirit.

Although its day in the sun lasted the decade following its 1934 creation, the Wisconsin Progressive party was ideological heir of the Progressive Movement in this century's earliest decades. More specifically, its lineage traced from Wisconsin's "Fighting Bob" La Follette and that elder La Follette's 1924 national third party venture at the twilight of his life. The Wisconsin Progressive party's principal architects were in fact Fighting Bob's sons, Philip and Robert, Jr., who had in 1924 directed their dad's national third-party campaign for the presidency.

Robert La Follette, Jr., won election as a Republican in 1925 to succeed his dead father in the U.S. Senate. Voters reelected him on that party's line in 1928. Philip La Follette won the governorship as the GOP nominee in 1930. Seeking reelection two years later, Philip was defeated in the Republican primary by a conservative challenger, who lost out in turn in the 1932 Democratic landslide.

Although they had inherited their father's place of leadership of the usually dominant progressive wing of the Wisconsin GOP, the two younger La Follettes in the early 1930s found themselves ideologically out of touch with the course of national Republicanism and far more in tune with the directions of FDR and the national Democrats. The La Follettes cherished the word progressive and also realized that Wisconsin voters approvingly linked it to the La Follette tradition of clean and affirmative government. When the decision came for a third party there really was no doubt what its name would be. Franklin Roosevelt, who regarded Philip and Robert, Jr., as good New Dealers, gave his blessing to their act of third-party creation.[37]

The new party enjoyed its peak success during the year of its birth. In 1934, the Progressives won the governorship (Philip), a seat in the U.S. Senate (Robert, Jr.), a majority in the state legislature, and most of the Wisconsin seats in the U.S. House. But the results of elections in the late 1930s and early 1940s brought to the party troubling signs that Wisconsin was not immune to a national trend toward the right. Philip won reelection as a Progressive in 1936. In 1938 he lost out to the Republican nominee. The Progressive party won the gubernatorial election of 1942; but its victorious candidate, Orland Loomis, died before inauguration day, and the Republican lieutenant governor-elect took the oath of office. Robert Jr. enjoyed the fruits of senatorial victory one last time in 1940. Although gubernatorial and other campaigns were offered to voters on a Progressive line until 1952, the party, drained of its life's blood, essentially disbanded in 1946.

Robert, Jr., ran in 1946 not as a Progressive but for nomination by a state Republican party that had fallen into conservative hands by the secession of progressives in 1934. Like Robert, Jr., many other Progressive leaders and followers deserted to the Republicans or Democrats in the 1940s. The candidate who defeated Robert, Jr., for the nomination and then took the "La Follette seat" was Joseph R. McCarthy. Senator McCarthy went on to renown or infamy as America's leading red baiter, and his memory still wins praise from some American conservatives. If that were not irony enough, there is one other fact little known to non-Wisconsinites. In 1946 McCarthy's candidacy won the backing of state Communists as well as conservatives. Senator La Follette had incurred the ire of Communists for his strong words against Soviet expansionism at the close of World War II.[38]

Despite its short life span, the Wisconsin Progressive party and the two La Follettes who led it amassed an extraordinary achievement record. Philip La Follette's first (Republican) administration secured passage of a public works program which put unemployed citizens to work and also improved Wisconsin's transportation infrastructure. In 1932 Wisconsin became the first state to provide unemployment insurance. This act was the precedent for federal social security legislation enacted in 1935. During his second and third terms Governor La Follette and his Progressive forces in the legislature established public agencies for electric power, to provide farmers with marketing assistance, to set fair standards for business competition, and for the settlement of labor disputes. In the Senate Robert, Jr., played important roles in the drafting and enactment of legislation for assistance to drought-stricken farmers and to people out of work. He also investigated employer use of spies to infiltrate labor organizations.[39]

The brevity of Wisconsin Progressive party existence underscores a very common theme in the record of third parties in America. In its prime possessing, and using, the power to determine the policy course in home state Wisconsin, this Progressive party saw many of its programs coopted by Franklin Roosevelt and the Democratic party in Congress.

Thus, in national policy the transient party staked claim to a considerable legacy.

## Significant Others in New York's "Modified Two-Party System"[40]

In this century Republicans and Democrats have held center place in New York state politics as continuously as anywhere in the country. No twentieth-century New York third party ever has intruded into the ranks of the major parties statewide. But New York is extraordinary in having had, and still having, third parties so significant that they modify the pattern of two-party dominance. The longevity of some New York third parties also is remarkable considering the rapid burnout of most American nonmajor parties.

When you ask why the significance of New York third parties, the answers lead in different directions. New York certainly is one of America's most heterogeneous states, and the wide range of political opinion coaxes some New Yorkers to break out of the confines of two-partyism. But much the same could be said about California, and in California "modified" is an unnecessary and inaccurate prefix in characterizing the party system.

The more potent explanation for the significance of New York third parties is institutional. New York law allows candidates for office to receive nominations from more than one party and to have their votes under the various party labels added together in determining the general election winner. This is a practice known as **cross-endorsement.** Except in judicial elections, it is rare for New York's major parties to join in endorsing the same candidate. The law's main effect is that New York elections frequently feature fusion candidacies in which third parties influence by rewarding, with their sometimes decisive endorsements, major party candidates for fidelity or promised devotion to what interests the third party.

Fusion candidacies were common in many parts of America in the nineteenth century, when parties printed and distributed their own election ballots. But when states took over the ballot-printing prerogative, most states prohibited the name of a candidate from appearing more than once in the same contest. Fusion candidacies virtually joined the dinosaurs as a result. New York's statute is quite extraordinary in allowing cross-endorsements on the ballot. Today, except for New York, just Connecticut and Vermont allow this practice.

The *Liberals* and *Conservatives*, New York's leading contemporary third parties, take full advantage of this law. The single issue *Right-to-Lifers* do likewise. So did the *American Labor party* until its 1956 demise. New York third parties often demand patronage returns for their endorsements of major party candidates. Liberals in particular have been inclined to covet judgeships as attractive returns for rendered service of this kind. Contributions to third-party treasuries often become the expected payoff for a candidate endorsement. The Liberal party agreed in 1980 to extend its ballot line to presidential candidate John Anderson, but only after the Liberals had forced Anderson's New York handlers to give up their plan to run their man on a separate, independent line too. (This Liberal demand was anything but beneficial to Anderson's campaign. But since Anderson's New York vote on the Liberal line was larger than the difference between Reagan's and Carter's there, Liberals could tout their party's significance in presidential politics as it is played New York-style.) The state's third parties also have ideological and policy agendas. Liberals have tried to pull the state Democratic party leftward. The Conservatives seek a rightward shift by the GOP. Key issues— capital punishment, for instance (Conservative party), or abortion (Right-to-Life party)—become litmus tests as these third parties query major party candidates seeking their endorsement and line.[41]

These parties also can and do punish. They may sit out the contest or run their own candidate. Sometimes Liberals even will endorse a progressive Republican or Conservatives will endorse an ideologically acceptable Democrat. It is never required that the third parties wait for major party endorsement to give their own. The Conservatives gave a real boost to U.S. Senate hopeful Alphonse D'Amato in 1980 and the Liberals to gubernatorial candidate Mario Cuomo in 1982 by endorsing them before the major parties got down to the business of deciding.

Thus, New York's law allows third parties to adjust themselves— even commit themselves—to the system of two major parties. At the same time they also enjoy some influence upon the electoral and the policy processes as well as returns in the patronage network. It also resolves a third-party problem of long standing: the argument that a third-party vote may contribute to the victory of the more ideologically incompatible major candidate. In fusion campaigns, New York third parties can support their ideological kin in a major party. On occasion they are able to demonstrate that their third-party's contribution at the polls made the difference between victory and defeat.

Most of the state lawmakers in Albany are elected on fusion tickets. In 1986 for example, 73.5 percent of the winners' names appeared more than once on the election ballots. But most are themselves Democrats or Republicans. As you might guess, they have been much less enthusiastic than are the third-party loyalists about this ballot procedure. Several times legislation has sought to reduce third-party electoral influence or even to eliminate the cross-endorsement ballot entirely. In 1947 the legislature did require a person enrolled in one party to secure permission of the committee of another party before running for the other party's nomination. Allegations that the American Labor party was aligned with the Communists prompted this legislation. What it meant immediately was that American Laborites no longer could seek to capture major party ballot lines without approval by the organization of the targeted major party.[42] The 1947 law continues in force today. But the New York judiciary has found constitutional arguments to overturn the other statutory assaults on cross-endorsement balloting.

The American Labor party was born in 1936, the progeny of New York labor leaders, particularly David Dubinsky of the International Ladies Garment Workers and Sidney Hillman of Amalgamated Clothing Workers. Although never a major statewide party, the ALP for some fifteen of its twenty-year life held near-major status in its New York City base. ALP was very active in anti-Tammany fusion politics in the late 1930s and early 1940s.[43] Its 1937 line contributed 482,790 votes (nearly the margin of victory) to the reelection of reform Mayor Fiorello La Guardia, a registered ALP member. Under the rules of a borough-based Proportional Representation (PR) system adopted in New York City in 1936 and used until 1947, ALP went on to elect members to the city council. ALP's most stunning success came in 1948 when American Labor Congressman Vito Marcantonio, running without major party endorsement, won reelection from New York's Eighteenth District. Marcantonio originally had won as a Republican in 1934 and in five later victories (1938, 1940, 1942, 1944, and 1946) he had benefitted from fusion campaigns. But New York's legislature passed its 1947 statute to "screw Marcantonio" and in 1948 the Congressman won without either Republican or Democratic help on the ballot.

Though city-based and thus drawing little support from upstate farmers, ALP bore many similarities to Minnesota Farmer-Labor. FDR gave ALP his blessing at the point of its birth just as he had blessed Olson era Farmer-Laborites and the Wisconsin Progressives. National Democrats believed ALP would help garner union and individual support for Roosevelt and the New Deal and they may have envisioned it as a satellite party in the national Democratic orbit. In some ways ALP fulfilled these expectations. But like Farmer-Labor, ALP's avowed socialism placed it to the left of the Democrats.

New York conservatives charged, as their Minnesota counterparts did about Farmer-Labor, that ALP was under the heavy influence of Communists. Evidence supporting this seems more conclusive with regard to ALP than to Farmer-Labor. In 1938 Communist leaders privately circulated their preference for the Democratic/American Labor fusion gubernatorial candidate Herbert Lehman, an act augmenting his electoral tally by an estimated 100,000 votes.[44] Lehman's margin of victory was less than 89,000, making plausible later Communist claims that their party had determined the winner of that important race. In 1940, at a time when the Comintern had interrrupted its popular front line, pro-Roosevelt APL'ers barely succeeded in securing their party's endorsement of the president's bid for a third term. Peter Cacchione and Benjamin Davis, two Communist party enrollees who held seats on New York's city council during World War II, enjoyed allied working relationships with ALP in election campaigns and while on council.[45]

It was evidence like this that led David Dubinsky and other anti-Communist leftists to withdraw from ALP in order to create the Liberal party in 1944. Their departure deepened Communist influence in the party they deserted. In 1948 Henry Wallace ran "against the Cold War" and for the presidency as a Progressive. His name appeared in New York on the ALP line. Wallace's campaign won active support from the Communist party as well as from some non-Communist leftists. Forty-four percent of his 1.2 million votes came from New York state, mostly from the Big Apple.

Of the two most important contemporary New York third parties, the Conservative party is the younger. Conservative Republicans alienated from their party and specifically from its progressive Rockefeller-Javits wing founded the Conservative party in 1962. Like the Democrats and Republicans, the New York Liberal and Conservative parties enjoy automatic ballot access. So does the Right-to-Life party. A third party achieves (and holds) that status when its gubernatorial candidate takes, on the party's line (the candidate may be endorsed by other parties too), at least 50,000 votes. (In a state the size of New York, that is a generously low threshold requirement. Someone taking just 50,000 votes today would be taking only about 1 percent of all votes cast.) Independents and candidates of every other third party in the state must collect and file petitions (20,000 signatures for a statewide race) to secure a place on the ballot.

Ideological compatibility increases the likelihood that Liberals and

Conservatives will enter into fusion candidacies with their "natural partners." During the Conservative party's pre-Reagan era, when Rockefeller-Javits progressivism usually prevailed in the New York GOP, Conservatives showed more estrangement from their natural partners (the Republicans) than Liberals did from the Democrats. But the Republican-Conservative quid pro quo has since become at least as intimate as the one between Democrats and Liberals.[46]

Bill Clinton ran in New York on both the Democratic and Liberal lines in 1992. Clinton took the state despite George Bush's cross-endorsement by Republicans, Conservatives, and Right-to-Lifers. Incumbent U.S. senator Alfonse D'Amato, running on the Republican, Conservative, and Right-to-Life lines, narrowly beat back a determined challenge by Democrat/Liberal Robert Abrams.

Fusion campaigns sometimes produce clear-cut triumphs for a third party. In 1988 S. R. Maltese, running on lines of the Conservative, Republican, and Right-to-Life parties for state senate, took 55 percent of the vote in his district in heavily Democratic Queens. That victory may have been 1988's sweetest for the Conservatives. Maltese was Conservative party's state chairman.[47] Bernhard H. Goetz, controversial patron of the vigilante spirit, caused a minor stir by attending Maltese's swearing in as invited guest of the new Senator.

Those occasions of Conservative and Liberal electoral independence sometimes produce impressive results. Liberals' proudest triumph may have come in 1969, when New York City Mayor John V. Lindsay won reelection on the Liberal line. Lindsay first won the office in 1965 as a Republican, but he lost the GOP primary in 1969. Success was sweeter still for the Conservatives a year later. In 1970 Conservative nominee James Buckley won the U.S. Senate seat held by Republican/Liberal Charles Goodell. Some elements of the GOP establishment dissociated themselves from Goodell and tacitly supported Buckley. Even so, the Buckley victory was a spectacular triumph for a third party. In 1990 Conservative gubernatorial nominee Herbert London, facing both the Democratic/Liberal incumbent Mario Cuomo and a Republican, took a most impressive 20.4 percent vote share.

New York Liberals and Conservatives occupy a tertiary level of partisan influence, well behind the Democrats and Republicans. Other third parties exist in the state, but they are more distant still from mainstream currents. In 1978 the gubernatorial nominee of the *Right-to-Life party* (RTL) polled 130,193 votes; thus, RTL joined the two major parties and the Liberals and Conservatives as a party entitled automatically to appear on the ballot.

RTL was born as a single issue component of the anti-abortion movement three years before the 1973 *Roe* v. *Wade* decision. It was the brainchild of a small group of homemakers in Merrick, a Long Island town forty miles east of New York City. Ellen McCormack, one of RTL's principal founding mothers, ran token campaigns for the presidency in 1976 and 1980.[48] A parochial school-educated suburban wife and mother of four children, McCormack had no political experience before her RTL days. RTL candidates, generally doctrinaire political novices, usually manage to take less than a third of the votes of New York's anti-abortion constituency.[49]

Robert Spitzer, an authority on RTL, conducted a survey in 1983 of thirty-two RTL leaders and 217 identifiers. He found that a majority of identifiers and 47 percent of the party's leaders were female. Most were New York state natives, married, and of moderate income. Their median age was thirty-something. The largest number were either professional-technical workers or full-time homemakers. The majority of followers had not graduated from college. Most of Spitzer's respondents labeled themselves either moderates or conservatives. Eighty-four percent of the leaders and 71 percent of the identifiers were Roman Catholics (most others were fundamentalist Protestants), and well over two-thirds said they were in church weekly. Most of the leaders would deny abortions to women under any circumstances; 70 percent of the identifiers said, about abortions, either never or only to save the mother's life.[50]

RTL fusion campaigns far more frequently link with Republicans and Conservatives than with Democrats. But Right-to-Lifers are a long way from the intimacy with other parties that Conservatives and Republicans now share. RTL did join the Republicans (and Conservatives) in fusion presidential and U.S. Senate campaigns in 1992. But RTL ran its own candidates for president and U.S. Senate in 1988. William Marra, the 1988 RTL presidential candidate, won just 22,148 votes, all of them in New York state.[51] U.S. Senate candidate Adell Nathanson did a bit better: 63,447, some 1 percent of the votes in a race against incumbent Democrat Moynihan and Republican Robert R. McMillan. In 1990 RTL weathered a threat to its automatic ballot access; under state law, a party must take at least 50,000 gubernatorial votes to retain that status.[52] RTL's vote, though just 3.4 percent of the total, was a comfortable 137,804.

## Conclusion

It is easy to think of American third parties as candles in the wind. Short-lived national parties often have given off considerable light, especially in their nineteenth-century golden age, before being snuffed out by the course of political events. Continuing doctrinal parties have been steady and interesting fixtures of our own century. But their glow usually has proven too weak and dim to penetrate the main arena of American politics.

But those single-state parties—the associations we have called the non-national significant others—are a different matter. Despite all barriers of culture and structure, some of these non-national parties have managed to scale the wall between periphery and mainstream. They have become, sometimes for decades, important, major, or even governing actors in states and communities. Episodes of their illumination cover the more than a century and a half of American third-party history. Despite the closure seen in this century—sometimes onerous state statutory requirements for ballot access, disincentives to fusion campaigns, the prohibitive costs of campaigning and of television advertising, wide use of nonpartisan local elections—recent prospects, if not exceedingly bright, have seemed brighter for single-state parties than for other third-party types. After all, Burlington's Progressives are alive and well, and New York's Conservatives, Liberals, and Right-to-Lifers are doing alright.

The nineteenth and twentieth centuries have fostered contrasting themes in the relationships held by single-state parties with the national major parties. In the last century, those periodic breaks and near-breaks in the national two-party system afforded true independence for some state third parties. Steady Republican and Democratic domination of national partisan electoral politics in the twentieth century produced the contrasting pattern of state satellite parties, important non-national third parties which, though formally independent, received the tacit or official blessing of some national major party. Often they returned the favor by backing the major party's nominees in presidential campaigns. Minnesota Farmer-Laborites, New York American Laborites, and in some sense the Wisconsin Progressives were satellites of the Democrats. Sometimes, as with Farmer-Labor, the major party coopting magnet eventually proved strong enough to suck all semblance of independence from the satellite party. Today's New York Conservatives and Liberals operate within the orbits of one or the other major party.

The two centuries also have occasioned contrasting ideological themes. Our century's most important state third parties have tended to the left. This generalization does bear exceptions, like the Conservatives and Right-to-Lifers in New York. But remember Minnesota Farmer-Labor and Wisconsin's Progressives, whose entry to the central arena came as a consequence both of regional culture and of the havoc rendered by the Great Depression. American Labor and Liberal in New York and today's Burlington Progressives likewise validate the observation about the success of the left in constructing single-state parties.

In the nineteenth century, both left and right met some success in crafting non-national third parties. Leftists built the Virginia Readjuster and Nevada Silver parties as well as some important independent Labor parties. But that century's tilt in single-state party construction and success was to the right. South Carolina Nullifiers, two important Virginia Conservative parties, and Rhode Island's Law and Order and Union parties all represented conservative reactions to the thrust of nineteenth-century change.

Most living Americans never encounter a significant non-national third party. Burlington's Progressives have fashioned for their city America's only true three-party system today. Third parties do reasonably well in New York, due in large part to the law allowing ballot cross-endorsement. Many political scientists who are acquainted with New York state politics propose cross-endorsement for consideration by other states. There are signs of new third-party life in neighboring Connecticut, in part because cross-endorsement exists there too.

It would be difficult to ensure that the adoption of cross-endorsement elsewhere would bring about the intended effect. California in 1960 abandoned a long-maintained cross-filing law that had authorized candidates to file in the primaries of more than one party. The results in the Golden State had proven far more burdensome than beneficial to the smaller parties, for most of the cross-filings had been with both major parties. The intricacies in crafting a law, sustainable in court, that would ensure New York rather than California results might prove finally insurmountable.

Even so, cross-endorsement's New York success seems to merit taking some risk. Wider adoption of cross-endorsement could substantially benefit the third-party cause. But the principal beneficiaries might well be the citizens of adopting states through the broadening and deepening of the representational process. It might even have some positive impact on our scandalously low rate of voter turn-out in America.

One should not count on the nation's legislators, virtually all of them Democrats and Republicans, volunteering to make such a reform. Improving the quality of representative government may rank lower on most politicians' priorities list than preserving their own prerogatives and influence. It seems more likely that New York would abandon cross-endorsement than that many other states would adopt it in the years soon coming.

Yet unforseen events occur all the time, and you should never think a resurgence of non-national third parties is impossible. Most people, after all, did not forecast the Great Depression. That sad occurrence was a boon to the third-party cause in America. Dislocating changes in the party system's environment, most likely resulting from a continuing failure of Washington politicians in the 1990s to resolve the nation's crushing distributive, debt, balance of trade, and savings-and-loan problems, could become the spark for important new non-national or even national parties as America moves into the next century.

# Notes

1. Nancy Shulins, "Socialist Mayor of Burlington" (Associated Press/National Distribution), July 3, 1988.

2. Allan R. Gold, "Exit a Socialist, to Let History Judge," New York Times, March 6, 1989.

3. Shulins, "Socialist Mayor."

4. October 1, 1988, telephone interview with George Thabault, Bernard Sanders's administrative assistant.

5. Bernard Sanders, "This Country Needs a Third Political Party," New York Times, January 3, 1989.

6. Gold, "Exit a Socialist," and Schulins, "Socialist Mayor."

7. Quoted by Schulins, "Socialist Mayor."

8. "Election '88: House of Representatives," USA Today, November 10, 1988.

9. Debbie Bookchin, "Mayor's Showing Makes History," Rutland (Vermont) Herald, November 10, 1988.

10. Ibid. A 1985 poll of Burlingtonians showed that fully a third of those who had voted for Reagan in 1984 intended to support Sanders for a third mayoralty term. A study of Sanders's 1990 statewide electoral base revealed a most extraordinary coalition of liberal Democrats, conservative Republicans, and single-issue voters. James W. Endersby and W. David Thomason, "Spotlight on Vermont: Third-Party Success in the 1990 Congressional Election," paper presented at convention of Southern Political Science Association, 1992.

11. Ian Polumbaum, "Coalition Redefines Its Stance," Burlington Free Press, October 2, 1988.

12. "The Greens of Vermont," Newsweek, 113 (February 27, 1989), 33.

13. See Kenneth C. Martis, The Historical Atlas of Political Parties in the United States Congress 1789–1989 (New York: Macmillan, 1989).

14. William Hesseltine, Third-Party Movements in the United States (New York: D. Van Nostrand, 1962), esp. 98–99.

15. The number 113 is derived by summing the number of seats held by third parties in all of the Congresses from 1901 through 1992 in which third parties secured representation in the House and/or Senate. Congress takes on a new number every two years. The One Hundred and Third Congress was elected in 1992. This means, of course, that a third-party Senator serving a six-year term was counted three times toward the number 113.

16. Daniel J. Elazar, *American Federalism: A View from the States*, 2d. ed. (New York: Thomas Y. Crowell, 1972), esp. 84–126.

17. Milwaukee's ethnic mix was such that in 1910 local Socialists were compelled to print their advertisements in twelve languages. Neal R. Peirce and Jerry Hagstrom, *The Book of the States* (New York: Warner Books, 1984), 269.

18. North Dakota has retained its open primary and no-registration procedures to this very day.

19. Robert P. Wilkins and Wynona H. Wilkins, *North Dakota* (New York: W. W. Norton, 1977), 143, 140.

20. James Manahan, *Trials of a Lawyer* (Minneapolis, Minn.: Farnham, 1933), 219–220.

21. Wilkins and Wilkins, *North Dakota*, 142–143.

22. *Ibid.*, 150. It is also ironic or at least puzzling that a year later, in 1922, North Dakota elected Frazier to the U.S. Senate. See Michael Barone and Grant Ujifusa, *The Almanac of American Politics 1992* (Washington, D.C.: National Journal, 1991), 942–943.

23. See J. David Gillespie, "Partisan Radicalism in the American Mainstream: the Farmer-Labor Party of Minnesota," *International Review of History and Political Science*, 22 (November, 1985), 13–34; Millard L. Gieske, *Minnesota Farmer-Laborism* (Minneapolis: University of Minnesota Press, 1979); and John E. Haynes, *Dubious Alliance* (Minneapolis: University of Minnesota Press, 1984).

24. Petersen was born in Denmark. Farmer-Labor's two other governors were sons of Scandinavian-born parents. Shipstead, Johnson, Lundeen, and many other prominent Farmer-Labor politicians had their ethnic roots in Norway, Sweden, or Denmark.

25. Hesseltine, *Third-Party Movements*, 98–99.

26. "Proposal to Use Troops if Necessary for Needy Applauded by Nation," *Farmer-Labor Leader*, April 30, 1933.

27. Benson was defeated in 1938 and Petersen in 1940 and 1942 by progressive Republican Harold Stassen. Stassen is better known to non-Minnesotans for his bids, serious in the 1940s but seemingly quixotic later on, for the Republican presidential nomination.

28. James M. Shields, *Mr. Progressive: A Biography of Elmer A. Benson* (Minneapolis, Minn.: T. S. Denison, 1971), 102.

29. *Ibid.*, 192. Benson maintained his radical perspective throughout life. He invited me to interview him on July 22, 1978, only a few years before his death. The interview took place at Lutsen, Minnesota, on the shore of Lake Superior, in a cabin built in the 1930s for Benson as a gift by appreciative members of a

miners' union. Speaking of the glory days of Farmer-Labor dominance, Benson recalled "it was the only time Minnesota wasn't controlled by U.S. Steel and the other interests." Of government ownership of factories, utilities, and monopolies, he remembered that "it was a dream of ours." Though still devoted to Franklin Roosevelt's memory, he expressed regret that the president had not taken more fundamental steps, especially to nationalize banking and the railroads. The legacy of FDR, as Benson unhappily saw it, was that Roosevelt had "saved" capitalism.

30. "1934 Farmer-Labor Platform," *Congressional Record*, 79 (August 17, 1935), 13525–13526.

31. "Analysis of the 1934 Farmer-Labor Platform," *Congressional Record*, 79 (August 17, 1935), 13526–13528.

32. One of the leading merger advocates on the Democratic side was a bright young politician named Hubert Humphrey.

33. Shields, *Mr. Progressive*, 161. To some it would seem indicative that Benson became national chairman of the Progressive party in 1948 and remained so until long after most of its non-Communist contingent, including Henry Wallace, had withdrawn at the opening of the Korean hostilities.

34. Arthur Naftalin, *A History of the Farmer-Labor Party of Minnesota* (Ph.D. diss., University of Minnesota, 1948), esp. 74 and 347. Also author's interviews with Naftalin, University of Minnesota, July 18–19, 1978.

35. James M. Youngdale, *Populism in a New Perspective* (Ph.D. diss., University of Minnesota, 1972), esp. 211–216. Also by Youngdale, ed., *Third Party Footprints* (Minneapolis, Minn.: Ross and Haines, 1966) and *Populism: A Psychohistorical Approach* (Port Washington, N.Y.: Kennikat Press, 1975).

36. For example, John B. Chapple, *La Follette Road to Communism* (privately published by author, 1936).

37. But perhaps mainly because of its strong German ethnic base, Wisconsin Progressivism was at odds with liberal national Democrats on U.S. entry into the two world wars. Senator Robert La Follette, Sr., had opposed Wilson's decision to join Britain and France in World War I and his two sons rejected FDR's machinations toward war with the Axis. In the Senate after Pearl Harbor Robert, Jr., did support Roosevelt's war policies.

38. Richard N. Current, *Wisconsin* (New York: W. W. Norton, 1977), 211.

39. *Ibid.*, 206–207.

40. The term "modified two-party system," as applied to New York, belongs to Daniel A. Mazmanian, *Third Parties in Presidential Elections* (Washington, D.C.: Brookings Institution, 1974), 115–135. Others have spoken of the state party configuration as multi-party in essence. For example, Robert J. Spitzer, "Multi-Party Politics in New York: A Cure for the Political System?" in *State Government*, ed. Thad L. Beyle (Washington, D.C.: Congressional Quarterly, 1989).

41. Howard A. Scarrow, *Parties, Elections, and Representation in the State of New York* (New York: New York University Press, 1983), 60–64.

42. V. O. Key Jr., *Politics, Parties, and Pressure Groups*, 5th ed. (New York: Thomas Y. Crowell, 1964), 276.

43. *Ibid.*, 275–276.

44. Rupert Hughes, *The Story of Thomas E. Dewey* (New York: Grosset and Dunlap, 1939), 200. Also see Mazmanian, *Third Parties*, 120.

45. See Simon W. Gerson, *Pete* (New York: International Publishers, 1976).

46. See "Election within Election," *New York Times*, November 13, 1988.

47. "Topic of the Times" (editorial), *New York Times*, January 4, 1989. Maltese must have enjoyed his experience in mainstream politics; he won his third consecutive state senatorial election in 1992.

48. Frank Smallwood, *The Other Candidates: Third Parties in Presidential Elections* (Hanover, N.H.: University Press of New England, 1983), 192–193. In 1976 McCormack qualified for federal matching funds (she eventually received $285,000) by collecting in small donations from givers in 20 states. Robert J. Spitzer, *The Right-to-Life Movement and Third-Party Politics* (Westport, Conn.: Greenwood Press, 1987), 59.

49. Spitzer, "Multi-Party Politics," 49.

50. Spitzer, *The Right-to-Life Movement*, 84–87.

51. "Election within Election," *New York Times*, November 13, 1988. Federal Election Commission returns for presidential 1988 show only 20,497 for Marra.

52. "Election within Election," *New York Times*, November 13, 1988.

✦

# What Manner of
# Men and Women?

## Beliefs and Personalities
## of Third-Party Leaders

*Two roads diverged in a wood, and I—*
*I took the one less traveled by.*
—from "The Road Not Taken" by Robert Frost

Fascinating people, folks with values and personalities sometimes very unlike those dominating the political mainstream, have been tempted out to the periphery to organize, become active in, or lead third parties. The foregoing pages introduced you to the likes of Strom Thurmond and George Wallace, to Belva Lockwood and Alice Paul, Eldridge Cleaver and Bobby Seale, Tom Watson and Floyd Olson and Eugene Debs, to George Lincoln Rockwell, and to some of the other interesting people important to the third-party tradition. Unfortunately, most studies of third-party personalities produce data that are anecdotal, not systematic, because a study of this kind almost always focuses biographically upon some particular third-party mover and shaker.

There have been a very few exceptions, each useful because it is so extraordinary. Robert Spitzer's 1983 survey of New York Right-to-Life Party leaders and identifiers illuminates his readers' understanding of the kinds of people commanding that party and also of the characters of folks attracted to RTL's rank and file.[1] The Green and Guth study of sixty-seven contributors to the Libertarian National Committee offers some rich insights into the characters, as well as the backgrounds and social standing, of Libertarian activists.[2] Frank Smallwood did extensive interviews with those men and women who had run in 1980 as third-party presidential nominees. In the course of these conversations, Smallwood sought to probe their backgrounds and personalities.[3] Like those of Spitzer, of Green and Guth, and of Smallwood, the study about which you will be reading in this chapter seeks to throw back the veil a little bit, to let you observe more closely the values and beliefs, even the personalities, of some people who have been in positions of third-party leadership.

Scholars dispute about the relative power of belief and personality in moving individuals and associations such as political parties. Ideas alone probably lack the motivational power we once thought they had. Today, some psychologists and other social scientists argue that personality characteristics far outstrip belief systems—ideologies in the broadest meaning of that term—in determining what individuals and groups will do. In this view, shared belief can provide the association's raison d'être as well as justification for followers of the leaders' dominance within the group. But justification is not the same as motivation. Some social scientists see ideologies as entirely synthetic; that is, they are manufactured by elites or leaders only for the purpose of undergirding their power and control.

There are other scholars who present a very different perspective. They say that (1) belief and personality both are important in motivating individuals and determining the inner dynamics of a group, and (2) personality and belief are so meshed together in human beings as to be virtually inseparable. Silvan Tomkins wrote that ideology, and with it left versus right divisions, may be found in educational theory, aesthetics, mathematics, and other areas, not just in politics. A left-wing mathematician is likely to say that people invented numbers. That leftist's right-wing colleague, on the other hand, believes that numbers were discovered. Tomkins contends that ideological posturing tends to carry over from one area to another; there is a very good chance that the leftist mathematician also selects progressive education for her children, likes abstract art, and votes for candidates on the left. If Tomkins is correct, a person's world view may be a very tight wrapping of personality and belief.[4]

## The Leader Study

In a 1982 study,[5] I set out to learn several things about third-party leaders' beliefs and values: What do such leaders believe? How distant (ideologically dissimilar) are their belief systems from each other? How much distance is there between each of the principal third-party belief systems and the core values—liberty, individualism, equal rights, constitutionalism, free enterprise, and others—that define and delineate the American political mainstream?[6]

Letters sent to the headquarters of many third parties requested that one or two leaders participate in a study in which leaders of various third parties would indicate their beliefs and values. One or two leaders in each of twelve third parties complied with my request and participated in the study. The design of the research instrument made it possible as well to make some important inferences about personalities of those leaders who participated.

The respondents were, at the time, leading parties with formal ideological perspectives positioned at virtually every point on the spectrum:

*Left or Radical Left*
>    Industrial Union party
>    Progressive Labor party
>    Social Revolutionary Anarchist Federation
>    Socialist party

*Right*
>    Conservative party of the State of New York
>    Expansionist party
>    National Hamiltonian party
>    Prohibition party

*Radical Right*
>    National Socialist Party of America
>    National Socialist White People's party

*Position on Ideological Spectrum Arguable or Unplaceable*
>    Archonist party
>    Libertarian party

Participating leaders received the assurance that neither their names nor their particular positions in specified parties would ever appear in resulting reports. They knew that in their responses they were to register their own beliefs and values, not (unless coincidentally) their party's ideological position or formal doctrine. A few people responded anonymously, identifying only the parties with which they were associated. Most, however, gave both their names and party titles. Some undoubtedly were proud that in their associations they held positions like Executive Director, National Chairman, National Leader, National Organizer, or General Secretary.

Each participant received a package of fifty-five statements dealing with beliefs, social outlook, and self-image.[7] Based upon the participant's own values and beliefs, each respondent arranged the statements into categories from "most disagree" to "most agree" and then recorded the appropriate statement numbers on a diagram like that in Figure 1.

**Figure 1: Score Sheet**

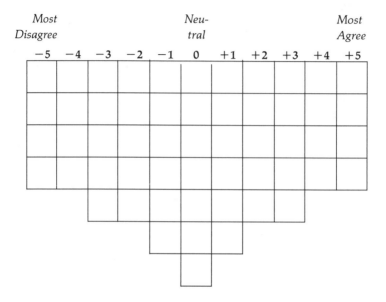

The procedure used in this study was **Q methodology.**[8] Factor analysis of the leaders' returns (their Q-sorts) uncovered three significant belief systems (factors) among those people guiding and directing third parties. Participants who were strongly identified with some particular factor also yielded, through their responses, evidence about personality types associated with that belief system.

Factor I represents a *Leftist/Libertarian belief system.* The returns of five leaders of leftist and radical leftist parties and of two Libertarian party leaders provided the Factor I scores for the fifty-five statements in the study. Factor II is a *Nazi factor.* Two of four participating Nazi leaders provided its statement scores, and the two other Nazis' returns identified them strongly with the Factor II belief system. Returns from Conservative, Expansionist, and National Hamiltonian leaders defined Factor III, which is a *Conservative factor.* Each factor's scores for the fifty-five statements appear in appendix 6 at the end of this book.

Table 7.1 reveals considerable distance—ideological dissimilarity— among the three factors. Writers who try to place ideologies on a straight line left-to-right continuum would be likely to guess that the Leftist/

# Q Methodology

Q Methodology is "an approach that determines the major points of agreement and disagreement—and their relative significance—in the population by analyzing the responses of a rather small number of people, selected to represent the major perspectives on an issue, to a set of statements chosen to cover a wide range of viewpoints on the subject (the Q-sample). Each respondent provides a Q-sort, a ranking of his agreement or disagreement with the statements. The statements are then correlated and factor-analyzed to isolate the various common attidues."

**Source:** Steven R. Brown and James G. Coke, *Public Opinion on Land Use Regulation* (Columbus, Ohio: Academy for Contemporary Problems, 1977), 3.

Libertarian and Nazi factors are most distant from each other, and that each is closer to the Conservative factor. The Table 7.1 findings defy this conventional wisdom. The Leftist/Libertarian and Nazi factors actually share more in common than either does with the Conservative. Some scholars reject positioning ideologies upon a straight line (as in Figure 2); they use instead a circle (Figure 3) to illustrate some value-sharing between left and right. The results of this study support their point of view.

**Figure 2**

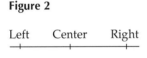

**Figure 3**

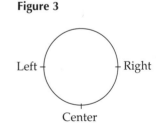

The table numbers indicate that the Conservative factor is a little closer ideologically to the Leftist/Libertarian than to the Nazi factor. There is no doubt that the Conservative factor also shares much more in common with the values of the American mainstream than the Nazi factor does. The Conservative may be no closer to mainstream values than the Leftist/Libertarian factor; but the leftist/libertarian participants indicated through their responses that they felt more alienated from the

**Table 7.1 Factor Correlation Scores***

|  | Factor I | Factor II | Factor III |
|---|---|---|---|
| Factor I | 1.000 | 0.238 | 0.077 |
| Factor II | 0.238 | 1.000 | −0.040 |
| Factor III | 0.077 | −0.040 | 1.000 |

*Range: 1.000 to −1.000. 1.000 indicates no distance at all, one belief system correlated with itself. −1.000 would indicate two belief systems, each the diametrical opposite of the other.

mainstream and its political system than the conservatives did. Voters and politicians who are in the mainstream probably feel just as alienated from leftist/libertarian leaders and their parties. Distance perceived may be just as important as real distance in securing one's place on the periphery.

### Leftist/Libertarian Belief System (Factor #I)

Four distinguishing elements characterize the Leftist/Libertarian belief system:

1. Factor I respondents rejected the view, widely held by mainstream American politicians and voters, that "politics is the art of the possible." Perhaps more than that of any other democratic nation, mainstream American politics adopts the pragmatic style. Successful American politicians seek day-to-day victories through compromise and accomodation. By contrast, these leftist/libertarian leaders found their political reality in the principles to which they subscribed, and specifically in their vision of the good society. In their preoccupation with principle and vision, Factor I folks shared something in common with those of the Nazi factor (II), though the Leftist/Libertarian vision is quite unlike that of the Nazis.[9] Factor I respondents believed in dreaming impossible dreams, even if in so doing they might be branded "quixotic." They were more likely than the Nazis or conservatives to say, of themselves, that "I dream of things that never were and ask 'why not?'" Like the Nazi, the Leftist/Libertarian belief system denies that "practical people," business people and manufacturers, for example, are more valuable than artists, professors, or other "people of ideas." Their commitment to principle and vision may have brought everyday political frustrations. Factor I adherents conceded that they wished they and their parties were closer to the American people. But if alienation is the price demanded for devotion to principle, that was a price they were willing to pay.

2. The Leftist/Libertarian belief system embraces principles generally identified as leftist; some of the Leftist/Libertarian values seem to have been influenced by Marxism. The leftist/libertarians denied that people of property are more dependable than the unpropertied, and that social mobility has created virtual classlessness in America. America's poor, said Factor I respondents, suffer not only poverty but "invisibility," a burden long ago chronicled in socialist Michael Harrington's *The Other America*. They believed it both true and unfortunate that most Americans, assuming a society of general affluence, lack a social consciousness. Leftist/Libertarianism maintains that in the United States producers consume little and consumers produce little or nothing; it embraces economic democracy, a term used in recent years almost as a synonym for socialism. Alongside classical Marxists, the leftist/libertarian leaders rejected the notion that "many people are just made to run a factory machine." These leftist/libertarian respondents generally devoted their loyalties to an international order of human beings instead of giving patriotic devotion to nation alone.

Other leftist elements of this belief system relate more directly to liberalism than to Marxism. With regard to matters of religious faith, Leftist/Libertarianism steers a secular middle course between the religiosity of traditional conservatives and Marxist atheism. It strongly favors women's liberation, just as it sharply repudiates racism. In common with liberal optimism about human nature, it denies the inevitability of war. Indeed, nothing in human history is predetermined or inevitable. Leftist/libertarians believe that humanity controls the course of history and, thus, its common future.

3. This belief system, rejecting authoritarianism, embraces libertarian values. This finding is particularly pertinent when it is remembered that traditional Marxist doctrine called for and also predicted a dictatorship of the proletariat. Leftist/Libertarianism rejects government by an elite, and it censures American government for violating human rights. This belief system upholds freedom of speech even for "people and groups that do not believe in free speech." It strongly concurs with Voltaire's famed aphorism, "I may not agree with what you have to say, but I'll defend to the death your right to say it." It vehemently denies propositions that "obedience and respect for authority are the most important virtues for children," and that more emphasis should be placed upon duties and less on rights.

4. Like the Nazi leaders in the study, the leftist/libertarians indicated a deep sense of alienation from the American political mainstream. "There is," they said, "not a dime's worth of difference" between the two

major parties, which in reality are "but one party with two virtually identical branches." Leftist/Libertarianism, alone among the three belief systems, registers a strong preference for a multi-party system. Leftist/libertarians said that the press is slanted, and that American presidents actually are selected by a small power elite. Leftist/libertarian participants in the study denied, somewhat less vigorously than the Nazis, that they have faith in the American political system.

### Nazi Belief System (Factor II)

1. Like the Leftist/Libertarian, this Nazi belief system devotes itself to principle and vision instead of pragmatism or expediency. The Nazi leaders in this study focused upon their image of a world to come. Even more than the leftist/libertarians, they rejected contentions that practical people should be more highly valued than the idealistic and creative.

2. This belief system denies that humanity possesses value in being able to chart the course of history. Perhaps borrowing from the anti-humanistic spirit of fascist and Nazi doctrine and from G. W. F. Hegel, whose philosophy strongly influenced classical fascist thought, these leaders espoused a deterministic view of history. "Human beings," they affirmed, "are the actors in history, but the course of history is determined by forces beyond human control." Believing change to be inevitable, they rejected one of the central tenets of traditional conservatism: "unless it is necessary to change, it is necessary not to change." But insisting as they did that people do not design the course of history, they denied that change comes from altering or elevating the state of human consciousness.

3. In common with classical fascists, especially those of Nazi Germany, the Nazi leaders in this study paid fealty to political authoritarianism, to dictatorship by a single top leader, and to racism (or racial idealism). They gave the highest possible assent to the proposition that "the world is made up of superior and inferior races." Embracing the fascist leader principle, they affirmed the legitimacy and destiny of the strong and dominant leader, the extraordinary person who is intelligent and exciting. Alone among the three belief systems revealed in this study, this Nazism rejects Voltaire's celebrated defense of free speech. It also rejects a multi-party system, its devotees presumably favoring a single elite nazi party.

4. Despite their authoritarian ideals, these Nazi leaders refused to defer to symbols of political authority in this country. They revealed that they were, if anything, even more deeply alienated than their leftist/libertarian counterparts from the American political order, a system

which they believed to be both weak and dominated by inferior minority races. They scorned Democrats and Republicans as two almost identical branches of a single party. These leaders even scuttled axioms about "America first" and "my country, right or wrong," despite the ultranationalism normally associated with Nazis and other fascists. It seems a safe bet that these Nazi respondents would resurrect aphorisms like those, should they and the Nazi movement attain the power to construct their Aryan New Order in this country.

### Conservative Belief System (Factor III)

1. The adherents of this Conservative belief system indicated by their responses that they were the most pragmatic third-party leaders in the study. They preferred "the practical person to the person of ideas." Visions of a world to come seemed rather irrelevant to these third-party conservatives, who believed that "politics is the art of the possible." They did wish it were possible for them to exercise more power and influence. But they strongly believed that control of history lies within the grasp of human beings.

2. Unlike the leftist/libertarians and nazis, these conservatives signaled little real sense of alienation from the American political system. Indeed, they registered the strongest possible "faith in the ... system," which they absolved of the charge that it regularly violates human rights. Conservative participants in this study believed that the press basically is informative and unbiased. They saw presidential elections as meaningful popular exercises.

What disaffection they did feel, they limited mainly to a few features of the political process that most constrain third parties. Like their leftist/ libertarian counterparts, they believed that "all third parties—not just my own—suffer unjustly under the restrictions of discriminatory state and federal legislation." They indicated, as did the leftist/libertarians and Nazis, that they respected leaders of other third parties more than Republican and Democratic politicians. But these conservatives were alone in admitting seeing some meaningful differences between the two major parties.

3. This Conservative belief system embraces many of the values that are associated with liberal democracy in America. These conservative respondents believed in free speech. They strongly repudiated racism in principle. Although unlikely to characterize themselves as feminists, they sought options for women beyond those of wife and mother alone. They denied that human nature makes wars inevitable. Despite their conservatism

(or maybe out of a sense of noblesse oblige), their belief system admits some individual responsibility to provide for the public good.

**4.** But these conservative third-party leaders' core values were values they shared with conservatives of the mainstream, including many Republican activists. Clearly this belief system is propertarian. Its adherents saw people with property as far more dependable than the propertyless, and they were not very sympathetic of the tears others shed about the invisibility of the poor. They defended religion against the contrary currents of secular society. Their attitudes toward the state seem somewhat contradictory. On the one hand, they expressed deep faith in the American political system as a general object. Their patriotism may have led them to embrace the controversial "my country, right or wrong" adage. Yet they strongly professed that government in Washington is a beast grown too large, one that is beyond control by the American people. If these be contradictions, they are contradictions also embraced by major party conservatives, by people like Reagan and Bush.

**5.** Some of the values registered by these conservative third-party leaders appear to be authoritarian or quasi-authoritarian. They professed quite strongly that "in each generation some extraordinary individuals are destined to become leaders." They saw governmental restrictions on the "strong and dominant" as illegitimate. Affirming though they did their belief in popular representative institutions, they would have preferred actual rulership by an enlightened, public-spirited aristocracy.

## Third Party Leader Personalities

Perhaps you remember the distinction that Harold Lasswell drew between the political agitator and political administrator types,[10] as well as our own conjecture that third parties draw into their midst more than their share of the political agitators. People of the political administrator type are flexible folks who set their sights on short-term goals, entering into skirmishes to achieve these objectives, while willingly compromising when accommodation seems needed.

Not all who enter the mainstream are political administrators. But it seems rather clear that many of the most successful political figures in this country have come closer to the administrator than to the agitator type. Of course, one personality often reveals ingredients of both these types.

If administrators tend to dominate the mainstream, agitators may reside in large numbers on the periphery. It is logical to speculate that many of them take the reins of third-party leadership. According to

Lasswell, political agitators are fervent people who exhort their comrades while sharply vilifying adversaries. They tend to be personally undisciplined, and they are repelled by administrative routine. They find their joy in the battle itself. Lasswell found the agitators to be narcissistic people. They find self-worth and significance in a sense of mission, and they tend strongly toward rigidity and principle rather than pragmatism and accommodation.

The third-party leader study about which you have been reading offers a lot of evidence that some of the leaders who participated tended toward the political agitator personality type. It is not the kind of evidence one could take like a lawyer to court. For that you would need, figuratively, to put these subjects on a couch and psychoanalyze them.

In search of political agitators among the third-party leader respondents, two indicators of the agitator type were built into this study: (1) a sense of mission and (2) the identification and vilification of adversaries. Selected statements from fifty-five study statements provide fragmentary clues about each of these indicators. For the selected statements, the composite scores of all leader participants whose responses defined each of the three third-party belief systems were examined. Taken together, these composite scores for the selected statements revealed patterns strongly supporting the conclusion that there were political agitator types among the study's respondents.

This study produced no substantial evidence to support any claim that conservative third parties attract large numbers of political agitators to their leadership ranks. The Conservative (Factor III) participants in the study did convey a sense of mission. But they showed no sign at all of scapegoating—of identifying and condemning devils or orgres.

Political agitators are far more likely to be found in the leadership of leftist/libertarian than of conservative third parties. It is quite likely, in fact, that some of the Leftist/Libertarian (Factor I) respondents possessed personalities of this type. The indicators show in Factor I respondents both a sense of mission and a tendency to posit devil theories about real or perceived adversaries.

The study reveals the clearest evidence of political agitators among the Nazi (Factor II) respondents. Factor II participants revealed a strong personal sense of mission. They also were very prone to vilify all those people and groups that they believed were impeding the fulfillment of that mission. It is very likely that a high percentage of those people attracted to ultraright third parties have personalities tending toward the agitator type.

This study provides abundant evidence as well that Nazi (Factor II)

**Table 7.2 Indications of "Political Agitator" Personalities Among Leaders Defining Each of the Three Third-Party Belief Systems**

| Indicators and Supportive Statements (Also statement numbers; see appendix 6) | Belief Systems | | |
|---|---|---|---|
| | Leftist/Liberation (Factor I) | Nazi (Factor II) | Conservative (Factor III) |
| *Sense of Mission* | Indicated | Strongly Indicated | Indicated |
| (10) I feel politically unfrustrated | No (−2) | Yes (+4) | No (−2) |
| (13) Dreaming "impossible dreams" | Yes (+2) | Yes (+1) | Yes (+1) |
| (15) I can affect course of events | Yes (+1) | Yes (+5) | Yes (+5) |
| (24) My party is significant | Yes (+2) | Yes (+5) | Yes (+3) |
| (42) I dream of things that never were | Yes (+3) | Yes (+1) | Yes (+1) |
| (47) I have tried to live extraordinary life | Neutral (0) | Yes (+3) | Yes (+4) |
| (55) Undisciplined, emotional person | Yes (+2) | Neutral (0) | Yes (+1) |
| *Vilification of Adversaries* | Indicated | Strongly Indicated | Not Indicated |
| ( 1) Slanted, misleading press | Yes (+3) | Yes (+5) | No (−3) |
| ( 5) Power elite | Yes (+3) | Yes (+4) | No (−5) |
| ( 9) Inferior races | No (−5) | Yes (+5) | No (−4) |
| (31) Dangerous conspirators | Yes (+1) | Yes (+3) | No (−5) |
| (34) American political system | Yes (+2) | Yes (+5) | No (−5) |
| (36) Major parties | Yes (+3) | Yes (+4) | No (−2) |
| (38) Secret plotters | Yes (+1) | Yes (+3) | No (−5) |

participants possess authoritarian personalities. It may be surprising that similar indications were not discovered among respondents associated with the two other belief systems. One of the Factor I respondents led a Marxist-Leninist party, the official doctrine of which continued at the time of the study to embrace the idea of the dictatorship of the proletariat. Moreover, the Factor III respondents endorsed certain principles that seem to be quasi-authoritarian if not authoritarian. It was, however, the Nazi (Factor II) participants alone whose responses reveal a lot of evidence that they were given by people with authoritarian personalities.

In 1950 T. W. Adorno co-authored with his team of social scientists *The Authoritarian Personality.*[11] That book remains to this day one of the definitive treatises on this personality type. Its authors observed that authoritarian personalities draw very sharp distinctions between in-group and out-group, between us and them. They indulge in stereotyping and make sweeping value judgments. They show extreme hostility toward out-groups, while deferring unquestioningly to the in-group. People with authoritarian personalities also see conflict and manipulation as central ingredients in the relationships of human beings. They seem sure that their survival, as well as that of their own group, requires them to engage in such conflict and manipulation.

The Nazi participants in this study clearly distinguished between in-group and out-group. This is most evident in their very strong support of the premise that "the world is made up of superior and inferior races." They also gave a lot of significance to divisions among social classes in America, and their beliefs included the thought that "there are many people who are just made to run a factory machine." The Nazi participants denied any personal responsibility to provide for others. Each seemed absolutely convinced of the rightness and significance of his own Nazi party. They indicated that the distance separating them from the American people bothered them not one bit.

If you remain unconvinced that Nazi (Factor II) respondents had authoritarian personalities, look at what they said about a world run through conflict and manipulation. The Nazis in this study, in stark contrast to the leftist/libertarians and conservatives, strongly affirmed that "human nature being what it is, there will always be war and conflict." They believed that the American press is slanted and manipulative, that presidential elections are controlled by a small power elite, that there are "dangerous conspirators" who are "hatching plots" in secret places. These Nazis found their remedy in their own fascist vision of the future. They professed considerable optimism about their own ability to "affect the course of events," and they believed that their own party was the last best, perhaps the only, hope for saving America from its social afflictions. They appeared to believe that their ends justify any means necessary, for they were willing to use "stringent methods," to play "political hardball."

## Conclusion: Third-Party Distance
## from the Mainstream

The American political mainstream imposes upon third parties formidable burdens, both of the structural and the cultural kinds. These constraints go some distance toward explaining why many such parties seem destined to dwell outside the mind and sight of most people. They do not, however, come close to completing the picture.

The study about which you have read in this chapter shows that among people in positions of third-party leadership, there are many who feel distinctly alienated from the political system and the American people. The study results found this especially true of the Nazi leaders, but also true of the leftist/libertarians. The conservatives, on the other hand, seemed rather tuned-in to mainstream processes and values. They may have been quite happy with the nation's general direction during the conservative Reagan era, the time during which this study was conducted.

The Nazi respondents in this study repudiated liberty, civil rights, and other fundamental democratic convictions, as these had been enunciated in Louis Hartz's 1955 treatise on the central values of mainstream America.[12] This study's conservaties did embrace most of these values, although these third-party conservatives vehemently affirmed that in America "we have overemphasized 'rights' and underemphasized 'duties.'" There may be many mainstream voters and politicians who share these conservative respondents' view of the proper places of rights and duties.

An objective analysis of leftist/libertarian beliefs must conclude that in those beliefs there is much that is strongly supportive of many of the core democratic values of the American mainstream. Two of the seven study participants whose responses defined the Leftist/Libertarian factor were Libertarian party leaders. Their party's credo quite clearly embraces many mainstream verities, especially liberty. It particularly venerates Thomas Jefferson, whom Libertarian partisans regard as the last and greatest libertarian president. Also helping to define the Leftist/Libertarian factor were two people who, at the time of the study, were leaders in the Socialist party. Recently published accounts of that party's venerable history persuasively show that the party and its democratic socialist ideology came "directly from the mainstream of American culture."[13]

The key political problem for many leftist/libertarians is not that they reject mainstream values; it is that they embrace some of them too radically. As a practical matter, this particularly aggrieves the Libertarian party. Andre Marrou, Libertarian's 1992 standardbearer, ran for the presidency on a platform calling for the repeal of anti-drug, anti-prostitution, and anti-pornography legislation; the elimination of farm subsidies; and the termination of compulsory school attendance. A program like that may, indeed, serve the cause of human liberty. But it does not play well in Peoria, or, for that matter, in Baton Rouge, Spokane, or Albuquerque.

## Notes

1. Robert J. Spitzer, *The Right-to-Life Movement and Third-Party Politics* (Westport, Conn.: Greenwood Press, 1987), 84–87.

2. John C. Green and James L. Guth, "The Socialization of a Third-Party Elite: the Case of the Libertarians," paper presented at annual meeting of the South Carolina Political Science Association, Charleston, April 2, 1983.

3. Frank Smallwood, *The Other Candidates: Third Parties in Presidential Elections* (Hanover, N. H.: University Press of New England, 1983).

4. Silvan Tomkins, "Left and Right: A Basic Dimension of Ideology and Personality," in *The Study of Lives*, ed. Robert W. White (New York: Atherton Press, 1964), 388–411.

5. J. David Gillespie, "Attitudes and Perspectives of Third-Party Leaders," paper presented at convention of the Southern Political Science Association, 1982; and Gillespie, "Third-Party Leaders and the American Ideological Mainstream," paper presented at convention of Northeastern Political Science Association, 1984.

6. See Louis Hartz, *The Liberal Tradition in America* (New York: Harcourt, Brace, and World, 1955), esp. 5–14.

7. See appendix 6 for a list of the 55 statements.

8. See Steven R. Brown, *Political Subjectivity: Applications of Q Methodology in Political Science* (New Haven, Conn.: Yale University Press, 1980); also *Operant Subjectivity*, an interdisciplinary Q methodology journal edited by Brown.

9. Glenn Tinder has contrasted the visionary "politics of redemption" with the pragmatic "politics of convenience." See Glenn Tinder, *Political Thinking: The Perennial Questions*, 4th. ed. (Glenview, Ill.: Scott Foresman and Co., 1986), 172–173. The major American political parties are strongly identified with the politics of convenience. The Leftist/Libertarian and Nazi belief systems revealed

in this study are much more closely identified with the politics of redemption than is the Conservative belief system (Factor III).

10. Harold D. Lasswell, *Psychopathology and Politics* (Chicago: University of Chicago Press, 1930).

11. T. W. Adorno, *et al.*, *The Authoritarian Personality* (New York: Harper and Row, 1950).

12. Hartz, *The Liberal Tradition.*

13. Elliott Shore, *Talkin' Socialism* (Lawrence: University Press of Kansas, 1988), 4. Also see Nick Salvatore, *Eugene V. Debs* (Urbana: University of Illinois Press, 1982).

# CHAPTER EIGHT

# Looking Back, Looking Ahead:

## *The Third-Party Legacy and the Future*

*Where there is no vision, the people perish.*
—Proverbs 29:18

*Our Democracy is but a name. We vote. What does that mean? It means that we choose between two . . . bodies of autocrats. We choose between Tweedledum and Tweedledee.*
—Helen Keller[1]

The spate of celebration and troop homecoming events following the Persian Gulf War of 1991 confirmed that Americans were in a patriotic mood, that they wanted to feel good about themselves as a nation. Given that fact, *The Day That America Told the Truth*, a book reaching the vendors that year, was not likely to win a warm reception in Middle America. It is a portrait of the nation in the 1990s, a disturbing, most troubling picture based upon one of the most elaborate and comprehensive opinion surveys ever conducted in the United States. If the authors' findings come even close to the truth, America has become a nation without vision, a country in deep peril.[1]

Sometimes the good sense of American voters has produced leaders, like Lincoln and Wilson, who used the presidency's "bully pulpit" to articulate a vision and to inspire the nation to undertake the quest toward its fulfillment. But the Republican and Democratic parties, those pragmatic, relatively nonideological practitioners of the politics of convenience,[2] are not in the business of selling visions. Michael Dukakis drew voters' attention in 1988 to a contest over "competence, not ideology."

Early in the course of his presidency, George Bush conceded that he had trouble with "that vision thing."

American third parties, drawing much closer to the politics of redemption,[3] have been far more inclined than the major parties to exposit visions. Not all third party visions have been positive and good; some were silly, demeaning, or even sinister. When a third party does showcase a good vision that is eventually fulfilled, it normally is almost impossible to certify a cause-and-effect connection between the third party's enunciation and the subsequent fruition of the vision. Even so, consider these past third-party visions of the future:

- An open polity freed of secrecy and elitism (Antimasonic party, People's party);
- A free society purged of the stain of slavery (Liberty party, Free Soil party);
- Structural democratization of the polity, an American version of what the Soviets called *perestroika* (Prohibition party, People's party, 1912 and 1924 Progressive parties);
- Women empowered by the franchise (Prohibition party, Greenback party, Equal Rights party, People's party, Socialist party, 1912 Progressive party, National Woman's party);
- A nonracial polity with full participation by African-Americans as well as whites (Greenback party, People's party, Communist party);
- An enlightened public policy attuned to the needs of producers and of society's least fortunate (People's party, 1912 and 1924 Progressive parties, Socialist party, others);
- A society freed from various social afflictions (Prohibition party, American Independent party, others);
- A peaceful and harmonious new world order, casting aside the Cold War, its frightful costs and horrifying dangers (1948 Progressive party).

Through most of the course of this century—at least since the demise of the Bull Moose Progressives—America's two-party system and its Republican and Democratic parties have been a citadel impregnable to the challenges of third-party and independent outsiders. If, as is likely, 1992 is recorded as a pivotal year in U.S. political history, it will be partly the result of the Perot phenomenon and of weighty inferences therefrom.

There were a thousand reasons to predict that Perot would go nowhere in 1992. He was a political novice, inexperienced, some said, at the way things are done inside the Washington beltway. There seemed to be quirks in the man's personality. People worried that, temperamentally if not philosophically, Perot might be an authoritarian. (Bumper stickers demanding "Ross for Boss" did nothing to reduce those fears.) The media (and Republicans) accused him of making bizarre charges. He was vague about whether to go for a campaign run by professionals or a more spontaneous movement of grassroots volunteers and fans. Perot even had trouble deciding whether to stay in or get out of the race. Although Perot chose in Stockdale a nice, admirable guy, Perot's running mate lent little or nothing to the strength of the ticket. Perot billed himself the populist outsider in a year when voters seemed eager to throw the rascals out; yet Perot's wealth and his huge campaign expenditure (Perot publicly resolved to "buy the presidency for the American people") appeared to some to belie Perot's claim to be the people's true voice. Unlike most third-party and independent campaigns, Perot's seemed devoid of ideological content. Perot sought, if anything, centrist ground in a year when both major-party candidates also were seeking to stake out the middle. Many of Perot's policy pronouncements seemed glittering generality; those that were not were filled with promises of austerity—new taxes and spending cuts. Opinion polls in the closing weeks left no doubt that Perot would lose.

Despite all this, in fact *because* of some of it, Perot took a larger share than any non-major-party presidential candidate in the eighty years that had passed since the Bull Moose campaign. Indeed he did better than any such candidate in history who had not previously served as U.S. president. Ross Perot's remarkable 1992 presidential campaign and his nearly 20 percent share on November 3 may be most important in what it has to say of the deep disaffection of voters and of the major parties' vulnerability as this century draws to a close.

Today the third-party impulse and a third-party legacy dating back to the 1820s are alive and kicking. Access to media and to money and an array of other problems confronting third parties seem as formidable as ever; but ballot access barriers have eased substantially in many states since the 1960s. Recent third-party electoral breakthroughs are among the most significant in a half-century. Not since 1936 had two states simultaneously elected third-party gubernatorial nominees who ran without the endorsement of one of the national major parties; the year 1990 brought both Lowell Weicker and Alaska's Wally Hickel.

Connecticut Governor Weicker brought a state income tax to his ungrateful constituents and, with it, shrill public demands for his political scalp. But by 1992 Weicker's A Connecticut Party was deeply involved in election campaigns and Weicker himself was networking with people who share his interest in building a progressive new third party on a national scale.[4] Late that year, Weicker, the distinguished political scientist Theodore J. Lowi, some veterans of the Perot campaign, and others from around the country announced they were giving birth to the Independence party.

Independent socialist Bernie Sanders won Vermont's U.S. House seat in 1990 and easily held onto it two years later. Burlington's Progressive Coalition, the local third party with which Sanders is connected, commanded a considerable share of local power and several Burlington seats in the Vermont legislature as of 1993. At the same time the Libertarian party could proudly claim three New Hampshire legislators and a hundred or more elected officials scattered around the country.[5]

The Greens, a network of activists and of some 450 local groups with interests and commitments ranging from environmentalism and the antinuclear and peace movements to feminism and Native American rights, can trace their history in America to 1974. Grassroots localists tried and true, Greens long ago adopted "think globally, act locally" as motto and ethos. Greens, especially the more leftist-minded of them, have felt uncomfortable calling themselves a party. Movement has been their term of choice. Thus, a summer 1991 happening may have portended substantial change in the Greens network as well as important third-party history about to be made: in August 200 delegates showed up in the West Virginia mountain town of Elkins for the first national Green Congress. The Congress set up, on paper at least, the Green Party of the U.S.A.[6]

Greens over the years have contested local elections. In 1992 thirty-seven Greens elected officials were serving on county commissions, city councils, and in other posts in at least ten states. The mayor of Cordova, Arkansas, as of 1992 was Green. Alaska, Hawaii, Arizona, New Mexico, and California today recognize the Greens as a statutory party entitled to ballot access.[7]

The Peace and Freedom party, a radical product of the 1960s, is electorally active in California more than a quarter of a century later. Conservatives, Liberals, and Right-to-Lifers continue their work in New York. The New Alliance Party, born in New York, has long since become a nationally active electoral party. Local coalitions like Hartford's People for Change claim a share of the power in some communities.

The Natural Law party sprouted in the reasonably congenial circumstances of 1992. Its creators devoted their new party to "bringing the light of science into politics." That was most ironic, some outsiders observed, because the party itself seemed so shrouded in fog.

Natural Law's defining attribute may be its intimate connection, spiritual and financial, with the transcendental meditation movement. John Hagelin, the party's 1992 presidential nominee, is said to be a Harvard-educated Ph.D. in nuclear physics. Qualifying for federal matching funds, Hagelin showcased his party on television and in major newspapers. Natural Law ran dozens of candidates in many states in 1992.

U.S. third parties sometimes become in effect—rarely by intent—corrective agencies that alter the course of one or the other major party. Strident and sometimes powerful voices inside the GOP were grousing at President Bush in 1992 for being an unfaithful relayer of Reagan conservatism. Offering themselves as rightist alternatives to Bush in 1992, Patrick Buchanan and David Duke each darkly hinted that someday he might bolt to lead a third-party charge. Bush took the nomination, but his November loss to Clinton virtually assured a bloody battle for the soul of the Republican party. Pat Robertson's Christian Coalition was but one of many conservative groups sharpening their spears for the fight.

On one of the flanks of the GOP two ultraright third parties are hoping to capitalize on what they expect will be Republican failure to steer clearly to the right. Inspired by its guts-and-glory nominee Bo Gritz, a revitalized Populist party took more votes in 1992 than in either of its two previous presidential tries.

As 1992 approached an infant Taxpayers party was threatening the security of these Populists' control of far right electoral turf. The Taxpayers party is the brainchild of right-activist Howard Phillips. It has been seeking to coalesce veteran John Birchers, Moral Majoritarians, George Wallaceites, and other rightists who feel alienated because of a centrist drift in the Republican party (and the GOP's cynical desertion, under Bush, of its "no new taxes" pledge) but who are disinclined to support a Populist party that is animated and stained by racism. Taxpayers party activists tried but failed to attract someone like Patrick Buchanan, or Oliver North, or Jesse Helms, as their 1992 standardbearer. Howard Phillips stood in himself as the party's presidential nominee. Like others on the far right, Taxpayers party movers sharply criticized the Persian Gulf War and other episodes of U.S. intervention. Domestically their party features opposition to taxes, welfare, abortion, and affirmative action.[8]

Long-term and equally serious threats came from the left as

disturbing signals to the Democratic party. Clearly a struggle has been under way for the ideological soul of that major party. It would be hard to say, later on, that the Democrats have not been given fair warning.

Initial signs that liberal energies within the Democratic party were beginning to dissipate prompted Jesse Jackson to observe that no longer were there differences that really counted for anything between America's two major parties. In Vermont early in the 1990s the Rainbow Coalition and Burlington's Progressive Coalition formally merged. The Progressive Vermont Alliance, the product of their union, set out on the very specific quest to become a major party in challenge to Vermont's "Republicrats." As the prospect grew that the new anti-choice Supreme Court majority soon might shift the abortion debate fully into the political arena (thus, into the hands of nervous Democratic and Republican lawmakers), third-party devotees in the National Organization for Women prepared to launch their 21st Century party.

Though far from enthusiastic about the bid of Bill Clinton, a prominent Democratic centrist, for his party's nomination, many leftists welcomed and worked for Clinton's victory in November 1992. As the Clinton administration began, progressives seemed very inclined to give the new president a chance. But the support these leftists offered Clinton was a conditional support. They already had sent the Democrats a message with singular clarity: feminists and Rainbow Coalition people and other progressives who long have supported the Democratic party now are more than capable of changing course. They may sustain their Democratic ties or journey instead into third-party territory. A lot will depend on that struggle for the Democratic party's soul.

## Notes

1. James Patterson and Peter Kim, *The Day America Told the Truth* (New York: Prentice Hall Press, 1991).

2. See Glenn Tinder, *Political Thinking: The Perennial Questions*, 4th. ed. (Glenview, Ill.: Scott Foresman and Co., 1986), 172–73.

3. *Ibid.*

4. See Mark Paziokas, "Weicker to Discuss Creation of New Party," *Hartford Courant*, August 19, 1992.

5. "What is the Libertarian party?", undated information sheet produced and periodically revised by Libertarian National Committee.

6. Phil Hill, "U.S. Greens Grow Beyond the Grass Roots," *Guardian*, September 18, 1991.

7. Jay Walljasper, "Why the Democrats Matter," *Utne Reader* (November/ December 1992), 150–151.

8. Sara Diamond, "New Taxpayers Party to Push Bush from the Right," *Guardian*, October 9, 1991.

# Returns from
# November 3, 1992,
# Presidential Election

|  | Ballot Position (50 states and D.C.) | Popular Votes Cast* |
|---|---|---|
| *Candidates of the Two Major Parties* | | |
| Bill Clinton, Democratic Party | 51 | 44,908,233 |
| George Bush, Republican Party | 51 | 39,102,282 |
| Combined major parties' shares of total presidential vote: just over 80%. | | |
| *Independent Candidate* | | |
| Ross Perot, Independent | 51 | 19,721,433 |
| Independent Perot's share to total presidential vote: nearly 19%. | | |
| *Other Candidates Appearing on One or More State Ballots**  | | |
| Andre Marrou, Libertarian Party | 51 | 291,612 |
| James "Bo Gritz, Populist Party" | 18 | 98,918 |
| Lenora Fulani, New Alliance Party | 40 | 73,248 |
| Howard Phillips, Taxpayers Party | 21 | 42,960 |
| John Hagelin, Natural Law Party | 29 | 37,137 |
| Ron Daniels, Independent | 9 | 27,396 |
| Lyndon La Rouche, Independent | 18 | 25,863 |
| James Mac Warren, Socialist Workers Party | 14 | 22,883 |

*Official counts as reported by states.

**For some minor candidates, party designations on ballots varied from state to state.

| | Ballot Position (50 states and D.C.) | Popular Votes Cast* |
|---|---|---|
| Drew Bradford, Independent | 1 | 4,749 |
| Jack Herer, Grassroots Party | 3 | 3,875 |
| Helen Halyard, Workers League | 2 | 3,050 |
| J. Quinn Brisben, Socialist Party | 4 | 2,909 |
| John Yiamouyiannis, Independent | 4 | 2,199 |
| Delbert Ehlers, Independent | 1 | 1,149 |
| Honest Jim Boren, Apathy Party | 1 | 956 |
| Earl Dodge, Prohibition Party | 3 | 935 |
| Eugene Hem, Third Party | 1 | 405 |
| Isabell Masters, Looking Back | 1 | 327 |
| Robert Smith, American Party | 1 | 292 |
| Gloria La Riva, Workers World Party | 1 | 181 |

Combined minor candidates' shares of total presidential vote: under 1%

| | |
|---|---|
| Write-in votes | 177,207 |
| None of the Above (Nevada Option) | 2,537 |
| Total | 104,552,736 |

Source: Federal Election Commission, "1992 Official Presidential General Election Results," January 11, 1993.

# Addresses of Third Parties

For the most complete lists of third parties, including state and local branches and publications available, as well as of thousands of other groups of the left and right in America, see Laird Wilcox, *Guide to the American Right* and *Guide to the American Left* (P.O. Box 2047, Olathe, Kans. 66061: Editorial Research Service, 1989). See also latest edition of *Encyclopedia of Associations* (Detroit, Mich.: Gale Research, Inc.)

ALL-AFRICAN PEOPLE'S REVOLUTIONARY PARTY. 1738 A St., S.E., Washington, D.C. 20003

AMERICAN INDEPENDENT PARTY. 8158 Palm St., Lemon Grove, Calif. 92045.

AMERICAN PARTY. P.O. Box 597, Provo, UT 84603. Or P.O. Box 22382, Lexington, Ky. 40522.

AMERICAN NAZI PARTY. 4375 North Peck Rd., El Monte, Calif. 91732.

AMERICAN WHITE NATIONALIST PARTY. P.O. Box 14083, Columbus, Oh. 43214.

AMERICAN WHITE SUPREMACIST PARTY. P.O. Box 2002, East Peoria, Il. 61611.

ANTI-LAWYER PARTY. 6308 24th Ave., Kenosha, Wis. 53140.

BLACK PANTHER PARTY. 7911 MacArthur Blvd., Oakland, Calif. 94605.

BOSTON TEA PARTY. 1051 North Grand, Mesa, Ariz. 85201.

COMMUNIST LABOR PARTY. P.O. Box 3705, Chicago, Ill. 60654.

COMMUNIST PARTY-USA. 235 W. 23d St., New York, N.Y. 10011.

CONSERVATIVE PARTY OF THE STATE OF NEW YORK. 486 78th St., Brooklyn, N.Y. 11209.

CONSERVATIVE PARTY OF THE UNITED STATES. 13131 W. Jamesville Rd., Hales Corner, Wis. 53130.

CONSTITUTION PARTIES OF THE UNITED STATES. P.O. Box 608, White Fish, Mont. 59937.

DANIEL DE LEON ELECTION COMMITTEE. P.O. Box 362, Newaygo, N.Y. 49337.

EXPANSIONIST PARTY. 446 W. 46th St., New York, N.Y. 10036.

FOURTH INTERNATIONAL TENDENCY. P.O. Box 1947, New York, N.Y. 10009.

GREEN PARTY. P.O. Box 127, Downers Grove, Ill. 60515.

INDUSTRIAL UNION PARTY. P.O. Box 80, New York, N.Y. 10159.

JEWISH LABOR BUND. 21 E. 21st St., New York, N.Y. 10010.

LA RAZA UNIDA PARTY. 483 Fifth St., San Fernando, Calif. 91340.

LIBERAL PARTY OF NEW YORK STATE. 381 Park Ave. S., New York, N.Y. 10016.

LIBERTARIAN PARTY. 1528 Pennsylvania Ave. SE, Washington, D.C. 20003.

MARXIST-LENINIST PARTY OF THE USA. P.O. Box 11942, Ontario St. Station, Chicago, Ill. 60611.

MISSISSIPPI FREEDOM DEMOCRATIC PARTY. P.O. Box 10837, Jackson, Miss. 39209.

NATIONAL BLACK INDEPENDENT POLITICAL PARTY. 370 St. Nicholas #2, New York, N.Y. 10027.

NATIONAL DEMOCRATIC POLICY COMMITTEE. P.O. Box 17729, Washington, D.C. 20041.

NATIONAL DETERMINATION PARTY. P.O. Box 3646, Manchester, N.H. 03105.

NATIONAL HAMILTONIAN PARTY. 3314 Dillian Rd., Flushing, Mich. 48433.

NATIONAL STATES' RIGHTS PARTY. P.O. Box 1211, Marietta, Ga. 30061.

NATIONAL WOMAN'S PARTY. 144 Constitution Ave. NE., Washington, D.C. 20002.

NATURAL LAW PARTY. 51 W. Washington Ave., Fairfield, Iowa 52556.

NEW ALLIANCE PARTY. 200 W. 72d St., Suite 30, New York, N.Y. 10023.

NEW DEMOCRATIC MOVEMENT. P.O. Box 295, 39 Bowery, New York, N.Y. 10002.

NEW FEDERALIST PARTY. 760 Lilian Way, Apt. 15, Los Angeles, Calif. 90038.

NEW ORDER. P.O. Box 27486, Milwaukee, Wis. 53227.

NEW PARTY. 324 Belleville Ave., Bloomfield, N.J. 07003.

PEACE AND FREEDOM PARTY. P.O. Box 42644, San Francisco, Calif. 94142.

POPULIST PARTY. P.O. Box 76737, Washington, D.C. 20013. Or P.O. Box 1992, Ford City, Pa. 16226.

PROHIBITION PARTY. P.O. Box 2635, Denver, Colo. 80201.

REVOLUTIONARY COMMUNIST PARTY. P.O. Box 3486, Chicago, Ill. 60654.

SOCIALIST LABOR PARTY. P.O. Box 50218, Palo Alto, Calif. 94303.

SOCIALIST PARTY. 516 W. 25th St., #404, New York, N.Y. 10001.

SOCIALIST WORKERS PARTY. 14 Charles Lane, New York, N.Y. 10014.

SPARTACIST LEAGUE. P.O. Box 1377, New York, N.Y. 10116.

UNITED STATES PACIFIST PARTY. 5729 S. Dorchester Ave., Chicago, Ill. 60637.

UNITED WORKERS PARTY. G.P.O. Box 1565, New York, N.Y. 10001.

WHITE PATRIOT PARTY. P.O. Box 56, Clementon, N.J. 08021.

WORKERS WORLD PARTY. 46 W. 21st St., New York, N.Y. 10010.

WORLD SOCIALIST PARTY OF THE UNITED STATES. P.O. Box 405, Boston, Mass. 02272.

YOUTH INTERNATIONAL PARTY (YIPPIES). P.O. Box 392, New York, N.Y. 10013.

# Third-Party and Independent Candidacies Receiving at Least One Percent of Popular Vote for President

| Election | Candidacy/Candidate | Popular Vote | Percent of Total | Electoral Vote | Percent of Total |
|----------|---------------------|-------------|------------------|---------------|------------------|
| 1832 | Antimasonic/ William Wirt | 100,715 | 7.78 | 7 | 2.43 |
| 1844 | Liberty/ James G. Birney | 62,103 | 2.30 | — | — |
| 1848 | Free Soil/ Martin Van Buren | 291,501 | 10.12 | — | — |
| 1852 | Free Soil/ John P. Hale | 155,210 | 4.91 | — | — |
| 1856 | American/ Millard Fillmore | 873,053 | 21.53 | 8 | 2.70 |
| 1860 | Southern Democrat/ John C. Breckinridge | 848,019 | 18.09 | 72 | 23.76 |
|  | Constitutional Union/ John Bell | 590,901 | 12.61 | 39 | 12.87 |
| 1872* | | | | | |

*In a fusion campaign the Democrats nominated Liberal Republican party nominee Horace Greeley and adopted LRP platform verbatim. Greeley won 2,834,761 popular votes (43.83%). Greeley died before the meeting of the electoral college, but electors to which he would have been entitled cast 66 votes. Congress refused to count three of these because they were cast for deceased nominee.

| Election | Candidacy/Candidate | Popular Vote | Percent of Total | Electoral Vote | Percent of Total |
|---|---|---|---|---|---|
| 1880 | Greenback/<br>James B. Weaver | 305,997 | 3.32 | — | — |
| 1884 | Greenback/<br>Benjamin F. Butler | 175,096 | 1.74 | — | — |
|  | Prohibition/<br>John P. St. John | 147,482 | 1.47 | — | — |
| 1888 | Prohibition/<br>Clinton B. Fisk | 249,813 | 2.19 | — | — |
|  | Union Labor/<br>Alson J. Streeter | 146,602 | 1.29 | — | — |
| 1892 | Populist/<br>James B. Weaver | 1,024,280 | 8.50 | 22 | 4.95 |
|  | Prohibition/<br>John Bidwell | 270,770 | 2.25 | — | — |
| 1896** |  |  |  |  |  |
| 1900 | Prohibition/<br>John C. Wooley | 209,004 | 1.50 | — | — |
| 1904 | Socialist/<br>Eugene V. Debs | 402,489 | 2.98 | — | — |
|  | Prohibition/<br>Silas C. Swallow | 258,596 | 1.91 | — | — |
| 1908 | Socialist/<br>Eugene V. Debs | 420,380 | 2.82 | — | — |
|  | Prohibition/<br>Eugene W. Chafin | 252,821 | 1.70 | — | — |
| 1912 | Progressive/<br>Theodore Roosevelt | 4,119,207 | 27.39 | 88 | 16.57 |
|  | Socialist/<br>Eugene V. Debs | 900,369 | 5.99 | — | — |
|  | Prohibition/<br>Eugene W. Chafin | 207,972 | 1.38 | — | — |

**Populists nominated Democratic nominee William Jennings Bryan, who had two vice presidential running mates, one Democratic and the other Populist. Bryan won 6,511,495 popular votes (46.73%) and 176 electoral votes (39.37%). Bryan's Populist running mate Thomas Watson received 27 electoral votes even though some Populist electors voted instead for the Democratic vice presidential nominee.

| Election | Candidacy/Candidate | Popular Vote | Percent of Total | Electoral Vote | Percent of Total |
|----------|---------------------|--------------|------------------|----------------|------------------|
| 1916 | Socialist/ Allan L. Benson | 589,924 | 3.18 | — | — |
| | Prohibition/ J. Frank Hanley | 221,030 | 1.19 | — | — |
| 1920 | Socialist/ Eugene V. Debs | 913,664 | 3.42 | — | — |
| 1924 | Progressive (& Socialist)/ Robert M. La Follette | 4,814,050 | 16.56 | 13 | 2.45 |
| 1932 | Socialist/ Norman M. Thomas | 883,990 | 2.22 | — | — |
| 1936 | Union/ William Lemke | 892,492 | 1.96 | — | — |
| 1948 | States' Rights Democrat/Strom Thurmond | 1,169,134 | 2.40 | 39 | 7.34 |
| | Progressive (& American Labor)/ Henry Wallace | 1,157,057 | 2.38 | — | — |
| 1968 | American Independent/ George C. Wallace | 9,901,151 | 13.53 | 46 | 8.55 |
| 1972 | American/John G. Schmitz | 1,090,673 | 1.40 | — | — |
| 1980 | National Unity (Independent)/John Anderson | 5,719,437 | 6.61 | — | — |
| | Libertarian/Ed Clark | 920,859 | 1.06 | — | — |
| 1992 | Independent/ Ross Perot | 19,721,433 | 18.86 | — | — |

**Sources:** *Presidential Elections Since 1789* (Washington, D.C.: Congressional Quarterly, 1975); *History of U.S. Political Parties,* ed. Arthur M. Schlesinger, Jr. (New York: Chelsea House, 1975); Federal Election Commission, "1980 Presidential Election Results," December 31, 1980; Federal Election Commission, "1992 Official Presidential General Election Results," January 11, 1993.

# Third-Party Presence (Excluding Independents) in U.S. Congress*

| Term | Senate<br>Party and Seats | House<br>Party and Seats |
|------|---------------------------|--------------------------|
| 1829–1831 | — | Antimasonic 5 (N.Y. 3, Pa., Vt.) |
| 1831–1833 | Nullifiers 2 (S.C.2) | Nullifiers 4 (S.C. 4)<br>Antimasonic 17 (N.Y. 8, Pas. 7, Vt. 2) |
| 1833–1835 | Nullifiers 2 (S.C. 2) | Nullifiers 9 (Ala., S.C. 8)<br>Antimasonic 25 (Mass. 2, N.Y. 8, Ohio 2, Pa. 10, R.I., Vt. 2) |
| 1835–1837 | Nullifiers 2 (S.C. 2) | Nullifiers 8 (Ala., S.C. 7)<br>Antimasonic 16 (Mass. 3, Ohio, Pa. 8, R.I. 2, Vt. 2) |
| 1837–1839 | — | Nullifiers 6 (S.C. 6)<br>Antimasonic 7 (Pa. 7) |
| 1839–1841 | — | Antimasonic 6 (Pa. 6)<br>Virginia Conservative 2 |
| 1843–1845 | — | Rhode Island Law and Order 2 |
| 1845–1847 | — | American 6 (N.Y. 4, Pa. 2) |
| 1847–1849 | — | American 1 (Pa.) |
| 1849–1851 | Free Soil 2 (N.H., Ohio) | Free Soil 9 (Conn., Ind., Mass; N.H., N.Y., Ohio 2, Pa. 2)<br>American 1 (Pa.) |

*No third party held a seat in either chamber prior to 1829; during 1841–1843, 1863–1869, 1875–1879, 1903–1911, or 1951–1971; or since 1977.

| Term | Senate Party and Seats | House Party and Seats |
| --- | --- | --- |
| 1851–1853 | Free Soil 3 (Mass., N.H., Ohio) | Free Soil 4 (Mass. 2, Ohio, Wis.) Unionist 10 (Ala., Ga. 6, Miss. 3) States Rights 3 (Ga. 2, Miss.) |
| 1853–1855 | Free Soil 2 (Mass., Ohio) | Free Soil 4 (Mass., N.Y., Ohio 2) |
| 1855–1857 | American 1 (Tex.) | American 51 (Ala. 2, Conn. 4, Del., Ga. 2, Ky. 6, La., Md. 4, Mass. 11, Miss., N.H. 3, N.Y. 3, N.C. 3, Pa., R.I. 2, Tenn. 5, Tex, Va.) |
| 1857–1859 | American 5 (Ky. 2, Md., Tenn., Tex) | American 14 (Ga. 2, Ky. 2, La., Md. 3, Mo. 2, N.C., Tenn. 3) |
| 1859–1861 | American 2 (Ky., Md.) | American 5 (La., Md. 3, Mo.) Opposition 19 (Ga. 2, Ky. 5, N.C. 4, Tenn. 7, Va.) |
| 1861–1863 | — | Constitutional Union 2 (Mass., Mo.) Rhode Island Union 2 |
| 1869–1871 | — | Virginia Conservative 5 |
| 1871–1873 | Liberal Republican 1 (Mo.) | Liberal Republican 2 (Mo. 2) |
| 1873–1875 | Liberal Republican 7 (Conn., Mass., Mo., Nebr., N.Y., R.I., Tex.) | Liberal Republican 4 (Ala., Ark., La., Ohio) |
| 1879–1881 | — | Greenback 13 (Ala., Ill., Ind., Iowa 2, Maine 2, Mo., N.C., Pa. 2, Tex., Vt.) |
| 1881–1883 | Virginia Readjuster 1 | Virginia Readjuster 2 Greenback 10 (Ala., Maine 2, Mo. 4., Pa. 2, Tex.) |
| 1883–1885 | Virginia Readjuster 2 | Virginia Readjuster 4 Greenback 2 (Iowa, Pa.) |
| 1885–1887 | — | Greenback 1 (Iowa) |
| 1887–1889 | — | Greenback 1 (Iowa) Labor (independent) 2 (Wis., Va.) |
| 1889–1891 | — | Labor (independent) 1 (Ark.) |
| 1891–1893 | People's 2 (Kans., S. Dak.) | People's 8 (Kans. 5, Mont., Nebr. 2) |

| Term | Senate Party and Seats | House Party and Seats |
|------|------------------------|------------------------|
| 1893–1895 | People's 3 (Kans., Nebr., S. Dak.) Nevada Silver 1 | People's 11 (Calif., Colo. 2, Kans. 5, Mont., Nebr. 2) Nevada Silver 1 |
| 1895–1897 | People's 4 (Kans., Nebr., N.C., S. Dak.) Nevada Silver 2 | People's 9 (Ala. 2, Colo., Kans., Nebr., N.C. 4) Nevada Silver 1 |
| 1897–1899 | People's 5 (Idaho, Kans., Nebr., N.C., S. Dak.) Nevada Silver 2 Silver Republican 5 (Colo., Mont., S. Dak., Utah, Wash.) | People's 22 (Ala., Ark. 2, Colo., Idaho, Kans. 6, Nebr. 4, N.C. 5, S. Dak. 2) Nevada Silver 1 Silver Republican 3 (Colo., Mont., Wash.) |
| 1899–1901 | People's 5 (Idaho, Kans., Nebr., N.C., S. Dak.) Nevada Silver 2 Silver Republican 3 (Colo., S. Dak., Wash.) | People's 6 (Colo., Kans., Nebr. 3, N.C.) Nevada Silver 1 Silver Republican 2 (Colo., Idaho) |
| 1901–1903 | People's 2 (Kans., Nebr.) | People's 5 (Colo., Idaho, Mont., Nebr. 2) |
| 1911–1913 | — | Socialist 1 (Wis.) |
| 1913–1915 | Progressive 1 (Wash.) | Progressive 9 (Ill. 2, Mich. 2, N.Y., Pa. 2, Wash. 2) |
| 1915–1917 | — | Progressive 6 (Calif. 2, Ill., La., Mich., N.Y.) Prohibition 1 (Calif.) Socialist 1 (N.Y.) |
| 1917–1919 | — | Progressive 3 (La., Mich., Pa.) Prohibition (Calif.) Socialist (N.Y.) |
| 1919–1921 | — | Prohibition 1 (Calif.) Minnesota Union-Labor 1 |
| 1921–1923 | — | Socialist 1 (N.Y.) |
| 1923–1925 | Minnesota Farmer-Labor 1 | Minnesota Farmer-Labor 2 Socialist 1 (Wis.) |

| Term | Senate Party and Seats | House Party and Seats |
|---|---|---|
| 1925–1927 | Minnesota Farmer-Labor 1 | Minnesota Farmer-Labor 3<br>Socialist 1 (Wis.)<br>New York American Labor 1** |
| 1927–1929 | Minnesota Farmer-Labor 1 | Minnesota Farmer-Labor 2<br>Socialist 1 (Wis.) |
| 1929–1931 | Minnesota Farmer-Labor 1 | Minnesota Farmer-Labor 1 |
| 1931–1933 | Minnesota Farmer-Labor 1 | Minnesota Farmer-Labor 1 |
| 1933–1935 | Minnesota Farmer-Labor 1 | Minnesota Farmer-Labor 5 |
| 1935–1937 | Minnesota Farmer-Labor 1<br>Wisconsin Progressive 1 | Minnesota Farmer-Labor 3<br>Wisconsin Progressive 7 |
| 1937–1939 | Minnesota Farmer-Labor 2<br>Wisconsin Progressive 1 | Minnesota Farmer-Labor 5<br>Wisconsin Progressive 8 |
| 1939–1941 | Minnesota Farmer-Labor 2<br>Wisconsin Progressive 1 | Minnesota Farmer-Labor 1<br>Wisconsin Progressive 2<br>New York American Labor 1 |
| 1941–1943 | Wisconsin Progressive 1 | Wisconsin Progressive 3<br>Minnesota Farmer-Labor 1<br>New York American Labor 1 |
| 1943–1945 | Wisconsin Progressive 1 | Wisconsin Progressive 2<br>Minnesota Farmer-Labor 1<br>New York American Labor 1 |
| 1945–1947 | Wisconsin Progressive 1 | Wisconsin Progressive 1<br>New York American Labor 1 |
| 1947–1949 | — | New York American Labor 2 |
| 1949–1951 | — | New York American Labor 1 |
| 1971–1973 | New York Conservative 1 | — |
| 1973–1975 | New York Conservative 1 | — |
| 1975–1977 | New York Conservative 1 | — |

**Source:** Kenneth C. Martis, *The Historical Atlas of Political Parties in the United States Congress 1789–1989* (New York: Macmillan, 1989).

**Fiorello La Guardia was nominated by the tiny New York City-based American Labor party. The ALP had not qualified for ballot position and La Guardia took his plurality (42.7%) running on the Socialist and Liberty Bell lines against Republican and Democratic opponents. Although precursor, the ALP of the 1920s should not be confused with the more important and influential ALP that was organized in the state of New York in 1936.

# Third-Party and

# Independent Gubernatorial

# Popular Elections

This table excludes successful fusion candidacies in which a third party entered into coalition with a recognized national major party. The only exceptions are in Kansas, where Populist governors Lewelling and Leedy headed a People's party leading in state politics and clearly prevailing over its fusion partners, the Democrats. Many other governors won office on fusion tickets bringing together a national major and a third party. These included, among others, Free Soil campaigns with Whigs or Republicans (Iowa, New York, and Wisconsin) in the 1850s; American links to Whigs or Republicans (Delaware, Maine, New York, Pennsylvania, and Rhode Island), mainly in the 1850s; a Rhode Island Democratic-Union Party fusion ticket in 1861; Liberal Republican-Democratic tickets (Georgia, Louisiana, Missouri, and Tennessee) in the 1870s; Greenback campaigns with Democrats (Maine, Massachusetts, and Michigan) in the 1880s; People's (Populist)-Democratic tickets (Colorado, Idaho, Minnesota, Montana, Nebraska, North Dakota, Oregon, South Dakota, Washington, and Wyoming) in the 1890s or early in this century; Silver-Democratic fusion candidacies (Nevada) in 1902 and 1906; Prohibition ballot lines supporting Republican candidates (California, Oregon, Rhode Island, and Vermont) episodically over a quarter-century; Progressive campaigns with Republicans or (in one case) a Democrat (California, Delaware, South Dakota, and Utah) in the years 1912–1918; and, from 1936 to the present, third-party links to New York Democrats and Republicans under that state's cross-endorsement procedure. Some of these unlisted fusion campaigns were clearly victories for the third party cause. For example, Massachusetts Greenback-Democratic fusion Governor Benjamin F. Butler was in essence a Greenbacker. Butler was to be the Greenback nominee for president in 1884.

| State | Election | Percent of Total Vote | Person Elected | Party Affiliation |
|---|---|---|---|---|
| Alaska | 1990 | 38.95 | Walter J. Hickel | Alaska Independence |
| California | 1855 | 52.55 | J. Neeley Johnson | American |
| | 1914 | 49.69 | Hiram Johnson | Progressive (Bull Moose) |
| Colorado | 1892 | 46.68 | Davis H. Waite[a] | Populist/ Silver Democrat |
| Connecticut | 1855 | 43.51 | William T. Minor | American/ Temperance |
| | 1856 | 38.98 | William T. Minor | American |
| | 1990 | 40.36 | Lowell P. Weicker | A Connecticut |
| Florida | 1916 | 47.71 | Sidney J. Catts[b] | Prohibition/ Independent Democrat |
| Georgia | 1851 | 59.66 | Howell Cobb | Constitutional Union |
| Kansas | 1892 | 50.04 | L. D. Lewelling[c] | People's (Populist) |
| | 1896 | 50.53 | John H. Leedy | People's (Populist) |
| Kentucky | 1855 | 51.59 | Charles S. Morehead | American |
| Louisiana | 1892 | 44.54 | Murphy J. Foster[d] | Anti-Lottery Democrat/Farm Alliance |
| Maine | 1974 | 39.14 | James B. Longley | Independent |
| Maryland | 1857 | 54.93 | Thomas H. Hicks | American |
| Massachusetts | 1854 | 62.57 | Henry J. Gardner | American |
| | 1855 | 37.80 | Henry J. Gardner | American |
| | 1856 | 58.93 | Henry J. Gardner | American |

[a] Waite's opponents included a regular Democrat.
[b] Catts's opponents included a regular Democrat.
[c] See headnote to this appendix.
[d] Foster's opponents included a regular Democrat.

| State | Election | Percent of Total Vote | Person Elected | Party Affiliation |
|-------|----------|------------------------|----------------|-------------------|
| Minnesota | 1930 | 59.30 | Floyd B. Olson | Minnesota Farmer-Labor |
| | 1932 | 50.57 | Floyd B. Olson | Minnesota Farmer-Labor |
| | 1934 | 44.61 | Floyd B. Olson | Minnesota Farmer-Labor |
| | 1936 | 60.74 | Elmer A. Benson | Minnesota Farmer-Labor |
| Nevada | 1894 | 49.87 | John E. Jones | Nevada Silver |
| | 1898 | 35.67 | Reinhold Sadler | Nevada Silver |
| New Hampshire | 1855 | 50.67 | Ralph Metcalf | American |
| | 1856 | 48.15 | Ralph Metcalf | American |
| North Dakota | 1921 | 50.94 | Regnvald A. Nestos[e] | Independent |
| | 1936 | 35.80 | William Langer | Independent |
| Oregon | 1930 | 54.51 | Julius L. Meier | Independent |
| Pennsylvania | 1835 | 46.91 | Joseph Ritner | Antimasonic |
| Rhode Island | 1843 | 55.21 | James Fenner | Law and Order |
| | 1844 | 96.39 | James Fenner | Law and Order |
| | 1845 | 50.44 | Charles Jackson[f] | Liberation-Whig |
| South Dakota | 1896 | 49.75 | Andrew E. Lee | People's (Populist) |
| Texas | 1859 | 56.84 | Sam Houston[g] | Independent Democrat/American |
| Vermont | 1831 | 44.00 | William A. Palmer | Antimasonic |
| | 1832 | 42.16 | William A. Palmer | Antimasonic |
| | 1833 | 52.86 | William A. Palmer | Antimasonic |
| | 1834 | 45.37 | William A. Palmer | Antimasonic |

[e] Successful recall of Gov. Lynn J. Frazier
[f] Jackson's principal opponent was a regular Whig.
[g] Houston's principal opponent was a regular Democrat.

| State | Election | Percent of Total Vote | Person Elected | Party Affiliation |
|-------|----------|-----------------------|----------------|-------------------|
| Virginia | 1869 | 54.15 | Gilbert C. Walker | Virginia Conservative |
| | 1881 | 52.97 | William E. Cameron | Virginia Readjuster |
| Wisconsin | 1934 | 39.12 | Philip F. La Follette | Wisconsin Progressive |
| | 1936 | 46.38 | Philip F. La Follette | Wisconsin Progressive |
| | 1942 | 49.67 | Orland S. Loomis[h] | Wisconsin Progressive |

**Source:** Joseph E. Kallenbach and Jessamine S. Kallenbach, *American State Governors, 1776–1976,* Vol. I (Dobbs Ferry, N.Y.: Oceana Publications, 1977).

[h] Loomis died before inaguration. Position went to Republican lieutenant governor-elect.

APPENDIX SIX

# Study Statements and Factor Scores

*Factor I:* Leftist/Libertarian
*Factor II:* Nazi
*Factor III:* Conservative

| | Factor I | Factor II | Factor III |
|---|---|---|---|
| 1. I would contend that most of the news from the press, radio, and T.V. in this country is deliberately slanted to mislead us. | +3 | +5 | −3 |
| 2. I believe that a multi-party system would be preferable to the kind of party system that exists in this country today. | +5 | −4 | 0 |
| 3. I feel a personal responsibility to provide for others. | 0 | −3 | +1 |
| 4. The impulse to production can be maintained only if there is a fair division of the product. Fair division can be maintained only by restrictions on the strong and dominant. | −1 | −4 | −3 |
| 5. Despite the myth of free elections, Reagan, Carter—all presidents—are really selected by a small group of powerful people. | +3 | +4 | −5 |
| 6. In this country the productive people consume little and the big consumers produce little or nothing. | +1 | −1 | 0 |
| 7. Human nature being what it is, there will always be war and conflict. | −4 | +4 | −2 |
| 8. I prefer the practical person to the person of ideas. | −2 | −3 | +2 |
| 9. Let's face facts. The world is made up of superior and inferior races. | −5 | +5 | −4 |
| 10. I sometimes feel frustrated in my political activities. | +2 | −4 | +2 |

|  | Factor | | |
|---|---|---|---|
|  | I | II | III |
| 11. When it comes down to it I'll put my faith in the uncommon person—the person of special abilities and effort, the person of intelligence, sophistication, and excitement. | −2 | +3 | +3 |
| 12. The only method of change that will work in today's society is to change the pattern of people's thinking—to eliminate their misconceptions and therefore make them more conscious. Only through this can government be changed for the better. | +4 | −2 | +5 |
| 13. So what if we're called "quixotic"? Dreaming "impossible dreams" is more ethical—and more socially significant—than accomodating oneself to expedient "reality." | +2 | +1 | +1 |
| 14. People and groups that do not believe in free speech should not be able to claim a constitutional right to speak freely themselves. | −3 | −1 | −3 |
| 15. I feel that there is little that I can do personally to affect the course of events. | −1 | −5 | −5 |
| 16. The federal government has moved into every field to which it believes its services are needed. The result is Leviathan, a vast national authority out of touch with people and out of their control. | +3 | −1 | +4 |
| 17. I may not agree with what you have to say, but I'll defend to the death your right to say it. | +4 | −1 | +1 |
| 18. Obedience and respect for authority are the most important virtues children should learn. | −5 | −1 | 0 |
| 19. Political democracy in America will never mean as much as it should until we're ready to take steps to democratize our economic system too. | +2 | −1 | 0 |
| 20. Unless it is necessary to change it is necessary not to change. | −2 | −3 | 0 |
| 21. Human beings are the actors in history but the course of history is determined by forces beyond human control. | −3 | +2 | −4 |

|  | I | II | III |
|---|:---:|:---:|:---:|
| 22. I would like to be more powerful and influential. | 0 | 0 | +2 |
| 23. The American class system is so fluid, with so much social mobility, that it is correct to say that we actually live in a classless society. | −5 | −4 | +1 |
| 24. My party is significant, far more so than you might conclude if you looked only at the rather small number of people who presently identify with it. | +2 | +5 | +3 |
| 25. People never accomplish anything worthwhile politically until they realize that politics is the art of the possible. | −1 | +1 | +2 |
| 26. I have a rather thick skin and am often amused to see how people react to me. | −1 | −1 | +3 |
| 27. Fundamental change may require stringent methods. There is nothing wrong with playing political hardball if your purpose is just. | 0 | +1 | +3 |
| 28. The business person and manufacturer are more important to society that the artist and professor. | −3 | −5 | −1 |
| 29. Anybody with the potential to become somebody should have the opportunity, but there are many people who are just made to run a factory machine. | −4 | +2 | 0 |
| 30. Violence is as American as cherry pie. | 0 | 0 | −3 |
| 31. There are dangerous conspirators in this country, powerful people who are unknown to most Americans. | +1 | +3 | −5 |
| 32. I wish that my party and I were closer to the American people. | +2 | −2 | −1 |
| 33. The best route to reform is through strong affirmative government controlled by the most educated, most intelligent, most expert people who can be found, devising and carrying out programs in the best interest of the people. | −3 | −2 | +3 |

|  | Factor | | |
|---|---|---|---|
|  | *I* | *II* | *III* |
| 34. I have an underlying faith in the American political system. | −2 | −5 | +5 |
| 35. My party is the best, probably the only, hope for saving the people from the social afflictions that are so evident. | 0 | +2 | +1 |
| 36. Actually America has not two major parties but one party with two virtually identical branches. | +3 | +4 | −2 |
| 37. I allow nothing to dull my spirit or dampen my ardor. | +1 | +1 | 0 |
| 38. Most people don't realize how much of our lives are controlled by plots hatched in secret places. | +1 | +3 | −5 |
| 39. We've become too accustomed to looking to government as the giver of rights. It's time to recognize that government is the greatest violator of rights in this country today. | +5 | +2 | −2 |
| 40. America's poor may be less poor than the Third World's poor but they're also less visible. It's hard to get help when most people don't know you exist. | +1 | 0 | −1 |
| 41. I sometimes wonder whether my party and I are doing the right thing. | −1 | −5 | −2 |
| 42. Some people see things as they are and ask "why?" I dream of things that never were and ask "why not?" | +3 | +1 | +1 |
| 43. All third parties—not just my own—suffer unjustly under the restrictions of discriminatory state and federal legislation. | +4 | +1 | +4 |
| 44. I really endeavor to uphold the principles in which I believe. | +5 | +5 | +4 |
| 45. People who own property are generally more dependable than people who don't. | −3 | −3 | +4 |
| 46. Religion is like a frontal lobotomy. It doesn't free you but it keeps you quiet and apathetic. | 0 | −3 | −4 |
| 47. I have always tried to live as normally as anyone else. | 0 | −3 | −4 |

|     |                                                                                                                                                                                                  | Factor |       |       |
|-----|--------------------------------------------------------------------------------------------------------------------------------------------------------------------------------------------------|:------:|:-----:|:-----:|
|     |                                                                                                                                                                                                  |   I    |  II   |  III  |
| 48. | Although American third parties really differ in their principles and programs, I tend to respect the leaders of other third parties more than I do mainstream Democratic and Republican politicians. |  +1    |  +2   |  +2   |
| 49. | You can't be a "citizen of the world" and also a devoted citizen of this county. Down with the one-worlders. I'm an American.                                                                      |  −4    |  −4   |  −1   |
| 50. | A woman's place is in the home.                                                                                                                                                                   |  −5    |   0   |  −3   |
| 51. | "My country, right or wrong" is so much bunk. When the country is wrong we are obliged to say so—loudly.                                                                                           |  +5    |  +4   |  −1   |
| 52. | There is not a dime's worth of difference between the Republican and Democratic parties.                                                                                                          |  +4    |   0   |  −2   |
| 53. | In each generation some extraordinary individuals are destined to become leaders.                                                                                                                 |  −1    |  +3   |  +5   |
| 54. | We have overemphasized "rights" and underemphasized "duties."                                                                                                                                     |  −4    |  +3   |  +5   |
| 55. | I think of myself as a self-disciplined, effective, and not very emotional person.                                                                                                               |  −2    |   0   |  −1   |

# Glossary

**Cadre Party:** A party in which only a small proportion of party identifiers in the electorate become active in the party organization.

**COINTELPRO:** The FBI's Counterintelligence Program launched in the late 1960s by J. Edgar Hoover and continued long after Hoover's 1972 death. Aiming to neutralize radicals and radical groups, nominally to protect national security and public safety, COINTELPRO violated the freedom of association and other basic constitutional liberties and fostered grave concerns about how to protect security without destroying freedom.

**Comintern:** The Communist International, a Soviet-dominated association of Communist parties. Established in 1919, the Comintern was formally ended by Stalin in deference to his wartime allies in 1943.

**Continuing Doctrinal Party:** A third party that sustains itself for several decades at least, not through rational hopes of electoral victory but because of faithful devotion to party doctrine or creed.

**Converting Election:** A very rare type of realigning election in which many voters permanently shift (i.e., for the long term) their party allegiances, the cumulative effect of the shifts being bi-directional and the more popular major party keeping or even enhancing its majority or plurality status (see Realignment).

**Cooptation:** The process whereby a major party appropriates the ideas of a third party and eventually absorbs the third party itself.

**Cross-endorsement:** A procedure, frequently used in New York state and available in Vermont and Connecticut, wherein two or more parties endorse or nominate the same candidate and place the candidate's name on the general election ballot. Votes for each candidate are added together from the various ballot lines on which the candidate's name appears. The procedure may encourage third-party activity and influence through the prospect of third-party entry into fusion campaigns with a major party and/or the threat to refrain from such fusion and thus to siphon votes from the major party nominee.

**Dealignment:** A movement by party identifiers toward independence or more independence of partisan loyalties and identifications.

**Deviating Election (also known as Idiosyncratic Election):** An election in which candidate identification, issue identification, or some other factor(s) leads to the victory of a nominee other than that of the party enjoying majority status in the electorate. Deviating elections occur less frequently than Maintaining Elections (also known as Sustaining Elections). In a maintaining election the nominee of the party holding majority status wins.

**Direct Action:** Illegal but nonviolent forms of dissent. Direct action is very akin to what people mean when they refer to civil disobedience.

**Eighteenth Amendment:** A 1919 addendum to the Constitution banning the manufacture, sale, transportation, importation, or exportation of "intoxicating liquors." The Twenty-first Amendment repealed the Eighteenth Amendment in 1932.

**Electoral College:** The presidential and vice-presidential selection process required by the Constitution. Typically state parties nominate electoral slates equal to the state's electoral vote. State and District of Columbia voters elect particular electoral slates in November and in December the electors formally choose the president and vice-president.

**Equal Rights Amendment (ERA):** A proposed constitutional amendment which, if it had been ratified, would have forbidden the national government or any state to deny or abridge "equality of rights under the law on account of sex." Offered by Congress in 1972, the proposal was defeated because only thirty-five of the thirty-eight states necessary for ratification approved it.

**Faction:** An eighteenth-century term connoting any interest-holding segment of society. In the twentieth century the term usually connotes more specifically a relatively cohesive portion of a divided party.

**Faithless Elector:** A member of the electoral college who violates his or her commitment and votes for someone else for president and/or vice-president.

**Fairness Doctrine:** A 1949 rule of the Federal Communications Commission which required broadcasters to cover issues of public importance and to reflect the range of differing views on these issues. The FCC repealed the Fairness Doctrine in 1988.

**Federal Election Campaign Act:** A series of legislative acts and amendments, beginning in 1971 (the most important coming in 1974), that Congress designed to clean up national elections and reduce the influence of wealthy campaign contributors upon national politics. FECA established the Federal Election Commission. FECA contains provisions disadvantageous to third parties.

**Fusion Strategy:** The coalition of two or more parties in support of a common candidate and sometimes a common program. In fusion campaigns, the nominee of one party is endorsed and sometimes listed on the ballot by the other party or parties (see Cross-endorsement).

**Gender Gap:** The recent tendency of women as a general group to be more inclined than men to liberal positions on some public policy issues and less inclined than men to vote Republican for president.

**Major Party:** A coalition of fairly stable, enduring, and frequently conflicting interests, organized to mobilize support in competitive elections in order to control policy making (from Nimmo and Ungs).

**Mass Membership Party:** A party in which many partisans in the electorate also hold formal membership in the party organization.

**Nationalist-Integrationist Duality:** Competing ideological perspectives in the African-American struggle for liberation. Nationalists have differed with integrationists on both ends and means. Integrationists target mainstreaming (e.g., school and residential integration) and economic justice for blacks (and other minorities), and they have embraced nonviolent (though not always exclusively legal) methods to accomplish these goals. Separatist goals of the nationalists range from an independent African-American entity to cultural identification by black Americans with Africa to autonomy for African-American communities. Though not always inclined to endorse violence as the method of first choice, many nationalists accept violence as a legitimate possibility.

**Nineteenth Amendment:** The woman suffrage amendment proposed in 1919 and added to the Constitution in 1920.

**Non-national Significant Other:** A third party that becomes an important player, sometimes even a major actor, in the politics of a state or community but remains confined by choice or circumstance to its own originating boundaries.

**Party-in-Government:** The participation and influence of a party, through its personnel elected and appointed to public office, in political leadership and in the making and administration of public policy.

**Party in the Electorate:** Partisan identification and loyalty among real and eligible voters.

**Party Organization:** Structures and personnel of a party outside the formal governmental institutions.

**Political Administrators:** Among political actors, one of two personality types identified and revealed by Harold Lasswell. Political administrators are pragmatic, goal-centered people who may find gratification and success in positions of leadership and influence.

**Political Agitators:** Among political actors, a second personality type presented by Lasswell. Political agitators pitch their appeals in emotional and exhortative language and they vituperate their adversaries. They find more gratification in the political contest or crusade than in daily routines of governing.

**Political Socialization:** The process whereby people, particularly nonadults, attain knowledge, feelings, and evaluations about the political system and their relation to it.

**Popular Front:** A strategy enunciated by Moscow-oriented Communists, including Communist Party-USA, of building coalitions with other "progressive" forces (liberals, socialists, and others) in common cause for the defeat of fascism. Set forth in 1935 and reintroduced after the 1941 German invasion of the Soviet Union, the Popular Front profoundly affected the 1948 Progressive party, Minnesota Farmer-Labor, New York American Labor, and various other American third parties of the left.

**Pragmatists:** Third-party people who are devoted to broadening the appeal of their party, its candidates, and program. Pragmatists generally are more willing than purists to broaden and soften their party's issue stands and to enter into fusion campaigns with other parties.

**Proportional Representation (PR):** An at-large election system in which seats go to groups or parties based upon their share of the total vote.

**Purists:** Third-party people who primarily devote themselves to their party and its own internally articulated program. Like third-party pragmatists, purists want their party to win; but when faced with two hard and mutually exclusive choices, purists normally prefer that their party be right than that it be victorious.

**Quid Pro Quo:** Latin for "something for something." In the American political lexicon, the term refers to agreements or understandings for returning favor for favor.

**Realignment:** A permanent or long-term shift by voters of their party identifications from one party to another and/or from nonpartisanship to identification with a particular party. A Realigning Election (also known as a Critical Election) is a rare election, or series of elections in a brief period of time, during which very substantial numbers of people assume new party loyalties without condition as to time. A realigning election may bestow majority status upon a party that did not have it before the realignment; or it may sustain or enhance the position of the previously prevailing party (see Converting Election).

**Red Baiting:** Vituperative rhetoric, often inflated or false, that associates one's political adversary with dangerous leftist radicalism. Other forms of baiting include race baiting, Jew baiting, and gay-bashing.

**Responsible Party:** A party that maintains internal cohesion and discipline and differentiates itself programmatically from its party opposition.

**Satellite Party:** A non-national third party exercising power locally while revolving in the orbit of a nationally acknowledged major party. (From Hesseltine.)

**Secessionist Party:** A short-lived third party born as a result of the deliberate withdrawal of a faction of leaders and followers from a major party in protest of the directions and/or policies of that major party.

**Short-lived Party:** A third party, usually originating either as a movement of economic protest or as a splinter from a major party, that is unable to sustain itself but that in its short existence may (1) affect election outcomes, (2) influence a major party, and thus (3) have an impact upon policy and policy making.

**Single Member District Plurality System:** An election system in which a single victor wins by taking the largest vote in the constituency.

**Southern Strategy:** A Republican party plan, developed and implemented by party planners such as Kevin Phillips, Harry Dent, and Lee Atwater and first set in motion in the 1968 Nixon campaign, to persuade southern whites (and Hispanics) to depart from historic loyalties to the Democrats and to realign with the GOP. The game plan may have broadened somewhat in the hands of Atwater and George Bush in an effort to reach some black voters as well. It has been part of a general GOP strategy to win the identification of a majority of the American electorate.

**Third Party:** An organized aggregate of leaders, members, and supporters that (1) designates itself a party, (2) articulates perceived interests of its devotees, (3) presses these interests upon or in contradistinction to the American political and party systems using electoral and/or other political methods, and (4) either never attains or is unable to sustain the primary or the secondary share of loyalties of people making up the national body politic.

**Twenty-second Amendment:** The constitutional provision, ratified in 1951, that sets a lifetime limit for U.S. presidents of two full terms or ten years.

**Utilitarianism:** The doctrine that "the greatest good (or happiness) for the greatest number" should be the aim of all state action. Classical Utilitarianism emphasized the individual's discretion to define and pursue pleasure/happiness, subject only to limits necessary to sustain every other individual's prerogative to do likewise.

# Suggestions for Further Reading

## General Works on Third Parties

Day, Glenn, *Minor Presidential Candidates and Parties of 1988* (Jefferson, N.C.: McFarland, 1988).

Hesseltine, William B., *Third-Party Movements in the United States* (Princeton, N.J.: D. Van Nostrand, 1962).

Hesseltine, William B., *The Rise and Fall of Third Parties* (Princeton, N.J.: D. Van Nostrand, 1948).

Kruschke, Earl R., *Encyclopedia of Third Parties in the United States* (Santa Barbaba, Calif.: ABC-CLIO, 1991).

Mazmanian, Daniel A., *Third Parties in Presidential Elections* (Washington, D.C.: Brookings Institution Press, 1974).

Nash, Jr., Howard, *Third Parties in American Politics* (Washington, D.C.: Public Affairs, 1959).

Rockwood, D. Stephen, *et al.*, *American Third Parties Since the Civil War* (New York: Garland Publishing, 1985). [annotated bibliography]

Rosenstone, Steven J., Roy L. Behr, and Edward H. Lazarus, *Third Parties in America* (Princeton, N.J.: Princeton University Press, 1984).

Schapsmeier, Edward L., and Frederick H. Schapsmeier, *Political Parties and Civic Action Groups* (Westport, Conn.: Greenwood Press, 1981).

Smallwood, Frank, *The Other Candidates* (Hanover, N.H.: University Press of New England, 1983).

## Other General Works Relevant to the Study of Third Parties

Beck, Paul A., and Frank J. Sorauf, *Party Politics in America*, 7th. ed. (New York: Harper Collins, 1992).

Black, Earl, and Merle Black, *Politics and Society in the South* (Cambridge, Mass.: Harvard University Press, 1987).

Epstein, Leon, *Political Parties in the American Mold* (Madison: University of Wisconsin Press, 1986).

Epstein, Leon, *Political Parties in Western Democracies* (New York: Frederick A. Praeger, 1967).

Kallenbach, Joseph E., and Jessamine S. Kallenbach, *American State Governors, 1776–1976* (Dobbs Ferry, N.Y.: Oceana Publications, 1977).

Key, V. O., *Politics, Parties, and Pressure Groups*, 5th ed. (New York: Thomas Y. Crowell, 1964).

Ladd, Jr., Everett Carll, and Charles D. Hadley, *Transformations of the American Party System* (New York: W. W. Norton, 1975).

Martis, Kenneth C., *The Historical Atlas of Political Parties in the United States Congress 1789–1989* (New York: Macmillan, 1989).

Murphy, Paul L., ed., *Political Parties in American History*, 4 vols. (New York: G. P. Putnam's Sons, 1974).

*National Party Conventions, 1831–1984* (Washington, D.C.: Congressional Quarterly, 1987).

Schlesinger, Jr., Arthur M., ed., *History of U.S. Political Parties*, 4 vols. (New York: Chelsea House, 1973).

Schlesinger, Arthur M., and Fred L. Israel, *History of American Presidential Elections*, 4 vols. (New York: McGraw Hill, 1971).

Sundquist, James L., *Dynamics of the Party System* (Washington, D.C.: Brookings Institution Press, 1973).

Thayer, George, *The Farther Shores of Politics* (New York: Simon and Schuster, 1967).

## Works Treating Particular Third Parties

Bart, Philip, ed., *Highlights of a Fighting History* (New York: International, 1979). [Communist]

Bernard, William D., *Dixiecrats and Democrats* (Tuscaloosa: University of Alabama Press, 1974).

Blackstock, Nelson, *COINTELPRO* (New York: Anchor Foundation, 1988).

Blue, Frederick J., *The Free Soilers* (Urbana: University of Illinois Press, 1973).

Breitman, George, ed., *The Founding of the Socialist Workers Party* (New York: Anchor Foundation, 1982).

Cannon, James P., *History of American Trotskyism* (New York: Pathfinder, 1972).

Clark, Ed, *A New Beginning* (Ottawa, Il.: Caroline House, 1980). [Libertarian]

Downs, Donald A., *Nazis in Skokie* (Notre Dame, Ind.: Notre Dame University Press, 1985).

Edsall, Thomas B., *Chain Reaction* (New York: W. W. Norton, 1991).

Edsall, Thomas B., and Mary D. Edsall, "Race," *Atlantic Monthly*, 267 (May 1991), 53–56ff.

Gable, John Allen, *The Bull Moose Years* (Port Washington, N.Y.: Kennikat Press, 1978).

Gieske, Millard L., *Minnesota Farmer-Laborism* (Minneapolis: University of Minnesota Press, 1979).

Goodwyn, Lawrence, *Democratic Promise* (New York: Oxford University Press, 1976). [Populist]

Harrington, Michael, *Socialism* (New York: Arcade Publishing, 1989).

Haynes, John E., *Dubious Alliance* (Minneapolis: University of Minnesota Press, 1984). [Minnesota Farmer-Labor]

Heath, G. Louis, ed., *Off the Pigs!* (Metuchen, N.J.: Scarecrow Press, 1976). [Black Panther]

Hobday, Charles, *Communist and Marxist Parties of the World* (Santa Barbara, Calif.: ABC-CLIO, 1986).

Hofstadter, Richard, *The Age of Reform* (New York: Vintage Press, 1955). [Populist and Progressive]

Howe, Irving, and Lewis Coser, *The American Communist Party* (New York: De Capo, 1974).

Irwin, Inez Haynes, *The Story of the Woman's Party* (New York: Kraus Reprint, 1971).

Jayko, Margaret, ed., *The FBI on Trial* (New York: Pathfinder, 1988).

Kelley, Robin D., *Hammer and Hoe* (Chapel Hill: University of North Carolina Press, 1990). [Communist]

Laidler, Harry W., *History of Socialism* (New York: Thomas Y. Crowell, 1968).

Langer, Elinor, "The American Neo-Nazi Movement Today," *The Nation*, 251 (July 16/23, 1990), 82–107.

Mackay, Kenneth C., *The Progressive Movement of 1924* (New York: Octagon, 1947).

Maolain, Ciaran O., *The Radical Right* (Santa Barbara, Calif., ABC-CLIO, 1987).

O'Neill, William L., *A Better World* (New York: Touchstone, 1982). [Communist]

O'Reilly, *Racial Matters* (New York: Free Press, 1989).

Ridgeway, James, *Blood in the Face* (New York: Thunder's Mouth, 1990).

Rorty, James, *McCarthy and the Communists* (Westport, Conn.: Greenwood Press, 1972).

Scarrow, Howard A., *Parties, Elections, and Representation in the State of New York* (New York: New York University Press, 1983).

Sewell, Richard H., *Ballots for Freedom* (New York: W. W. Norton, 1975).

Shapiro, Bruce, "The New Alliance Party: Dr. Fulani's Snake-Oil Show," *The Nation*, 254 (May 4, 1992), 585–594.

Shore, Elliott, *Talkin' Socialism* (Lawrence: University Press of Kansas, 1988).

Spitzer, Robert J., *The Right to Life Movement and Third Party Politics* (Westport, Conn.: Greenwood Press, 1987).

Storms, Roger C., *Partisan Prophets* (Denver, Colo.: Prohibition National Foundation, 1972). [Prohibition]

Valelly, Richard M., *Radicalism in the States* (Chicago, Ill.: University of Chicago Press, 1989). [Minnesota Farmer-Labor]

Vaughn, William Preston, *The Antimasonic Party in the United States* (Lexington: University Press of Kentucky, 1983).

Walton, Jr., Hanes, *Black Political Parties* (New York: Free Press, 1975).

Walton, Jr., Hanes, *The Negro in Third-Party Politics* (Philadelphia: Dorrance, 1969).

Walton, Richard J., *Henry Wallace, Harry Truman, and the Cold War* (New York: Viking, 1976).

Weinstein, James, *The Decline of Socialism in America* (New York: Monthly Review Press, 1967).

Wilcox, Laird, *Guide to the American Left* (Olathe, Kans.: Editorial Research Service, 1989).

Wilcox, Laird, *Guide to the American Right* (Olathe, Kans.: Editorial Research Service, 1989).

*Yearbook on International Communist Affairs*, annual, various editors (Stanford, Calif.: Hoover Institution Press).

Youngsdale, James M., *Populism* (Port Washington, N.Y.: Kennikat Press, 1975).

Youngsdale, James M., *Third Party Footprints* (Minneapolis, Minn.: Ross and Haines, 1966).

Zeidler, Frank P., *Ninety Years of Democratic Socialism* (Privately printed monograph available from Socialist Party, New York, 1991).

## Biographies of Third Party Leaders and Activists

Cleaver, Eldridge, *Soul on Ice* (New York: Dell Publishing, 1968).

Davis, Angela, *Angela Davis* (New York: Random House, 1974).

Davis, Julia, "A Feisty Schoolmarm Made the Lawyers Sit Up and Take Notice," *Smithsonian Magazine*, 11 (March, 1981), 133ff. [Belva Lockwood]

Dennis, Peggy, *The Autobiography of an American Communist* (Berkeley, Calif.: Lawrence Hill, 1977).

Duram, James C., et al., *Norman Thomas* (New York: Irving Publishers, 1974).

Frady, Marshall, *Wallace* (New York: World Publishing, 1968). [George Wallace]

Flynt, J. Wayne, *Cracker Messiah* (Baton Rouge: Louisiana State University Press, 1977). [Sidney Catts]

Gerson, Simon W., *Pete* (New York: International Publishers, 1976).

Ginger, Ray, *The Bending Cross* (New Brunswick, N.J.: Rutgers University Press, 1949). [Eugene V. Debs]

Gross, Ken, *Ross Perot* (New York: Random House, 1992).

King, Dennis, *Lyndon La Rouche and the New American Fascism* (New York: Doubleday, 1988).

Kutcher, James, *The Case of the Legless Veteran* (New York: Anchor Foundation, 1973).

Lachicotte, Alberta, *Rebel Senator* (New York: Devon-Adair, 1966). [Strom Thurmond]

Mayer, George H., *The Political Career of Floyd B. Olson* (Minneapolis: University of Minnesota Press, 1951).

Meyer, Gerald, *Vito Marcantonio* (Albany, N.Y.: SUNY Press, 1989).

Nash, Jr., Howard P., *Stormy Petrel* (Rutherford, N.J.: Fairleigh Dickinson University Press, 1969). [Benjamin Butler]

Reeve, Carl, *The Life and Times of Daniel DeLeon* (New York: Humanities, 1972).

Salvatore, Nick, *Eugene V. Debs* (Champaign: University of Illinois Press, 1982).

Sheilds, James M., *Mr. Progressive* (Minneapolis, Minn.: T. S. Denison, 1971). [Elmer Benson]

Spender, Dale, *Women of Ideas* (London: Routledge and Kegan Paul, 1982).

Wallace, George C., *Stand Up for America* (Garden City, N.Y.: Doubleday, 1976).

Woodward, C. Vann, *Tom Watson* (New York: Macmillan, 1938).

# Index of Parties, Associations, and People